HUMAN RIGHTS OBLIGATIONS OF NON-STATE ARMED GROUPS

This book is concerned with the international regulation of non-state armed groups. Specifically, it examines the possibility of subjecting armed groups to international human rights law obligations.

First addressed is the means by which armed groups may be bound by international law. Of particular interest is the de facto control theory and the possibility that international law may be applied in the absence of direct treaty regulation. Application of this theory is dependent upon an armed group's establishment of an independent existence, as demonstrated by the displacement of state authority. This means that armed groups are treated as a vertical authority, thereby maintaining the established hierarchy of international regulation. At issue therefore is not a radical approach to the regulation of non-state actors, but rather a modification of the traditional means of application in response to the reality of the situation.

The attribution of international human rights law obligations to armed groups is then addressed in light of potential *ratione personae* restrictions. International human rights law treaties are interpreted in light of the contemporary international context, on the basis that an international instrument has to be applied within the framework of the entire legal system prevailing at the time of interpretation. Armed groups' status as vertical authorities facilitates the vertical application of international human rights law in a manner consistent with both the object and purpose of the law and its foundation in human dignity.

Finally, if international human rights law is to be applied to armed groups, its application must be effective in practice. A context-dependent division of responsibility between the territorial state and the armed group is proposed. The respect, protect, fulfil framework is adapted to facilitate the application of human rights obligations in a manner consistent with the control exerted by both the state and the armed group.

Volume 57 in the series Studies in International Law

Studies in International Law

Recent titles in this series

Integration at the Border: The Dutch Act on Integration Abroad and International Immigration Law
Karin de Vries

An Equitable Framework for Humanitarian Intervention
Ciarán Burke

Democratic Statehood in International Law: The Emergence of New States in Post-Cold War Practice
Jure Vidmar

International Law and the Construction of the Liberal Peace
Russell Buchan

The OIC, the UN, and Counter-Terrorism Law-Making: Conflicting or Cooperative Legal Orders?
Katja Samuel

Statelessness: The Enigma of the International Community
William E Conklin

The Reception of Asylum Seekers under International Law: Between Sovereignty and Equality
Lieneke Slingenberg

International Law and Child Soldiers
Gus Waschefort

The Contractual Nature of the Optional Clause
Gunnar Törber

Non-State Actors in International Law
Edited by Math Noortmann, August Reinisch and Cedric Ryngaert

The Rule of Law at the National and International Levels: Contestations and Deference
Edited by Machiko Kanetake and André Nollkaemper

For the complete list of titles in this series, see 'Studies in International Law' link at www.hartpub.co.uk/books/series.asp

Human Rights Obligations of Non-State Armed Groups

Daragh Murray

·HART·
PUBLISHING
OXFORD AND PORTLAND, OREGON
2016

Published in the United Kingdom by Hart Publishing Ltd
16C Worcester Place, Oxford, OX1 2JW
Telephone: +44 (0)1865 517530
Fax: +44 (0)1865 510710
E-mail: mail@hartpub.co.uk
Website: http://www.hartpub.co.uk

Published in North America (US and Canada) by
Hart Publishing
c/o International Specialized Book Services
920 NE 58th Avenue, Suite 300
Portland, OR 97213-3786
USA
Tel: +1 503 287 3093 or toll-free: (1) 800 944 6190
Fax: +1 503 280 8832
E-mail: orders@isbs.com
Website: http://www.isbs.com

Hart Publishing is an imprint of Bloomsbury Publishing plc.

British Library Cataloguing in Publication Data
Data Available

Library of Congress Cataloging-in-Publication Data

Names: Murray, Daragh, author.

Title: Human rights obligations of non-state armed groups / Daragh Murray.

Description: Oxford ; Portland, Oregon, Hart Publishing Ltd, 2016. | Series: Studies in international law ; volume 57 | Includes bibliographical references and index.

Identifiers: LCCN 2015048263 (print) | LCCN 2015048698 (ebook) | ISBN 9781509901630 (hardback : alk. paper) | ISBN 9781509901654 (Epub)

Subjects: LCSH: Non-state actors (International relations) | War (International law) | International criminal law.

Classification: LCC KZ6405.N66 M87 2016 (print) | LCC KZ6405.N66 (ebook) | DDC 341.6/7—dc23

LC record available at http://lccn.loc.gov/2015048263

ISBN: 978-1-50990-163-0

Typeset by Compuscript Ltd, Shannon
Printed and bound in Great Britain by
CPI Group (UK) Ltd, Croydon CR0 4YY

Foreword

It is by now a well-known fact that non-state actors have been at the heart of a vast number of conflicts in recent decades. Attempts to regulate the conduct of parties during armed conflicts are therefore doomed to failure if we do not account for the fact that so many of the actors on the ground are not state militaries, but rather armed groups. The treaty rules of International Humanitarian Law (IHL) applicable to non-international armed conflicts and to armed groups are relatively sparse in comparison to those for states engaged in international armed conflict, and progress has needed to come through the identification of customary rules and detailed studies of practice. As far as the protection of civilians affected by conflict is concerned, even these developments in IHL are not enough. Recent years have also seen the increased acceptance of the vital role played by International Human Rights Law during armed conflict. Human rights obligations apply alongside IHL and the two branches of international law must be interpreted in a manner which reinforces their respective purpose, employing a practicable approach which balances the reality of conflict with the need to protect the civilian population from the ravages of war. Yet, while IHL is readily assumed to impose obligations on armed groups, it is often said that human rights obligations only apply to states. If this were the case, the millions of people affected by conflicts involving armed groups stand to lose the potential protection of human rights and to be subject to a legal vacuum. It is on this point that this book steps forward and introduces a novel approach which could have far-reaching implications.

In the book, Daragh Murray goes beyond the confines of the IHL obligations of armed groups, and instead focuses on the question of whether such groups can be directly bound by International Human Rights Law. He proceeds to lay out a well-reasoned argument presenting the legal foundations for the proposition, followed by a detailed analysis of how this would work in practice. It is a complex topic, and no doubt some may find certain conclusions to be controversial. It is however precisely on those points that this book stands out as an insightful work capable of making a truly important contribution to the field.

The book is based upon Daragh Murray's PhD thesis, of which I had the pleasure of being supervisor. Having witnessed up close the dedication and rigour he has applied to his work, it is no surprise that Daragh Murray has produced an exceptional book which deserves to be widely read and seriously considered by all those working in this field.

Professor Noam Lubell
Wivenhoe 2016

Acknowledgements

It is only on rare occasions that you get the chance to thank those who help, support and inspire you. I am grateful for this opportunity.

First, and foremost, thanks go to my family: to my parents, Máire and Paraic, and to my sister, Áine. I wouldn't be who I am without you, and if I could be more like you I would be better for it. Thank you so much.

This book began as a PhD thesis, initiated at the Irish Centre for Human Rights and brought to fruition at the University of Essex Human Rights Centre. The constant throughout was the supervision of Professor Noam Lubell. It has been an absolute privilege to work with Noam, and the opportunity to engage with, and to learn from, such an inspiring scholar immeasurably enriched the PhD process. Noam was one of the first people I met as I took my initial tentative steps towards the field of international law and human rights, and I couldn't have asked for a better mentor. I am delighted to now call Noam a colleague, and a friend, and to have the opportunity to continue to collaborate with—and to continue to learn from!—such a leader in the field.

I would like to thank all those who read through this manuscript—in whole or in part—and who provided insightful comments and food for thought. In particular, I would like to thank Professor Andrew Clapham and Professor Sheldon Leader. Both provided comments that have enriched this manuscript, and as my examiners they provided a viva that was challenging but hugely memorable. Thanks also go to the anonymous reviewers at Hart publishing, who provided valuable, and sometimes challenging, comments. Again, this manuscript is better for their insights.

I am now based at the Human Rights Centre at the University of Essex, and I could not ask for a better, or more inspiring, work environment. The opportunity to engage with colleagues here, both academic and administrative, is something that I appreciate each day. Particular mention must be made of Professor Lorna McGregor and Professor Françoise Hampson who are sources of both inspiration and support. Mention must also be made of the students we are privileged to teach and to learn from.

There are too many people to thank individually. I feel that I have been incredibly lucky in relation to the people I have worked with, and the friends that I have made over the last few years. I would like to extend particular thanks to Raji Sourani, my first boss, and a man who taught me so much about what the practice of human rights really means. His continued work, and that of his staff and colleagues, is a testament to perseverance and the importance of human rights work. A few others who deserve special mention are Nathan Derejko, Gen Sander, Eyad Al Alami, Jehan Al Alami, Chantal Meloni, Josh Curtis, Waseem El-Sarraj, Hannah Baumann, Daniel Machover, Dr Kathleen Cavanaugh and Professor Ray Murphy.The process of finalising this book could not have been easier, and I am thankful for the assistance and support of all at Hart publishing.

My doctoral research was enabled by a scholarship from the Irish Research Council for Humanities and Social Science. I am indebted to their support.

Last, but most definitely not least, I must thank my partner, Sara. Words can't even begin to describe how I feel. You are the touchstone for everything that I do, and I am just incredibly lucky to have you in my life.

Daragh Murray
Wivenhoe
January 2016

Contents

Table of Abbreviations

ANC	African National Congress
APRD	People's Army for the Restoration of Democracy
APWé	Patriotic Alliance of the Wé People
BRN-C	National Revolution Front-Coordinate
BSF	Border Security Force
CNDP	National Congress for the Defence of the People
CNF	Chin National Front
COBRA	Commando Battalions for Resolute Action
CPJP	Convention of Patriots for Justice and Peace
CPN-M	Communist Party of Nepal-Maoist
CPP/NPA/NDF	Communist Party of the Philippines/New People's Army/National Democratic Front
CRPF	Central Reserve Police Force
DRC	Democratic Republic of the Congo
ELN	National Liberation ARmy
EPLF	Eritrean People's Liberation Front
ESCR	Economic, Social and Cultural Rights
ETA	Basque Homeland and Freedom
EU	European Union
EZLN	Zapatista Army of National Liberation
FAFN	Armed Forces of the New Forces
FARC	Revolutionary Armed Forces of Colombia
FDLR	Democratic Forces for the Liberation of Rwanda
FDN	Nicaraguan Democratic Force
FIDH	International Federation for Human Rights
FLGO	Liberation Front for the Great West
FMLN	Farabundo Marti National Liberation Front
GAM	Free Aceh Movement
ICC	International Criminal Court
ICCPR	International Covenant on Civil and Political Rights
ICESCR	International Covenant on Economic, Social and Cultural Rights
ICJ	International Court of Justice
ICRC	International Committee of the Red Cross
ICTY	International Criminal Tribunal for the Former Yugoslavia
IDF	Israeli Defence Forces
IDU	Internal Defence Unit (See RUF)

IED	Improvised Explosive Device
IHL	International Humanitarian Law
IHRL	International Human Rights Law
ILO	International Labour Organization
IMF	International Monetary Fund
IRA	Irish Republican Army
ITC	International Tin Council
KLA	Kosovo Liberation Army
KNPP	Karen National Progressive Party
KNU	Karen National Union
LRA	Lord's Resistance Army
LTTE	Liberation Tigers of Tamil Eelam
MILF	Moro Islamic Liberation Front
MILOCI	Ivorian Liberation Movement for the West of Cote d'Ivoire
MLC	Movement for the Liberation of Congo
MNJ	Niger Movement for Justice
MNLA	National Movement for the Liberation of Azawad
MRT	Moldovan Republic of *Transdniestra*
MSF	Doctors Without Borders
NATO	North Atlantic Treaty Organization
NDFP	National Democratic Front of the Philippines
NGO	Non-Governmental Organisation
NIAC	Non-International Armed Conflict
OAS	Organization of American States
OCHA (UN)	Office for the Coordination of Humanitarian Affairs
ODA	Overseas Development Assistance
OHCHR (UN)	Office of the High Commissioner for Human Rights
ONUSAL	United Nations Observer Mission in El Salvador
PDS	Planning and Development Secretariat
PKK	Kurdistan Workers' Party
POLISARIO	Popular Front for the Liberation of Saguia el-Hamra and Río de Oro
PYD	Democratic Union Party
RCD	Rally for Congolese Democracy
RNA	Royal Nepalese Army
RUF	Revolutionary United Front
SLA	Sudan Liberation Army
SLA-Abu-Gasim	Sudan Liberation Army-Abu Gasim
SLA-Free Will	Sudan Liberation Army-Free Will
SLM-Unity	Sudan Liberation Movement-Unity
SPLA	Sudan Peoples' Liberation Army
SPLM/A	Sudan Peoples' Liberation Movement/Army
TNC	Transnational Corporation

TRNC	Turkish Republic of Northern Cyprus
UN	United Nations
UNICEF	United Nations Children's Fund
UNSC	United Nations Security Council
UPC/FPLC	Union of Congolese Patriots/Patriotic Forces for the Liberation of Congo
UPRGO	Patriotic Resistance Union of the Great West
WHO	World Health Organization

Table of Cases

1

Introduction

THIS MONOGRAPH IS concerned with the protection of individuals' human rights in situations affected by the activities of non-state armed groups, and with the international regulation of armed groups themselves.[1] It intends to establish whether non-state armed groups may be directly bound by obligations under international law—and, in particular, by obligations under international human rights law—and if so, under what circumstances. This subject is approached from the understanding that if international law is to be effective, it must be capable of both responding to the realities of international life, and of being implemented in practice. As such, if non-state armed groups are subject to international human rights law obligations, it is essential that the content of these obligations reflects the reality of the situation at hand and the capacity of the armed group in question: any imposed obligations must strike a balance between the needs of the affected population and the capability of the armed group.

Non-state armed groups exert an ever-increasing influence on the lives of individuals throughout the world, as demonstrated, inter alia, by the post-World War II trend evidencing increased instances of non-international armed conflict (which involve at least one non-state actor) when compared with instances of international armed conflict (which occur between states).[2] Indeed, the Human Security Report notes that international armed conflicts 'have become extremely rare.'[3] The reality of non-international armed conflicts, such as the current conflicts in Syria,[4]

[1] A definition of non-state armed groups is discussed below in section II. The key requirement is that the armed group in question exists independently; ie that it is not a de facto organ of a third state.

[2] See, Human Security Report Project, *Human Security Report 2005: War and Peace in the 21st Century* (Oxford, OUP, 2005) 23; Human Security Report Project, *Human Security Report 2009/2010: The Causes of Peace and the Shrinking Costs of War* (Oxford, OUP, 2011) 160.

[3] See *Human Security Report 2009/2010* above n 2, 160.

[4] See 'More than 191,000 people killed in Syria with "no end in sight"', *UN News Centre* (22 August 2014); Edith M Lederer, 'Death Toll in Syria Rises To 100,000 UN Chief Ban Ki-Moon Says', *Associated Press* (25 July 2013).

Iraq,[5] the 2011 conflict in Libya,[6] or the longstanding and ongoing conflict in the Democratic Republic of Congo,[7] illustrate the potentially devastating impact that non-state armed groups can have on the lives and livelihoods of civilian populations.[8]

Armed groups also exert an often significant influence outside situations of armed conflict.[9] For example, in India the Naxalite movement has been reported as being active in 90 of the country's 636 districts,[10] and in 2006 the Indian prime minister described the Naxalites as 'the single biggest internal security challenge ever faced' by India.[11] The group exercises de facto control in a number of areas,[12] and has established a state-like apparatus that includes judicial, health, and educational components.[13] In Lebanon, Hezbollah has established a sophisticated parallel infrastructure, providing services such as health care, education, and social welfare, and even establishing a telephone network.[14] In Colombia,

[5] See, for instance, 'Battle for Iraq and Syria in Maps', *BBC News* (London, 10 July 2015); 'Struggle for Iraq: In maps', *BBC News* (London, 17 June 2014); John Simpson, 'Iraq: Not falling apart. Yet', *BBC News* (London, 17 June 2014); Martin Chulov, 'Isis insurgents seize control of Iraqi city of Mosul', *The Guardian* (London, 10 June 2014).

[6] See Ian Black, 'Libyan revolution casualties lower than expected, says new government', *The Guardian* (London, 8 January 2013).

[7] See for example, International Crisis Group, 'Eastern Congo: Why Stabilisation Failed' (2012); MONUSCO and United Nations Office of the High Commissioner for Human Rights, 'Final Report of the Fact-Finding Missions of the United Nations Joint Human Rights Office into the Mass Rapes and Other Human Rights Violations Committed by a Coalition of Armed Groups Along the Kigua-Mpofi Axis in Walikale Territory, North Kivu, From 30 July to 2 August 2010' (2011); United Nations Office of the High Commissioner for Human Rights, 'Report of the Mapping Exercise documenting the most serious violations of human rights and international humanitarian law committed within the territory of the Democratic Republic of the Congo between March 1993 and June 2003' (2010).

[8] A significant number of additional examples exist. For example, reference may be made to the conflict in Sri Lanka which ended in 2009, the ongoing insurgency in southern Thailand, or the continuing conflict in Colombia.

[9] See, eg 'Q&A: Mexico's drug-related violence', *BBC News* (London, 25 November 2013); International Crisis Group, 'Peña Nieto's Challenge: Criminal Cartels and Rule of Law in Mexico (2013).

[10] Arnaud Blin, 'Armed groups and intra-state conflicts: the dawn of a new era?' (2011) 93 *International Review of the Red Cross* 22. See also Human Rights Watch, 'Sabotaged Schooling: Naxalite Attacks and Police Occupation of Schools in India's Bihar and Jharkhand States' (2009) 23. A 2015 newspaper article reports that Naxalites are active in 76 districts across 10 states. See Yatish Yadav, 'Police vs Maoists: Are Indian Security Forces Strong Against Naxals?', *The New Indian Express* (25 April 2015).

[11] Quoted in, Human Rights Watch, ''Being Neutral is Our Biggest Crime': Government, Vigilante, and Naxalite Abuses in India's Chhattisgarh State' (2008) 5.

[12] ibid 22.

[13] See further, Arundhati Roy, *Walking With the Comrades* (London, Penguin Books 2011); Rishi Chhikara, 'People's Liberation Guerrilla Army of CPI (Maoist)' Manekshaw Paper No 35 (New Delhi, Centre for Land Warfare Studies, 2012).

[14] Michael T Kindt, 'Hezbollah: A State within a State' in Michael T Kindt, Jerrold M Post, and Barry R Schneider (eds), *The World's Most Threatening Terrorist Networks and Criminal Gangs* (London, Palgrave Macmillan, 2009) 132; International Crisis Group, *'Lebanon: Hizbollah's Weapons Turn Inward'* (Brussels, International Crisis Group, 2008) 3.

the Urabeños—the country's largest paramilitary group, with an estimated 1,300-2,000 fighters[15]—have taken control over large areas along the Caribbean coast.[16] The extent of the group's influence is demonstrated by a 'strike' called in 2012 in response to the killing of the group's leader, during which the group effectively shut down business and public transport in six of Colombia's 32 provinces.[17] The Office of the Prosecutor at the International Criminal Court has also launched preliminary investigations into the conduct of non-state actors in Nigeria and the Central African Republic, where armed groups are suspected of committing crimes against humanity in situations outside non-international armed conflict.[18]

It is important to note that non-state armed groups actively engage with the civilian population, both during and outside non-international armed conflict, inter alia, through measures intended to ensure public order—involving the establishment of courts or arbitration tribunals, or the detention of individuals—the collection of taxes,[19] or the provision of

[15] See International Criminal Court, The Office of the Prosecutor, 'Report on Preliminary Examination Activities' (2013) para 129.

[16] Adriaan Alsema, 'Profiles: Urabeños' (*Colombia Reports*) http://colombiareports.co/urabenos/.

[17] Jeremy McDermott, 'Urabeños Flex Their Muscles in North Colombia' *InSight Crime* (9 January 2012). See also, Aylish O'Driscoll, '"Urabeños" bring northern Colombia to a halt' (*Colombia Reports*) http://colombiareports.co/urabenos-bring-northern-colombia-to-a-halt-as-police-struggle-to-control-armed-strike/.

[18] See International Criminal Court, Office of the Prosecutor, 'Report on Preliminary Examination Activities', (November 2012) para 89; 'Report on Preliminary Examination Activities' above n 15, para 218; International Criminal Court, The Office of the Prosecutor, 'Statement of the Prosecutor of the International Criminal Court, Fatou Bensouda, on opening a new Preliminary Examination in Central African Republic' (7 February 2014); International Criminal Court, Office of the Prosecutor, 'Situation in the Central African Republic II: Article 53(1) Report', 24 September 2014, paras 130–31.

[19] In Sri Lanka the LTTE imposed a range of direct and indirect taxation measures. Other groups who have imposed taxes include the Forces Nouvelles in Cote d'Ivoire, Hezbollah in Lebanon, the GAM in Indonesia, the NPA in the Philippines, the Shining Path in Peru, the National Congress for the Defence of the People ('CNDP') in the Democratic Republic of Congo, Hamas in the Gaza Strip, the FMLN in El Salvador, and the Afghan Taliban. See Kristian Stokke, 'Building the Tamil Eelam State: emerging state institutions and forms of governance in LTTE-controlled areas in Sri Lanka' (2006) 27 *Third World Quarterly* 6, 1034; Human Rights Watch, 'Afraid and Forgotten: Lawlessness, Rape, and Impunity in Western Cote d'Ivoire' (2010) 66–68; Olivier Bangerter, 'Internal Control: Codes of Conduct within Insurgent Armed Groups' (2012) Small Arms Survey Occasional Paper No 31, 47; International Crisis Group, 'Hizbollah and the Lebanese Crisis' (2007) 20; International Crisis Group, 'Aceh: Escalating Tension' (2000) 3; Soliman M Santos, Jr and Paz Verdades M Santos, 'Primed and Purposeful: Armed Groups and Human Security Efforts in the Philippines' (Small Arms Survey and South-South Network for Non-State Armed Group Engagement, 2010) 52; Bruce H Kay, 'Violent Opportunities: The Rise and Fall of "King Coca" and Shining Path' (1999) 41 *Journal of Interamerican Studies and World Affairs*, 103; Louise Arimatsu, 'The Democratic Republic of the Congo 1993–2010' in Elizabeth Wilmshurst (ed), *International Law and the Classification of Conflicts* (Oxford, OUP, 2012) 186; Rory McCarthy, 'Hamas imposes new Gaza taxes to pay for burgeoning bureaucracy' *The Guardian* (London, 8 April 2010);

services. For example, the New People's Army (NPA) in the Philippines established a system of people's courts,[20] while the Free Aceh Movement (GAM) in Indonesia convened councils (*majelis*) at the village, sub-district, and district level. Lower-level councils reportedly handled petty crime, while higher-level councils were convened for offences regarded as more serious, such as collaboration.[21] In Iraq, the Mahdi movement created a network of institutions called *Makatib al-Shahid al-Thani* (Offices of the Second Martyr), which ran arbitration committees comprised of local tribal chiefs. These committees were reportedly well organised, and more effective with respect to dispute resolution than the police.[22] The Afghan Taliban has also established a court system in areas under their influence.[23] These courts are reported as being increasingly popular, apparently to the point of 'rendering official government courts all but inoperable'.[24] One journalist reported that in Taliban areas 'a new saying prevails: "[g]overnment courts for the rich (because the judges are bribable), Taliban justice for the poor."'[25] A court system established by the Communist Party of Nepal-Maoist (CPN-M) in Nepal is also reported as having enjoyed popularity amongst the population,[26] consequent to a distrust of state courts and the perception that CPN-M courts were able to dispense with cases quickly and cheaply.[27] A number of other groups also established courts, including the Liberation Tigers of Tamil Eelam (LTTE),[28] the Sudan Peoples' Liberation Army (SPLA),[29] the Revolutionary Armed Forces of

'Third Report of the United Nations Observer Mission in El Salvador (ONUSAL)', UN Doc A/46/876, 10 February 1992, para 148; International Crisis Group, 'The Insurgency in Afghanistan's Heartland' (2011) 8.

[20] 'Report of the Special Rapporteur on extrajudicial, summary or arbitrary executions, Philip Alston, Mission to Philippines', UN Doc A/HRC/8/3/Add.2, 16 April 2008, para 32. In India, the Naxalites have also established people's courts (*jan adalat*). See Human Rights Watch, '"Being Neutral is our Biggest Crime:" Government, Vigilante, and Naxalite Abuses in India's Chhattisgarh State' (2008) 20; Arundhati Roy, 'Walking With the Comrades' *Outlook India* (29 March 2010) www.outlookindia.com/article.aspx?264738-0.

[21] Human Rights Watch, 'Indonesia: The War in Aceh' (2001) 22.

[22] International Crisis Group, 'Iraq's Muqtada Al-Sadr: Spoiler or Stabiliser?' (2006) 20; International Crisis Group, 'Iraq's Civil War, the Sadrists and the Surge' (2008) 7.

[23] International Crisis Group, 'The Insurgency in Afghanistan's Heartland' (2011) 8.

[24] ibid 17.

[25] Tim McGirk, 'Behind the Taliban's Resurgence in Afghanistan' *TIME* (16 September 2009).

[26] Office of the High Commissioner for Human Rights in Nepal, 'Human rights abused by the CPN-M: Summary of Concerns' (2006) 4.

[27] Sandesh Sivakumaran, 'Courts of Armed Opposition Groups: Fair Trials or Summary Justice' (2009) 7 *Journal of International Criminal Justice*, 493.

[28] See, 'Building the Tamil Eelam State' above n 19, 1027; 'Courts of Armed Opposition Groups' above n 27, 494.

[29] Claire Metelits, 'Reformed Rebels? Democratization, Global Norms, and the Sudan People's Liberation Army' (2004) 51 *Africa Today* 1, 74.

Colombia (FARC),[30] the Forces Nouvelles,[31] Al Nusrah,[32] Hezbollah,[33] and the Farabundo Marti National Liberation Front (FMLN).[34] Interestingly, elements of the Syrian opposition have established courts that continue to apply the Syrian criminal law system.[35]

A number of non-state armed groups have also engaged in various levels of service provision, ranging from ad hoc support, to the provision of society-wide, state-like, services. For example, the Democratic Union Party (PYD) in Syria provides direct aid, such as fuel, gas, and flour, to families in their territory affected by the Syrian civil war,[36] the Eritrean People's Liberation Front (EPLF) in Ethiopia established a system of 'barefoot doctors' who worked throughout EPLF territory,[37] while both the EPLF and the Popular Front for the Liberation of Saguia el-Hamra and Río de Oro (POLISARIO) in Western Sahara established schools and medical facilities.[38] In Nigeria, Boko Haram provided welfare hand-outs, food, and shelter in their base area,[39] and in Libya Ansar al-Sharia has provided welfare support and social services such as road cleaning and repair.[40] The G-5 unit established by the Revolutionary United Front (RUF) was also responsible for the welfare of civilians in base areas, and appropriated foodstuffs from the frontlines to this end.[41] At lower levels of group sophistication, it is reported that drug factions in Rio de Janeiro distribute food and provide other kinds of social programmes within

30 See Human Rights Watch, 'Colombia: Beyond Negotiation International Humanitarian Law and its Application to the Conduct of FARC-EP' (2001) 6; Human Rights Watch, 'War Without Quarter: Colombia and International Humanitarian Law' (1998).

31 'Twenty-fourth report of the Secretary-General on the United Nations Operation in Cote d'Ivoire', UN Doc S/2010/245, 20 May 2010, para 24.

32 Bill Roggio, 'Al Nusrah Front poised to take over last major city on Euphrates River' *The Long War Journal* (13 March 2013).

33 See 'Hezbollah: A State within a State' above n 14, 133.

34 'Third Report of the United Nations Observer Mission in El Salvador (ONUSAL)', UN Doc A/46/876, 10 February 1992, para 113.

35 Human Rights Watch, 'Syria: End Opposition Use of Torture, Executions', (17 September 2012) 3.

36 International Crisis Group, 'Syria's Kurds: A Struggle Within a Struggle' (2013) 21.

37 David Pool, *From Guerrillas to Government: The Eritrean People's Liberation Front* (Athens, Ohio University Press, 2001) 100. It is noted that a significant portion of this territory now forms part of modern-day Eritrea.

38 See, respectively, Michael Bhatia, 'The Western Sahara under Polisario Control' (2001) 28 *Review of African Political Economy* 88, 297, and above n 37, 100.

39 Andrew Walker, 'What is Boko Haram?' (2012) United States Institute of Peace, Special Report 308, 3, 9.

40 Alison Pargeter, 'Islamist Militant Groups in Post Qadhafi Libya', *Combating Terrorism Center at West Point* (20 February 2013) www.ctc.usma.edu/posts/islamist-militant-groups-in-post-qadhafi-libya.

41 *Prosecutor v Sesay, Kallon and Gbao*, Trial Chamber, Special Court for Sierra Leone, Case No SCSL-04-15-T, 2 March 2009) para 692.

the territory under their control.[42] At more advanced levels, the Islamic State provides services, including health, welfare and the administration of justice to approximately 6 million people in those areas of Syria and Iraq under its control.[43] In Lebanon, Hezbollah oversee an advanced social network,[44] providing welfare support (including allowances paid to families of deceased fighters), food aid, housing, compensation for damage occurring as a result of hostilities,[45] vocational training and professional support,[46] as well as running schools, and hospitals.[47] Indeed, it is reported that in southern Lebanon over 400,000 patients are treated per year in Hezbollah facilities.[48]

I. THE IMPORTANCE OF PROTECTING INDIVIDUALS AFFECTED BY ARMED GROUPS

Even these brief examples demonstrate that non-state armed groups can exert a significant impact on the lives of individuals subject to their influence. It is submitted that the protection of such individuals must necessarily be of international concern.[49] Life goes on for individuals affected by armed group activity, and despite the uncertain circumstances in which they live, it is essential that efforts be undertaken to ensure that their fundamental human rights are respected and protected. Article 2 of the Universal Declaration of Human Rights states simply that '[e]veryone is entitled to all the rights and freedoms set forth in this Declaration, without distinction of any kind'.[50] International human rights law does

[42] Sven Peterke, 'Urban Insurgency, "Drug War" and International Humanitarian Law: The Case of Rio de Janeiro' (2010) 1 *International Humanitarian Legal Studies* 169 fn 22.

[43] Michael Weiss and Hassan Hassan, *ISIS: Inside the Army of Terror* (New York, Regan Arts, 2015) 224–28; Richard Barrett, 'The Islamic State', The Soufan Group, November 2014.

[44] Human Rights Watch, 'Why They Died: Civilian Casualties in Lebanon during the 2006 War' (2007) 41.

[45] 'Hizbollah and the Lebanese Crisis' above n 19, 20; Eitan Azani, *Hezbollah: The Story of the Party of God: From Revolution to Institutionalization* (London, Palgrave Macmillan, 2008) 117; International Crisis Group, 'Israel/Hizbollah/Lebanon: Avoiding Renewed Conflict' (2006) 7.

[46] *Hezbollah: The Story of the Party of God* above n 45, 72, 117.

[47] 'Hizbollah and the Lebanese Crisis' above n 19, 20.

[48] See 'Hezbollah: A State within a State' above n 14, 132.

[49] The Human Rights Council has held Special Sessions to address the activities of the Islamic State (22nd Special Session, 1 September 2014) and Boko Haram (23rd Special Session, 1 April 2015). The UN Security Council has also called on armed groups to respect human rights, or condemned human rights violations committed by armed groups. See, for instance, UNSC Res 2031 (2011) para 13; UNSC Res 2088 (2013) para 13.

[50] See also, Art 2(1) International Covenant on Civil and Political Rights; Art 2(2) International Covenant on Economic, Social and Cultural Rights.

not contain any provisions excluding individuals affected by either armed conflict or the activities of non-state armed groups. Rather, human rights are considered to be universal and applicable at all times.[51]

When giving effect to human rights in situations involving armed groups, the protection of individuals' human rights requires more than protection against the immediate effects of hostilities: day-to-day life for the affected individuals does not come to a halt. In Mexico, for example, although the level of armed violence is extremely high, individuals continue to live their lives in areas subject to the influence of armed groups, attempting to earn a living, ensure their children's education, and so on; these individuals' rights must also be protected. Equally—and perhaps contrary to popular perception—not all situations involving armed groups are characterised by violence. As noted above, armed groups are active outside armed conflict, while even in situations of non-international armed conflict, the scope of active hostilities is often restricted, and armed groups frequently exercise relatively stable control in areas removed from the frontlines; ie in situations replicating 'normalcy' to the extent possible under the circumstances. In Sri Lanka, for instance, the LTTE maintained the rule of law in areas subject to their control,[52] as did the RUF in their base areas in Sierra Leone.[53]

Efforts to ensure the overall protection of individuals' human rights must therefore address not only the 'typical' rights associated with armed group activity, such as the right to life and the prohibition of torture, but also rights of a more general application, such as the prohibition of arbitrary detention, the right to a fair trial, the right to the highest attainable standard of health, the right to education, the right to an adequate standard of living, and so on. The entire spectrum of human rights protections remains relevant.

II. WHAT IS A NON-STATE ARMED GROUP?

Of concern is the question of if, and how, non-state armed groups may be bound by international law, and international human rights law in particular. As a starting point, it is noted that if direct international rights or obligations are to be applied to non-state armed groups, international law requires that no other entity be legally responsible for the actions of the

[51] Louise Doswald-Beck, *Human Rights in Times of Conflict and Terrorism* (Oxford, OUP, 2011) 5–12.

[52] 'Courts of Armed Opposition Groups' above n 27, 493; 'Building the Tamil Eelam State' above n 19, 1022.

[53] See, *Prosecutor v Sesay, Kallon and Gbao*, above n 41, para 707.

armed group in question: the group must exist independently. If an armed group is 'completely dependent'[54] on a third state (or other entity), then it is considered to be an organ of that state, and is bound on the basis of that state's international obligations. The armed group is not directly bound in its own right. As the direct international regulation of armed groups is of interest, independence is thus a key criterion required of non-state armed groups for the purposes of this work.

This requirement does not preclude the possibility that an armed group may come under the partial authority of a third state. For instance, a third state may exercise effective control over certain of an armed group's activities.[55] In this situation, however, the armed group remains independent in relation to those activities not subject to the effective control of the third state. As such, the direct international law obligations of the armed group exist concurrent to the obligations of the third state.

Of course, none of the above implies that an armed group cannot share an ideology with, or be supported by, a state. Indeed, an overlapping of interests is relatively common in practice. For instance, Hezbollah in Lebanon receives support from Iran,[56] the United States supported the Contras in Nicaragua,[57] while a number of countries—including the United Kingdom, the United States, and Saudi Arabia—have extended support to elements of the armed opposition in Syria.[58] Of concern is whether the armed group is completely dependent on a third state:[59] in these circumstances the conduct of the armed group in question cannot be considered non-state conduct, and so the group will not be considered to be a non-state armed group.[60]

[54] *Case Concerning Application of the Convention on the Prevention and Punishment of the Crime of Genocide (Bosnia and Herzegovina v Serbia and Montenegro)*, Judgment, International Court of Justice, 26 February 2007, para 392.

[55] ibid paras 399–400.

[56] For example, 'Iran's Rohani affirms support for Syria and Hezbollah in "confronting Zionist regime"' *Haaretz* (16 July 2013).

[57] *Case Concerning Military and Paramilitary Activities In and Against Nicaragua (Nicaragua v United States of America)*, Merits, International Court of Justice, 27 June 1986.

[58] For example, Kim Sengupta, 'Revealed: What the West has given Syria's rebels' *The Independent* (London, 11 August 2013); 'Syria Conflict: UK to give extra £5m to opposition groups' *BBC News* (London, 10 August 2012); Michael R Gordon, 'US Steps Up Aid to Syrian Opposition, Pledging $60 Million' *New York Times* (New York, 28 February 2013); Anne Barnard, 'Syrian Rebels Say Saudi Arabia Is Stepping Up Weapons Deliveries' *New York Times* (New York, 12 September 2013).

[59] This is discussed further below, see Ch 5 section III.

[60] This work is primarily concerned with non-international armed conflict, and situations outside armed conflict. It is possible that a situation otherwise amounting to non-international armed conflict may be internationalised consequent to the intervention of a third state in circumstances where the level of control exercised by the third state is insufficient to negate the non-state armed group's independence. See *Case Concerning Military and Paramilitary Activities in and Against Nicaragua (Nicaragua v United States of America)* above n 57 para 115; *Case Concerning Application of the Convention on the Prevention and Punishment*

The specific criteria required in order for an armed group to demonstrate an independent existence are left deliberately vague at this point. These criteria are central to the discussion of international legal personality, and are examined further in Chapter 2 section IV.A, in relation to the attribution of direct international rights or obligations on the basis of treaty law, and in Chapter 5 section III, in relation to the displacement of state authority. Equally, issues relating to an armed group's level of organisation—or other internal characteristics—are linked to the group's capacity to possess international rights or obligations, and are discussed in Chapter 3.

The absence of a precise definition means that a potentially diverse range of non-state armed groups may be addressed: this is deliberate. For present purposes, it is the impact of the armed group that is decisive, and not its motive, ideology, or *modus operandi*. As such, guerrilla groups in advanced stages of insurgency, such as the FARC in Colombia or the Moro Islamic Liberation Front ('MILF') in the Philippines, are equally as relevant as drug gangs like the Zetas or Knights Templar in Mexico, or transnational networks such as Al Qaeda or Jemaah Islamiyah. For ease of reading, the phrases non-state armed group, armed group, and armed opposition group will be used interchangeably herein.

Before proceeding to the substantive analysis, it is important to note that although this book is concerned with non-state armed groups, these entities' existence as a subset of the broader category of non-state actors is acknowledged. As such, care has been taken to ensure that any suggestions presented herein remain cognisant of the reality of non-state actors more generally, and that their application to other non-state actors (if possible) remains legally sound.

III. TRADITIONAL UNDERSTANDINGS OF INTERNATIONAL LAW AS IT RELATES TO ARMED GROUPS

In light of the issues raised above, the question arises as to how international law can address the influence exerted by non-state armed groups and ensure—or attempt to ensure—the conditions necessary for the protection of individuals' human rights. A traditional reading of international law results in the conclusion that it cannot: the international

of the Crime of Genocide (Bosnia and Herzegovina v Serbia and Montenegro) above n 54 paras 398–406; *Prosecutor v Tadic*, Judgment, Appeals Chamber, International Criminal Tribunal for the former Yugoslavia, Case No IT-94-1-A, 15 July 1999, para 137. However, this situation is unresolved and this book proceeds on the basis that only states may be party to an international armed conflict. See Noam Lubell, *Extraterritorial Use of Force Against Non-State Actors* (Oxford, OUP, 2010) 97–99.

legal order is a predominantly state-centric system, and non-state actors are typically regarded as subject to states' exclusive domestic jurisdiction.[61] In practice this results in a legal vacuum: the state is incapable of enforcing its domestic law, as by definition armed opposition groups exist beyond state authority, while the armed groups themselves are not subject to direct international regulation.[62] Affected individuals are left without any effective international legal protection.[63]

This apparent lack of international regulation gives rise to a number of concerns both in relation to the affected civilian populations and to the validity of international law itself. From the perspective of international law, the consequences of a legal vacuum are significant: by allowing a vacuum to exist, international law fails to respond to the realities of international life, undermining the law's effectiveness. Significantly, the fact that non-state armed groups are not acknowledged by international law effectively grants these groups a status superior even to that enjoyed by states.[64] While states enjoy a wide freedom of action, they remain subject to the restrictions imposed by international law.[65] Conversely, non-state armed groups are not subject to international regulation and are thus free to act as they choose: they enjoy a form of supreme sovereignty.

Turning to the affected civilian populations, who is responsible for their wellbeing? Is it appropriate that individuals' best interests, and the protection of their human rights, be left unregulated and at the discretion of armed groups? For instance, should it be at an armed group's discretion whether or not they ensure the continued operation of social services, or refrain from indirectly interfering with the right to health? Likewise, if armed groups do undertake activities with respect to the civilian population, do they have complete freedom of action? Can they issue new laws, or restructure the health or education systems? Are they required to address the needs of the population in any way?

IV. THE INADEQUACY OF THE LAW OF NON-INTERNATIONAL ARMED CONFLICT VIS-À-VIS THE REGULATION OF ARMED GROUPS

A limited exception to this legal vacuum does exist with respect to armed groups party to a non-international armed conflict. These groups are

[61] This is discussed further below. See Ch 2 section I.C.

[62] With the limited exception of those treaties discussed below in Ch 6 section I.

[63] Note that the legal protection referred to is not restricted to remedy in the event of a violation, but also includes the existence of laws regulating armed group activity.

[64] See discussion below in Ch 5 section I.E.

[65] *Customs Regime between Germany and Austria (Protocol of March 19th, 1931)*, Separate Opinion of Judge Anzilotti, Permanent Court of International Justice, 5 September 1931, para 81.

bound, inter alia, by Article 3 common to the Geneva Conventions of 1949,[66] the customary international law of armed conflict, and—where applicable—Additional Protocol II to the Geneva Conventions.[67] However, while the law of non-international armed conflict offers essential protection in times of conflict, it is inadequate with respect to the effective international regulation of non-state armed groups for a number of reasons.

First, the application of the law of armed conflict is restricted to situations of armed conflict. As such, it does not apply to a (potentially significant) number of situations involving armed groups.[68] Second, the law of non-international armed conflict predominantly consists of rules relating to the conduct of hostilities and negative obligations relating to the treatment of civilians.[69] For instance, while the law of international armed conflict contains specific rules regulating a state's treatment of civilian populations subject to its control,[70] these rules do not extend to the regulation of armed group activity in non-international armed conflict.[71] With the limited exception of rules relating to the treatment of detainees, there are no positive obligations governing the treatment of individuals, or the civilian population at large. Issues relating to the needs of civilians, such as the provision of health care, or the maintenance of public order and civil life, are not addressed. For example, while it is prohibited to attack foodstuffs and agricultural areas,[72] no complementary obligations exist in relation to the overall wellbeing of the population in this

[66] See, Convention (IV) relative to the Protection of Civilian Persons in Time of War (adopted 12 August 1949, entered into force 21 October 1950) 75 UNTS 287 Art.3.

[67] Protocol Additional to the Geneva Conventions of 12 August 1949, and relating to the Protection of Victims of Non-International Armed Conflicts (Protocol II), (adopted 8 June 1977, entered into force 7 December 1978) 1125 UNTS 609.

[68] The examples presented above (see nn 9–18) are recalled, and it is highlighted that the impact of armed group activity in these situations can be significant. As noted, the Office of the Prosecutor of the International Criminal Court believes that Boko Haram may have committed crimes against humanity. 'Report on Preliminary Examination Activities' above n 15, para 89.

[69] For example, Pt IV of Additional Protocol II—which concerns the civilian population—establishes rules prohibiting direct attacks targeting: civilians, objects indispensable to the survival of the civilian population, works or installations containing dangerous forces, cultural objects and places of worship. Art 18 does allow for relief action if 'the civilian population is suffering undue hardship owing to a lack of the supplies essential for its survival' but the scope of this provision is necessarily limited.

[70] See, inter alia, Arts 27–78 Geneva IV; Arts 42–56 Regulations Respecting the Laws and Customs of War on Land, Annex to Convention (IV) respecting the Laws and Customs of War on Land (adopted 18 October 1907, entered into force 26 January 1910).

[71] The International Committee of the Red Cross's Customary International Humanitarian Law Study does not recognise any such rules as forming part of the customary international law of non-international armed conflict. See Jean-Marie Henckaerts and Louise Doswald-Beck, *Customary International Humanitarian Law, Vol 1: Rules* (Geneva, International Committee of the Red Cross and CUP, 2005).

[72] See, Art 14 Additional Protocol II.

regard, such as obligations with respect to the right to food, the right to the highest attainable standard of living, or the right to work. Third, the law of non-international armed conflict does not clarify the scope and content of an armed group's authority as it relates to civilians subject to its control. Specifically, it is unclear as to whether armed groups can take legislative or judicial measures to enforce the rule of law in the interests of the affected population. Similarly, the law of armed conflict does not clarify whether armed groups can promulgate a new penal code, or introduce legislation intended to avoid stagnation with respect to the local economy.

Clearly—and indeed unsurprisingly—the law of non-international armed conflict is incapable of effectively ensuring the overall protection of the civilian population, and of individuals' human rights. However, it is important to note that the fact that this body of law exists confirms that international law is, in principle, capable of responding to the activities of non-state armed groups.[73]

V. MOVING FORWARD: THE EVOLUTION OF INTERNATIONAL LAW

Returning to the issue of international regulation, it is submitted that developments in contemporary international law may demand that the law's perceived inability to address non-state armed groups be re-evaluated. While the conclusion that international law cannot effectively respond to the reality of non-state armed groups may once have been true, and indeed remains widely accepted, this may no longer actually be the case. The international legal order has undergone significant development since World War II: inter alia, International Organisations have been authoritatively recognised as possessing international legal personality;[74] it is now confirmed that individuals (non-state entities) can be directly addressed by international law;[75] and, as mentioned above, non-state armed groups party to a non-international armed conflict are subject to direct international regulation.[76] Equally significant has been the development of international human rights law and the emergence

[73] See further, Jean S Pictet (ed), *Commentary: IV Geneva Convention Relative to the Protection of Civilian Persons in Time of War* (Geneva, International Committee of the Red Cross, 1958) 26.

[74] *Reparations for injuries suffered in the services of the United Nations*, Advisory Opinion, International Court of Justice, 11 April 1949, 179; *Legality of the use by a State of Nuclear Weapons in Armed Conflict*, Advisory Opinion, International Court of Justice, 8 July 1996, para 25.

[75] See, *LaGrand (Germany v United States of America*, Judgment, International Court of Justice, 27 June 2001, para 77; *Avena and Other Mexican Nationals (Mexico v United States of America)*, Judgment, International Court of Justice, 31 March 2004, para 40.

[76] As evidenced, for example, by the application of common Art 3 to the four Geneva Conventions of 1949.

of 'community obligations';[77] obligations that are not purely reciprocal, but rather are owed to either the international community as a whole,[78] or—in the case of multilateral treaties—to all other contracting parties.[79] Explaining this concept, the International Court of Justice stated in *Barcelona Traction* that:

> [A]n essential distinction should be drawn between the obligations of a State towards the international community as a whole, and those arising vis-à-vis another State … By their very nature the former are the concern of all States. In view of the importance of the rights involved, all States can be held to have a legal interest in their protection; they are obligations *erga omnes*.[80]

While the above paragraph referred to the field of diplomatic protection, the International Court of Justice clarified that community obligations include 'the principles and rules concerning the basic rights of the human person',[81] as well as those obligations 'conferred by international instruments of a universal or quasi-universal character'.[82] Prominent instruments in this regard include the major human rights treaties,[83] such as the International Covenant on Civil and Political Rights,[84] and the International Covenant on Economic, Social and Cultural Rights.[85] The fact that certain obligations are considered to reflect fundamental values, the protection of which is a legal interest of the international community as a whole, suggests that it may be necessary for international law to respond when protection of these obligations is undermined,[86] for instance in situations where the authority of the state has been displaced by that of an armed group.

[77] See *The Effect of Reservations on the Entry Into Force of the American Convention on Human Rights (Arts 74 and 75)*, Advisory Opinion, Inter-American Court of Human Rights, 24 September 1982, para 29.

[78] Antonio Cassese, *International Law*, 2nd edn (Oxford, OUP, 2005) 64.

[79] See, Arnold D McNair, 'The Functions and Differing Legal Character of Treaties'(1930) 11 *British Yearbook of International Law* 116.

[80] *Barcelona Traction, Light and Power Company, Limited*, Judgment, International Court of Justice, 5 February 1970, para 33.

[81] ibid, para 34.

[82] ibid, para 34.

[83] It is noted that international human rights law treaties form a subset of the body of multilateral treaties. Other areas regulated by multilateral treaties include, for example, treaties related to the protection of the environment, and traffic in endangered species. See further, James Crawford, *Brownlie's Principles of Public International Law*, 8th edn (Oxford, OUP, 2012) 361–64.

[84] International Covenant on Civil and Political Rights (adopted 16 December 1966, entered into force 23 March 1976) 999 UNTS 171 (ICCPR).

[85] International Covenant on Economic, Social and Cultural Rights (adopted 16 December 1996, entered into force 3 January 1976) 993 UNTS 3 (ICESCR). See, in support, *Brownlie's Principles of Public International Law* above n 83, 638.

[86] *Barcelona Traction, Light and Power Company, Limited*, Judgment, International Court of Justice, 5 February 1970, para 33.

Relevant in this regard is the recognition of human rights' foundation in the inherent dignity of the human person.[87] The Vienna Declaration and Programme of Action adopted by the World Conference on Human Rights recognised and affirmed 'that all human rights derive from the dignity and worth inherent in the human person',[88] and this was endorsed by the Trial Chamber of the International Criminal Tribunal for the former Yugoslavia:

> The general principle of respect for human dignity is the basic underpinning and indeed the very *raison d'être* of international humanitarian law and human rights law; indeed in modern times it has become of such paramount importance as to permeate the whole body of international law.[89]

Recognition of human dignity as the source of human rights necessarily implies that human rights must be concerned with the protection of human dignity. Establishing a distinction between state and non-state armed group authorities in relation to the attribution of human rights obligations purely on the basis of their distinct international legal personality seems inconsistent with this requirement.[90] If international human rights law is intended to protect the individual, then the entity exercising authority over that individual must be regulated. If one accepts this proposition, 'there is little room left for arguments about the state or non-state character of the assailant.'[91]

Reflecting this concern for the continued protection of individuals' rights, irrespective of the governing authority, the Human Rights Committee stated in General Comment 26 that:

> The rights enshrined in the Covenant belong to the people living in the territory of the State party. The Human Rights Committee has consistently taken the view, as evidenced by its long-standing practice, that once the people are accorded the protection of the rights under the Covenant, such protection devolves with territory and continues to belong to them.[92]

In *Elmi v Australia* the Committee against Torture held that a non-state actor—in this case one of the warring factions in Somalia—should be

[87] This is discussed in greater detail below, see Ch 6.

[88] Vienna Declaration and Programme of Action, adopted by the World Conference on Human Rights, Vienna, 25 June 1993, Preamble.

[89] *Prosecutor v Furundzija*, Judgment, Trial Chamber, International Criminal Tribunal for the former Yugoslavia, Case No IT-95-17/1-T, 10 December 1998, para 183. See also, *Prosecutor v Zlatko Aleksovski*, Judgment, Trial Chamber, International Criminal Tribunal for the former Yugoslavia, Case No IT-95-14/1-T, 25 June 1999, para 54.

[90] See generally, MJ Bossuyt, *Guide to the 'Travaux Preparatoires' of the International Covenant on Civil and Political Rights* (The Hague, Martinus Nijhoff, 1987) 6. See further, n 78, 397.

[91] Andrew Clapham, *Human Rights Obligations of Non-State Actors* (Oxford, OUP, 2006) 534.

[92] Human Rights Committee, 'General Comment No 26: Continuity of obligations', UN Doc CPR/C/21/Rev.1/Add.8/Rev/1, 8 December 1997, para 4.

regarded as equivalent to a public authority, in light of the specific circumstances of the situation, which included the absence of a central government, and the factions' establishment of quasi-governmental institutions.[93] The Committee concluded that: 'the members of those factions can fall, for the purposes of the application of the Convention, within the phrase "public officials or other persons acting in an official capacity" contained in article 1.'[94]

It is suggested that, when considered holistically, developments such as those mentioned above may have had a potentially profound impact on the international legal order, raising the intriguing possibility that contemporary international law is now capable of responding to the realities of international life and subjecting non-state armed groups to international regulation. This monograph is concerned with exploring this possibility, and determining whether non-state armed groups may be subject to direct obligations under international law. Three issues are of central importance in this regard. First, the conditions under which non-state armed groups may be bound by international law must be determined. Of interest are issues such as the legal basis underpinning the application of international treaty law to non-state armed groups and the possibility that international law may apply in situations not addressed by international treaty law on the basis of the de facto control theory. Second, if armed groups can be bound by international law, it remains to be determined whether they may then be subject to direct obligations under international human rights law; for instance, is the application of international human rights law limited *ratione personae*? Third, if non-state armed groups can indeed be subject to international human rights law obligations, the content of any resultant obligations and how they may be implemented in practice must be understood.

VI. STRUCTURE

Part I: Subjecting Armed Groups to International Legal Regulation

International legal personality indicates direct comprehension by the international legal order: entities devoid of personality simply do not exist (directly at least) in the eyes of the law,[95] and are therefore excluded

[93] This issue is discussed further below, see Ch 5 section IV.

[94] *Sadiq Shek Elmi v Australia*, Committee against Torture, Communication No 120/1998, UN Doc CAT/C/22/D/120/1998, 14 May 1999, para 6.5. This is discussed further below in Ch 5 section IV.

[95] Jan Klabbers, 'The Concept of Legal Personality' (2005) 11 *Ius Gentium* 35.

from the international legal system.[96] Accordingly, if armed groups are to be subject to direct international obligations, it must first be determined whether they can possess international legal personality, and so Chapter 2 examines the criteria necessary for the acquisition of personality. Three key criteria are identified in this regard. First, an entity must have the capacity to possess direct international rights or obligations. This requirement is derived from the principle of effectiveness and is necessary to avoid the existence of a legal fiction.[97] Second, international legal personality indicates direct comprehension by the international legal order, and so for an entity to be acknowledged as an active participant on the international plane, it must actually possess direct international rights or obligations. Third, entities possessing international legal personality must exist independently: if an entity is subject to the exclusive authority of a superior entity, it is that entity's legal personality that is of relevance on the international legal plane. When these three criteria are present, a non-state entity is recognised as possessing international legal personality and is directly bound by international law.[98]

The remaining chapters in Part I examine whether non-state armed groups can satisfy these criteria. Chapter 3 looks at the organisational criteria necessary to demonstrate the capacity to possess direct international rights or obligations. The dominant entities of concern to the international system—states, International Organisations, armed groups, and transnational corporations—are evaluated in order to identify the specific characteristics required vis-à-vis each entity's acquisition of legal personality.[99] These entity-specific criteria are then evaluated in order to determine whether any criteria common to each entity, and thus to international legal persons generally, may be identified.

The question of whether non-state armed groups can actually possess direct international obligations is then considered. In order to answer this question, chapter four first considers the legal basis underpinning the potential application of international law to armed groups, and

[96] Roland Portmann, *Legal Personality in International Law* (Cambridge, CUP, 2010) 5.

[97] The principle of effectiveness requires 'that only those claims and situations which are effective can produce legal consequences. A situation is effective if it is solidly implanted in real life.' See further, n 78, 12–13.

[98] International legal personality is a construct indicative of a certain status under international law. International legal personality is not a prerequisite to being directly bound by international obligations. Rather, independence and capacity are prerequisites to the applicability of direct international rights or obligations. The presence of the three criteria confirms an entity's international legal personality.

[99] Although not all of these entities are recognised as possessing international legal personality, the potential international legal personality of each has been raised, and it is submitted that they are of relevance herein.

four principal theories in this regard are examined: customary law,[100] general principles,[101] third party consent,[102] and legislative (or prescriptive) jurisdiction.[103] Where appropriate, these theories are discussed and analysed in relation to the law of armed conflict as it has been authoritatively accepted that law of armed conflict treaties can bind non-state armed groups.[104] It is noted that the utility of these theories is not restricted to this body of law.

However, the theories discussed in Chapter 4 all ultimately require that armed groups be directly regulated by international treaty law. Chapter 5 examines another possibility: can the specific circumstances of a given situation—such as the existence of a legal vacuum—require that international law be applied to non-state armed groups in the absence of directly applicable international treaty law, on the basis of the de facto control theory? This chapter initially looks at the legal basis underpinning the de facto control theory,[105] before examining the international legal obligations applicable to armed groups consequent to its application. Finally, as independence is a prerequisite for the possession of international legal personality—and thus for application of the de facto control theory—the circumstances under which an armed group may establish an independent existence are addressed. This issue is approached in light of the requirement that, in order to possess international legal personality, an armed group cannot be subject to the exclusive authority of a superior entity, such as the territorial state. Independence is considered both in the context of and outside situations of non-international armed conflict. Outside armed conflict, an armed group's independence is considered in relation to the displacement of state authority, as demonstrated, for instance, by a state's inability to reasonably impose its will.

[100] Armed groups are bound by customary international humanitarian law, as opposed to any treaty-based obligations undertaken by the state.

[101] Similar to the customary law theory, but refers instead to the binding force of general principles of international law.

[102] Armed groups may be bound by international treaty law if this was the intent of the drafters, and the individual groups in question consent to be bound.

[103] A state has the authority to bind all those subject to its territorial or nationality-based jurisdiction.

[104] *Case Concerning Military and Paramilitary Activities in and Against Nicaragua (Nicaragua v United States of America)* above n 57, para 218.

[105] The de facto control theory holds that non-state entities are bound by international law on the basis of the exclusive control over a specific territory. This requires that certain acts of the de facto authority be acknowledged as legitimate, and the scope of a de facto authority's legitimate activity is referred to as an implied mandate in international jurisprudence. See further below, Ch 6 section V.

Part II: Can Armed Groups be Bound by International Human Rights Law?

Having established in Part I that armed groups may be bound by international law, Part II looks specifically at the application of international human rights law to armed groups. It is widely accepted that international human rights law treaties exclusively regulate the relationship between states and the individuals subject to their jurisdiction, and so Chapter 6 examines whether the application of this body of law is restricted *ratione personae*. Discussion in this regard relates to the object and purpose of international human rights law, the evolutionary nature of international law, and ascertaining whether an armed group—in situations where the authority of the state has been displaced—may be regarded as a vertical authority, thereby maintaining the traditional vertical application of international human rights law and overcoming potential *ratione personae* restrictions.

If international human rights law is to be applied to armed groups, the precise scope and content of any resultant obligations must be determined. Of course, it is necessary that any imposed obligations be responsive to the needs and rights of the affected population. However, armed groups are not equivalent to states, and it cannot be assumed that they possess the same ability to give effect to international obligations in all circumstances. As such, in order to ensure that any imposed obligations are effective in practice, it is also essential that they be realistic vis-à-vis the capability of the group in question. Chapter 7 therefore explores a context-dependent approach to the obligations of non-state armed groups. This requires a means of determining the specific obligations imposed in any given situation, and the possibility of adapting the respect, protect, fulfil framework is examined in this regard. At issue is the gradated application of obligations, beginning with the negative obligation to respect, and then progressing to include the positive obligations to fulfil and protect. In order to avoid a gap in protection with respect to those rights that are outside an armed groups' responsibility, this approach involves a division of responsibility between the state and the armed group, and so the territorial state's continuing international human rights law obligations with respect to territory outside its de facto control are examined. This chapter also addresses the means by which armed groups may be made aware of any obligations arising under international law.

Part III: Testing the Application of International Human Rights Law to Armed Groups in Practice

Part III brings together the work undertaken in previous chapters by examining how international human rights law obligations can be applied to non-state armed groups in practice. In particular, the context-dependent approach to human rights obligations developed in Chapter 7 is tested in relation to a number of specific issues, namely: prosecutions undertaken by armed groups, instances of armed group detention, and armed group obligations vis-à-vis the right to health. These issues have been chosen not only out of concern for the immediately implicated human rights (i.e. the right to a fair trial, the prohibition on arbitrary detention, and the right to health) but because they also raise broader concerns in relation to, inter alia, the potential legislative authority of an armed group, and how an armed group interacts with, and provides services for, the population subject to its authority.

Part I

Subjecting Armed Groups to International Legal Regulation

2

International Legal Personality

THE DIRECT ATTRIBUTION of international rights or obligations to a non-state armed group is dependent upon international legal personality,[1] and so a clear understanding of this concept is of central importance for the purposes of this work. However, despite the central role played by international legal personality within the international legal order, this area of law is shrouded in remarkable uncertainty, inhibiting an accurate understanding of the contemporary legal reality. If issues relating to the application of international obligations to non-state armed groups are to be addressed, it is essential that this uncertainty be overcome. This chapter therefore intends to clarify the relevant law in light of recent legal developments. In particular, it must be determined whether non-state armed groups may in principle possess international legal personality and, if so, the criteria necessary in order to acquire this status must be identified.

I. CORE CONCEPTS RELATING TO INTERNATIONAL LEGAL PERSONALITY

A. Legal Subjects

Traditionally, a distinction is made between legal subjects and objects. An object is an entity that is addressed by the law but which does not possess legal rights or duties.[2] For example, cats and dogs are often cited as examples of objects under municipal law, while the sea may be considered an object of international law, regulated by the Law of the Sea, but without distinct rights or duties.[3] A subject on the other hand, is an

[1] Although the attribution of either rights or obligations is relevant for the purposes of international legal personality, given the focus of this work, the attribution of international obligations is of principal concern.

[2] Robert Jennings and Arthur Watts (eds), *Oppenheim's International Law, vol 1*, 9th edn (Oxford, OUP, 2008) 120.

[3] United Nations Convention on the Law of the Sea (adopted 10 December 1982, entered into force 16 November 1994) 1833 UNTS 3.

'active participant' in the international legal order,[4] possessing direct international rights and duties.[5] States have long been regarded as the principal subjects of international law. The continued validity of the subject/object dichotomy has been questioned;[6] however, for present purposes the pertinent point is that the subjects of international law are the active participants of the international legal order, possessing direct rights or obligations.

B. International Legal Persons

All legal systems must determine their participants: those entities who are endowed with legal rights and obligations and whose actions are given legal significance. To this end municipal law typically establishes the concept of legal personality.[7] This is a construction used to identify an entity as a distinct and independent actor on the legal plane,[8] and may be regarded as a status that recognises an entity's ability to function in the legal order.[9] A characteristic definition thus holds that 'inside the system "legal personality" is the attire which enables an entity to function in a legal order; more importantly, this attire is awarded by that same legal order, which determines which entities participate in its sphere and which do not.'[10]

This definition may be extended to the international level: international legal persons are distinct, independent actors, who possess direct rights or obligations under international law.[11] International legal personality

[4] Karsten Nowrot, 'Legal Consequences of Globalization: The Status of Non-Governmental Organizations under International Law' (1999) 2 *Indiana Journal of Global Legal Studies* 622.

[5] Robert McCorquodale, 'The Individual and the International Legal System' in Malcolm Evans (ed), *International Law*, 2nd edn (Oxford, OUP, 2006) 308.

[6] Rosalyn Higgins, *Problems and Processes: International law and how we use it* (Oxford, OUP, 1994) 50.

[7] Roland Portmann, *Legal Personality in International Law* (Cambridge, CUP, 2010) 1. See also, ibid 7.

[8] Fergus Green, 'Fragmentation in Two Dimensions: The ICJ's Flawed Approach to Non-State Actors and International Legal Personality' (2008) 9 *Melbourne Journal of International Law* 50.

[9] Janne E Nijman,'Non-state actors and the international rule of law: Revisiting the "realist theory" of international legal personality' (2010) Amsterdam Center for International Law Research Paper Series, 5.

[10] Catherine Brolman, *The Institutional Veil in Public International Law: International Organisations and the Law of Treaties* (Oxford, Hart, 2007) 68.

[11] See, eg entry for 'international legal personality' in Jonathan Law and Elizabeth A Martin (eds), *Oxford Dictionary of Law* 5th edn (Oxford, OUP, 2002); Rein A Mullerson, 'Human Rights and the Individual as Subject of International Law: A Soviet View' (1990) 1 *European Journal of International Law*, 35; MNS Sellers, 'International Legal Personality' (2005) 11 *Ius Gentium* 67; DP O'Connell, *International Law* (London, Stevens & Sons, 1970) 80.

is thus a construct indicative of a certain status under international law. Specifically, international legal personality indicates direct comprehension by the international legal order: entities devoid of personality simply do not exist (directly at least) in the eyes of the law,[12] and are excluded from the international legal system.[13] An entity's independent existence is an essential underlying requirement with respect to international legal personality. In order to warrant direct cognition by the international legal order, an entity must establish itself as a distinct participant. If it is subject to the exclusive authority of another subject of international law, then it is that subject's personality that is decisive on the international plane, and the entity in question may more appropriately be regarded as a legal person under national and not international law, or simply as an extension of the dominant subject's personality.[14]

Although 'international legal personality' and 'subjects of international law' may, strictly speaking, be distinct concepts,[15] there has been a trend in modern international law to treat them as equivalent,[16] and, as noted by Klabbers, 'there is nothing particularly wrong with treating them as such in a pragmatic fashion.'[17] It is this contemporary, pragmatic understanding that is adopted herein: all subjects of international law possess international legal personality, while all international legal persons are subjects of international law. For present purposes these two concepts may be legitimately treated as synonymous.[18]

C. Non-State Entities and International Legal Personality

States have traditionally been considered to be the exclusive subjects of international law,[19] and the sole entities endowed with international legal personality.[20] However, this understanding no longer holds true today. Indeed, while state-exclusivity once formed a central component of the international legal order, it is important to note that there have nonetheless

[12] See, Jan Klabbers, 'The Concept of Legal Personality' (2005) 11 *Ius Gentium* 35.

[13] Above n 7, 5.

[14] See, eg Antonio Cassese, 'The Status of Rebels under the 1977 Geneva Protocol on Non-International Armed Conflicts' (1981) 2 *International and Comparative Law Quarterly* 429. See further above, Ch 1 section V.

[15] See, Jan Klabbers, *An Introduction to International Institutional Law* (Cambridge, CUP, 2003) 43.

[16] See eg, above n 7, 1.

[17] Above n 15, 43.

[18] Thus, the terms 'international subject', 'international legal personality', and 'international person' may be used interchangeably herein.

[19] Above n 2, 16.

[20] Colin Warbrick, 'States and Recognition in International Law' in Malcolm Evans (ed), *International Law*, 2nd edn (Oxford, OUP, 2006) 229.

long been notable exceptions. Frequently cited examples of non-state subjects of international law pre-dating the establishment of the United Nations include the Holy See,[21] the Sovereign Order of Malta,[22] the Central Commission for the Navigation of the Rhine,[23] and the Lighthouse at Cape Spartel.[24] Two other exceptions to state exclusivity—belligerent and insurgent groups—are of pertinent interest, given the subject matter of this monograph.

As a response to their forceful assertion of de facto power and authority,[25] since at least the early nineteenth century armed groups recognised as belligerents—and to a lesser extent insurgents—have been treated as possessing certain international law rights and duties,[26] and thus as subjects of international law.[27] For example, captured members of belligerent armed group forces were granted prisoner of war status,[28] while ships sailing under a belligerent's flag were granted access to the ports of recognising states, and 'had the right to visit and search at sea.'[29] Similarly, belligerent entities were granted the right to 'enter into legal relations and conclude agreements on the international plane with states and other belligerents/insurgents',[30] while certain acts of belligerent forces with respect to the territory they controlled were recognised as valid.[31] Belligerent entities could also be held liable for their acts. For instance, during the Spanish civil war, the British government addressed three reparations claims to the nationalist government—a belligerent entity—in relation to the destruction of British property by nationalist forces.[32] Interestingly—and

[21] Ian Brownlie, *Principles of Public international Law*, 7th edn (Oxford, OUP, 2008) 64.

[22] Malcolm Shaw, *International Law*, 6th edn (Cambridge, CUP, 2008) 243.

[23] O'Connell, above n 11, 94.

[24] David J Bederman, 'The Souls of International Organizations: Legal Personality and the Lighthouse at Cape Spartel' (1995) *Virginia Journal of International Law*, 367.

[25] See, eg, Antonio Cassese, *International Law*, 2nd edn (Oxford, OUP, 2005) 71.

[26] Jean Gabriel Castel, *International Law: Chiefly as Interpreted and Applied in Canada*, 3rd edn (London, Butterworths, 1976) 47. See further, Yair M Lootsteen, 'The Concept of Belligerency in International Law' (2000) 166 *Military Law Review*; Hersch Lauterpacht, 'Recognition of Insurgents as a De Facto Government' (1939) 3 *Modern Law Review*; Robert R Wilson, 'Recognition of Insurgency and Belligerency' (1937) 1 *Proceedings of the American Society of International Law at its Annual Meeting*.

[27] Hans Kelsen, *Principles of International Law* (New Jersey, Lawbook Exchange, 2003) 161.

[28] Sandesh Sivakumaran, *The Law of Non-International Armed Conflict* (Oxford, OUP, 2012) 16.

[29] 'The Concept of Belligerency in International Law' above n 26, 110.

[30] James Crawford, *Brownlie's Principles of Public International Law*, 8th edn (Oxford, OUP, 2012) 118.

[31] See discussion on *O'Neill v Central Leather Co*, and *US (George W Hopkins claim) v United Mexican States* in O'Connell, above n 11, 88–89.

[32] A similar claim was made with respect to acts committed by Confederate forces during the American civil war. 'Fourth Report on State Responsibility, by Mr Robert Ago, Special Rapporteur—The internationally wrongful act of the State, source of international responsibility (continued)' (1972) *Yearbook of International Law Commission* Vol II, UN Doc A/Cn.4/264, para 181.

indicative of the extent of this exception to state exclusivity—when belligerents have been recognised as de facto regimes,[33] it has been held that 'as far as international law and the recognizing State are concerned, a *de facto* government is a *de jure* government.'[34]

In the modern era,[35] states' status as the exclusive subjects of international law has been authoritatively rejected. In the *Reparations* Advisory Opinion, the International Court of Justice held the United Nations to be a subject of international law,[36] and in a subsequent Advisory Opinion this was extended to include all International Organisations.[37] Other non-state entities considered to possess international legal personality include the International Committee of the Red Cross,[38] the European Coal and Steel Community,[39] and the European Union.[40] Accordingly, the traditional view that states are the sole entities endowed with international legal personality is no longer valid, and today it is accepted that non-state entities may, under certain circumstances, possess international legal personality.

D. Determining the Consequences of International Legal Personality

Having established in principle that non-state actors may acquire international legal personality, the consequences of this personality—ie the scope of an entity's competence to act on the international plane—must be determined. Traditionally, it was accepted that states alone possessed 'the totality of international rights and duties recognised by international law',[41] and so issues relating to international legal personality and

[33] Above n 2, 162.

[34] Herbert W Briggs, 'De Facto and De Jure Recognition: The Arantzazu Mendi' (1939) 33 *American Journal of International Law* 690. For an analysis of relevant case law see O'Connell above n 11, 89–93.

[35] For present purposes, the modern era of international law is considered to be that era commencing with the establishment of the United Nations.

[36] *Reparations for injuries suffered in the services of the United Nations*, Advisory Opinion, International Court of Justice, 11 April 1949, 179.

[37] *Legality of the use by a State of Nuclear Weapons in Armed Conflict*, Advisory Opinion, International Court of Justice, 8 July 1996, para 27. The question as to whether International Organisations may be considered non-state actors has been raised. States do play a central role vis-à-vis such entities. However, International Organisations are characterised by an independent will—they are not merely a collection of states—and have the ability to bind a state against its will. Thus, while International Organisations exhibit characteristics that differentiate them from other non-state actors (this is not a homogenous category) they are not states, and significantly, possess a personality distinct from that of their member states.

[38] *Prosecutor v Simic*, Decision on the Prosecution Motion under Rule 73 for a Ruling concerning the Testimony of a Witness, Trial Chamber, International Criminal Tribunal for the former Yugoslavia, Case No IT-95-9, 27 July 1999, para 35.

[39] O'Connell above n 11, 98.

[40] Consolidated Version of the Treaty on European Union [2010] OJ C83/41, Art 47.

[41] Dr Manuel Rama-Montaldo, 'International Legal Personality and Implied Powers of International Organizations' (1970) 44 *British Yearbook of International Law* 133.

statehood were treated as synonymous. This historical conflation of international legal personality and statehood meant that it was not essential to differentiate between legally distinct issues such as the criteria regulating the acquisition of statehood or international legal personality, or, indeed, the consequences thereof.[42] In part as a result of the principle of the sovereign equality of states, international legal personality was thus treated as a uniform concept, and all international subjects were regarded as possessing the same competence to act on the international plane. The consequences of confusing these two legally distinct concepts became apparent with the emergence of non-state subjects of international law. For example, rights arising consequent to statehood, such as the capacity to bring an international claim, were considered to be indicators of personality,[43] while consequences of states' personality were presumed to be equally applicable to non-state international legal persons. Confusion in this regard has been generated, inter alia, in relation to the right to issue passports,[44] and individual immunity.[45]

In seeking clarity on this issue recourse may be had to the case law of the International Court of Justice. In the *Reparations* Advisory Opinion the Court stated that: 'the subjects of law in any legal system are not necessarily identical in their nature *or in the extent of their rights*.'[46] This was subsequently underlined in the *Nuclear Weapons* Advisory Opinion: 'international organizations are subjects of international law which do not, unlike states, possess a general competence'.[47] Accordingly, the International Court of Justice held that the extent to which a subject of international law may legitimately act on the international plane must be determined on the basis of factors specific to that subject: 'the rights and duties of an entity such as the Organization *must depend upon its purposes and functions* as specified or implied in its constituent documents and *developed in practice*.'[48] Thus, while the International Court of Justice noted that the World Health Organization could, in principle, request an Advisory Opinion, it held that the organisation did not have the specific competence required to request an Advisory Opinion on the legality of

[42] ibid, 133.
[43] Above n 41, 133.
[44] Above n 15, 159, fn 56.
[45] See *Difference Relating to Immunity from Legal Process of a Special Rapporteur of the Commission on Human Rights*, Advisory Opinion, International Court of Justice, 19 April 1999.
[46] *Reparations for injuries suffered in the services of the United Nations* above n 36, 178. Emphasis added.
[47] *Legality of the Use By a State of Nuclear Weapons in Armed Conflict* above n 37, para 25.
[48] *Reparations for injuries suffered in the services of the United Nations* above n 36, 180. Emphasis added.

nuclear weapons in armed conflict.[49] This subject-specific approach was also evident in *Simic* where the International Criminal Tribunal for the former Yugoslavia held that the role and function of the International Committee of the Red Cross (ICRC) included a right to confidentiality,[50] and in the *Bank for International Settlements* arbitration, where the Bank's treaty origin and public international functions were decisive in finding that it constituted a *sui generis* international organisation.[51] Similarly, Article 6 of the Treaty Establishing the European Coal and Steel Community states that '[i]n its international relationships, the Community shall enjoy the juridical capacity necessary to the exercise of its functions and the attainment of its ends.'[52] Accordingly, the consequences of international legal personality are not uniform and an entity's ability to act on the international plane is determined on the basis of factors specific to that entity; ie on the basis of an entity's subject-specific competence.

II. THE ACQUISITION OF INTERNATIONAL LEGAL PERSONALITY

Within the international legal system there is no centralised law of persons.[53] As a result, and distinct from the situation vis-à-vis municipal law, international law lacks a mechanism capable of definitively stipulating which entities have legal personality.[54] This has led to significant uncertainty, and a variety of competing conceptions based on various philosophical approaches to international law have emerged.[55] The dominant conceptions have recently been grouped into five distinct categories: the states-only, recognition, individualistic, formal, and actor conceptions.[56] This constitutes a slightly more nuanced classification—albeit based on similar tenets—than the objective and inductive conceptions previously presented by Rama-Montaldo.[57] These different conceptions will now be discussed in order that the traditional approaches to the acquisition of international legal personality may be understood.

[49] *Legality of the Use By a State of Nuclear Weapons in Armed Conflict* above n 37, para 27.

[50] *Prosecutor v Simic*, above n 38, para 73.

[51] *Reineccius et al v Bank for International Settlements*, Permanent Court of Arbitration, 22 November 2002, para 123. See further, above n 7, 228–32.

[52] Treaty establishing the European Coal and Steel Community, Paris, 18 April 1951, Art 6.

[53] Above n 7, 9.

[54] Above n 9, 19.

[55] Above n 8, 53.

[56] Above n 7, 2.

[57] Above n 41, 112.

A. The States-only and Recognition Conceptions

The states-only and recognition conceptions are founded on a positivist approach to international law. The states-only conception holds that states are the exclusive subjects of international law, and thus that there are no conditions necessary for the acquisition of international legal personality other than the acquisition of statehood.[58] This conception is no longer valid, having been authoritatively rejected by the International Court of Justice.[59] However, the states-only approach may be regarded as having evolved into the recognition conception, which retains the view of states as the original and dominant subjects of international law. According to this approach states have the exclusive power to create other international subjects through an act of explicit or implicit recognition. Once recognised, these secondary or derivative subjects have rights, duties, and capacities 'limited in accordance with the parameters defined in the act of recognition.'[60] This approach is similar to the inductive conception whereby certain international rights and duties may be expressly conferred by states, and from these particular rights and duties a general international personality may be derived.[61] Justification for the recognition approach is typically founded on the *Reparations* judgment, where it is argued that the Court based the United Nation's international status on the basis of implicit recognition on the part of the founding states.[62]

By ignoring the determinative relevance of objective legal criteria, however, the recognition conception suffers from faults similar to those associated with the constitutive theory of statehood, namely that political considerations may lead to legally unsound situations:[63] in practice, states will often choose not to acknowledge the legal consequences of a factual situation as they do not want those consequences to follow.[64] This restricts the international legal order's ability to effectively address the continuous evolution of international life as the emergence of international subjects is not regulated by international law, but rather is dependent upon state will, and thus, inevitably, on states' political considerations. This means, for example, that an entity may be regarded as a legitimate subject of

[58] Above n 7, 14.

[59] *Reparations for injuries suffered in the services of the United Nations* above n 36, 179; *Legality of the Use By a State of Nuclear Weapons in Armed Conflict* above n 37, para 25.

[60] Above n 7, 83.

[61] Above n 41, 112.

[62] Above n 7, 105.

[63] With respect to the constitutive theory of statehood it is noted that the act of recognition is often dependent upon political considerations, rather than legal criteria. See, eg above n 22, 445. Examples of the influence of political factors on the process of recognition include Arab states' refusal to recognise Israel, and the United States' refusal to recognise the People's Republic of China.

[64] Above n 22, 445.

international law for the purposes of some states but not for others, while equally, an entity identical to a 'recognised' subject, in terms of objective criteria, may not be granted such status, resulting in a legally untenable situation.

B. The Individualistic Conception

The individualistic conception regards the individual human being as the ultimate international person, capable of holding international rights and being subject to international duties.[65] The individual is considered to be an a priori international subject,[66] and status is not dependent upon an act of state recognition. Indeed, the state itself is regarded as a corporate entity created by individuals for pursuing their own interests.[67] Accordingly, states may become a posteriori subjects of international law if there are international norms addressing them, and the specific consequence of international personality is international responsibility.[68] The principles propounded at the Nuremberg trials—and subsequently in international criminal law—are a principal justification for this conception: '[c]rimes against international law are committed by men, not by abstract entities'.[69]

However, the individualistic conception fails to acknowledge the role of states—considered by the individualistic conception to be abstract entities—as the 'direct subjects'[70] of the international legal order. The distinct standing of states is illustrated, inter alia, by the primacy accorded to states in Article 2(1) of the United Nations Charter,[71] states' longstanding role with respect to the creation of international law,[72] the ability of a state to assert its own right following the violation of a citizen's right,[73] the obligations which states owe to other states,[74] and the concept of state responsibility distinct from the individual responsibility of state agents.[75]

[65] Above n 7, 128.
[66] ibid, 126.
[67] ibid, 129.
[68] ibid, 14.
[69] *Trial of the Major War Criminals before the International Military Tribunal*, Nürnberg, 14 November 1945-1 October 1946, [1957] 223.
[70] *Reparations for injuries suffered in the services of the United Nations* above n 36, 178.
[71] Charter of the United Nations (adopted 26 June 1945, entered into force 24 October 1945) 1 UNTS XVI.
[72] See, eg *North Sea Continental Shelf*, Judgment, International Court of Justice, 20 February 1969.
[73] *The Mavrommatis Palestine Concessions*, Judgment, Permanent Court of International Justice, 30 August 1924, 12.
[74] *Barcelona Traction, Light and Power Company, Limited*, Judgment, International Court of Justice, 5 February 1970, para 33.
[75] See, eg Draft Articles on State Responsibility for Internationally Wrongful Acts, UNGA Res A/56/49(Vol 1)/Corr 4.

C. The Formal Conception

The formal conception regards international law as an open system. There are no a priori subjects of international law. Accordingly, any entity may become an international person provided it is addressed by a norm of international law, and there are no specific consequences attached to being an international person.[76] In many ways this conception resembles the objective approach as defined by Rama-Montaldo, wherein 'it is the international legal order which automatically ascribes personality to an entity fulfilling certain conditions.'[77] Portmann argues that the decisions of the International Court of Justice in the *LaGrand*[78] and *Avena*[79] judgments are the principal justifications for this conception.[80] The principal fault with respect to the formal conception is its failure to acknowledge the continued importance—even to a mitigated degree—of state will (and thus recognition) in the contemporary legal order;[81] in this regard, the International Court of Justice's finding that states may create new subjects of law is particularly relevant.[82]

D. The Actor Conception

The actor conception is primarily the product of the New Haven school,[83] with Higgins as its most prominent contemporary advocate.[84] International law is not seen as a set of rules, but rather as an authoritative decision-making process based on effective participation.[85] Consequently, this approach sees the concept of international legal personality as irrelevant, instead considering the international system to be composed of 'participants'. For present purposes, however, the participants of the actor conception may be regarded as subjects of international law.[86] Within this

[76] Above n 7, 177.
[77] Above n 41, 112. An analogy may also be made to the declarative approach as regards the acquisition of statehood.
[78] *LaGrand (Germany v United States of America)*, Judgment, International Court of Justice, 27 June 2001.
[79] *Avena and Other Mexican Nationals (Mexico v United States of America)*, Judgment, International Court of Justice, 31 March 2004.
[80] Above n 7, 197.
[81] See, eg above n 25, 71, and similar discussion with respect to the individualistic conception, above Ch 2 section II.B.
[82] *Legality of the Use By a State of Nuclear Weapons in Armed Conflict* above n 37, para 19.
[83] Above n 7, 215.
[84] See, above n 6, 50.
[85] Above n 7, 213.
[86] ibid, 208.

approach, participation—or becoming a subject of international law—is not based on any act of recognition or the fulfilment of specific criteria; rather it is founded on the effective power to participate. All actors effectively participating on the international scene are regarded as relevant.[87]

The actor conception, however, fails to acknowledge the continued dominance of states in the international legal order,[88] and the fact that, as Higgins herself has noted, despite significant changes in recent years states remain 'at the heart of the international legal system'.[89] Equally, international case law, particularly the *Reparations* and *Western Sahara* Advisory Opinions, has relied upon legal criteria in evaluating an entity's status and not—in contradistinction to the actor approach—the mere fact of effective power to participate.[90]

E. Conclusions Regarding the Different Conceptions of International Legal Personality

The above-mentioned approaches to international legal personality are the product of philosophically distinct understandings of international law, and may be grouped into two broad categories analogous to the constitutive and declarative theories utilised in relation to the recognition of statehood. Personality may thus be regarded as dependent upon either state will (the states-only and recognition conceptions) or the satisfaction of objective legal criteria (the individualistic, formal, and actor conceptions). At its most simple the problem with each conception, when considered distinctly, is that they fail to acknowledge the presence and influence of the other category, with the consequence that no single approach accurately reflects the contemporary international reality. While at one time certain of these conceptions—such as the states-only approach—may have enjoyed a dominant role within the international legal order, this does not hold true today, and the modern international legal order exhibits elements of both categories.[91] To persist with one of these traditional approaches

[87] Above n 6, 50.

[88] For similar discussion with respect to the individualistic and formal conceptions, see above Ch 2 sections II.B and II.C.

[89] Above n 6, 39.

[90] *Reparations for injuries suffered in the services of the United Nations* above n 36, 178; *Western Sahara*, Advisory Opinion, International Court of Justice, 16 October 1975, para 148.

[91] The issue of recognition of statehood serves as a relevant analogy. While the declarative approach may be dominant, in practice the declarative and constitutive theories coexist to a certain extent: in instances of overwhelming international recognition, less attention may be paid to satisfaction of the objective criteria, whereas in situations of limited recognition, satisfaction of the objective criteria is of greater importance. See Malcolm Shaw, *International Law*, 5th edn (Cambridge, CUP, 2003) 186, 207, 445. See further, the reasoning utilised by the International Court of Justice in *Western Sahara*, above n 90.

would be to ignore the realities of modern international law and international life, and—to paraphrase Higgins—to persist within an intellectual prison of our own making.[92] Clearly, an alternative approach is required. Before proceeding further, however, a question specific to armed groups' acquisition of international legal personality must be addressed.

III. COMMON ARTICLE 3's 'LEGAL STATUS CLAUSE' AND THE INTERNATIONAL LEGAL PERSONALITY OF ARMED GROUPS

Article 3(4) common to the four Geneva Conventions of 1949 holds that:[93] '[t]he application of the preceding provisions shall not affect the legal status of the Parties to the conflict.'[94] This clause is widely regarded as 'essential' with respect to the extension of international humanitarian law to non-international armed conflicts, and thus to non-state armed groups.[95] According to the International Committee of the Red Cross *Commentary*, '[w]ithout it neither Article 3, nor any other Article in its place, would ever have been adopted.'[96] It was intended to address states' concerns regarding the consequences of extending international law to previously unregulated internal affairs; concerns relating to, inter alia, state sovereignty and states' ability—or right—to quell an insurrection.[97] Indicative of its importance, this clause was inserted at the very outset of the common Article 3 drafting process.[98]

However, Article 3(4)'s specific legal consequences remain ambiguous.[99] What is meant by a group's 'legal status'? Given that international legal personality is sometimes referred to as 'legal status', are the two considered synonymous?[100] If this is the case, this clause may preclude the

[92] Above n 6, 49.

[93] Although not present in the text of Additional Protocol II, this clause remains applicable, inter alia, on the basis that the Protocol 'develops and supplements Article 3 common to the Geneva Conventions'. See Art 1(1), Additional Protocol II.

[94] Art 3, Convention (IV) relative to the Protection of Civilian Persons in Time of War (adopted 12 August 1949, entered into force 21 October 1950) 75 UNTS 287.

[95] A similar clause has been included in a number of subsequent treaties addressing armed groups. See for instance, Art 1(6), Protocol on Prohibitions or Restrictions on the Use of Mines, Booby-Traps and Other Devices as amended on 3 May 1996; Art 7(1), African Union Convention for the Protection and Assistance of Internally Displaced Persons in Africa (Kampala Convention); Art 4(3), Optional Protocol to the Convention on the Rights of the Child on the involvement of children in armed conflict.

[96] Jean S Pictet, *Commentary to the IV Geneva Convention Relative to the Protection of Civilian Persons in Time of War* (Geneva, International Committee of the Red Cross, 1960) 44.

[97] ibid, 44.

[98] See Jean S Pictet (ed), *Commentary: III Geneva Convention Relative to the Treatment of Prisoners of War* (Geneva, International Committee of the Red Cross, 1960) 43.

[99] David P Forsythe, 'Legal Management of Internal War: The 1977 Protocol on Non-International Armed Conflicts' (1978) 72 *American Journal of International Law* 273.

[100] See, eg above n 25, 150.

international legal personality of armed groups addressed by common Article 3. This conclusion would mean that common Article 3 does not establish direct obligations vis-à-vis armed groups, as this is impossible absent international legal personality. Rather, common Article 3 would have to be interpreted as exclusively establishing obligations vis-à-vis states, the provisions of which are to be implemented via the medium of national law.[101] Accordingly, armed groups would be bound by national and not international law. This interpretation would have a decisive impact in relation to both the direct application of international law to armed groups,[102] and the international legal personality of such groups. Clearly, the specific legal consequences of Article 3(4) must be understood.

The drafting history of common Article 3 indicates that the legal status clause was included to address two principal concerns: that the attribution of international law obligations to armed oppositions groups would (a) not grant legitimacy to, or (b) not constitute recognition of, such groups.[103] These two concerns will now be addressed. This section will deal primarily with common Article 3; however, it is noted that these issues are also relevant vis-à-vis Additional Protocol II, which 'develops and supplements' common Article 3.[104]

A. The Desire to Avoid Legitimising Armed Groups

A principal motivation underlying the legal status clause was a desire to avoid legitimising armed opposition groups and their political aims.[105] By definition, these groups stand in violent opposition to states, and it was feared that their legitimisation would imply, inter alia, the illegitimacy of the state, an erosion of state authority, or the legitimacy of using force against the state.[106] States were determined to maintain their supremacy at the national level, and a key theme throughout the drafting process was states' intention to ensure that their right to criminalise and suppress insurrection would not be unduly restricted.[107] However, while states'

[101] See, generally, Alfred P Rubin, 'The Status of Rebels under the Geneva Conventions of 1949' (1972) 21 *International and Comparative Law Quarterly* 475.

[102] Discussed further in Ch 4.

[103] See, above n 96, 44.

[104] Art 1(1), Additional Protocol II.

[105] David A Elder, 'The Historical Background of Common Article 3 of the Geneva Conventions of 1949' (1979) 11 *Case Western Reserve Journal of International Law* 68.

[106] Above n 96, 44.

[107] See, eg above n 14, 421. See further Pakistan, 'Official Records of the Diplomatic Conference on the Reaffirmation and Development of International Humanitarian Law Applicable in Armed Conflicts (Geneva 1974–1977)' Vol VII, CDDH/SR.49, draft art 1, 61, para 11; Zaire, ibid, p 219, para 124.

desire to avoid legitimising armed opposition groups is understandable, it does not require that such groups' international legal personality be restricted or precluded: such a stance conflates the separate concepts of legitimacy and international legal personality.[108]

The application of direct international rights or obligations does not affect the political or moral legitimacy of an entity as such, but rather acknowledges the reality of the situation,[109] and the fact of the entity's participation in the international system.[110] Indeed, it is evident that certain states—entities unquestionably enjoying 'full' international legal personality—are often regarded as illegitimate.[111] Equally, the fact that an armed group possesses international legal personality does not imply that all of the group's actions must be considered legal, that the activities of its members cannot be criminalised, or that states are no longer entitled to suppress the group's insurrection: both international and domestic law remain applicable. The example of individual criminal responsibility for the commission of war crimes is pertinent in this regard. Individuals are addressed by the law, and certain actions are criminalised, without influencing their perceived legitimacy or that of the party to the conflict to which they belong. Any legitimacy-related concerns must therefore be regarded as purely political considerations, and without influence as regards the legal effects of common Article 3(4).

B. The Desire to Avoid Recognition of Belligerency

The second and more legally pertinent motivation underpinning Article 3(4) was a desire to avoid the legal recognition of armed opposition groups.[112] This desire is related to the concept of belligerency, whereby states—by extending recognition of belligerent status—may elevate an

[108] JK Kleffner, 'The applicability of international humanitarian law to organized armed groups' (2011) 93 *International Review of the Red Cross* 455.

[109] States are often reluctant to acknowledge the existence of a non-international armed conflict on their territory. Nonetheless, international law classifies such situations on the basis of objective criteria.

[110] On the basis of the maxim that in order to be effective, the law must reflect the realities of international life.

[111] See, eg the international reaction to, and sanctioning of, the apartheid regimes in Rhodesia and South Africa. See further, *Legal Consequences for States of the Continued Presence of South Africa in Namibia (South West Africa) Notwithstanding Security Council Resolution 276 (1970)*, Advisory Opinion, International Court of Justice, 21 June 1971, paras 119–26; United Nations Security Council Resolution 591 (1986).

[112] See, eg 'Final Record of the Diplomatic Conference of Geneva of 1949', Vol II Section B, UK, 10; ibid, Burma, 15; ibid, UK, 47; GIAD Draper, *The Red Cross Conventions* (London, Stevens & Sons, 1958) 103.

armed group to the level of a *pro tanto* international subject, bringing into effect the application of international law, including what is now referred to as the law of international armed conflict.[113] Recognition of belligerent status thus gives rise to a number of significant legal consequences, a fact specifically mentioned during the drafting process.[114] For example, captured rebels must be granted prisoner of war status, rebel ships have the right to visit and search at sea and the right to confiscate contraband, while third states are under an obligation of neutrality and non-intervention.[115] As noted by the UK, belligerent status 'implied rights exceeding the scope of the Convention.'[116] Significantly, in light of states' concerns as expressed above, recognition of belligerency would, to a certain extent, limit a state's right to suppress an insurgency; for example, rebel fighters could not be prosecuted for 'legitimate acts of warfare'.[117]

Pertinently, belligerent status can never be acquired by armed groups themselves:[118] an act of state is the key determinant. This act typically took the form of recognition.[119] States' potential legal recognition of armed groups by virtue of the application of the Conventions was thus an important issue during the drafting process. For instance, the United Kingdom made it clear that what was to become common Article 3 'was a source of serious difficulties ... because the application of the Convention would appear to give the status of belligerents to insurgents',[120] while Burma 'could not agree to the recognition of the status of belligerency to insurgents.'[121] This viewpoint was also expressed in the drafting of Additional Protocol II. For example, Pakistan—which took a lead role in

[113] The concept of belligerency arose prior to the legal regulation of non-international armed conflict. Recognition of belligerency elevated the situation to one broadly equivalent to international armed conflict. See further, 'The Concept of Belligerency in International Law' above n 26; Hans Kelsen, 'Recognition in International Law: Theoretical Observations' (1941) 35 *American Journal of International Law* 616. Belligerency is also briefly discussed below, see Ch 3 section I.C.

[114] Final Record of the Diplomatic Conference of Geneva of 1949, Vol II Section B, Norway, 11.

[115] 'The Concept of Belligerency in International Law' above n 26, 10; above n 27, 292; Hersch Lauterpacht, 'The Subjects of International Law' in Andrea Bianchi (ed), *Non-State Actors and International Law* (Farnham, Ashgate 2009) 5; above n 2, 165.

[116] Final Record of the Diplomatic Conference of Geneva of 1949, Vol II Section B, UK, 47.

[117] Above n 28, 16. The extent of this restriction is limited. Other activities, including membership of the armed group, treason, and illegitimate acts of war, can still be criminalised.

[118] Rudiger Wolfrum and Christiane E Philipp, 'The Status of the Taliban: Their Obligations and Rights under International Law' (2002) 6 *Max Planck Yearbook of United Nations Law* 580.

[119] It has been suggested that it may also arise by other means, for example, through the imposition of a blockade. Iain Scobbie, 'Gaza' in Elizabeth Wilmshurst (ed), *International Law and the Classification of Conflicts* (Oxford, OUP, 2012) 302.

[120] Final Record of the Diplomatic Conference of Geneva of 1949, Vol II Section B, UK, 10.

[121] ibid, Burma, 50.

the drafting process—stated that, 'nothing in the Protocol should suggest that dissidents must be treated legally other than as rebels'.[122]

Given the significant consequences associated with recognition of belligerency, states' concerns at Geneva are entirely understandable.[123] The legal status clause must thus be regarded as a means of addressing these concerns, and stating within the Conventions themselves that the application of the Conventions did not confer belligerent status on armed groups.[124] This was in fact made explicit by states present at Geneva in a resolution of the Final Conference:[125]

> The Conference considers that the conditions under which a Party to a conflict can be recognized as a belligerent by Powers not taking part in this conflict, are governed by the general rules of international law on the subject and are in no way modified by the Geneva Conventions.[126]

This role of the legal status clause in precluding recognition of belligerency was also made clear in the draft of Additional Protocol II to the Geneva Conventions prepared by the International Committee of the Red Cross in 1973.[127] Equally, the Commentary to the finalised Protocol confirmed that Protocol II's 'implementation does not constitute recognition of belligerency even implicitly'.[128] The drafting history thus indicates that the principal motivations underlying the legal status clause were a desire to ensure that the application of the Conventions to non-international armed conflict did not confer recognition of belligerent status, and did not interfere with a state's ability to quell an insurrection.[129] As stated by Draper:

> This vital paragraph makes it clear that the application of Article 3 in no way constitutes any legal recognition by the *de jure* Government of the rebel party, nor limits the former's right to quell the rebellion and to punish, in accordance with its laws, the criminal acts committed by those who took part in it.[130]

[122] 'Official Records of the Diplomatic Conference on the Reaffirmation and Development of International Humanitarian Law Applicable in Armed Conflicts (Geneva 1974–1977)' Vol VII, CDDH/SR 49, 61, Pakistan, para 11.

[123] Recognition of belligerency would result in the application of a legal framework far beyond the minimum requirements of common Art 3. See comments of the UK, Final Record of the Diplomatic Conference of Geneva of 1949, Vol II Section B, 47.

[124] *The Red Cross Conventions* above n 112, 103. See also, above n 98, 44; Joyce AC Gutteridge, 'The Geneva Conventions of 1949' (1949) 26 *British Yearbook of International Law* 301.

[125] See also, Denmark, Final Record of the Diplomatic Conference of Geneva of 1949, Vol II Section B, 332.

[126] Resolution 10, Final Record of the Diplomatic Conference of Geneva of 1949, Vol I, 362.

[127] See, International Committee of the Red Cross, 'Draft Additional Protocols to the Geneva Conventions of August 12, 1949, Commentary' (1973) 134.

[128] Yves Sandov, Christophe Swinarski and Brun Zimmermann (eds), *Commentary on the Additional Protocols of 8 June 1977 to the Geneva Conventions of 12 August 1949* (The Hague, Martinus Nijhoff, 1987) 1344.

[129] See further, above n 28, 207.

[130] *The Red Cross Conventions* above n 112, 17.

C. The Legal Status Clause and International Legal Personality

Having established the principal motivation underpinning the legal status clause, its impact on the international legal personality of armed groups addressed by the Conventions must now be considered. Specifically, by stating that the legal status of armed groups is not affected by the application of the Conventions, does Article 3(4) preclude, or restrict, armed groups' international legal personality? The Vienna Convention on the Law of Treaties—the relevant parts of which are considered to form part of customary international law[131]—requires that treaties be interpreted in good faith, in accordance with the ordinary meaning associated with the terms of the treaty in their context, and in light of the treaty's object and purpose;[132] in the absence of clarity, recourse may be had to supplementary means of interpretation.[133] Ultimately, the principle of effective interpretation (*ut res magis valeat quam pereat*) presumes that states do not undertake exercises in futility,[134] and that a treaty is intended to produce effects consistent with its overall object and purpose.

During the drafting process some states expressed the belief that—in general—armed groups could not possess international legal personality.[135] For example, with respect to draft common Article 3, Italy noted that a proposal to include a delegation 'to be made by the rebels presupposes a legal personality which they could not possess',[136] while, similarly, during the drafting of Additional Protocol II, Zaire made the distinction between states as subjects of international law, and armed groups as subjects of domestic law.[137] However, the impact of common Article 3(4) with respect to a group's international legal personality was not explicitly discussed, and the drafting history is unclear on this point. Discussion in Geneva focused primarily on the impact of the Conventions on the legitimacy and belligerent status of armed groups, and it cannot be concluded that states intended Article 3(4) to preclude the international legal personality of a group. It is noted that recognition of belligerent status would result in international legal personality. However, states were concerned with

131 Above n 25, 167.

132 Art 31(1), Vienna Convention on the Law of Treaties (23 May 1969, entered into force 27 January 1980) 1155 UNTS. 331.

133 Art 32, Vienna Convention on the Law of Treaties.

134 Above n 25, 179.

135 The drafting and codification of the Geneva Conventions of 1949 predominantly took place prior to the International Court of Justice's landmark decision in *Reparations*.

136 Final Record of the Diplomatic Conference of Geneva of 1949, Vol II Section B, 47.

137 Thus precluding the international legal personality of armed groups. 'Official Records of the Diplomatic Conference on the Reaffirmation and Development of International Humanitarian Law Applicable in Armed Conflicts, Geneva, (1974–1977)', Vol VII, CDDH/SR56, 219.

the subject-specific consequences of this personality—and in particular the implications vis-à-vis their ability to quell an insurrection—and not with armed groups' acquisition of international legal personality per se.[138] Significantly, with respect to the rules on treaty interpretation, an interpretation that precludes armed groups' international legal personality does not emerge clearly from the text of Article 3(4) itself.

Reference to the principle of effective interpretation further reinforces this conclusion. The purpose of common Article 3 as a whole is unquestionably to ensure international regulation of non-international armed conflicts, achieved through the attribution of international obligations to armed groups. This application of direct international obligations to armed groups will necessarily result in international legal personality.[139] For instance, Draper notes that, '[w]hen individuals group themselves in a certain way so that they become party to an internal conflict, then they are given collectively a sufficient legal personality to enable them to be subject to obligations and to hold rights conferred or imposed on them by these Conventions.'[140] This conclusion was endorsed by Sivakumaran,[141] who further noted that armed groups possess, inter alia, 'the right to conclude international humanitarian law agreements';[142] a right restricted to subjects of international law.[143] Similarly, Shaw refers to a 'community need' to ensure the operation of the laws of war, and thus to accept 'some form of qualified personality in this area',[144] while a similar view, referring to 'some measure of recognition as an international subject'[145] has been expressed by Cassese. For Article 3(4) to explicitly preclude such personality would contradict the very object and purpose of common Article 3 as a whole,[146] namely the application of international legal obligations to armed opposition groups. This would negate the utility of the article, leading 'to a result which is manifestly absurd or unreasonable'.[147]

This is not to say, however, that application of the Conventions elevates armed groups to the status of full subjects of international law. Indeed, a desire to preclude groups' status as 'full subjects' was pertinent to the

[138] See above Ch 2 section III.B.
[139] See further below Ch 2 section IV.
[140] *The Red Cross Conventions* above n 112, 17.
[141] Sandesh Sivakumaran, 'Binding Armed Opposition Groups' (2006) 55 *The International and Comparative Law Quarterly* 374.
[142] ibid, 380.
[143] See above Ch 2 section I.
[144] Above n 91, 244.
[145] Above n 25, 124.
[146] Jan Klabbers, '(I Can't Get No) Recognition: Subjects Doctrine and the Emergence of Non-State Actors' in Andrea Bianchi (ed), *Non-State Actors and International Law* (Farnham, Ashgate, 2009) 45.
[147] Art 32(b), Vienna Convention on the Law of Treaties.

context of the discussions at Geneva, given that recognition as a belligerent or de facto government implied significant consequences on the international legal plane, in many respects similar to those of a state.[148] Rather, any international legal personality associated with armed groups is demarcated by the Conventions themselves, and relates to the groups' subject-specific competence.[149]

D. Summary

It is submitted that the legal status clause was intended to preclude the granting of either legitimacy or belligerent status to armed opposition groups. As such, it does not affect their international legal personality, and so allows for the direct attribution of international law to those groups addressed by common Article 3. This conclusion is cognisant of states' intentions at Geneva—to the extent that they may be determined from the drafting history—and the text of Article 3 itself. Importantly, it also allows Article 3(4) to remain consistent with the overall object and purpose of Article 3, namely the international regulation of armed group activity. Having established that common Article 3 does not prevent armed groups' acquisition of international legal personality, the general criteria necessary for the establishment of international legal personality must now be addressed.

IV. DETERMINING THE CRITERIA NECESSARY FOR THE ACQUISITION OF INTERNATIONAL LEGAL PERSONALITY IN THE CONTEMPORARY ERA

If a clear understanding of international legal personality is to be developed, the contemporary international law criteria regulating the acquisition of international legal personality must first be determined. As a starting point, it is recalled that an international legal person must be subject to direct international rights or obligations. As such, an entity's independent existence must be regarded as an essential criterion vis-à-vis the acquisition of international legal personality.[150] As the remainder of the criteria are not explicitly specified,[151] they must be ascertained from

148 See below Ch 3 section I.C.

149 See above Ch 2 section I.D.

150 See above Ch 1 section II. This is also discussed further below, see Ch 2 section IV.A and Ch 5 section III.

151 There is, for example, no Vienna Convention on the Law of International Legal Personality. Above n 9, 19.

an analysis of the relevant case law and legal literature. In *Reparations*, the International Court of Justice held that the UN possessed international legal personality, which it stated as meaning that 'it is a subject of international law and capable of possessing international rights and duties, and that it has the capacity to maintain its rights by bringing international claims.'[152] From this statement, two potential criteria for international legal personality may be identified:[153] (a) the capacity to possess international rights and duties, and (b) the capacity to bring an international claim. However, a number of commentators focus on another—albeit related—criterion: the actual possession of international rights or duties.[154] These four criteria—independence, the capacity to possess direct international rights or obligations, the actual possession of such rights or obligations, and the capacity to bring an international claim—will be examined in order to accurately determine the specific criteria necessary for the acquisition of international legal personality.

A. The Independence Requirement

The direct attribution of international rights or obligations is essential to international legal personality:[155] if the attribution of rights or obligations is not direct, but rather occurs exclusively through the medium of another entity, then it is that entity's legal personality that is relevant on the international plane.[156] Accordingly, an entity must exist independently to possess international legal personality. This independence may be demonstrated by the absence of an exclusive superior authority.[157] Examples in this regard include: states, who have no authority over them other than that of international law;[158] armed groups party to a non-international armed conflict and de facto communities, who have 'broken the bonds of society'[159] and removed themselves from the authority

[152] *Reparations for injuries suffered in the services of the United Nations*, above n 36, 179.
[153] See, eg Ian Brownlie, *Principles of Public International Law*, 6th edn (Oxford, OUP, 2003) 58; above n 5, 309.
[154] 'The Subjects of International Law' above n 115, 147; above n 41, 138.
[155] See, eg above n 2, 16; above n 22, 196; Dapo Akande, 'International Organizations' in Malcolm Evans (ed), *International Law*, 2nd edn (Oxford, OUP, 2006) 281.
[156] See, eg above n 14, 429; Marek St Korowicz, 'The Problem of the International Personality of Individuals' (1956) 50 *American Journal of International Law* 3, 535.
[157] See further below Ch 5 section III.
[158] *Customs Regime between Germany and Austria (Protocol of March 19th, 1931)*, Separate Opinion of Judge Anzilotti, Permanent Court of International Justice, 5 September 1931, para 81.
[159] *Sambiaggio Case (of a general nature)* (1903) Reports of International Arbitral Awards, Vol X, p 513.

of the state; and International Organisations, which possess a will independent of their member states.[160] As these entities are not exclusively subject to any superior authority, the attribution of international rights or obligations must be direct: there is no other entity capable of acting as a medium. It is noted that an entity may be partially subject to the authority of a superior entity but still retain its independence. For instance, a de facto authority such as the Turkish Republic of Northern Cyprus exists independently and as such is subject to direct international regulation, while at the same time remaining partially subject to Turkey's authority.[161] As long as the entity in question retains its independence—ie as long as the superior authority exerts only partial and not exclusive authority—then an entity may continue to be regarded as an international legal person.

Exceptionally, the direct attribution of international rights or obligations by means of international treaty law will also generate a form of rights- or obligations-specific independence, in and of itself. In this situation, while the entity may be subject to a superior authority, the authority exercised will not be exclusive, by virtue of the direct application of international treaty law. An example is the direct attribution of international rights to individuals.[162] While the individual remains subject to the jurisdiction of the state, the fact that they possess direct international rights means that—from the perspective of international law—these rights exist independently of the state, and may, for example, be invoked by the individual in their own right.[163]

B. The Capacity to Possess International Rights or Obligations

The capacity to possess direct international rights or obligations as a criterion for an entity's acquisition of international legal personality is a

[160] See, Viljam Engstrom, 'Powers of organizations and the many faces of autonomy' in Richard Collins and Nigel D White (eds), *International Organizations and the Idea of Autonomy: Institutional Independence in the International Legal Order* (Abingdon, Routledge, 2011) 216; *Western Sahara* above n 90, para 148.

[161] Similarly, states retain their international legal personality despite being subject to the authority of International Organisations—such as the United Nations—in certain circumstances. Another example concerns the direct attribution of international rights to individuals. While the individual remains subject to the authority of the state, the fact that they possess direct international rights means that—from the perspective of international law—these rights exist independently of the state, and may, for example, be invoked by the individual in their own right.

[162] See, *LaGrand (Germany v United States of America)* above n 78, para 77.

[163] See *Avena and Other Mexican Nationals (Mexico v United States of America)* above n 79, para 40. Equally, under some circumstances an individual may be able to bring a claim directly, as is the case vis-à-vis the European Court of Human Rights, the Inter-American Court of Human Rights, and the African Court of Human and Peoples' Rights.

feature of the International Court of Justice's case law,[164] and a consistent element in the legal literature:[165] as stated by O'Connell, 'capacity implies personality'.[166] The necessity of this criterion is underlined by reference to the principle of effectiveness, which holds 'that only those claims and situations which are effective can produce legal consequences.'[167] Consequently, and in order to avoid a legal fiction:[168] 'if an entity is to possess international rights and duties, it must have the factual capacity to possess those rights and duties'.[169]

In *Reparations* the International Court of Justice held that the UN 'is a subject of international law and *capable of possessing* international rights and duties'.[170] The Court established that the UN's international legal personality was dependent upon its possession, in regard to its members, of 'rights which it is entitled to ask them to respect.'[171] This finding was subsequently endorsed in the *Western Sahara* Advisory Opinion, where the Court held that 'it expresses the essential test where a group, whether composed of states, of tribes or of individuals, is claimed to be a legal entity distinct from its members.'[172] Accordingly, it is submitted that it is an entity's organisational characteristics that will determine its capacity to possess international rights or obligations: the entity must be structured in such a way that it is capable 'of availing itself of obligations incumbent on its Members.'[173] For instance, without the ability to bind member states, International Organisations—as distinct entities—could not be effectively subject to international obligations, as they would be incapable of ensuring compliance with those same obligations; this capacity is dependent upon the organisational structure of the International Organisation and the existence, for example, of majority voting or an autonomous decision-making organ. Similarly, an armed group's capacity to enforce obligations under international humanitarian law is recognised as dependent upon its ability to bind the individuals under its command, which in turn is dependent upon the existence of a command and control structure.[174]

164 *Western Sahara* above n 90, para 148; *Reparations for injuries suffered in the services of the United Nations* above n 36, 178.

165 See, eg 'The Subjects of International Law' above n 115, 14; 'International Organizations' above n 155, 281.

166 O'Connell above n 11, 81.

167 Above n 25, 12–13.

168 See, above n 25, 13.

169 Above n 8, 72.

170 *Reparations for injuries suffered in the services of the United Nations* above n 36, 179. Emphasis added.

171 ibid, 178. It is submitted that the ability to bind members is a manifestation of an entity's independent will (*volonté distincte*).

172 *Western Sahara* above n 90, para 148.

173 *Reparations for injuries suffered in the services of the United Nations* above n 36, 178.

174 This is discussed further below, see Ch 3 section III.A.2.

Equally the two most decisive criteria with respect to statehood, government and independence, are intrinsically related to the organisational characteristics of the state.[175]

C. The Actual Possession of International Rights or Obligations

Although the capacity to possess international rights or obligations is essential, on its own this criterion is incapable of generating international legal personality. While a large corporation may exhibit organisational characteristics similar to an International Organisation such as the World Health Organization, a drug gang might share organisational characteristics with an armed group party to a non-international armed conflict, or an autonomous region might share characteristics with a state,[176] it does not necessarily follow that these entities are—or should be—recognised as international legal persons. In particular, it has not been determined whether these entities are active participants on the international plane subject to direct comprehension by the international legal order, as demonstrated by the possession of direct international rights or obligations. For example, before confirming the international legal personality of the UN in *Reparations*, the International Court of Justice evaluated the entity's actual possession of direct international rights or obligations as demonstrated by the provisions of the UN Charter and the intent of the drafters.[177] Similarly, Oppenheim's Law states that, to 'the extent that bodies other than states directly possess some rights, powers and duties in international law they can be regarded as subjects of international law, possessing international personality'.[178] The *Oxford Dictionary of Law* also adopts this approach: 'entities who are endowed with rights and obligations under public international law are said to have international legal personality.'[179] The possession of direct international rights or obligations may occur consequent to the application of international treaty law,[180] or customary international law.[181]

[175] This is discussed further below, see Ch 3 section I.B.

[176] Member states within a federation—such as the cantons in Switzerland—provide a related example.

[177] See *Reparations for injuries suffered in the services of the United Nations* above n 36, 178–79.

[178] Above n 2, 16. See, further above n 27, 100; above n 41, 138; 'International Organizations' above n 155, 281.

[179] 'International Legal Personality' in Jonathan Law and Elizabeth A Martin (eds), *Oxford Dictionary of Law* 5th edn (Oxford, OUP, 2002).

[180] For example, armed groups party to a common Art 3 conflict are subject to a number of direct international obligations.

[181] See, eg *Interpretation of the Agreement of 25 March 1951 Between the WHO and Egypt*, Advisory Opinion, International Court of Justice, 20 December 1980, para 37.

D. The Capacity to Bring an International Claim

A number of commentators have identified the capacity to bring an international claim as a prerequisite criterion vis-à-vis an entity's acquisition of international legal personality.[182] Support for this proposition is typically drawn from the text of the *Reparations* Advisory Opinion, wherein the International Court of Justice stated that the UN's international legal personality means that it 'is a subject of international law and capable of possessing international rights and duties, and that it has capacity to maintain its rights by bringing international claims.'[183] However, it is submitted that having established the UN's international personality, the Court then went on to refer to the specific consequences of this personality (ie the UN's subject-specific competence), which included the capacity to bring international claims.[184] The process whereby the Court evaluated the UN's legal status demonstrates the appropriateness of this conclusion.[185] In determining whether the UN had legal personality, the Court focused on examining whether the UN exhibited an independent will.[186] Only once this was confirmed and personality established was the competence to bring an international claim addressed: '[t]he next question is whether the sum of the international rights of the Organization comprises the right to bring the kind of international claim described in the Request for this Opinion.'[187] Similarly, in the *Western Sahara* Advisory Opinion, the Court did not address the Bilad Shinguitti or Mauritanian entity's capacity to bring an international claim when assessing its legal nature, enquiry being restricted to discussion of the entity's independent will.[188]

The capacity to possess rights and duties must be differentiated from the standing to vindicate those rights and duties, which is a subject-specific consequence of personality.[189] Lauterpacht notes that, '[t]he quality of a subject of international law—i.e. the capacity of being a subject of rights created or recognized by international law—does not, as already stated, depend upon the capacity to claim or enforce such rights in the beneficiary's own name.'[190] Similarly, the Permanent Court of

[182] Above n 30, 115; above n 22, 196; Nkambo Mugerwa, 'Subjects of International Law' in Max Sorensen (ed), *Manual of Public International Law* (London, Macmillan, 1968) 249.

[183] *Reparations for injuries suffered in the services of the United Nations* above n 36, 179.

[184] See Andrew Clapham, *Human Rights Obligations of Non-State Actors* (Oxford, OUP, 2006) 65.

[185] For example, in asking whether the UN had the capacity to bring an international claim, the Court stated that it 'must first enquire' whether the UN had international legal personality, in *Reparations for injuries suffered in the services of the United Nations* above n 36, 178. See also, above n 41, 125.

[186] *Reparations for injuries suffered in the services of the United Nations* above n 36, 178.

[187] ibid, 179.

[188] *Western Sahara* above n 90, para 148.

[189] Sellers above n 11, 67.

[190] 'The Subjects of International Law' above n 115, 14.

International Justice held that, 'it is scarcely necessary to point out that the capacity to possess civil rights does not necessarily imply the capacity to exercise those rights oneself.'[191] Ultimately, the absence of standing cannot be taken to imply the absence of rights or personality.[192] The decisions of the International Court of Justice in *LaGrand* and *Avena*—where the Court explicitly held that individuals can directly possess international rights[193]—reinforce this point. In reaching this conclusion—which some commentators hold amounts to recognition of international legal personality[194]—the Court exclusively analysed the international rights in question and the legal situation surrounding their attribution: the individuals' capacity to bring a claim in their own right was not addressed. Indeed, in this case, the claim was brought on behalf of the individuals by the state. Thus, it appears safe to conclude that '[t]he fact that the beneficiary of rights is not authorized to take independent steps in his own name to enforce them does not signify that he is not a subject of the law or that the rights in question are vested exclusively in the agency which possesses the capacity to enforce them.'[195] The ability to bring an international claim should appropriately be regarded as a possible consequence of, but not a prerequisite to, international legal personality.[196]

E. Summary

Contemporary international law establishes three criteria that must be satisfied if an entity is to acquire international legal personality: an entity must exist independently, be capable of possessing direct international rights or obligations, and actually be in possession of such rights or obligations.[197] Clarification of these criteria provides a more accurate understanding of

[191] *Appeal from a Judgment of the Hungaro-Czechoslovak Mixed Arbitral Tribunal (The Peter Pazmany University v The State of Czechoslovakia)*, Judgment, Permanent Court of International Justice, 15 December 1933, 231.

[192] See, Sellers above n 11, 146.

[193] *LaGrand (Germany v United States of America)* above n 78, para 77; *Avena and Other Mexican Nationals (Mexico v United States of America)* above n 79, para 40.

[194] International Law Commission, 'First Report on Responsibility of International Organizations', UN Doc A/Cn.4/532, 26 March 2003, para 17; See further, above n 7, 197.

[195] Hersch Lauterpacht, 'International Law and Human Rights', quoted in above n 6, 53.

[196] See, above n 27, 152; 'International Organizations' above n 155, 281.

[197] As noted above, the direct attribution of international rights or obligations by means of international treaty law will generate a form of rights- or obligations-specific independence, and as such, the actual possession criterion and the independence criterion are related. The principal importance of the distinction between these two criteria arises in relation to those entities not directly addressed by international treaty law, and is of relevance, for example, when considering the application of international law on the basis of the de facto control theory. This is discussed further below, see Ch 5 section I.

international legal personality, facilitating the application of this concept in practice. Having established these criteria, the means by which their fulfilment may be evaluated must now be determined: this is central to the acquisition of international legal personality.

V. A FUNCTIONAL APPROACH TO INTERNATIONAL LEGAL PERSONALITY

International law does not contain specific rules regulating the acquisition—or consequences of—international legal personality: there is no 'Vienna Convention on the law of international legal persons.'[198] Accordingly, in order to determine whether the three criteria for international legal personality have been satisfied, a functional approach should be adopted:[199] 'when there is no constitutional system for, as it were, recognizing and registering associations as legal persons, the primary test is functional.'[200] By developing an understanding of international legal personality based upon an objective analysis of the current state of the law—thereby avoiding the intellectual prisons associated with inflexible traditional conceptions or philosophies—a functional approach will ensure the greatest possible symmetry between international life and the legal system which purports to regulate it. Importantly, the objective nature of this approach encompasses the principle of effectiveness.[201]

The functional approach proposed herein builds upon the understanding of international legal personality developed above, with an entity's acquisition of international legal personality dependent upon the establishment of an independent existence, the capacity to possess direct rights or obligations under international law, and the actual possession of such rights or obligations.[202] The capacity and actual possession criteria combine the previously distinct conceptions of international

[198] Above n 9, 19.

[199] This builds on proposals by a number of writers. See, O'Connell above n 11, 98; above n 146, 49; above n 8, 71.

[200] Above n 153, 676.

[201] See, eg above n 153, 64.

[202] This approach is primarily derived from the jurisprudence of the International Court of Justice, and in particular the *Reparations* and *Western Sahara* Advisory Opinions; it builds upon frameworks developed, in particular, by Klabbers, Akande, Seyersted and Green; and combines elements of the objective and inductive approach to personality presented by Rama-Montaldo, the formal, actor and recognition conceptions presented by Portmann, and, by analogy, the declarative and constitutive approaches to statehood. See further, above n 146, 54; 'International Organizations' above n 155, 281; Finn Seyersted, 'Objective International Personality of Intergovernmental Organizations: Do their capacities really depend upon the conventions establishing them?' (1964) 34 *Nordisk Tidsskrift Int'l Ret*; above n 8, 71; above n 7; above n 41, 112. For further discussion, see above Ch 2 section I.D.

legal personality. Determining an entity's satisfaction of the capacity criterion involves an objective assessment of the facts, in order to evaluate the capacity of the entity in question.[203] However, the importance of recognition—ie state will—is also acknowledged, and assessment of the actual possession criterion evaluates whether states have, through the direct attribution of international rights or obligations, recognised the entity as a distinct participant in the international legal order.[204] States may 'recognise' the international legal personality of an entity (or categories of entities) either directly,[205] for example, through the conventional treaty-based attribution of international obligations,[206] or indirectly, as evidenced, for example, by the intent of states in the form of the 'implied powers' doctrine advanced in *Reparations*,[207] or through the application of customary international law.[208]

This approach overcomes the problems that occur when international legal personality is addressed solely through the lens of one of the distinct conceptions outlined above.[209] Significantly, while potential legal inconsistencies associated with recognition-only conceptions are avoided, the primary role of state will is nonetheless acknowledged. As noted by Klabbers, an argument based solely on objective criteria:

> can be countered by an argument based on (lack of) recognition, and thus needs to incorporate recognition in order to survive; an argument based on mere recognition, on the other hand, is always vulnerable to the argument that even if an entity has been recognized as a subject, such was never really necessary to begin with or, more importantly perhaps, to the consideration that even non-recognized entities do play a role, and sometimes an important one.[210]

The proposed functional approach is reflective of the requirements of international life, and the realities of contemporary international law, and rests upon an acknowledgment that '[i]nternational personality is participation plus some form of community acceptance.'[211] As distinct from the

[203] Reflective of the declarative approach.

[204] Reflective of the constitutive approach.

[205] Although it is noted that express recognition is rare in practice. See, above n 7, 99.

[206] As demonstrated, for example, by the application of common Art 3 to armed groups party to a non-international armed conflict.

[207] *Reparations for injuries suffered in the services of the United Nations* above n 36, 190. See also, *Legality of the Use By a State of Nuclear Weapons in Armed Conflict* above n 37, para 25.

[208] The UN Security Council has subjected non-state armed groups to international obligations (see for example, UNSC Res 1244 (1999) operative para 15; UNSC Res 1267 (1999) operative paras 2–3; UNSC Res Resolution 1564 (2004) operative para 10; UNSC Res 20136 (2012) operative para 16) and that states have also created the customary international law that binds non-state armed groups. Further issues arising in this regard are discussed in greater detail below. See Ch 4 section III.A and Ch 5 section I.

[209] See further, above Ch 2 section II.E.

[210] Above n 146, 51.

[211] Above n 91, 197.

traditional positivist conception, the proposed approach does not view the international legal order as a closed system, with participation exclusively dependent upon state discretion. Rather, international legal personality may be attributed to any entity fulfilling the required legal criteria.

VI. CONCLUSION

The traditional approaches to international legal personality have been discussed, resulting in the conclusion that none of these approaches—when considered distinctly—accurately reflect the reality of contemporary international law. Accordingly, the current role of international legal personality has been examined in light of recent legal developments, and three criteria essential to the acquisition of international legal personality have been identified: an entity must have the capacity to possess direct international rights or obligations, must actually possess such rights or obligations, and must exist independently. The actual possession of rights or obligations is a key element as this criterion recognises an entity's active participation in the international system, and its direct comprehension by the international legal order; possession of rights or obligations may arise consequent to the application of either treaty-based or customary international law. When these three criteria are present, a non-state entity possesses international legal personality, and is directly bound by international law. In this sense, international legal personality is a construct indicative of a certain status under international law. It is not a prerequisite to being bound by direct international obligations. Rather, independence and capacity are prerequisites to the applicability of direct international obligations, and the presence of all three criteria results in international legal personality.

The approach to international legal personality developed herein requires that an entity's satisfaction of the three criteria must be determined on the basis of a functional assessment, and so the specific content of each criterion as they relate to non-state armed groups must be identified. Accordingly the remaining chapters in Part I examine: the criteria that must be satisfied in order for an entity to demonstrate the capacity to possess international obligations, how an entity can acquire (ie actually possess) direct obligations under international law, and the conditions under which a non-state entity can be said to exist independently. This discussion is centred around two questions: can armed groups be directly subject to international regulation and, if so, under what circumstances?

3

Determining the Criteria Necessary to Satisfy the Capacity Requirement Associated with International Legal Personality

THIS CHAPTER EVALUATES an entity's capacity to possess direct international obligations. As discussed previously, this is primarily dependent upon organisational characteristics:[1] is an entity structured in such a way that it is capable of fulfilling obligations arising under international law? In order to better understand how this requirement can be satisfied, the dominant entities of concern to the international system—states, International Organisations, armed groups, and transnational corporations[2]—will be evaluated in turn, so that the specific criteria required of each entity vis-à-vis the capacity criterion may be ascertained.[3] The final component of this chapter then evaluates these entity-specific criteria, in order to determine whether any criteria common to each entity, and thus to international persons in general, may be identified.

[1] See above Ch 2 section IV.

[2] While individuals may possess international legal personality, they remain unitary entities with respect to whom any discussion of organisational capacity or structure is irrelevant. With respect to individuals' possession of international personality, see 'First Report on responsibility of international organizations by Mr Giorgio Gaja, Special Rapporteur', International Law Commission, UN Doc A/CN.4/532, 26 March 2003, para 17.

[3] Although transnational corporations are not currently accepted as possessing international legal personality, they are nonetheless considered to be an appropriate subject for the current study: their international legal personality is currently subject to debate, and they are recognised as possessing legal personality under municipal law, and so specific requirements exist vis-à-vis these entities' acquisition of legal personality. Issues relating to the international legal personality of armed groups are discussed further below, see Ch 3 section III.

I. STATES

States are recognised as the original international legal persons, and the direct subjects of international law.[4] Indeed, it was only as recently as 1949 that the International Court of Justice confirmed that non-state entities could possess international legal personality.[5] As a result of this historical reality, the concepts of statehood and international personality have long been intertwined,[6] and so in order to accurately understand the concept of international legal personality it is necessary that issues relating to the international legal personality of states be addressed.

A. States' Acquisition of Statehood/International Legal Personality

The international legal system does not include an authoritative piece of legislation regulating the acquisition of statehood,[7] and two approaches to the issue have been developed: the constitutive and the declarative theories.[8] Today, the declarative theory enjoys the widest support.[9] Significantly, this does not undermine the importance of recognition as a political act, as evidenced, for example, by the current status of Taiwan.[10] Nonetheless, if the acquisition of statehood is declarative, it must be dependent upon identifiable criteria.

B. The Criteria Regulating the Acquisition of Statehood

The most commonly referenced criteria regulating the acquisition of statehood are contained in the Montevideo Convention on the Rights and

[4] See *Reparations for injuries suffered in the services of the United Nations*, Advisory Opinion, International Court of Justice, 11 April 1949, 178; Manuel Rama-Montaldo,' International Legal Personality and Implied Powers of International Organizations' (1970) 44 *British Yearbook of International Law* 140.

[5] *Reparations for injuries suffered in the services of the United Nations*, above n 4.

[6] See above, Ch 2 section I.C.

[7] Antonio Cassese, *International Law*, 2nd edn (Oxford, OUP, 2005) 73. Although, as discussed below, the Montevideo Convention does provide commonly referenced criteria in this regard. See n 14.

[8] According to the constitutive theory an entity acquires statehood when it is recognised as such by other states. The declarative theory holds that an entity acquires statehood upon satisfaction of identified criteria. See further, James Crawford, *The Creation of States in International Law*, 2nd edn (Oxford, OUP, 2006) 19–26.

[9] See eg Art 3 of the Montevideo Convention on the Rights and Duties of States; See also the reasoning utilised in *Western Sahara*, Advisory Opinion, International Court of Justice, 16 October 1975, 178; *Reference Re Secession of Quebec* (1998) 115 ILR 536, 589–90. See forcefully, above n 7, 73–77. See also, above n 8, 22–28, and James Crawford, *Brownlie's Principles of Public International Law*, 8th edn (Oxford, OUP, 2012) 145.

[10] See Crawford above n 9, 125.

Duties of States.[11] Article 1 thereof holds that: '[t]he state as a person of international law should possess the following qualifications: a) a permanent population; b) a defined territory; c) government; and d) capacity to enter into relations with the other states.'[12] Although these elements are not regarded as definitive,[13] there is broad consensus regarding a number of derivative criteria: a permanent population, defined territory, government, and independence.[14]

These criteria may be further broken down and grouped into two determinative elements. The first element is the existence of a central structure, or governmental authority, capable of exercising control over a specific population in a given territory; this requirement recognises the importance attributed to the existence of a stable community and the necessary flexibility associated with the territory and population criteria.[15] In this regard the significance of a governmental authority must be emphasised, and it is noted that—with respect to the creation of states—international law defines territory in relation to the extent of governmental power exercised, or capable of being exercised, within a specific territory: '[t]erritorial sovereignty is not ownership of but governing power with respect to territory.'[16] The second element is independence: a state must not be exclusively subject to any superior authority (other than that of international law). Given the fundamental principle of the equality of states, this is an essential requirement. As stated by the Permanent Court of International Justice: 'the principle of the exclusive competence of the State [is] the point of departure in settling most questions that concern international relations.'[17]

A state's acquisition of international legal personality is thus dependent upon independence, and the existence of a governmental structure or central authority. The independence requirement marks a state as a distinct actor on the international plane, capable of being subject to direct international rights and obligations. The government requirement evidences a state's ability to fulfil, or give effect to, its rights and obligations under international law, thereby constituting the capacity requirement.

[11] Crawford above n 9, 128.

[12] Montevideo Convention on the Rights and Duties of States (adopted 26 December 1933, entered into force 26 December 1934).

[13] Crawford above n 9, 128.

[14] See Crawford above n 9, 128–30; above n 7, 73. Crawford also refers to: a degree of permanence; willingness to observe international law; sovereignty; and that the entity function as a state. However, these criteria are not decisive. See Crawford above n 9, 134–36.

[15] See eg above n 7, 73; Crawford above n 9, 129. See generally, ibid, 128–30.

[16] Above n 8, 56. This requirement applies in the context of the creation of states, and does not refer to a limitation on a state's territorial sovereignty once statehood is established.

[17] *The Island of Palmas Case (or Miangas) (United States of America v The Netherlands)*, Award, Permanent Court of Arbitration, 4 April 1928, 8.

For the purposes of international legal personality, the requirements of territory and population must be regarded as factors external to the entity, as these are elements subject to the state's authority and not intrinsic to the organisation of the state itself.[18]

C. The Concept of Belligerency

Traditionally, recognition of belligerent status elevated an insurgent community to the international plane, conferring a state-like status.[19] As this was a legitimate means of acquiring an international legal personality with certain competences equivalent to that of states, it is appropriate that the criteria necessary for recognition of belligerency be briefly evaluated herein.[20] However, it must be acknowledged that, particularly since the codification of the Geneva Conventions in 1949, there have been no clear cases of recognition of belligerency, and it has been suggested that the concept has now fallen into desuetude.[21]

In 1900, the Institute of International Law adopted a resolution on the subject of insurrection wherein it specified three criteria necessary for lawful recognition of belligerent status:

> Article 8. Third Parties cannot recognize the character of belligerent in a revolutionary party:
>
> *Section 1.* If it has not acquired a distinct territorial existence through the possession of a definite portion of the national territory;
>
> *Section 2.* If it has not the elements of a regular government exercising in fact the manifest rights of sovereignty over this portion of the territory;
>
> *Section 3.* If the fight is not carried on in its name by organized troops, subject to military discipline and conforming to the laws and customs of war.[22]

[18] Of course, these factors remain central to the determination of statehood.

[19] See Hans Kelsen, *Principles of International Law* (New Jersey, Lawbook Exchange, 2003) 292.

[20] In relation to the consequences of recognition of belligerency see further, Sandesh Sivakumaran, *The Law of Non-International Armed Conflict* (Oxford, OUP, 2012) 15–16.

[21] Above n 8, 419. However, as a counterpoint, states' stances with respect to the insurgent groups in Libya in 2011 and Syria in 2012 are worth investigating. See also Iain Scobbie, 'Gaza' in Elizabeth Wilmshurst (ed), *International Law and the Classification of Conflicts* (Oxford, OUP, 2012) 302.

[22] Quoted in PK Menon, *The Law of Recognition in International Law* (New York, Edwin Mellen Press, 1994) 115.

These criteria have been somewhat developed in order to incorporate an explicit requirement of armed conflict, and broad consensus now exists regarding the following criteria:[23]

1. There must exist a state of general, as opposed to localised, armed conflict.
2. The insurgent body must have established a governmental structure exercising control over a part of the national territory.
3. The insurgent forces must fight in accordance with the laws and customs of war.[24]

It is apparent that a high threshold is required with respect to recognition of belligerency, reflecting the significant consequences thereof, namely the conferring of a status equivalent in certain respects to that of states. Indeed, clear correlations exist with respect to the requirements of statehood, in particular those of territorial control, government, and independence.[25] Ultimately, the insurgent entity must be, 'if left to itself … reasonably capable of discharging the duties of a State.'[26] As such, the capacity requirements associated with a belligerent entity may be regarded as equivalent to that of a state, and dependent upon the existence of a governmental structure.[27]

II. INTERNATIONAL ORGANISATIONS

For present purposes, International Organisations are defined as organisations established by a treaty or other instrument governed by international law, with a membership that may include both state and non-state entities.[28] Other criteria associated with the definition of International

[23] See eg above n 19, 291; above n 22, 114; Yair M Lootsteen, 'The Concept of Belligerency in International Law' (2009) 166 *Military Law Review* 10; Ann Van Wynen Thomas and AJ Thomas Jr, 'International Legal Aspects of the Civil War in Spain, 1936–39' in Richard Falk (ed), *The International Law of Civil War* (Baltimore MD, Johns Hopkins University Press, 1971) 141; Rogier Bartels, 'Timelines, borderlines and conflicts: The historical evolution of the legal divide between international and non-international armed conflicts' (2009) 91 *International Review of the Red Cross* 50; above n 20, 11.

[24] See further above n 20, 9–20.

[25] By definition, a belligerent entity must be independent of the control of the territorial state, although the possibility that the belligerent entity is subject to the effective control of a third state must be acknowledged.

[26] Quoting Dana, in above n 22, 113.

[27] In this regard the link between de facto authorities and belligerent entities is noted.

[28] This is a widely accepted definition. See eg, Art 2(a) Draft Articles on the Responsibility of International Organizations (2011) *Yearbook of the International Law Commission*, Vol II, Pt Two; Art 2(i), Vienna Convention on the Law of Treaties between States and International Organizations or between International Organizations (adopted 21 March 1986, not yet in force) UN Doc A/CONF.129/15.

Organisations include a permanent system of organs and autonomy.[29] However, as these elements relate to the capacity criterion, they will be addressed below.

Before proceeding, two preliminary issues relating to International Organisations must be raised. First, International Organisations were the first non-state entities to be authoritatively recognised as possessing international legal personality,[30] and, to date, remain the only non-state entities explicitly recognised as international persons by the International Court of Justice.[31] Second, as they are created by states—and are thus a clear manifestation of state will—International Organisations may be regarded as a relatively non-contentious instance of non-state international legal personality; the decisive role of the state is maintained.[32] Questions relating to the international legal personality of International Organisations therefore avoid a number of the issues associated with the international legal personality of other entities—such as armed groups—whose existence might arise contrary to state will.[33]

A. The Organisational Characteristics of International Organisations

In determining the criteria necessary for an International Organisation to fulfil the capacity requirement, reference must be made to the case law of the International Court of Justice. In *Reparations*, the Court established that the UN's international legal personality was dependent upon it being in 'such a position that it possesses, in regard to its Members, rights which it is entitled to ask them to respect.'[34] This approach was subsequently confirmed in the *Western Sahara* Advisory Opinion:

> Some criterion has ... to be employed to determine in any particular case whether what confronts the law is or is not legally an 'entity'. The Court, moreover, notes that in the *Reparation* case the criterion which it applied was to enquire whether the United Nations Organization—the entity involved—was in 'such a position that it possesses, in regard to its Members, rights which it is entitled to ask them

[29] Henry G Schermers and Neils M Blokker, *International Institutional Law*, 4th edn (The Hague, Martinus Nijhoff, 2003) para 33; Philippe Sands and Pierre Klein, *Bowett's Law of International Institutions*, 6th edn (London, Sweet & Maxwell, 2009) para I-028.

[30] *Reparations for injuries suffered in the services of the United Nations*, above n 4, 179.

[31] It may be argued that in *LaGrand* and *Avena* the International Court of Justice implicitly recognised the legal personality of individuals, however, this was not explicit. See eg above n 2, para 17.

[32] See eg discussion related to the 'recognition conception' of international legal personality in Roland Portmann, *Legal Personality in International Law* (Cambridge, CUP, 2010) ch 6.

[33] These issues are primarily political, relating, for example, to a state's reluctance to recognise a non-state actor as this may challenge, or indicate a restriction of, its own authority.

[34] *Reparations for injuries suffered in the services of the United Nations*, above n 4, 178.

> to respect' ... In that Opinion, no doubt the criterion was applied in a somewhat special context. Nevertheless, it expresses the essential test where a group, whether composed of States, of tribes or of individuals, is claimed to be a legal entity distinct from its members.[35]

It is clear from *Reparations* that the Court regarded recognition of the UN's international legal personality as dependent upon the Organisation's autonomous position vis-à-vis its members, coupled with its ability to bind the membership.[36] In *Western Sahara,* this conclusion was endorsed and clarified as referring to an entity's existence 'distinct from its members'.[37] These characteristics are encapsulated in the concept of independent will or *volonté distincte.* Although the definition of *volonté distincte* is 'admittedly of a somewhat metaphysical character',[38] at its core it refers to the capacity for independent action,[39] and thus the ability to make binding decisions absent unanimous consent:[40] it is the manifestation of an independent will.

The existence of a *volonté distincte* establishes an International Organisation's capacity to possess direct international rights or obligations. It is the capacity for independent action—and in particular the ability to bind its membership—that enables an International Organisation to fulfil its international obligations:[41] without the capacity for independent action, an International Organisation will remain bound solely by the will of its members.[42] As noted by Schermers and Blokker: '[t]he requirement that the organ in question have a will of its own (*volonté distincte*) distinguishes organizations from bilateral or multilateral treaties, whereby parties lay down a common will, which remains their own'.[43] Ultimately, the absence of independent will precludes the possession of international legal personality.[44]

[35] *Western Sahara,* above n 9, para 148.

[36] *Reparations for injuries suffered in the services of the United Nations,* above n 4, 178.

[37] *Western Sahara,* above n 9, para 148. See also, *Legality of the Use by a State of Nuclear Weapons in Armed Conflict,* Advisory Opinion, International Court of Justice, 8 July 1996, para 19.

[38] Catherine Brolman, *The Institutional Veil in Public International Law: International Organisations and the Law of Treaties* (Oxford, Hart, 2007) 21.

[39] DP O'Connell, *International Law* (London, Stevens & Sons, 1970) 98.

[40] See eg Viljam Engstrom, 'Powers of organizations and the many faces of autonomy' in Richard Collins and Nigel D White (eds), *International Organizations and the Idea of Autonomy: Institutional Independence in the International Legal Order* (Abingdon, Routledge, 2011) 216.

[41] See eg *Maclaine Watson & Co Ltd v International Tin Council* [1990] BCLC 102, 133 (HL). See also, M Marchegiano, 'The Juristic Character of the International Commission of Cape Spartel Lighthouse' (1931) 25 *American Journal of International Law*; CF Amerasinghe, 'International Legal Personality Revisited' (1995) 47 *Austrian Journal of Public and International Law* 127.

[42] For instance, if an organisation's ability to act is dependent upon unanimity, then a state's ability to veto a decision means that no state can be bound against its will. This is not the case, for example, when an organisation acts on the basis of majority voting.

[43] Above n 29, para 44A.

[44] Above n 38, 76.

B. How is Independent will Determined?

Ascertaining how an International Organisation's independent will is determined is therefore essential with respect to determining the criteria associated with the capacity requirement. Here again recourse must be had to the *Reparations* Advisory Opinion. In determining whether the UN exhibited an independent will, the International Court of Justice looked to the Organisation's characteristics. In particular, the Court noted that:

> The Charter has not been content to make the Organization created by it merely a centre 'for harmonizing the actions of nations in the attainment of these common ends' (Article 1, para. 4). It has equipped that centre with organs, and has given it special tasks. It has defined the position of the Members in relation to the Organization by requiring them to give it every assistance in any action undertaken by it (Article 2, para. 5), and to accept and carry out the decisions of the Security Council; by authorizing the General Assembly to make recommendations to the Members; by giving the Organization legal capacity and privileges and immunities in the territory of each of its Members; and by providing for the conclusion of agreements between the Organization and its Members.[45]

The Court then noted that subsequent practice had confirmed these characteristics of the UN, 'which occupies a position in certain respects in detachment from its Members, and which is under a duty to remind them, if need be, of certain obligations.'[46] The evaluation of the UN's independent will was thus based upon an evaluation of the characteristics of the UN, as determined by its organisational structure:[47] ie whether it possessed institutional autonomy both by virtue of the Charter, and 'in fact'.[48]

The same approach was adopted by the Advocate General in *MacLaine Watson*, a case concerning the International Tin Council (ITC). Referring to the organisational characteristics identified in *Reparations*, the Advocate General noted that the International Tin Council exercised 'its own decision-making power distinct from that of the Members who make up the Organization';[49] that 'the position of the members in relation to the ITC is defined inasmuch as they are bound by all decisions of the Council (Article 41(2))';[50] and that the Chairman is an independent organ of the organisation, with its own powers.[51] Equally, the Italian Court of

[45] *Reparations for injuries suffered in the services of the United Nations*, above n 4, 178–79.

[46] ibid, 179.

[47] This approach was also adopted in the *Western Sahara* Advisory Opinion, however, the entity in question (the Mauritanian entity/Bilad Shinguitti) was not an International Organisation. See *Western Sahara*, above n 9, para 149.

[48] *Reparations for injuries suffered in the services of the United Nations*, above n 4, 179.

[49] Case C-241/87 *Maclaine Watson & Co Ltd v Council and Commission of the European Communities* [1990] ECR I-01797, Opinion of Advocate General, para 135.

[50] ibid, para 135.

[51] ibid.

Cassation held that the International Institute of Agriculture possessed international legal personality, as it was 'free from interference by the sovereign power of the States composing the Union'.[52]

The organisational criteria required to prove the existence of an independent will—and thus the capacity to possess direct international rights or obligations—thus hinge upon an International Organisation's ability to take independent decisions which bind the membership,[53] potentially against their will.[54] This is typically demonstrated through the existence of an independent organ with decision-making powers,[55] or through an organ which acts of the basis of majority—and not unanimous—vote.[56]

III. ARMED GROUPS

Although not authoritatively settled, the international legal personality of non-state armed groups is most commonly recognised consequent to the application of international humanitarian law, should an armed group become party to a non-international armed conflict.[57] However, armed groups may also be subject to international obligations outside armed conflict, in the context of crimes against humanity, with potential implications vis-à-vis international legal personality.[58] This section will therefore address the capacity requirement associated with armed groups, first in the context of armed conflict, and then in the context of crimes against

[52] Referred to in, Hersch Lauterpacht, 'The Subjects of the Law of Nations' (1947) 63 *Law Quarterly Review* 449.

[53] See eg above n 38, 76.

[54] See eg Nigel D White, 'Layers of autonomy in the UN system' in Richard Collins and Nigel D White (eds), *International Organizations and the Idea of Autonomy: Institutional Independence in the International Legal Order* (Abingdon, Routledge, 2011) 301; Jean d'Aspermont, 'The multifaceted concept of autonomy of international organizations and international legal discourse' in Richard Collins and Nigel D White (eds), *International Organizations and the Idea of Autonomy: Institutional Independence in the International Legal Order* (Abingdon, Routledge, 2011) 69; above n 38, 21.

[55] Such as the Chairman of the International Tin Council. See *Maclaine Watson & Co Ltd v Council and Commission of the European Communities* (Advocate General's Opinion), above n 49, para 135.

[56] See eg discussion relating to the International Sugar Agreement (1902) in ES Fawcett, 'The Function of Law in International Commodity Agreements' (1970) 44 *British Yearbook of International Law* 166. See also Art 19, Constitution of the World Health Organization (22 July 1946, as amended 15 September 2005).

[57] See eg Marco Sassoli, 'Taking Armed Groups Seriously: Ways to Improve Compliance with International Humanitarian Law' (2010) *International Humanitarian Legal Studies*, 31; Liesbeth Zegveld, *Accountability of Armed Opposition Groups in International Law* (Cambridge, CUP, 2002) 57. See also, Hans Aufricht, 'Personality in International Law' (1943) 37 *American Political Science Review* 221.

[58] See Art 7(2)(a), Statute of the International Criminal Court.

humanity. The identified requirements will then be analysed in order to determine whether it is possible to identify any core criteria applicable to armed groups both during, and outside, armed conflict.

A. Situations of Armed Conflict

The authoritative definition of armed conflict was established by the Appeals Chamber of the International Criminal Tribunal for the former Yugoslavia in *Tadic*:[59] 'an armed conflict exists whenever there is a resort to armed force between States or protracted armed violence between governmental authorities and organized armed groups or between such groups'.[60] This book is concerned with non-state armed groups who do not act on behalf of a state, and so the criteria relating to non-international armed conflict—'protracted armed violence between governmental authorities and organized armed groups or between such groups'—are of principal relevance. From the *Tadic* definition, it is apparent that the existence of a non-international armed conflict—essential to a group's acquisition of international legal personality—is established on the basis of a two-part test, evaluating: '(1) the organisation of the parties to the conflict and (2) the intensity of the conflict.'[61]

(i) Requirements Associated with the Intensity Criterion

Satisfaction of the intensity requirement is necessarily dependent upon the actions of other actors engaged in the hostilities, and not solely upon the activity of the group itself.[62] As such—and although decisive with respect to establishing the application of international humanitarian law—intensity-related criteria must be regarded as primarily external factors, and not as elements intrinsic to the group. They are therefore not decisive for present purposes. That said, it is noted that an armed group's capacity to engage in hostilities—and thus to satisfy the intensity

[59] See also *Prosecutor v Lubanga*, Judgment, Trial Chamber, International Criminal Court, Case No ICC-01/04-01/6, 14 March 2012, para 533; Anthony Cullen, *The Concept of Non-International Armed Conflict in International Humanitarian Law* (Cambridge, CUP, 2010) 137.

[60] *Prosecutor v Tadic*, Decision on the Defence Motion for Interlocutory Appeal on Jurisdiction, Appeals Chamber, International Criminal Tribunal for the former Yugoslavia, 2 October 1995, para 70.

[61] *Prosecutor v Milosevic*, Decision on Motion for Judgment of Acquittal, Trial Chamber, International Criminal Tribunal for the former Yugoslavia, Case No IT-02-54-T, 16 June 2004, para 17. See also, Eve La Haye, *War Crimes in Internal Armed Conflicts* (Cambridge, CUP, 2008) 13.

[62] In relation to the indicators associated with the intensity criterion, see *Prosecutor v Boskoski*, Judgment, Trial Chamber, International Criminal Tribunal for the former Yugoslavia, Case No IT-04-82-T, 10 July 2008, para 177.

threshold—will to a certain extent depend upon its organisational capacity.[63] For example, in *Limaj*, the Trial Chamber interpreted the ability of the Kosovo Liberation Army (KLA) to engage in armed clashes across Kosovo as an indicator of its level of organisation,[64] while similarly the *Lubanga* Trial Chamber of the International Criminal Court noted the relevance to the organisation test of 'the extent, seriousness, and intensity of any military involvement'.[65]

(ii) Requirements Associated with the Organisation Criterion

The criteria associated with the organisation requirement are intrinsic to an armed group, and are thus decisive with respect to satisfaction of the capacity requirement. Yet, despite the centrality of the organisation requirement to the classification of armed conflict, there is a distinct lack of specificity as to what it entails. While it is clear that 'some degree of organisation'[66] is necessary, '[t]he precise degree of organization required of the armed group is rather opaque.'[67] In keeping with the principle of effectiveness, however, there is general consensus that the degree of organisation, although ostensibly minimal,[68] must be sufficient to allow the group to fulfil any applicable international humanitarian law obligations.[69] This capacity to fulfil international obligations must appropriately be regarded as dependent upon the existence of an internal structure,[70] capable of exerting authority over its members.[71] As stated by the *Boskoski* Trial Chamber, 'the leadership of the group must, as a minimum, have the ability to

[63] *Prosecutor v Haradinaj*, Judgment, Trial Chamber, International Criminal Tribunal for the former Yugoslavia, Case No IT-04-84-T, 3 April 2008, para 60.

[64] *Prosecutor v Limaj*, Judgment, Trial Chamber, International Criminal Tribunal for the former Yugoslavia, Case No IT-03-66-T, 30 November 2005, para 172.

[65] *Prosecutor v Lubanga*, above n 59, para 537.

[66] *Prosecutor v Limaj*, above n 64, para 89.

[67] Above n 20, 170.

[68] See eg *Prosecutor v Akayesu*, Judgment, Trial Chamber, International Criminal Tribunal for Rwanda, Case No ICTR-96-4-T, 2 September 1998, para 620.

[69] Jelena Pejic, 'The protective scope of Common Article 3: more than meets the eye' (2011) 93 *International Review of the Red Cross* 191–92. See further, Lindsay Moir, *The Law of Internal Armed Conflict* (Cambridge, CUP, 2002) 36; *The Concept of Non-International Armed Conflict in International Humanitarian Law* above n 59, 124.

[70] This does not necessarily equate to a traditional military hierarchy in terms of the decision-making process. For instance, collaborative decision-making may be adopted by some armed groups. However, even with a collaborative structure, decisions made must be adhered to. See Abraham Guillen, *Philosophy of the Urban Guerrilla: The Revolutionary Writings of Abraham Guillen* (Donald C Hodges (ed), New York, William Morrow & Company Inc, 1973) 268.

[71] See eg International Committee of the Red Cross, 'International Humanitarian Law and the Challenges of Contemporary Armed Conflicts', Report of the 28th International Conference of the Red Cross and Red Crescent (2003) 19. See also, International Committee of the Red Cross, 'Armed conflicts linked to the disintegration of State structures' (23 January 1998).

exercise some control over its members so that the basic obligation of Common Article 3 of the Geneva Conventions may be implemented.'[72] Similarly, the International Law Association Committee on the Use of Force noted that the 'underlying theme'[73] with respect to the organisation requirement 'is that there must be a sufficient level of organisation through a command structure'[74] so that common Article 3 may be implemented. Moir has similarly suggested that fulfilment of common Article 3 obligations is 'unlikely without the insurgents being organised (at least to a degree) along military lines, including a responsible command structure and controlling authority.'[75] A group's ability to fulfil international humanitarian law obligations (ie to satisfy the capacity requirement) is thus tied to its ability to exert control over the membership of the group.[76]

A number of further factors have been identified with respect to the organisation requirement. In *Lubanga* the Trial Chamber stated that relevant indicators include: the group's internal hierarchy, the command structure and rules, the availability of military equipment, the ability to plan and execute military operations, and the extent and intensity of the conflict.[77] However, the Chamber noted that '[n]one of these factors are individually determinative';[78] rather they serve as a non-exhaustive list of indicators. As such, each armed group must be evaluated on a case-by-case basis.[79] On the basis of a review of the relevant case law, the *Boskoski* Trial Chamber subsequently grouped the indicators into five broad categories:

— factors signalling the existence of a command structure;[80]
— factors indicating that the group could carry out operations in an organised manner;[81]

[72] *Prosecutor v Boskoski*, above n 62, para 196.
[73] International Law Association Committee on the Use of Force, 'Final Report on the Meaning of Armed Conflict in International Law', *The Hague Conference* (2010) 29.
[74] ibid, 29.
[75] *The Law of Internal Armed Conflict* above n 69, 36. See also, Noam Lubell, *Extraterritorial Use of Force Against Non-State Actors* (Oxford, OUP, 2010) 110.
[76] See discussion relating to responsible command, below Ch 3 section III.A(ii)(a).
[77] *Prosecutor v Lubanga*, above n 59, para 537.
[78] *ibid*, para 537.
[79] *Prosecutor v Oric*, Judgment, Trial Chamber, International Criminal Tribunal for the former Yugoslavia, Case No IT-03-68-T, 30 June 2006, para 254. See further, Sylvain Vite, 'Typology of armed conflicts in international humanitarian law: legal concepts and actual situations' (2009) 91 *International Review of the Red Cross* 76.
[80] *Prosecutor v Boskoski*, above n 62, para 199. Factors include, the existence of a military-like hierarchy, with the ability to distribute orders and internal regulations, authorise military operations, appoint commanders, and keep the command and other units informed of operational developments. Other relevant indicators include: the existence and dissemination of internal regulations, the existence of a headquarters or headquarters' staff, and a formalised internal hierarchy. See further, *Prosecutor v Boskoski*, above n 62, para 199; *Prosecutor v Haradinaj*, above n 63, paras 65–68; *Prosecutor v Milosevic*, Decision on Motion for Judgment of Acquittal above n 61, para 23.
[81] *Prosecutor v Boskoski*, above n 62, para 200. Factors include the ability to plan and execute a unified military strategy, potentially over a large area; and the capacity to control territory.

— factors indicating a level of sophistication with respect to logistics;[82]
— factors indicating internal discipline;[83] and
— factors indicating the ability to speak with 'one voice'.[84]

While potentially helpful in gaining a broad overview of the elements involved in evaluating the organisation requirement, the five *Boskoski* categories—considered as such—do not provide assistance in establishing the essential criteria necessary for an entity to qualify as an 'organised armed group'. Indeed, a large degree of overlap between the identified categories is apparent. For example, the command structure category includes as indicators the dissemination of internal regulations and the organisation of a weapons supply, both of which are essential to the internal discipline and logistics categories respectively; the ability to speak with one voice—which includes the ability to ensure cease fire orders are implemented—will necessarily be dependent upon a command structure capable of enforcing internal discipline; while the capacity to carry out organised operations is dependent, inter alia, on the dissemination of internal orders and the division of forces into zones of responsibility, elements of which are also associated with the command structure category. It is submitted that these categories of indicators may be collapsed down into one essential criterion: the existence of a responsible command.[85]

(a) The Existence of a Responsible Command

At first glance this proposition may appear contentious: the responsible command requirement is traditionally associated, not with the minimum

Other relevant indicators include the division of territory into zones of responsibility, units' capacity to coordinate their actions, and the effective dissemination of internal communications. See further, *Prosecutor v Limaj*, above n 64, paras 105–08; *Prosecutor v Boskoski*, above n 62, para 200; *Prosecutor v Haradinaj*, above n 63, para 87.

[82] *Prosecutor v Boskoski*, above n 62, para 201. This category centres upon the ability to transport and supply troops and equipment. Relevant indicators therefore include the ability to recruit new members, the provision of military training, the use of uniforms, the organised supply of weapons, and the existence of internal communications. See further, *Prosecutor v Limaj*, above n 64, paras 118–23; *Prosecutor v Haradinaj*, above n 63, paras 76–86; *Prosecutor v Milosevic*, Decision on Motion for Judgment of Acquittal above n 61, para 23.

[83] *Prosecutor v Boskoski*, above n 62, para 202. This category centres upon the ability to ensure that orders are implemented, thereby maintaining operation as a cohesive military organisation. Other relevant indicators include the existence and dissemination of disciplinary rules and regulations and proper training. See further, *Prosecutor v Sesay, Kallon, Gbao*, Judgment, Trial Chamber, Special Court for Sierra Leone, Case No. SCSL-04-15-T, 2 March 2009, para 706.

[84] *Prosecutor v Boskoski*, above n 62, para 203. Typically, this category is evaluated in the context of political negotiations or the ability to conclude—and, importantly, to respect—ceasefire or peace agreements. Also relevant are communications-related criteria, such as the ability to issue communiqués and political statements on behalf of the group. See further, *Prosecutor v Haradinaj*, above n 63, para 88.

[85] For a similar analysis, see above n 20, 174–76.

threshold of non-international armed conflict, but rather with the higher threshold of Additional Protocol II.[86] However, it is recalled that the essential criterion with respect to an entity's level of organisation is the ability to fulfil obligations arising consequent to the application of international humanitarian law, and that this is understood as the ability to enforce internal discipline.[87] It is difficult to envisage how this criterion may be satisfied save on the basis of responsible command. In order to enforce discipline, a military-like structure is required, comprising persons responsible for their subordinates:

> [F]or an army to even function, troops must obey given orders. As such, a commander must ensure compliance with his orders. ... The obligation to ensure compliance with orders is not limited to combat orders but encompasses all orders given by a commander to his troops, including those intended to ensure compliance with international humanitarian law.[88]

As stated by the US Supreme Court in *Yamashita*, 'the law of war presupposes that its violation is to be avoided through the control of the operations of war by commanders who are to some extent responsible for their subordinates.'[89] Similarly, the *Commentary* to Additional Protocol II notes that '[t]he existence of a responsible command implies some degree of organization ... It implies an organization capable of ... imposing discipline in the name of a *de facto* authority.'[90] This was endorsed by the *Akayesu* Trial Chamber of the International Criminal Tribunal for Rwanda,[91] and its evolution in modern international law may be traced back to the recognition of belligerent status, which required that an entity be commanded by a person responsible for his subordinates.[92] A responsible command may thus be appropriately regarded as a command with the capacity to enforce internal discipline (i.e. to fulfil international humanitarian law obligations), and, on this basis, as the essence of military—or military-like—organisation. This conclusion is equally applicable to

[86] See eg *Prosecutor v Boskoski*, above n 62, para 197.

[87] See eg, Final Record of the Diplomatic Conference of Geneva of 1949, Vol II Section B, France, 10.

[88] *Prosecutor v Hadzihasanovic*, Judgment, Trial Chamber, International Criminal Tribunal for the former Yugoslavia, Case No IT-01-47-T, 15 March 2006, para 87. Discussing the concept of 'effective control' in the context of a common Art 3 conflict.

[89] *Yamashita v Styer*, Supreme Court, 317 US 1, 4 February 1946, 15. This case concerned an international armed conflict. However, the comment in question is equally applicable vis-à-vis the law of non-international armed conflict.

[90] Yves Sandov, Christophe Swinarski and Brun Zimmermann (eds), *Commentary on the Additional Protocols of 8 June 1977 to the Geneva Conventions of 12 August 1949* (The Hague, Martinus Nijhoff, 1987) para 4463.

[91] *Prosecutor v Akayesu*, above n 68, para 626.

[92] See above n 20, 11. See also, Art 1(1), Regulations Respecting the Laws and Customs of War on Land, Annex to 'Convention (IV) respecting the Laws and Customs of War on Land' (adopted 18 October 1907, entered into force 26 January 1910). The Hague Regulations address what is now referred to as international armed conflict.

common Article 3 conflicts.[93] For example, in *Hadzihasanovic* the Appeals Chamber of the International Criminal Tribunal for the former Yugoslavia held that the existence of a responsible command was integral to the prohibitions contained in common Article 3,[94] stating further that: '[i]t is evident that there cannot be an organized military force save on the basis of responsible command.'[95] It is noted that this requirement does not necessarily imply a traditional hierarchical structure, or one equivalent to that of a state's armed forces, rather '[i]t simply requires that there be some sort of relationship of effective control by which one individual has the power to control the acts of another, in particular the power to prevent or punish particular acts of that individual.'[96]

Significantly, however, in both *Lubanga* and *Katanga,* Trial Chambers of the International Criminal Court rejected the requirement of responsible command vis-à-vis the non-international armed conflict threshold test—exclusively associating this requirement with Additional Protocol II—while requiring instead that: 'the "organised armed groups" must have a sufficient degree of organisation, in order to enable them to carry out protracted armed violence.'[97] It is submitted that the Trial Chamber adopted an unwarranted distinction between the concept of responsible command and that of a 'sufficient degree of organisation'. As has been established, the two concepts are effectively synonymous: the level of organisation required is dependent upon the capacity to fulfil international humanitarian law obligations, which in turn, is dependent upon the existence of a responsible command. Indeed, in both *Katanga* and *Lubanga* the Trial Chamber noted that indicators of organisation include, inter alia: 'the force or group's internal hierarchy; its command structure and the rules applied within it'.[98] As discussed above, these are central elements of a responsible command. Similarly, in *Gombo* the Pre-Trial Chamber of the International Criminal Court held that, with respect to the non-international armed conflict threshold, organised armed groups 'must be

[93] See eg *Prosecutor v Strugar,* Judgment, Trial Chamber, International Criminal Tribunal for the former Yugoslavia, Case No IT-01-42-T, 31 January 2005, para 357. See also, Statute of the International Criminal Court Art 8, Statute of the International Criminal Tribunal for the former Yugoslavia Art 7(3), Statute of the International Criminal Tribunal for Rwanda Art 6(3).

[94] *Prosecutor v Hadzihasanovic,* Decision on Interlocutory Appeal Challenging Jurisdiction in Relation to Command Responsibility, Appeals Chamber, International Criminal Tribunal for the former Yugoslavia, Case No IT-01-47-AR72, 16 July 2003, para 15.

[95] ibid, para 16.

[96] Above n 20, 175.

[97] *Prosecutor v Lubanga,* above n 59, para 536; *Prosecutor v Germain Katanga,* Judgment pursuant to Art 74 of the Statute, Trial Chamber, International Criminal Court, Case No ICC-01/04-01/7, 7 March 2014, paras 1185–86.

[98] *Prosecutor v Germain Katanga,* above n 97, para 1186; *Prosecutor v Lubanga,* above n 59, para 537.

under responsible command. In this regard, responsible command entails some degree of organization of those armed groups, including the possibility to impose discipline'.[99] The above-mentioned conclusion in *Hadzihasanovic*—'that there cannot be an organized military force save on the basis of responsible command'[100]—is thus seen as convincing.

To summarise, responsible command denotes a command capable of imposing internal discipline, thereby evidencing a minimum level of organisation. This definition does not conflate the non-international armed conflict threshold test with the higher threshold associated with Additional Protocol II,[101] which involves an assessment of other factors such as, for example, the capacity to carry out sustained and concerted military operations.[102] Neither does it require that responsible command per se entail command responsibility,[103] although the two are related, with command responsibility recognised as having its roots in the principle of responsible command.[104] Rather it states that the concept of responsible command is essential to determining the organisational requirement associated with the minimum threshold of non-international armed conflict. Returning to the five categories of indicia developed by the *Boskoski* Trial Chamber,[105] further analysis indicates that they may all be regarded as elements of, or derived from, the concept of responsible command. The core element of a responsible command is the existence of a command structure capable of enforcing internal discipline, thereby encapsulating two of the *Boskoski* groupings. Reference to the indicia associated with these two categories confirms this conclusion. Identified factors include the presence of a military-like hierarchy, the ability to distribute orders and internal regulations,[106] the ability to ensure that orders are implemented, and the existence of disciplinary rules and regulations.[107] These factors are all indicative of responsible command. The three remaining

[99] *Prosecutor v Gombo*, Decision Pursuant to Art 61(7)(a) and (b) of the Rome Statute on the Charges of the Prosecutor against Jean-Pierre Bemba Gombo, Pre-Trial Chamber, International Criminal Court, Case No ICC-01/05-01/08, 15 June 2009, para 234.

[100] *Prosecutor v Hadzihasanovic*, Decision on Interlocutory Appeal Challenging Jurisdiction in Relation to Command Responsibility, above n 94, para 16.

[101] See *The Concept of Non-International Armed Conflict in International Humanitarian Law* above n 59, 155. See further above n 20, 170–80, 184–85.

[102] Art 1(1), Additional Protocol II.

[103] See Chantal Meloni, *Command Responsibility in International Criminal Law* (The Hague, TMC Asser Press, 2010) 36.

[104] *Prosecutor v Hadzihasanovic*, Decision on Joint Challenge to Jurisdiction, Trial Chamber, International Criminal Tribunal for the former Yugoslavia, Case No IT-01-47-PT, 12 November 2002, para 93.

[105] The five categories are: responsible command, the ability to impose internal discipline, the ability to speak with one voice, the ability to conduct organised operations, and a logistics capability.

[106] *Prosecutor v Boskoski*, above n 62, para 199.

[107] ibid, para 202.

Boskoski groupings are also dependent upon the existence of a responsible command: a group's ability to speak with one voice is necessarily dependent upon the ability to enforce internal discipline,[108] the conduct of organised operations is dependent upon a command structure capable of, inter alia, effectively distributing orders,[109] as is the ability to organise logistics.[110] Accordingly, it is suggested that it is the existence of a responsible command that demonstrates an armed group's ability to fulfil obligations arising under international humanitarian law.

B. Situations Outside Armed Conflict

Outside armed conflict, armed groups may be subject to international obligations in relation to the customary international law prohibition on crimes against humanity,[111] a central element of which is the existence of an organisational policy or plan.[112] For example, the Rome Statute of the International Criminal Court states that:[113] an '"[a]ttack directed against a civilian population" means a course of conduct involving the multiple commission of acts ... against any civilian population, pursuant to or in furtherance of a State *or organizational* policy to commit such attack'.[114] In this context the prohibition of crimes against humanity is discussed in relation to international criminal law and is concerned with the issue of individual criminal responsibility and not the responsibility of the group as such. However, international law does not preclude the possibility that an organisation engaged in the commission of a crime against humanity (or a war crime) may be internationally responsible in its own right.[115]

108 As indicated, for example, by the requirement that ceasefire orders be respected. See *Prosecutor v Boskoski*, above n 62, para 203.

109 Other indicators are regarded as emerging from the responsible command requirement. For example, the ability to define a unified strategy, division of territory into zones of responsibility, and the capacity to coordinate actions are all dependent upon the basic responsible command requirement that orders are effective.

110 Similarly, the ability to coordinate logistics will depend upon the communications network necessary to ensure a responsible command exists in practice.

111 *Prosecutor v Tadic*, Decision on the Defence Motion for Interlocutory Appeal on Jurisdiction, above n 60, para 141.

112 The prohibition of crimes against humanity applies to all groups capable of committing such acts, regardless of their actual commission or not.

113 Art 7(1) Statute of the International Criminal Court.

114 ibid, Art 7(2)(a).

115 See International Law Commission, 'Draft Articles on Responsibility of States for Internationally Wrongful Acts, with commentaries' (2001) *Yearbook of the International Commission* Vol II, 52. See also, Andrew Clapham, 'The Question of Jurisdiction Under International Criminal Law Over Legal Persons: Lessons from the Rome Conference on an International Criminal Court' in Menno T Kamminga and Saman Zia-Zarifi (eds), *Liability of Multinational Corporations under International Law* (Alphen aan den Rijn, Kluwer Law International, 2000) 191.

For instance, although the US Military Tribunals at Nuremberg did not have jurisdiction over legal persons, the Tribunal clearly held that:

> Where private individuals, *including juristic persons*, proceed to exploit the military occupancy by acquiring private property against the will and consent of the former owner, such action, not being expressly justified by an applicable provision of the Hague Regulations, is in violation of international law.[116]

This established, the Tribunal concluded that a number of corporations had violated international law.[117] Significantly, although individual criminal responsibility was at issue, this was addressed 'only after a lengthy and detailed explication of the actions of the Krupp firm as the prime actor and perpetrator of the various war crimes and crimes against humanity.'[118] The Tribunals regarded the corporations as instruments of cohesion, in the name of whom the illegal acts were committed.[119] In *Farben*, for instance, it was held that 'acts of spoliation and plunder, constituting offenses against property as defined in Control Council Law No. 10, were committed *through Farben* with respect to three properties located in Poland.'[120]

It follows that if organisations can violate international law prohibitions relating to crimes against humanity and war crimes they must be subject to a corresponding obligation, and so may acquire international legal personality on this basis.[121] Irrespective of whether it is accepted that an organisation acquires international legal personality in this manner, as a determination regarding an entity's qualification as an organisation is required vis-à-vis a finding related to the crime itself, the associated criteria are relevant for present purposes.[122]

Certain controversy exists over whether non-state actors may commit crimes against humanity, and thus whether armed groups may fall within

[116] *The IG Farben Trial, The United States of America v Carl Krauch et al,* Judgment, US Military Tribunal Nuremberg, 30 July 1948, 1132. Emphasis added. See further, 'The Question of Jurisdiction Under International Criminal Law Over Legal Persons' above n 115, 167; Beth Stephens, 'The Amorality of Profit: Transnational Corporations and Human Rights' (2002) 20 *Berkeley Journal of International Law* 76. *Cf* Kevin Jon Heller, *The Nuremberg Military Tribunals and the Origins of International Criminal Law* (Oxford, OUP, 2011) 253.

[117] See eg, *United States v Krupp et al,* Judgment, US Military Tribunal Nuremberg, 31 July 1948, 1353; *The IG Farben Trial,* above n 116, 1139.

[118] Anita Ramasastry, 'Corporate Complicity: From Nuremberg to Rangoon, An Examination of Forced Labor Cases and Their Impact on the Liability of Multinational Corporations' (2002) 20 *Berkeley Journal of International Law* 108. This reasoning applies equally with respect to *Farben.*

[119] *The IG Farben Trial,* above n 116, 1152.

[120] ibid, 1140. See also *United States v Krupp et al,* above n 117, 1353. Emphasis added.

[121] In order to acquire international legal personality the organisation must exist independently and have the capacity to possess international rights and obligations (see above Ch 2 section IV.E).

[122] This should not be read as dismissing the possibility that the organisation itself may be held responsible.

the scope of the prohibition.[123] Yet, despite the academic controversy, it is presented that the matter is now settled in the case law. In *Kayishema and Ruzindana* the Trial Chamber of the International Criminal Tribunal for Rwanda confirmed that it had jurisdiction with respect to crimes against humanity over 'both State and non-State actors',[124] and a similar finding was made by the International Criminal Tribunal for the former Yugoslavia in *Kupreskic*.[125] Similarly, in *Katanga and Chui*, the Pre-Trial Chamber of the International Criminal Court clearly stated that the policy to commit a crime against humanity, 'may be made either by groups of persons who govern a specific territory or by any organisation with the capability to commit a widespread or systematic attack against a civilian population.'[126] Addressing the situation in Kenya, the Pre-Trial Chamber stated that:

> Whereas some have argued that only State-like organizations may qualify, the Chamber opines that the formal nature of a group and the level of its organization should not be the defining criterion. Instead, as others have convincingly put forward, a distinction should be drawn on whether a group has the capability to perform acts which infringe on basic human values.[127]

It is clear that the case law of the international tribunals recognises that non-state groups may commit crimes against humanity. As such, it is possible that non-traditional groups such as organised criminal gangs, or private criminal organisations, may be included in this category. Indeed, developing the Pre-Trial Chamber's reasoning,[128] this seems inescapable; if a group has the capability to commit a crime against humanity, then it seems appropriate that this capability should be the decisive factor.

(i) Requirements Associated with the Organisation Criterion

Having established that non-state entities may commit crimes against humanity on the basis of an organisational policy, the criteria required for an entity to qualify as an 'organisation' must be identified. It is noted

[123] See William Schabas, *The International Criminal Court: A Commentary on the Rome Statute* (Oxford, OUP, 2010) 152.

[124] *Prosecutor v Clement Kayishema and Obed Ruzindana*, Judgment, Trial Chamber, International Criminal Tribunal for Rwanda, Case No ICTR-95-1-T, 21 May 1999, para 126.

[125] *Prosecutor v Kupreskic*, Judgment, Trial Chamber, International Criminal Tribunal for the former Yugoslavia, Case No IT-95-16-T, 14 January 2000, para 551.

[126] *Prosecutor v Germain Katanga and Mathieu Ngudjolo Chui*, Decision on the Confirmation of Charges, Pre-Trial Chamber, International Criminal Court, Case No ICC-01/04-01/07, 30 September 2008, para 396.

[127] Decision Pursuant to Art 15 of the Rome Statute on the Authorization of an investigation into the Situation in the Republic of Kenya, Pre-Trial Chamber, International Criminal Court, Case No ICC-01/09, 31 March 2010, para 90.

[128] ibid, para 90.

that case law and academic thought in this area remains relatively underdeveloped as the requirement of an organisational policy was only explicitly introduced with the codification of the Rome Statute of the International Criminal Court;[129] neither the Statute of the International Criminal Tribunal for the former Yugoslavia[130] nor the Statute of the International Criminal Tribunal for Rwanda[131] require the existence of an organisational policy.[132]

In *Ntaganda* the Pre-Trial Chamber of the International Criminal Court identified a number of criteria which should be taken into account when determining whether an entity qualifies as an 'organisation',[133] and these have subsequently been referred to by other Chambers:[134]

(i) whether the group is under a responsible command, or has an established hierarchy;
(ii) whether the group possesses, in fact, the means to carry out a widespread or systematic attack against a civilian population;
(iii) whether the group exercises control over part of the territory of a state;
(iv) whether the group has criminal activities against the civilian population as a primary purpose;
(v) whether the group articulates, explicitly or implicitly, an intention to attack a civilian population;
(vi) whether the group is part of a larger group, which fulfils some or all of the above-mentioned criteria.[135]

Similar to the evaluation of the organisation requirement associated with non-international armed conflict, these factors serve as indicators,

[129] Art 7(2)(a), Rome Statute.

[130] See Art 5, Statute of the International Criminal Tribunal for the former Yugoslavia.

[131] See Art 3 Statute of the International Criminal Tribunal for Rwanda.

[132] This requirement was, however, elaborated in the jurisprudence. See eg *Prosecutor v Naletilic and Martinovic*, Judgment, Trial Chamber, International Criminal Tribunal for the former Yugoslavia, Case No IT-98-34-T, 31 March 2003, para 236. See also, *Prosecutor v Kunarac, Kovac and Vukovic*, Judgment, Appeals Chamber, International Criminal Tribunal for the former Yugoslavia, Case No IT-96-23 & IT-96-23/1-A, 12 June 2002, para 94; *Prosecutor v Semanza*, Judgment, Trial Chamber, International Criminal Tribunal for Rwanda, Case No ICTR-97-20-T, 15 May 2003, para 329.

[133] Decision Pursuant to Art 15 of the Rome Statute on the Authorization of an Investigation into the Situation in the Republic of Kenya, above n 127, para 93.

[134] See for example, *Prosecutor v Bosco Ntaganda*, Decision on the Prosecutor's Application under Art 58, Pre-Trial Chamber, International Criminal Court, Case No ICC-01/04-02/06, 13 July 2012, para 24; *Prosecutor v William Samoei Ruto, Heny Kiprono Kosgey and Joshua Arap Sang*, Decision on the Confirmation of Charges Pursuant to Art 61(7)(a) and (b) of the Rome Statute, Pre-Trial Chamber, International Criminal Court, Case No ICC-01/09-01/11, 23 January 2012, para 185; Decision Pursuant to Art 15 of the Rome Statute on the Authorisation of an Investigation into the Situation in the Republic of Cote d'Ivoire, Pre-Trial Chamber, International Criminal Court, Case No ICC-02/11, 3 October 2011, para 46.

[135] Decision Pursuant to Art 15 of the Rome Statute on the Authorization of an Investigation into the Situation in the Republic of Kenya, above n 127, para 93.

not as exhaustive criteria, and any evaluation must be undertaken on a case-by-case basis.[136] It is submitted that the first three criteria are the most pertinent for present purposes, and these will be analysed individually below. Criteria (iv) and (v) respectively relate to the purpose—or motivation—of the organisation, and whether it has made clear an intention to attack a civilian population. These criteria are not intrinsic to an organisation's structure, but rather relate more to other elements of the crime, such as establishing the existence of a 'policy'. Criterion (vi) notes that the previously mentioned criteria remain relevant should the group form part of a larger group which may qualify as an 'organisation'.

(a) The Existence of a Responsible Command

The existence of a responsible command has been a consistent requirement in the developing case law of the International Criminal Court. Although the Court has not gone into extensive detail in this regard, it appears to conceive a responsible command as involving an identifiable, typically hierarchical, organisational structure. For example, in *Ruto, Kosgey and Sang* the Court stated:

> The evidence reveals that the Network was under responsible command and had an established hierarchy, with Mr Ruto as the designated leader, in charge of securing the establishment and efficient functioning of the Network as well as the pursuit of its criminal purposes. The evidence available to the Chamber establishes substantial grounds to believe that the hierarchical structure of the Network was comprised of three commanders (or generals), in charge of the attack ... as well as four divisional commanders, who were responsible for the execution of the attack in the field.[137]

A similar finding was made in *Muthaura, Kenyatta and Ali*, where the Court noted that the entity in question 'operated at the relevant time as a hierarchical organization with defined roles for members at different levels.'[138] This was reiterated in *Ntaganda*, where the Pre-Trial Chamber held that the UPC/FPLC 'was an organization under responsible command and had an established hierarchy'.[139]

[136] ibid, para 93.

[137] *Prosecutor v William Samoei Ruto, Heny Kiprono Kosgey and Joshua Arap Sang*, Decision on the Confirmation of Charges Pursuant to Art 61(7)(a) and (b) of the Rome Statute, above n 134, para 197.

[138] *Prosecutor v Francis Kirimi Muthaura, Uhuru Muigai Kenyatta and Mohammed Hussein Ali*, Decision on the Confirmation of Charges Pursuant to Article 61(7)(a) and (b) of the Rome Statute, Pre-Trial Chamber, International Criminal Court, Case No ICC-01/09-02/11, 23 January 2012, para 190.

[139] *Prosecutor v Bosco Ntaganda*, Decision on the Prosecutor's Application under Article 58, above n 134, para 26.

The other element identified with respect to the existence of a responsible command is a group's ability to ensure compliance with its rules and orders. As stated in *Muthaura, Kenyatta and Ali*: 'the evidence further demonstrates the existence, at the relevant time, of an effective system of ensuring compliance by the members of the Mungiki with the rules of the organization.'[140] This internal discipline requirement was not made explicit in other decisions of the Court, but it may be read into the Court's reasoning with respect to the responsible command requirement, bearing in mind that—perhaps as a result of the pre-trial nature of the proceedings—the issue was not discussed in great detail. For example, in *Ntaganda*, reference was made to the existence of an established hierarchy, a pool of trained military personnel, and tiers of communication with those responsible in the field.[141] Taken together, these elements indicate the existence of a group capable of effectively communicating orders, and it may be reasonably assumed that such orders were to be complied with. Similarly, in *Ruto, Kosgey and Sang*, the Court noted the entity's hierarchical structure, which included distinct levels of responsibility,[142] and highlighted members' commitment to complying with orders.[143]

(b) The Capacity to Carry Out a Widespread or Systematic Attack

The capacity to carry out a widespread or systematic attack has also been a consistent requirement in the early decisions of the International Criminal Court. In *Gombo* the Court stated that a policy may be made 'by any organization with the capability to commit a widespread or systematic attack against a civilian population',[144] echoing a similar statement in *Katanga and Chui*.[145] In evaluating a specific group's satisfaction of this criterion, the Chamber in *Ruto, Kosgey and Sang* noted that the Mungiki Network had the capacity to carry out a widespread or systematic attack, 'as its members had access to and utilised a considerable amount of

140 *Prosecutor v Francis Kirimi Muthaura, Uhuru Muigai Kenyatta and Mohammed Hussein Ali*, Decision on the Confirmation of Charges Pursuant to Article 61(7)(a) and (b) of the Rome Statute, above n 138, para 207.

141 *Prosecutor v Bosco Ntaganda*, Decision on the Prosecutor's Application under Article 58, above n 134, para 26.

142 *Prosecutor v William Samoei Ruto, Heny Kiprono Kosgey and Joshua Arap Sang*, Decision on the Confirmation of Charges Pursuant to Article 61(7)(a) and (b) of the Rome Statute, above n 134, para 192.

143 ibid, para 193.

144 *Prosecutor v Gombo*, Decision Pursuant to Article 61(7)(a) and (b) of the Rome Statute on the Charges of the Prosecutor against Jean-Pierre Bemba Gombo, above n 99, para 81.

145 *Prosecutor v Germain Katanga and Mathieu Ngudjolo Chui*, above n 126, para 396.

capital, guns, crude weapons and manpower'.[146] Similarly, in *Ntaganda* the Chamber noted the UPC/FPLC's 'access to a significant amount of weapons, to a manpower pool of trained military personnel, and to lines of communication with those responsible on the field.'[147]

It is submitted that a group's capacity to carry out a widespread or systematic attack is necessarily dependent upon the existence of a responsible command.[148] A systematic attack,[149] denoted by the existence of a preconceived policy or plan,[150] will necessarily require a responsible command given the level of organisation required: there must be an organisational structure capable of ensuring that the policy to commit a crime against humanity is implemented.[151] As stated in *Akayesu*, '[t[he concept of systematic may be defined as *thoroughly organised* and following a regular pattern on the basis of a common policy'.[152]

The commission of a widespread attack must also be regarded as dependent upon the presence of a responsible command capable of ensuring the necessary level of planning and coordination:[153] 'in the context of a widespread attack, the requirement of an organisational policy pursuant to article 7(2)(a) of the Statute ensures that the attack … must still be thoroughly organised.'[154] This conclusion is supported by further reference to the decisions of the International Criminal Court. For example, in *Ntaganda*, the Pre-Trial Chamber held that, '[t]here are also reasonable grounds to believe that the UPC/FPLC possessed the means to carry out a widespread or systematic attack against the civilian population, as it had access to a significant amount of weapons, to a manpower pool of trained military personnel, and to lines of communication with those responsible in the field.'[155] These requirements—which are similar to those

[146] *Prosecutor v William Samoei Ruto, Heny Kiprono Kosgey and Joshua Arap Sang*, Decision on the Confirmation of Charges Pursuant to Article 61(7)(a) and (b) of the Rome Statute, above n 134, para 200.

[147] *Prosecutor v Bosco Ntaganda*, Decision on the Prosecutor's Application under Article 58, above n 134, para 26.

[148] See further above Ch 3 section III.A(ii)(a).

[149] See *Prosecutor v Popovic et al*, Judgment, Trial Chamber, International Criminal Tribunal for the former Yugoslavia, Case No IT-05-88-T, 10 June 2010, para 756.

[150] See *Prosecutor v Semanza*, above n 132, para 329. See also, *Prosecutor v Kunarac, Kovac and Vukovic*, above n 132, para 94.

[151] See further, the reasoning utilised by the Pre-Trial Chamber in *Prosecutor v William Samoei Ruto, Heny Kiprono Kosgey and Joshua Arap Sang*, Decision on the Confirmation of Charges Pursuant to Article 61(7)(a) and (b) of the Rome Statute, above n 134, para 179. See also the discussion above relating to responsible command in the context of an armed conflict, Ch 3 section III.A(ii)(a).

[152] *Prosecutor v Akayesu*, above n 68, para 580. Emphasis added.

[153] See *Prosecutor v Popovic et al*, above n 149, para 756.

[154] *Prosecutor v Germain Katanga and Mathieu Ngudjolo Chui*, above n 126, para 396.

[155] *Prosecutor v Bosco Ntaganda*, Decision on the Prosecutor's Application under Article 58, above n 134, para 26.

listed in *Ruto, Kosgey and Sang*[156] and *Muthaura, Kenyatta and Ali*[157]—are ultimately dependent upon responsible command: the supply of weapons is primarily a logistics issue, dependent upon planning, coordination, and communication; in order to be effective—ie capable of committing the required attack on behalf of the group—a military wing or pool of personnel must be subject to effective command and control; while effective communications require an identifiable organisational structure with assigned areas of responsibility, and the ability to ensure compliance with instructions. Significantly, in *Muthaura, Kenyatta and Ali*, the Pre-Trial Chamber concluded that the Mungiki qualified as an organisation, on the basis that:

> [T]he Mungiki was a hierarchically structured organization; (ii) there existed an effective system of ensuring compliance by the members with the rules and orders imposed by the higher levels of command; (iii) the Mungiki was a large organization and included a trained quasi-military wing; and (iv) it controlled and provided, in certain parts of Kenya, essential social services, including security.[158]

The first two factors are inherent in the concept of responsible command, while the second two are consequences of the organisational capacity that this command makes possible.[159]

(c) The Exercise of Territorial Control

The final element to be considered is the requirement of territorial control.[160] Subsequent to its initial identification, the territorial requirement has not been a consistent feature in the decisions of the International Criminal Court; in finding that the entity under discussion satisfied the organisational criteria, territorial control was not mentioned in *Katanga*,[161]

[156] *Prosecutor v William Samoei Ruto, Heny Kiprono Kosgey and Joshua Arap Sang*, Decision on the Confirmation of Charges Pursuant to Article 61(7)(a) and (b) of the Rome Statute, above n 134, para 200.

[157] *Prosecutor v Francis Kirimi Muthaura, Uhuru Muigai Kenyatta and Mohammed Hussein Ali*, Decision on the Confirmation of Charges Pursuant to Article 61(7)(a) and (b) of the Rome Statute, above n 138, para 222.

[158] *Prosecutor v Francis Kirimi Muthaura, Uhuru Muigai Kenyatta and Mohammed Hussein Ali*, Decision on the Confirmation of Charges Pursuant to Article 61(7)(a) and (b) of the Rome Statute, above n 138, para 228.

[159] The responsible command requirement applies to the organisation involved in the preparation of the policy or plan. It is not required that all individuals involved in the commission of a crime against humanity be members of that organisation. For example, individual perpetrators may have been mobilised by the organisation.

[160] Decision Pursuant to Article 15 of the Rome Statute on the Authorization of an Investigation into the Situation in the Republic of Kenya, above n 127, para 93.

[161] *Prosecutor v Germain Katanga*, above n 97, paras 1119–20, 1139–41.

Ruto, Kosgey and Sang,[162] *Ntaganda*,[163] or *Katanga and Chui*.[164] It must thus be concluded that territorial control—while indicative of the required organisational sophistication—is not an essential criterion.[165] This would appear appropriate: the test should rest not on a formal requirement of territorial control,[166] but rather upon whether an organised group has the 'capability to perform acts which infringe on basic human values'.[167] For present purposes the exercise of territorial control cannot be considered as a characteristic intrinsic to the group, but must be regarded as an external factor.

C. Summary

From the above analysis, it is apparent that the decisive factor in determining an armed group's capacity to directly possess international obligations—whether during or outside armed conflict—is the existence of a responsible command. A responsible command is defined by the existence of an organisational structure capable of ensuring internal discipline, and thus capable of ensuring the group's fulfilment of any obligations arising under international law.[168] In situations of armed conflict, the intensity criteria must also be satisfied; however, satisfaction of these criteria is dependent to a large extent upon external factors, such as the actions of other entities engaged in the hostilities. Outside armed conflict, the customary law prohibition of crimes against humanity applies to all armed groups capable of committing such acts.

In light of this requirement it is noted that the establishment and maintenance of internal discipline is widely regarded as essential to

[162] *Prosecutor v William Samoei Ruto, Heny Kiprono Kosgey and Joshua Arap Sang*, Decision on the Confirmation of Charges Pursuant to Article 61(7)(a) and (b) of the Rome Statute, above n 134, para 208 and preceding discussion.

[163] *Prosecutor v Bosco Ntaganda*, Decision on the Prosecutor's Application under Article 58, above n 134, para 26.

[164] *Prosecutor v Germain Katanga and Mathieu Ngudjolo Chui*, above n 126.

[165] A territorial requirement was not a feature of the International Law Commission's Draft Code of Crimes against the Peace and Security of Mankind. See Art 18, International Law Commission, 'Draft Code of Crimes against the Peace and Security of Mankind, with Commentaries' (1996) *Yearbook of the International Law Commission*, Vol II, Pt Two.

[166] *cf* above n 123, 152; M Cherif Bassiouni, *Crimes against Humanity in International Criminal Law*, 2nd edn (Alphen aan den Rijn, Kluwer Law International, 1999) 245.

[167] Decision Pursuant to Article 15 of the Rome Statute on the Authorization of an Investigation into the Situation in the Republic of Kenya, above n 127, para 90.

[168] The existence of a responsible command does not depend upon a traditional military top-down hierarchy, and that other forms of organisation—such as 'internal democracy'—may exist. However, it is required that, once made, decisions be obeyed. See eg above n 70, 268.

the effective functioning of armed groups. In *Prosecutor v Sesay, Kallon and Gbao* the Special Court for Sierra Leone held that 'the RUF's disciplinary system was critical to maintaining its operation as a cohesive military organisation'.[169] Similarly, Che Guevara, Vo Nguyen Giap, and Mao Tse-tung have underlined the importance of discipline in guerrilla organisations,[170] while the UN Secretary-General has noted that, in order to ensure respect for international norms, states and non-state parties to an armed conflict should: '[e]nsure that orders and instructions are observed by establishing effective disciplinary procedures.'[171]

Practice demonstrates that a large number of diverse armed groups do establish an internal disciplinary system. In Iraq the Mahdi army established *Al-Ma'had al-Mahdawi* (the Mahdist Institute) to teach the purposes of the group,[172] and a 'Judgment Committee' was also established to question and punish those suspected of violating the rules.[173] The Islamic State has established a mechanism capable of receiving complaints directed against its fighters and commanders,[174] and has also established an elaborate intelligence system to monitor its members' activities.[175] Similarly, in Sierra Leone the RUF established an Internal Defence Unit (IDU) to investigate misconduct by fighters. Members of the IDU were dispatched to the front lines and attached to most battalions and companies, while an IDU commander was appointed at the brigade level.[176] It is noted that the RUF disciplinary system sought to ensure internal command and control, and not respect for general rules or principles. Thus, while attacks against civilians in base areas were punished, on the front lines commanders routinely

[169] *Prosecutor v Sesay, Kallon and Gbao*, Trial Chamber, Special Court for Sierra Leone, Case No SCSL-04-15-T, 2 March 2009, para 706.

[170] For example, 'When this discipline is violated, it is necessary always to punish the offender, whatever his rank': Ernesto 'Che' Guevara, *Guerrilla Warfare* (USA, BN Publishing, 2007) 85; 'The Vietnam People's Army practices a strict discipline … He who speaks of the army speaks of strict discipline': Vo Nguyen Giap, *The Military Art of People's War: Selected Writings of General Vo Nguyen Giap* (Russell Stetler (ed), New York, Monthly Review Press, 1970) 112; 'A revolutionary army must have discipline that is established on a limited democratic basis. In all armies, obedience of the subordinates to their superiors must be exacted … Although discipline in guerrilla ranks is not as severe as in the ranks of orthodox forces, the necessity for discipline exists.' Mao Tse-tung, *Mao Tse-tung on Guerrilla Warfare* (Washington DC, US Marine Corps, 1989) 90.

[171] 'Report of the Secretary-General on the protection of civilians in armed conflict', UN Doc S/2009/277, 29 May 2009, para 65.

[172] International Crisis Group, 'Iraq's Muqtada Al-Sadr: Spoiler or Stabiliser?' (2006) 14.

[173] ibid, 20.

[174] Charles C Caris and Samuel Reynolds, 'ISIS Governance in Syria', Middle East Security Report 22, Institute for the Study of War, July 2014, 19.

[175] Christoph Reuter, 'The Terror Strategist: Secret Files Reveal the Structure of Islamic State', *Der Spiegel* (18 April 2015).

[176] *Prosecutor v Sesay, Kallon and Gbao*, above n 169, para 682.

ordered brutal attacks against the civilian population.[177] Ultimately, the Special Court for Sierra Leone concluded that 'the RUF's disciplinary system was critical to maintaining its operation as a cohesive military organisation',[178] and that it 'functioned essentially to allow the leadership to maintain control over all the RUF fighters and impose and maintain order in RUF territory.'[179] Internal disciplinary systems have also been established by groups including Hezbollah,[180] FARC,[181] the FMLN,[182] and the ELN;[183] groups such as the Democratic Forces for the Liberation of Rwanda (FDLR)[184] and the KLA[185] have also established military police units.

IV. TRANSNATIONAL CORPORATIONS

This section addresses the potential international legal personality of transnational and multinational corporations. Regarding the definition of such entities, UN terminology initially distinguished between 'transnational corporations', entities owned and controlled by persons from one state but operating across state borders, and 'multinational corporations', entities owned or controlled by persons from more than one state. In practice, however, this distinction is no longer maintained,[186] and, adopting Muchlinski's definition, the term 'transnational corporation' will be used herein to cover all forms of cross-border business associations engaged in

[177] See for example, 'S Leone trio guilty of war crimes', *BBC News* (25 February 2009). The Special Court for Sierra Leone concluded that 'the RUF operated on the basis that criminal conduct was inherently acceptable in certain situations.' *Prosecutor v Sesay, Kallon and Gbao,* above n 169, para 709.

[178] *Prosecutor v Sesay, Kallon and Gbao,* above n 169, para 706.

[179] *ibid,* para 712.

[180] International Crisis Group, 'Hizbollah: Rebel Without a Cause?' (2003) 3; Human Rights Watch, 'Why They Died: Civilian Casualties in Lebanon during the 2006 War' (2007) 42.

[181] See Human Rights Watch, 'Colombia: Beyond Negotiation International Humanitarian Law and its Application to the Conduct of FARC-EP' (2001) 6; Human Rights Watch, 'War Without Quarter: Colombia and International Humanitarian Law' (1998).

[182] Sandesh Sivakumaran, 'Courts of Armed Opposition Groups: Fair Trials or Summary Justice' (2009) 7 *Journal of International Criminal Justice*, 491.

[183] Human Rights Watch, 'War Without Quarter: Colombia and International Humanitarian Law' (1998).

[184] International Crisis Group, 'Rwandan Hutu Rebels in the Congo: a New Approach to Disarmament and Reintegration' (2003) 8.

[185] *Prosecutor v Limaj,* International Criminal Tribunal for the former Yugoslavia, IT-03-66-T, 30 November 2006, para 113.

[186] Peter T Muchlinksi, *Multinational Enterprises and the Law,* 2nd edn (Oxford, OUP, 2007) 6.

direct investment.[187] It is noted that a characteristic common to all such entities is their possession of limited liability.[188] At the outset, it must be highlighted that the international legal personality of transnational corporations is by no means a settled issue. De Schutter has noted that transnational corporations are typically only subject to indirect rights or obligations[189]—ie through the medium of the state[190]—while the United States Court of Appeals stated in *Kiobel* that:

> Looking to international law, we find a jurisprudence, first set forth in Nuremberg and repeated by every international tribunal of which we are aware, that offenses against the law of nations (i.e., customary international law) for violations of human rights can be charged against States and against individual men and women but not against juridical persons such as corporations. As a result, although international law has sometimes extended the scope of liability for a violation of a given norm to individuals, it has *never* extended the scope of liability to a corporation.[191]

However, as transnational corporations are established under municipal law, clear criteria exist regarding the acquisition of legal personality, and these criteria are necessarily of relevance herein.

A. The Organisational Characteristics of Transnational Corporations

A corporation, under both municipal and international law,[192] is defined by the existence of an independent personality: registering a company as a corporation will transform it into an entity in its own right, possessing rights and obligations distinct from that of its members.[193] As stated by the House of Lords in the landmark UK case of *Salomon v Salomon*, 'once the company is legally incorporated it must be treated like any other independent person with its rights and liabilities appropriate to itself'.[194]

[187] See further Menno T Kamminga and Saman Zia-Zarifi, 'Liability of Multinational Corporations under International Law: An Introduction' in Menno T Kamminga and Saman Zia-Zarifi (eds), *Liability of Multinational Corporations under International Law* (Alphen aan den Rijn, Kluwer Law International, 2000) 2.

[188] Beth Stephens, 'The Amorality of Profit: Transnational Corporations and Human Rights' (2002) 20 *Berkeley Journal of International Law* 55.

[189] Olivier De Schutter, 'The Accountability of Multinationals for Human Rights Violations in European Law' in Philip Alston (ed), *Non-State Actors and Human Rights* (Oxford, OUP, 2005) 233.

[190] Under such circumstances transnational corporations would be subjects of municipal and not international law.

[191] *Kiobel v Royal Dutch Petroleum Co*, United States Court of Appeals Second Circuit, 621 F 3d 111, 17 September 2010, 120.

[192] See eg *Case Concerning the Barcelona Traction, Light and Power Company, Limited*, Judgment, International Court of Justice, 5 February 1970, para 38.

[193] LE Talbot, *Critical Company Law* (London, Routledge-Cavendish, 2008) 23.

[194] *Salomon v Salomon* [1897] AC 22 (HL), 30.

This principle has been endorsed by the International Court of Justice: 'international law has repeatedly acknowledged the principle of domestic law that a company has a legal personality distinct from that of its shareholders.'[195] As such, it is the company alone, acting through the directors or management, which is entitled to take action with respect to matters of a corporate character:[196] '[t]he concept and structure of the company are founded on and determined by a firm distinction between the separate entity of the company and that of the shareholder'.[197] The decisive criterion with respect to a corporation's organisational structure is thus that it has a legal personality distinct from its members.[198] This characteristic, inherent in the structural composition of transnational corporations, constitutes the capacity to possess direct rights or obligations under international law.

V. CONCLUSION

The above analysis addressed a variety of distinct non-state entities, identifying the organisational criteria necessary for each entity to satisfy the capacity requirement associated with international legal personality. It concluded that international organisations must exhibit an independent will (*volonté distincte*), armed groups—whether inside or outside armed conflict—must be subject to a responsible command, and transnational corporations must possess a distinct legal personality with respect to their members or shareholders. It is submitted that these criteria centre on the same underlying requirement, namely that the organisational characteristic required of each entity in order to satisfy the capacity requirement may be demonstrated by the existence of an independent will. As discussed below, although this concept must necessarily be evaluated on a slightly different basis dependent upon the entity in question, it remains the determinative criterion.

To recap, an independent will is defined by the existence of an organisational will independent to that of the individual member entities, whether they are states, individuals, or other legal persons. This is an internal requirement, dependent upon an entity's relationship with its members. As such, it is distinguished from the independence criterion of international legal personality, which concerns an entity's external relationships.

195 *Case Concerning Ahmadou Sadio Diallo (Republic of Guinea v Democratic Republic of the Congo)*, Judgment, International Court of Justice, 30 December 2010, para 155.

196 *Case Concerning Barcelona Traction, Light and Power Company, Limited*, above n 192, para 42.

197 ibid, para 41.

198 See eg *Case Concerning Ahmadou Sadio Diallo (Republic of Guinea v Democratic Republic of the Congo)*, above n 195, para 61.

An independent will is typically determined on the basis of an organisation's power to bind its members, if necessary against their will.[199] As stated by the International Court of Justice, an organisation must be in 'such a position that it possesses, in regard to its Members, rights which it is entitled to ask them to respect.'[200] This requirement is held to 'express the essential test where a group, whether composed of States, of tribes or of individuals, is claimed to be a legal entity distinct from its members.'[201]

While the relevance of the independent will requirement to international organisations is unequivocal—this was the essential criterion specified by the International Court of Justice in *Reparations*[202]—the situation is less clear-cut with respect to armed groups and transnational corporations. Regarding transnational corporations, it is recalled that it is the company alone which is entitled to take action with respect to matters of a corporate character,[203] and that the members or shareholders are bound by any decisions of the corporation.[204] This autonomous capacity, and the ability to bind the membership, is directly equivalent to the existence of an independent will, and thus satisfies the 'essential test' by which an entity may be said to exist as an independent legal personality.[205] Indeed, an independent will is inherent in the corporate structure itself.[206] Equally, it is recalled that a responsible command is defined by the existence of a central structure, capable of enforcing internal discipline. It is the combination of these two elements that allows armed groups both to manifest a distinct will, and to bind the membership to that will. The ability to enforce internal discipline places an armed group in a position with respect to its members whereby it possess rights which it is entitled to ask them to respect. Indeed this is the very essence of a military, or a military-like structure: 'for an army to even function, troops must obey given orders.'[207] An armed group's ability to impose its will—through ensuring respect for its commands and orders—also confirms the existence of a group will, distinct from that of its individual members. It must be concluded that the

[199] See Rosalyn Higgins, *Problems and Processes: International Law and How We Use It* (Oxford, OUP, 1994) 46.

[200] *Reparations for injuries suffered in the services of the United Nations*, above n 4, 178.

[201] *Western Sahara*, above n 9, para 148.

[202] *Reparations for injuries suffered in the services of the United Nations*, above n 4, 178.

[203] *Case Concerning Barcelona Traction, Light and Power Company, Limited*, above n 192, para 42.

[204] See eg *Case Concerning Barcelona Traction, Light and Power Company, Limited*, above n 192, para 41.

[205] *Western Sahara*, above n 9, para 148.

[206] *Case Concerning Ahmadou Sadio Diallo (Republic of Guinea v Democratic Republic of the Congo)*, above n 195, para 155.

[207] *Prosecutor v Hadzihasanovic*, above n 88, para 87. Discussing the concept of 'effective control' in the context of a common Art 3 conflict.

existence of a responsible command satisfies the 'essential test' advanced in *Western Sahara*. The government/central authority requirement associated with the acquisition of statehood is also evidence of an independent will, allowing the state to control its population and to subject them to state authority.

Necessarily, the independent will criterion must be assessed on a slightly different basis depending on the entity in question. With respect to armed groups, for example, a central structure's ability to impose internal discipline will be decisive, whereas for international organisations it will be the existence of an independent organ with decision-making powers, or decision-making on the basis of majority vote. Equally, the organisational structure of transnational corporations and international organisations will typically be legally defined, for instance in an establishing treaty or in articles of incorporation, while for an armed group its function in practice may be more relevant. That said, the existence of an independent will remains the underlying criterion, upon which an entity's capacity to possess direct international rights or obligations will depend. The next criterion of international legal personality, the actual possession of international rights or obligations, will now be addressed.

4

Establishing a Legal Basis for the Application of International Law to Armed Groups

IN ORDER TO determine whether non-state armed groups may 'actually possess' direct international rights or obligations,[1] the legal basis underpinning the application of direct international rights or obligations to non-state armed groups must first be understood.[2] Today, it is authoritatively accepted that international humanitarian law treaties can bind non-state armed groups.[3] However, the legal basis underpinning this direct application of international law was uncertain in 1949, and remains so today; in many respects, the application of international humanitarian law to armed opposition groups is regarded as a fait acompli, happily, if somewhat disbelievingly, accepted.[4] Yet, the importance of understanding the legal basis underpinning the establishment of direct international obligations is evident, not only in terms of legal clarity and principles such as *nullum crimen sine lege*, but also, and perhaps more significantly, as a means of facilitating the future regulation of non-state armed groups, and indeed other non-state actors. Surprisingly, despite its fundamental importance,[5] this issue has not been addressed in a fully satisfactory manner to date, and has only been subject to in-depth analysis on a few notable occasions.[6]

[1] See above, Ch 2 section IV.C.

[2] Elements of this chapter originally appeared in, Daragh Murray, 'How International Humanitarian Law Treaties Bind Non-State Armed Groups' (2015) 20 *Journal of Conflict & Security Law*.

[3] *Case concerning military and paramilitary activities in and against Nicaragua (Nicaragua v United States of America)*, Merits, International Court of Justice, 27 June 1986, para 218.

[4] Conversely, while the attribution of international humanitarian law to non-state actors may be accepted, the potential attribution of other bodies of law is typically rejected as a matter of course.

[5] Evidenced by the significant global impact of armed groups. See above Ch 1 section I.

[6] Antonio Cassese, 'The Status of Rebels under the 1977 Geneva Protocol on Non-International Armed Conflicts' (1981) 30 *International and Comparative Law Quarterly* 2; Sandesh Sivakumaran, 'Binding Armed Opposition Groups' (2006) 55 *International and Comparative Law Quarterly*. See also, JK Kleffner, 'The applicability of international humanitarian law to organized armed groups' (2011) 93 *International Review of the Red Cross* 882.

Five principal theories have been put forward to explain the legal basis underpinning the direct application of international law to non-state armed groups: customary law,[7] general principles,[8] de facto control,[9] third party consent,[10] and legislative (or prescriptive) jurisdiction.[11] The de facto control theory is distinguished from the other theories of attribution as it has the potential to generate international legal personality in the absence of applicable international treaty law. As such, it will be discussed in the next chapter. Where relevant, these theories will be analysed in relation to international humanitarian law in order that they may be understood by reference to a body of law widely accepted as binding armed groups. However, it is important to note that these theories are equally applicable with respect to other bodies of law: if they can be used to explain the direct application of international humanitarian law treaties they can also be used to underpin the application of new treaties, in fields such as international human rights law, or international environmental law.

I. THE CUSTOMARY LAW THEORY

The customary law theory holds that where international rights or obligations form part of customary international law, they bind armed opposition groups *qua* customary law, with or without their consent, and irrespective of any actions undertaken by the territorial state.[12] This theory was utilised by the Appeals Chamber of the Special Court for Sierra Leone in the *Decision on Challenge to Jurisdiction: Lomé Accord Amnesty*: 'a convincing theory is that [armed groups] are bound as a matter of international customary law to observe the obligations declared by Common Article 3'.[13] The question is whether armed opposition groups—as non-state entities—can be bound by customary international law. As a source

[7] Armed groups are bound by customary international humanitarian law, as opposed to any treaty-based obligations undertaken by the state.

[8] Similar to the customary law theory, but refers instead to the binding force of general principles of international law.

[9] Armed groups which seize an element of state territory are bound in a manner similar to that of a seceding state.

[10] Armed groups may be bound by international treaty law if this was the intent of the drafters, and the individual groups in question consent to be bound.

[11] A state has the authority to bind all those subject to its territorial or nationality-based jurisdiction.

[12] See Heather Wilson, *International Law and the Use of Force by National Liberation Movements* (Oxford, Clarendon, 1988) 51; 'Binding Armed Opposition Groups' above n 6, 372; 'The Status of Rebels under the 1977 Geneva Protocol on Non-International Armed Conflicts' above n 6, 430.

[13] *Decision on Challenge to Jurisdiction: Lomé Accord Amnesty*, Appeals Chamber, Special Court for Sierra Leone, Case Nos SCSL-2004-15-AR72(E), SCSL-2004-16-AR72(E), 13 March 2004, para 47.

of law, custom is typically defined as 'general practice accepted as law',[14] and thus sometimes referred to as 'general rules'.[15] It is determined on the basis of 'State practice (*usus* or *diuturnitas*) and the corresponding views of States (*opinion juris* or *opinio necessitatis*).'[16] As is evident from this definition, customary law is typically regarded as emerging from (a) the practice and (b) the opinion of states:[17] the centrality of states with respect to customary international law is clear. Consequently, two distinct arguments against the customary law theory may be made. The first argument holds that customary international law applies exclusively to states and as such cannot bind non-state actors, including armed groups. The second argument holds that while customary law may bind armed groups this custom must be specific to such groups: armed groups should be bound by custom established by other armed groups.[18]

A. Can Customary Law Bind Non-State Armed Groups?

As discussed previously, states were traditionally regarded as the exclusive subjects of international law, possessing 'the totality of rights and duties recognised by international law.'[19] As such, states were the only entities involved in the creation of customary international law, and the only entities to which customary international law applied. However, in the post-World War II era it has been authoritatively confirmed that non-state entities may become subjects of international law.[20] Accordingly, it is submitted that, properly understood, customary international law binds not just states, but all subjects of international law. As held by the International Court of Justice, by their very nature customary law rules and obligations must have equal force for all members of the international community.[21] The definitive factor is not statehood, but international legal personality.

[14] Art 38(1), Statute of the International Court of Justice.

[15] Antonio Cassese, *International Law*, 2nd edn (Oxford, OUP, 2005) 154.

[16] ibid, 157.

[17] See PE Corbett, 'The Consent of States and the Sources of the Law of Nations' (1925) 6 *British Yearbook of International Law*, 26; IC MacGibbon, 'Customary International Law and Acquiescence' (1957) 33 *British Yearbook of International Law* 120.

[18] See Mark E Villiger, *Commentary on the 1969 Vienna Convention on the Law of Treaties* (The Hague, Martinus Nijhoff, 2009) 104; 'Binding Armed Opposition Groups' above n 6, 373.

[19] Dr Manuel Rama-Montaldo, 'International Legal Personality and Implied Powers of International Organizations' (1970) 44 *British Yearbook of International Law* 133.

[20] *Reparations for injuries suffered in the services of the United Nations*, Advisory Opinion, International Court of Justice, 11 April 1949, 179; *Legality of the use by a State of Nuclear Weapons in Armed Conflict*, Advisory Opinion, International Court of Justice, 8 July 1996, para 27.

[21] *North Sea Continental Shelf Cases*, Judgment, International Court of Justice, 20 February 1969, para 63.

This conclusion is supported by the case law of international and regional courts, and the writings of international law publicists.[22] Most authoritatively, the International Court of Justice has held that: '[i]nternational organizations are subjects of international law and, *as such*, are bound by any obligations incumbent upon them under general rules of international law'.[23] In this instance the Court clearly held customary international law to be applicable on the basis of international legal personality. Similarly, the European Court of Justice has referred to *jus cogens* 'as a body of higher rules of public international law binding on all subjects of international law',[24] and has noted that the European Union 'is required to comply with the rules of customary international law'.[25] The International Criminal Tribunal for the former Yugoslavia has also applied customary international law to a non-state entity, holding that the ICRC 'has a right under customary international law to non-disclosure',[26] while the US Court of Appeals has stated that: '[w]e do not agree that the law of nations, as understood in the modern era, confines its reach to state action.'[27] In this regard, reference was made to one of the first examples of customary international law, the prohibition of piracy.[28]

B. Can Custom Established by States Bind Armed Groups?

The second argument contends that armed groups are not bound by custom derived from the practice of states; inter alia as they were not involved in its creation.[29] Rather, any applicable custom is restricted to

[22] Lindsay Moir, *The Law of Internal Armed Conflict* (Cambridge, CUP, 2002) 53; 'Binding Armed Opposition Groups' above n 6, 373; August Reinisch, 'The Changing International Legal Framework for Dealing with Non-State Actors' in Philip Alston (ed), *Non-State Actors and Human Rights* (Oxford, OUP, 2005) 46.

[23] *Interpretation of the Agreement of 25 March 1951 Between the WHO and Egypt*, Advisory Opinion, International Court of Justice, 20 December 1980, para 37. Emphasis added. The phrases customary rules and general rules are often used interchangeably, see above n 15, 154.

[24] Case T-315/01 *Yusuf Abdullah Kadi v Council of the European Union & Commission of the European Communities*, Judgment (CFI, 21 September 2005), para 226.

[25] Case C-162/96 *A Racke GmbH & Co v Hauptzollamt Mainz* (ECJ, 16 June 1998), para 45. See also, Case C-286/90 *Poulsen & Diva Navigation Corp* (ECJ, 24 November 1992), para 9.

[26] *Prosecutor v Simic*, Decision on the Prosecution Motion Under Rule 73 for a Ruling Concerning the Testimony of a Witness, Trial Chamber, International Criminal Tribunal for the former Yugoslavia, Case No IT-95-9, 27 July 1999, para 35.

[27] *Kadic v Karadzic*, US Court of Appeals, 13 October 1995, 6.

[28] ibid, 6. It was highlighted elsewhere that 'piracy in violation of the law of nations is by definition perpetrated by nonstate actors'. *Shafi v Palestinian Authority*, US Court of Appeals, District of Columbia Circuit, No 10-7024, 14 June 2011, 15.

[29] See in addition to those sources cited above, n 18, for example, *The Geneva Convention and the Treatment of Prisoners of War in Vietnam* (1966–67) 80 *Harvard Law Review*, 856. The consent of armed groups is also relevant to this discussion, see below Ch 4 section III.

that established by armed groups. Again it is presented that this argument relates to the historical conception of states as the exclusive subjects of international law: as states were the only subjects of international law, and states created international law, it was assumed that the competence to create international law was a consequence of international legal personality.[30] However, this is not necessarily the case. As has been established, the modern international legal order recognises a number of different categories of international legal person, each possessing a subject-specific competence.[31] It is thus entirely possible that certain subjects of international law possess the right to create law, while others do not.[32]

It is unequivocal that states, the principal subjects of international law, possess the right to create law. With respect to armed groups, support for their role in the law creation process may be derived from the decision of the International Criminal Tribunal for the former Yugoslavia in *Tadic*,[33] which discussed the practice of armed groups as part of its analysis regarding the customary law of non-international armed conflicts.[34] However, there is very little other support for this proposition. For example, the ICRC's recent study on customary international humanitarian law considered the legal significance of armed group practice to be 'unclear', and did not conflate it with state practice.[35] Similarly, in order to enter into force, the *Vienna Convention on the Law of Treaties between States and International Organisations or between International Organisations*—to which international organisations could become a party[36]—requires ratification by 35 states; ratification or accession by international organisations was not determinative, implying that only states were considered relevant to the law creation process.[37] International courts, such as the International Court of Justice and the European Court of Justice, have held that non-state entities are bound by customary international law, without commenting on any potential ability of these entities to contribute to the creation of

[30] Roland Portmann, *Legal Personality in International Law* (Cambridge, CUP, 2010) 8–9.

[31] See above Ch 2 section I.D.

[32] Above n 30, 176.

[33] *Prosecutor v Tadic, Decision on the Defence Motion for Interlocutory Appeal on Jurisdiction*, Appeals Chamber, International Criminal Tribunal for the former Yugoslavia, Case No IT-94-1, 2 October 1995, paras 103, 107, 108.

[34] Liesbeth Zegveld, *The Accountability of Armed Opposition Groups in International Law* (Cambridge, CUP, 2002) 26.

[35] Jean-Marie Henckaerts and Louise Doswald-Beck, *Customary International Humanitarian Law, Volume 1: Rules* (Geneva, International Committee of the Red Cross/CUP, 2005) xlii. It is noted that this statement may have been made for reasons relating to the acceptance of the customary study as a whole, and as such it is not necessarily a legally valid conclusion.

[36] Art 84(1), Vienna Convention on the Law of Treaties between States and International Organizations or between International Organizations (adopted 21 March 1986, not yet in force) UN Doc A/CONF.129/15.

[37] ibid, Art 85.

such law.[38] Simply, while international law does not grant armed groups a role in the creation of customary international law,[39] this does not affect the actual application of this body of law. This is not to comment on the potential, or the desirability, of armed groups being granted a role in the customary process.[40]

C. Determining the Content of the Customary Law Applicable to Armed Groups

Having established that armed groups can be bound by customary international law, the extent of the applicable customary law must be determined. For instance, is an armed group party to a non-international armed conflict only bound by the customary law of armed conflict, or do other bodies of law also apply? Before examining this issue further, it is noted that the application of customary law to non-state entities gives rise to a potential difficulty as the customary rule in question may have been developed consequent to the regulation of state behaviour. However, this fact alone does not necessarily preclude the application of the customary rule to non-state actors.[41] For instance, although the treaty law relating to the conduct of hostilities in international armed conflict was developed solely to regulate state behaviour, these rules are now recognised as applying to non-state entities engaged in non-international armed conflict on the basis of customary law.[42]

It is submitted that customary international law should be regarded as a unitary body of law, binding all entities possessing international legal personality. In *North Sea Continental Shelf Cases* the International Court of Justice clearly stated that: 'customary law rules and obligations … by their very nature, must have equal force for all members of the international community',[43] while in *Interpretation of the Agreement of 25 March 1951 Between the WHO and Egypt* the Court linked the application of customary law to legal personality: '[i]nternational organizations

[38] *Interpretation of the Agreement of 25 March 1951 Between the WHO and Egypt*, above n 23; *Poulsen & Diva Navigation Corp*, above n 25; *A Racke GmbH & Co v Hauptzollamt Mainz*, above n 25.

[39] 'Binding Armed Opposition Groups' above n 6, 374.

[40] See eg Anthea Roberts and Sandesh Sivakumaran, 'Lawmaking by Nonstate Actors: Engaging Armed Groups in the Creation of International Humanitarian Law' (2012) 37 *Yale Journal of International Law*.

[41] This issue is returned to below. See Ch 6 section III.

[42] See *Prosecutor v Tadic*, Decision on the Defence Motion for Interlocutory Appeal on Jurisdiction, above n 33, para 127. See generally, Jean-Marie Henckaerts and Louise Doswald-Beck, *Customary International Humanitarian Law, Vol 1: Rules* (Geneva, International Committee of the Red Cross/CUP, 2005).

[43] *North Sea Continental Shelf Cases* above n 21, para 63.

are subjects of international law and, *as such*, are bound by *any obligations* incumbent upon them under general rules of international law'.[44] Accordingly, although an armed group's international personality may have been recognised consequent to the application of a particular branch of public international law—such as the law of armed conflict—once recognised as an international legal person, the group is bound by customary international law as a whole.[45] To hold otherwise would be to dismiss the concept of international law as a unitary system, and establish unwarranted distinctions within the corpus of public international law.[46]

This conclusion applies more broadly. For instance, states are bound by the entire body of customary international law, irrespective of whether the state is actually involved in the activity in question: landlocked states are bound by the customary international Law of the Sea, while states without a space programme are nonetheless bound by the customary international Law of Space. Individuals are similarly bound by the entire corpus of customary international law regardless of whether they engage in the activity in question. For instance, all individuals are bound by the prohibition on piracy, genocide, and crimes against humanity, irrespective of their participation in any of the constituent acts. Of course, the relevance of any imposed obligations will necessarily depend upon the context and the activity of the individual or entity in question, and so while a landlocked state or armed group may in principle be bound by the customary international Law of the Sea, the effect of this obligation is necessarily limited until such a time as the state or armed group engages in naval activities.

Ultimately, it is concluded that all international legal persons are bound by the entire spectrum of customary international law, as applicable *ratione personae*. Specific issues relating to *ratione personae* restrictions are discussed further below in the context of international human rights law.[47]

D. Summary

Customary international law can bind non-state armed groups. However, in order for international law to apply to an armed group, the group must possess international legal personality. This raises a potential obstacle with respect to the validity of the customary law theory as a means of

[44] *Interpretation of the Agreement of 25 March 1951 Between the WHO and Egypt*, above n 23, para 37. Emphasis added. The phrases customary rules and general rules are often used interchangeably, see above n 15, 154.

[45] To the extent that it is not limited *ratione personae*.

[46] See for example, the lack of any such distinction in Art 38 of the Statute of the International Court of Justice.

[47] See below Ch 6 section III.

explaining the application of common Article 3: in order to acquire international legal personality an armed group must be subject to direct cognition by the international legal order. This cognition is typically demonstrated by the direct application of treaty-based international rights or obligations, such as those arising consequent to the application of common Article 3.[48] Clearly, the customary law theory cannot be used to satisfactorily explain the application of common Article 3, if the treaty-based application of common Article 3 is first required in order to establish the requisite international legal personality.

Another possible explanation for the application of common Article 3 on the basis of customary law—and in the absence of treaty law—does exist. If the criteria necessary for an armed group to qualify as a party to a non-international armed conflict are satisfied,[49] this situation may demand direct cognition by the international legal order in order to facilitate the effective operation of international law:[50] in effect, customary international law may be applied on the basis of the de facto control theory, thereby satisfying the direct cognition requirement, and confirming the international legal personality of the armed group in question. This possibility is discussed in greater detail below.[51] Of course, this does not explain the initial application of the law, as the provision in question must first become a norm of customary international law in order to be applicable. However, irrespective of whether the customary law theory can be used to explain the initial application of direct treaty-based international rights or obligations, it is evident that all non-state armed groups possessing international legal personality are bound by customary international law.

II. THE GENERAL PRINCIPLES THEORY

A variation of the customary law theory holds that armed opposition groups are bound by the general principles of international law. These

[48] All international humanitarian law treaties applicable to armed groups occur in situations wherein common Art 3 is applicable, and no other body of international law subjects armed groups to direct regulation, with the limited exception of the Kampala Convention. See below Ch 6 section I.

[49] Satisfaction of these criteria will also denote satisfaction of the capacity and independence criteria associated with the acquisition of international legal personality, see above Ch 2 section IV.

[50] This scenario is less relevant today consequent to the universal ratification of the Geneva Conventions. However, it is the legal basis underpinning the application of the law that is at issue herein.

[51] See below Ch 5 sections I and II.

'fundamental standards'—listed as a source of law in the Statute of the International Court of Justice[52]—are the 'overriding legal standards that may be regarded as the constitutional principles of the international community.'[53] Examples of general principles include the principles of consent, reciprocity, equality of states, finality of awards and settlements, the legal validity of agreements, good faith, freedom of the seas, and domestic jurisdiction.[54] Like customary international law, general principles 'do not address themselves to states solely, but are binding on other international subjects as well, (in particular, insurgents, peoples represented by liberation movements, and international organizations).'[55] However, general principles, by their very nature, are not detailed regulations. Rather, they are constitutional principles—'abstractions from a mass of rules'[56]—intended to accommodate potential gaps in the law.[57] For example, Sivakumaran notes that distinction and proportionality are considered to be the general principles of international humanitarian law, but highlights that: 'when a rule expands on and gives substance to a general principle, it is no longer a general principle but is based on one. The rules governing internal armed conflict are built on general principles but are not general principles in and of themselves.'[58] As such, while potentially relevant—and binding on armed opposition groups—the exclusive application of general principles is incapable of effectively regulating the day-to-day intricacies of non-international armed conflict.[59] Equally, and as with the customary law theory, general principles of international law are only applicable to those armed groups with established international legal personality.

III. THE THIRD PARTY CONSENT THEORY

The 'third party consent' theory is one of the two dominant theories with respect to the application of international rights and obligations to armed opposition groups.[60] It is based upon the *pacta tertiis nec nocent nec prosunt*

52 Art 38(c), Statute of the International Court of Justice.

53 Above n 15, 48. Emphasis in original omitted.

54 James Crawford, *Brownlie's Principles of Public international Law*, 8th edn (Oxford, OUP, 2012) 37.

55 Above n 15, 64.

56 Ian Brownlie, *Principles of Public international Law*, 7th edn (Oxford, OUP, 2008) 19.

57 See for example the reference to general principles utilised in the Martens clause, contained in the preamble to the Hague Regulations of 1907.

58 'Binding Armed Opposition Groups' above n 6, 376.

59 Similar to the customary international law theory, this approach also fails to explain how armed groups are bound by international law in the first instance.

60 The other theory being the 'legislative jurisdiction' theory discussed below in Ch 4 section IV.

principle,[61] and the conception that, in principle, 'most rules of international law are only authoritative for those subjects who have accepted them.'[62] Drawing on the law of treaties,[63] this theory holds that armed opposition groups—classified as 'third parties' given the impossibility of accession—may only be bound by international treaty law if two conditions are met: first, that the drafters intended to bind armed opposition groups and, second, that the armed groups consented to be bound.[64]

One of the principle benefits associated with third party consent is the acquiescence of armed opposition groups.[65] It is generally held that if groups consent to international obligations—as opposed to being bound against their will, possibly consequent to an act of the very state that they are in conflict with—then this will translate to increased compliance with international law. As such, third party consent is presented as a 'forward-looking' theory, and one which grants insurgents 'the proper role they deserve' based on the factual reality of the conflict.[66] However, as discussed below, the significance of this assumption may be overstated.[67] Additionally, it is noted that by requiring armed group consent this principle grants non-state armed groups a state-like freedom of choice with respect to potential obligations arising under international law.[68]

A. The Legal Basis for the Third Party Consent Theory

The legal basis for the third party consent theory is derived from the Roman law maxim, *pacta tertiis nec nocent nec prosunt*,[69] which expresses 'the fundamental principle that a treaty applies only between the parties to it.'[70] On the international legal plane, this principle was endorsed by the Permanent Court of International Justice in the *German Interests in Polish Upper Silesia* case: '[a] treaty only creates law as between the States parties

[61] This principle holds that 'treaties neither harm nor benefit third parties'.

[62] Juan Antonio Carriollo Salcedo, 'Reflections on the Existence of a Hierarchy of Norms in International Law' (1997) 8 *European Journal of International Law* 584.

[63] See for example, Arts 26, 34–37, Vienna Convention on the Law of Treaties.

[64] Above n 15, 130.

[65] See 'The applicability of international humanitarian law to organized armed groups' above n 6, 459–60; Marco Sassoli, 'Taking armed groups seriously: ways to improve their compliance with international humanitarian law' (2010) *International Humanitarian Legal Studies* 29–32.

[66] 'The Status of Rebels under the 1977 Geneva Protocol on Non-International Armed Conflicts' above n 6, 439.

[67] See below Ch 4 section IV.D.

[68] See Alexandru Bolintineanu, 'Expression of Consent to be Bound by a Treaty in the Light of the 1969 Vienna Convention' (1974) 68 *American Journal of International Law* 673.

[69] *Commentary on the 1969 Vienna Convention on the Law of Treaties* above n 18, 468.

[70] Above n 54, 384.

to it'.[71] It has also been codified in the Vienna Convention on the Law of Treaties,[72] many of the provisions of which are said to reflect customary international law.[73] Article 34 states simply that: '[a] treaty does not create either obligations or rights for a third state without its consent';[74] Articles 35–36 codify the two-part test referred to above, based upon the intention of the drafters and the consent of third states.[75] Interestingly, the *pacta tertiis* principle was referred to during the drafting process of the Geneva Conventions.[76] For example, the United Kingdom supported the United States in expressing the opinion that 'insurgents could not be bound by an agreement to which they were not party.'[77] Burma emphasised this point: '"[t]he Convention should only be applied if the insurgent civil authority accepted it": this was said by the honourable Delegate for the United States of America at a meeting on the 11th May. I repeat: it says that the insurgent civil authority should accept the Convention.'[78]

(i) Relationship to Sovereignty, Equality, and Independence of States

The *pacta tertiis* principle is 'traditionally viewed as a corollary of the principles of the sovereignty, equality and independence of States'.[79] The underlying basis for this correlation is illustrated by reference to the *Lotus* case:

> International law governs relations between independent States. The rules of law binding upon States therefore emanate from their own free will as expressed in conventions or by usages generally accepted as expressing principles of law … Restrictions upon the independence of States cannot therefore be presumed.[80]

Accordingly, the concept that 'no State can be legally bound without or against its will'[81] is regarded as intrinsic to the equality of states,[82] while

[71] *Case concerning certain German interests in Polish Upper Silesia (The Merits) (Germany v Poland)*, Permanent Court of International Justice, 25 May 1925, para 82.

[72] *Vienna Convention on the Law of Treaties*, 23 May 1969, UNTS vol 115, 331.

[73] See above n 15, 170, 179–80.

[74] Art 34, Vienna Convention on the Law of Treaties.

[75] 'The Status of Rebels under the 1977 Geneva Protocol on Non-International Armed Conflicts' above n 6, 423.

[76] Final Record of the Diplomatic Conference of Geneva of 1949, Vol II Section B, United States, 83.

[77] ibid, United Kingdom, 94.

[78] ibid, Burma, 328.

[79] *Commentary on the 1969 Vienna Convention on the Law of Treaties* above n 18, 468.

[80] *The Case of the SS Lotus (France v Turkey)*, Judgment, Permanent Court of International Justice, 7 September 1927, para 44.

[81] Hans Kelsen, 'The Principle of Sovereign Equality of States as a Basis for International Organization' (1944) 53 *Yale Law Journal* 2, 209.

[82] The importance of the principle of sovereign equality is reflected in Art 2(1) of the UN Charter.

the act of concluding a treaty is recognised as 'one of the oldest and most characteristic exercises of independence or sovereignty on the part of States.'[83] Treaties to which a state is not a party are therefore typically regarded as *res inter alios acta (alteri nocere non debet)*; a matter between others, which shall not affect third parties. It is from this basis that the twin requirements of intent and consent are derived.

(ii) The Intent to Bind Requirement

The operative assumption is that treaties do not create third party effects. As explained by the Permanent Court of International Justice in the *Free Zones of Upper Savoy* case: '[i]t cannot be lightly presumed that stipulations favourable to a third State have been adopted with the object of creating an actual right in its favour.'[84] However, the Court noted that it is within the sovereign competence of states to create such rights, should they so intend:

> There is however nothing to prevent the will of sovereign States from having this object and this effect ... it must be ascertained whether the States which have stipulated in favour of a third State meant to create for that State an actual right.[85]

The Court affirmatively held that the Powers intended 'to create in favour of Switzerland a right, on which that country could rely.'[86] Similarly, in 1965, the Berlin Court of Appeal upheld this right to create agreements in favour of third parties, provided that this was the drafters' intent.[87] The intent of the drafters is thus regarded as determinative with respect to whether a third party right or obligation has been created, and the identity of the potential addressee.[88]

[83] Lord McNair, *The Law of Treaties* (Oxford, Clarendon Press, 1961) 35.

[84] *Case of the Free Zones of Upper Savoy and the District of Gex (France v Switzerland)*, Permanent Court of International Justice, 7 June 1932, para 125.

[85] ibid para 125. It is noted that Lord McNair considered this passage to be *obiter dictum*, above n 83, 312.

[86] *Case of the Free Zones of Upper Savoy and the District of Gex (France v Switzerland)* above n 84, para 147.

[87] Christine Chinkin, *Third Parties in International Law* (Oxford, Clarendon Press, 1993) 28. See also, *LaGrand Case (Germany v United States of America)*, Judgment, International Court of Justice, 27 June 2001, para 77.

[88] *Third Parties in International Law* above n 87, 33; Jan Klabbers, *The Concept of Treaty in International Law* (Alphen aan den Rijn, Kluwer Law International 1996) 68; Ulf Linderfalk, *On The Interpretation of Treaties: The Modern International Law as Expressed in the 1969 Vienna Convention on the Law of Treaties* (The Netherlands, Springer, 2007) 205.

(iii) The Consent to be Bound Requirement

Following the *pacta tertiis* and *res inter alios acta* principles, consent is regarded as 'the pivotal act by which a State expresses its commitment to a treaty.'[89] This was endorsed with respect to third state rights and obligations by the Permanent Court of International Justice in the *Free Zones of Upper Savoy*: 'it is certain that, in any case, Article 435 of the Treaty of Versailles is not binding upon Switzerland, who is not a Party to that Treaty, *except to the extent to which that country accepted it*.'[90] The International Court of Justice confirmed the consent requirement in the *North Sea Continental Shelf Cases*.[91] Generally speaking, it may be said that 'nothing can be done without or against the will of a sovereign State.'[92] Indeed, it has been held that 'every rule of international law derives its legal authority solely from the consent of states.'[93] With respect to third party obligations it is required that the consent of the addressee be explicitly expressed,[94] whereas with respect to third party rights the consent of the addressee may be implicit, and expressed, for example, through acquiescence.[95]

B. Critiques Relating to the Third Party Consent Theory

Two principal critiques of the third party consent theory may be presented, relating first to the evolutionary development of customary international law and the associated erosion of the consent principle, and second to the status of armed opposition groups and other non-state actors as international legal persons distinct from states.

(i) Modern International Law Establishes Obligations Without Consent

International law has undergone an evolutionary process with respect to the concept of obligations without consent. Traditionally, it was unequivocally held that the legal basis for international law was the consent of states, and that states could not be subject to international

[89] Commentary on the 1969 Vienna Convention on the Law of Treaties above n 18, 176.

[90] *Case of the Free Zones of Upper Savoy and the District of Gex (France v Switzerland)*, above n 84, para 125. Emphasis added.

[91] *North Sea Continental Shelf Cases* above n 21 at, para 28.

[92] Above n 15, 170. See also, Malcolm Shaw, *International Law*, 5th edn (Cambridge, CUP, 2003) 817.

[93] 'The Consent of States and the Sources of the Law of Nations' above n 17, 23.

[94] Art 35, Vienna Convention on the Law of Treaties.

[95] ibid, Art 36(1).

obligations against their will.[96] As stated by Roxburgh in 1917, 'strictly speaking, neither conventional nor customary rule can bind any State, however, insignificant, which has not consented to it.'[97] However, the course of the twentieth century saw significant changes to the international order, as evidenced in particular by the advent of the League of Nations and the United Nations. By 1956 a progressive trend had been noted:

> During the last century the international community has been trying to expand its contractual methods in order to find a way through which it could reach subjects which do not participate in the agreements, and give sanction to rules of law susceptible to general application.[98]

The emergence of international values, considerations of humanity, and obligations *erga omnes*, meant that the concept of obligations without consent became essential to the modern international legal order:[99]

> If sovereignty and autonomy prevailed in all areas of international law, however, one could hardly hope to develop rules to bind all states. In a community of nearly two hundred diverse states, it is virtually impossible to obtain the acceptance of all to any norm, particularly one that requires significant expense or changes in behavior.[100]

Thus, as will be shown below, while the consent of states remains the general rule, international law has evolved and there exist clear exceptions.[101] Ultimately, it must be concluded that 'the actual conduct of States has made a major inroad into the *pacta tertiis* rule.'[102]

(a) International Treaty Law Establishes Obligations Without Consent

There exist certain categories of treaty, such as those relating to neutrality or the conditional establishment of new states, which are recognised as imposing obligations on third states.[103] Similarly, the non-intervention

[96] Above n 83, 309; 'The Consent of States and the Sources of the Law of Nations' above n 17, 23.

[97] Ronald Roxburgh, *International Conventions and Third States* (London, Longmans, Green and Co, 1917) 103. See also, 'Customary International Law and Acquiescence' above n 17, 120; PJ Baker, 'The Doctrine of Legal Equality of States' (1923) 4 *British Yearbook of International Law* 11.

[98] Eduardo Jimenez de Arechage, 'Treaty Stipulations in Favour of Third States' (1956) 50 *American Journal of International Law* 357.

[99] See eg Philippe Sands and Pierre Klein, *Bowett's Law of International Institutions*, 6th edn (London, Sweet & Maxwell, 2009) 3.

[100] Jonathan I Charney, 'Universal International Law' (1993) 87 *American Journal of International Law* 530.

[101] *International Law* above n 92, 834.

[102] *Third Parties in International Law* above n 87, 141.

[103] Above n 81, 210. See also, above n 83, 269.

pact signed during the Spanish civil war, and treaties establishing international organisations—including the UN—are also of interest. A number of states have been established by means of a treaty.[104] These treaties established states—necessarily third parties to the constitutive treaties—while at the same time imposing obligations upon them.[105] For instance, the Free City of Cracow was established by the Congress of Vienna in 1815. It was placed under the protection of an international commission composed of representatives of Austria, Prussia and Russia, and subject to a number of obligations including neutrality,[106] and a prohibition on the granting of asylum.[107] The Free City's constitution was also created on its behalf—thereby establishing third party rights and obligations—and annexed to the constitutive Treaty.[108]

Similarly, the Free City of Danzig was established in Section XI of the Treaty of Versailles, its 'legal birth certificate.'[109] According to the terms of the Treaty, Danzig was subject to a number of obligations restricting its sovereignty.[110] For example, the City was placed under the protection of the League of Nations;[111] a High Commissioner was appointed to supervise issues relating to the Treaty of Versailles 'or any arrangements or agreements made thereunder';[112] the City's constitution was subject to the High Commissioner's approval, and Danzig could not serve as a military base, erect fortifications, or manufacture munitions without the League's approval.[113] Poland was also granted a number of rights with respect to the City's international relations,[114] and internal autonomy,[115] such as, for example, 'the free use and service of all waterways, docks, basins, wharves and other works'.[116] Thus, while the case law of the Permanent Court of International Justice confirmed the international legal personality

104 Cracow, Danzig and Trieste are discussed below, while it is noted that Belgium was also established consequent to the London Conference of 1839, with its sovereignty and neutrality guaranteed by the Great Powers of Europe. See further, above n 83, 268. These examples are not intended to be exhaustive, for example the Lateran Treaty of 1929 established the Vatican State, see above n 15, 131–32.

105 Above n 81, 210.

106 Art VI, Final Act of the Congress of Vienna/General Treaty, 1815.

107 ibid, Art IX.

108 ibid, Art X.

109 Ian FD Morrow, 'The International Status of the Free City of Danzig' (1937) 18 *British Yearbook of International Law* 116.

110 See Malcolm M Lewis, 'The Free City of Danzig' (1924) 5 *British Yearbook of International Law*; Ian Brownlie, *Principles of International Law*, 7th edn (Oxford, OUP, 2008) 59.

111 Art 102, Treaty of Versailles.

112 ibid, Art 103.

113 'The Free City of Danzig' above n 110, 91, 94.

114 Art 104(6), Treaty of Versailles.

115 See generally, ibid, Art 104.

116 ibid, Art 104(2).

of Danzig, the state's status was similar to that of a protectorate, subject to external supervision.[117]

In the post-World War II era, the Italian Peace Treaty of 1947 provided for the establishment of a Free Territory at Trieste under the protection of the UN Security Council.[118] Similar to Danzig, a number of obligations were imposed by virtue of a Protocol to the Treaty.[119] For example, Trieste's constitution was subject to Security Council approval,[120] a Governor was appointed by the Security Council (with significant power in relation to inter alia, governance, legislation, and security),[121] and the Territory was declared demilitarised and neutral.[122] It is noted that, inter alia, as a result of these restrictions, entities such as Cracow, Danzig, and Trieste have sometimes not been regarded as full sovereign states. However, Brownlie concludes that, 'legally the distinction is not very significant.'[123]

The example of Swiss neutrality may also be discussed in relation to the capacity of treaties to impose obligations on third states. In 1815, as part of the Vienna settlement, Switzerland was neutralised,[124] and this neutrality was 'recognised and guaranteed by the Powers' party to the Congress of Vienna.[125] McNair, referencing Westlake, has suggested that the fact that the parties required third states to respect Swiss neutrality—described as 'a system of permanent neutrality created for the benefit of all Europe'[126]—is evidence of 'a tendency for [neutralisation treaties] to produce exceptions to the rule that a treaty cannot confer benefits or impose burdens upon third parties.'[127]

In contemporary international law the UN Charter has been regarded as creating obligations without consent vis-à-vis third states in two respects: (a) by virtue of the establishment of the UN itself, and (b) as a result of the Security Council's apparent ability to bind non-member states. In the *Reparations* Advisory Opinion the International Court of Justice was asked to consider whether the UN has the capacity to bring an international

[117] Above n 56, 59.

[118] Art 21, Treaty of Peace with Italy, 10 February 1947.

[119] See Annex VI: Permanent Statute of the Free Territory of Trieste, Treaty of Peace with Italy, 10 February 1947.

[120] ibid, Art 10.

[121] ibid, Art 11.

[122] ibid, Art 3.

[123] *Principles of International Law* above n 110, 59. See also, Christian Hattenhauer, 'Danzig, Free City of' in *Max Planck Encyclopaedia of International Law*.

[124] Art XCII, Final Act of the Congress of Vienna/General Treaty, 1815. See also, Art IV, Protocol of the Conference of Paris of 3 November, 1815.

[125] Art XCII, Final Act of the Congress of Vienna/General Treaty, 1815.

[126] Arnold D McNair, 'The Functions and Differing Legal Character of Treaties' (1930) 11 *British Yearbook of International Law* 113.

[127] ibid, 113.

claim against a non-member state.[128] As Israel was not a party to the UN Charter, the traditional view would hold that the Charter should be regarded as *res inter alios acta*, incapable of generating effects vis-à-vis Israel. However, the Court held that the UN was created with objective international legal personality:

> [F]ifty States, representing the vast majority of the members of the international community, had the power, in conformity with international law, to bring into being an entity possessing objective international personality, and not merely personality recognized by them alone, together with capacity to bring international claims.[129]

Israel was thus required to acknowledge the UN's personality, and the UN's standing to bring an international claim against a non-member was confirmed. The *Reparations* decision would not have been possible if the traditional law relating to treaties was applied: the 'Court's reasoning was based on personality, capacity, and functionalism, not the treaty law principle of *res inter alios acta*.'[130]

Equally, some consider Article 2(6) of the UN Charter as binding upon third states.[131] According to Widdows, 'it seems clear from the San Francisco discussions and from the plain meaning of Article 2(6) that all the Article 2 principles are to apply to non-members as far as may be necessary for the maintenance of international peace and security.'[132] Indeed, this provision is presumably the mechanism through which the UN purports to bind non-members,[133] although whether the UN actually has this authority is not settled.[134] The text of Article 2(6) would appear to indicate that the obligation is placed on the organisation rather than non-members.[135] However, the Security Council has consistently acted on the basis that it can bind non-members (in issues relating to international peace and security) imposing numerous Chapter VII Resolutions in this regard.[136] For example, operative paragraph 1 of Security Council Resolution 1989 (2011), enacted under Chapter VII of the UN Charter:

[128] *Reparations for injuries suffered in the services of the United Nations*, above n 20, 184.

[129] ibid, 185.

[130] *Third Parties in International Law* above n 87, 89.

[131] ibid, 33.

[132] Kelvin Widdows, 'Security Council Resolutions and Non-Members of the United Nations' (1978) 27 *International & Comparative Law Quarterly* 460.

[133] Myres McDougal and W Reisman, 'Rhodesia and the United Nations: The Lawfulness of International Concern' (1968) 62 *American Journal of International Law* 11.

[134] See generally, Christian Henderson and Noam Lubell, 'The Contemporary Legal Nature of UN Security Council Ceasefire Resolutions' (2013) 26 *Leiden Journal of International Law*.

[135] 'The Organisation shall ensure…'. See above n 132, 460.

[136] See Security Council Resolution 418 (1977); Security Council Resolution 661 (1990); Security Council Resolution 1540 (2004); Resolution 1127 (1997); Resolution 1173 (1998).

'*Decides* that all States shall take the measures as previously imposed by paragraph 8 (c) of resolution 1333 (2000), and paragraphs 1 and 2 of resolution 1390 (2002), with respect to Al-Qaida …'.[137] It is significant that, when referring to the binding force of Security Council Resolutions declaring an end to the mandate and the illegality of South Africa's continued presence, the International Court of Justice in the *Namibia* Advisory Opinion stated that:

> The Mandate having been terminated by decision of the international organization in which the supervisory authority over its administration was vested, and South Africa's continued presence in Namibia having been declared illegal, it is for non-member States to act in accordance with those decisions.[138]

(b) Customary International Law and *Jus Cogens* Establish Obligations Without Consent

Finally, it is noted that the formulation of customary international law was traditionally regarded as dependent upon state consent; as stated by Roxburgh 'neither conventional nor customary rule can bind any State, however, insignificant, which has not consented to it.'[139] The judgment of the Permanent Court of International Justice in the *Lotus* case may be cited in support of this proposition: 'rules of law binding upon States therefore *emanate from their own free will* as expressed in conventions or by usages generally accepted as expressing principles of law'.[140] However, in the modern era, international law has evolved such that the consent requirement associated with customary law relates to the consent of the international community, and not that of each individual state.[141] Today, customary law must be regarded as derived from general agreement, and not unanimity of will.[142] The evolution of this trend towards obligations without consent was authoritatively confirmed by the International Court of Justice in the *North Sea Continental Shelf Cases*. Here, the Court explicitly held that the rules of customary international law are binding

[137] Security Council Resolution 1989 (2011). See further, operative para 7, Security Council Resolution 1572 (2004); operative paras 7 and 8, Security Council Resolution 1556 (2004); and operative paras 5, 8, 10, 11, Security Council Resolution 1333 (2000).

[138] *Legal Consequences for States of the Continued Presence of South Africa in Namibia (South West Africa) Notwithstanding Security Council Resolution 276 (1970)*, Advisory Opinion, International Court of Justice, 21 June 1971, para 126. The relevant paragraph of this Opinion is, however, somewhat unclear.

[139] *International Conventions and Third States* above n 97, 103; See also 'Customary International Law and Acquiescence' above n 17, 120.

[140] *The Case of the SS Lotus (France v Turkey)*, above n 80, para 44. It is noted that 'usage' in this sense may be regarded as equivalent to custom. Emphasis added.

[141] Josef L Kunz, 'The Nature of Customary International Law' (1953) 47 *American Journal of International Law* 4, 666.

[142] *Commentary on the 1969 Vienna Convention on the Law of Treaties* above n 18, 10.

'independent of any specific assent, direct or indirect',[143] and are capable of 'becoming binding even for countries which have never, and do not, become parties'[144] to the treaty from which the customary rules are derived. The Court further stated that customary international law obligations, 'by their very nature, must have equal force for all members of the international community, and cannot therefore be the subject of any right of unilateral exclusion exercisable at will by any one of them in its own favour.'[145]

It is thus accepted that, today, customary international law may bind states without their consent, and that a treaty rule may bind a non-state party if it becomes part of international custom.[146] The only possible exception is the persistent objector rule.[147] This rule holds that: 'a state that has persistently objected to a rule of customary international law during the course of the rule's emergence is not bound by the rule.'[148] However, the application of this rule is severely restricted, and its continued relevance has been questioned.[149] With respect to consent, it is noted that the possibility of persistent objector status only arises while the relevant rule is in the process of crystallising as customary law. States which come into existence after the emergence of the rule cannot give effect to their lack of consent:[150] they are bound as a consequence of their statehood.[151] Equally, any lack of consent is irrelevant with respect to existing states who only later become involved in the activity regulated by the crystallised rule.[152] Similarly, the emergence and acceptance of the concept of *jus cogens*[153] has confirmed that states may be subject to obligations without their consent, and against their will. Norms of *jus cogens* are regarded as 'intransgressible principles of international law'[154] binding on

143 *North Sea Continental Shelf Cases* above n 21, para 37.

144 ibid, para 71.

145 ibid, para 63.

146 Art 38, Vienna Convention on the Law of Treaties (23 May 1969, entered into force 27 January 1980) 1155 UNTS 331.

147 See above n 54, 28.

148 Ted L Stein, 'The Approach of the Different Drummer: The Principle of Persistent Objector in International Law' (1985) 26 *Harvard International Law Journal* 457.

149 See eg Jonathan I Charney, 'The Persistent Objector Rule and the Development of Customary International Law' (1986) 57 *British Yearbook of International Law* 16. See further, above n 15, 163.

150 Above n 15, 163.

151 Above n 148, 458.

152 International Law Association, Committee on Formation of Customary (General) International Law, London Conference (2000) 27.

153 *Yusuf Abdullah Kadi v Council of the European Union & Commission of the European Communities*, above n 24, para 226. See also, Art 53, Vienna Convention on the Law of Treaties.

154 *Legality of the Threat or Use of Nuclear Weapons*, Advisory Opinion, International Court of Justice, 8 July 1996, para 79.

all members of the international community, and from which no legitimate derogation is possible.[155]

(c) Summary

Both state practice and the authoritative decisions of the International Court of Justice confirm that, today, states may be subject to obligations under international law without their consent. The untenability of an absolutist application of the *pacta tertiis* rule is evident with respect to customary international law, which no longer requires uniform consent.[156] In certain circumstances this also applies in relation to treaties and the establishment of third state obligations, as evidenced by state practice regarding the conditional establishment of new states by treaty, and the application of the UN Charter to non-members. Kelsen notes that membership of the UN—a defining marker of membership of the international community of states in the modern era—itself evidences the erosion of the *pacta tertiis* principle:

> The fact that the contracting State remains legally bound by the treaty without regard to a unilateral change of will clearly proves that a State can be bound even against its will and that the autonomy of the State under international law is not, and cannot be, unlimited.[157]

(ii) Non-State Actors as Subjects of International Law with a Competence Distinct to that of States

While it has been shown that the *pacta tertiis* rule is subject to notable exceptions with respect to inter-state relations, the actual applicability of this rule to state–non-state actor relationships may also be questioned, particularly given the rule's grounding in the principles of state sovereignty and equality. The fact that non-state armed groups possess an international legal personality distinguished from that of states means that the *pacta tertiis* principle may not translate to state-armed group relationships.[158]

State practice demonstrates exceptions to the *pacta tertiis* rule vis-à-vis non-state actors. For instance, states have consistently used international treaties to create entities with international legal personality and to subject them to obligations.[159] International Organisations are a case on point. The International Court of Justice has authoritatively confirmed

[155] Case T-306/01 *Ahmed Ali Yusuf & Al Barakaat International Foundation v Council of the European Union & Commission of the European Communities* (CFI, 21 September 2005), para 282.

[156] Above n 141, 666.

[157] Above n 81, 211.

[158] See eg above n 15, 72.

[159] See above Ch 4 section III.B.1.a.

that International Organisations may possess objective international legal personality, and such organisations are unquestionably third parties with respect to their constitutive treaty:[160] they did not exist at the time the treaty was drafted. States subject International Organisations to a number of obligations absent consent, inter alia by means of their founding treaties. In the *Reparations* Advisory Opinion the International Court of Justice held that: 'the rights and duties of an entity such as the [UN] must depend upon its purposes and functions as specified or implied in its constituent documents and developed in practice.'[161] Equally, the Permanent Court of International Justice has held that: '[a]s the European Commission is not a State, but an international institution with a special purpose, it only has the functions bestowed upon it by the Definitive Statute with a view to the fulfilment of that purpose'.[162]

The Law of State Responsibility may be cited as a further example of the imposition of international obligations on armed opposition groups, absent their consent. The relevant paragraphs of Article 10 of the Draft Articles on Responsibility of States for Internationally Wrongful Acts hold that:

> 1. The conduct of an insurrectional movement which becomes the new Government of a State shall be considered an act of that State under international law.
> 2. The conduct of a movement, insurrectional or other, which succeeds in establishing a new State in part of the territory of a pre-existing State or in a territory under its administration shall be considered an act of the new State under international law.[163]

The International Law Commission's Commentary to the Draft Articles note that, '[a]rbitral decisions, together with State practice and the literature, indicate a general acceptance of the two positive attribution rules in article 10.'[164] The *Bolivar Railway Company* claim explained the motivation underlying these rules as follows: '[t]he nation is responsible for the obligations of a successful revolution from its beginning, because in theory, it represented ab initio a changing national will, crystallizing in

[160] *Third Parties in International Law* above n 87, 12.

[161] *Reparations for injuries suffered in the services of the United Nations*, above n 20, 180. See also, *Legality of the Threat or Use of Nuclear Weapons*, above n 154, para 19.

[162] *Jurisdiction of the European Commission of the Danube Between Galatz and Braila*, Advisory Opinion, Permanent Court of International Justice, 8 December 1927, para 64.

[163] Draft Articles on State Responsibility for Internationally Wrongful Acts, UNGA Res A/56/49(Vol 1)/Corr 4.

[164] International Law Commission, 'Draft Articles on Responsibility of States for Internationally Wrongful Acts, with commentaries' (2001) *Yearbook of the International Commission* Vol II, Art 10, para 12. See further, *Sambiaggio Case (of a general nature)* (1903) Reports of International Arbitral Awards, Vol X, 513; *GL Solis (USA) v United Mexican States*, 3 October 1928, in Reports of International Arbitral Awards, Vol IV, 361.

the finally successful result.'[165] In this regard, 'acts committed during the struggle for power by the apparatus of the insurrectional movement should be attributable to the State, alongside acts of the then established Government'.[166] Under such circumstances international obligations are imposed on an armed opposition group absent the possibility of consent on the group's part.

Examples of restricted international legal persons have been presented above,[167] and these may be augmented by reference to protected or federal states, whose rights—for example, to enter into international treaties—are restricted, or in some instances, denied.[168] Armed groups necessarily fall into this restricted category: it is evident that armed groups are not states and, to paraphrase the *Reparations* opinion, their legal personality and rights and duties are not the same as those of states.[169]

(iii) The Inapplicability of the Pacta Tertiis *Rule to Non-State Actors*

The third party consent theory holds that the application of international humanitarian law to armed opposition groups should correctly be considered in light of the *pacta tertiis* rule, as codified in Articles 34–36 of the Vienna Convention on the Law of Treaties.[170] Article 1 of this Convention explicitly restricts its application to states, and so these rules may not be applied to armed groups *qua* treaty.[171] However, while acknowledging that the Convention regulates inter-state relationships, Cassese believes that the 'customary rules on the matter have a broader scope, in that they govern the effects of treaties on *any international subject* taking the position of a third party *vis-a-vis* a treaty.'[172] While it is uncertain that these rules do form part of customary international law[173]—inter alia as demonstrated by the state practice referred to above—should they do so, their application to non-state entities may be questioned.[174] While customary law

[165] *Bolivar Railway Case (on merits)* (1903) Reports of International Arbitral Awards, Vol IX, 453.

[166] International Law Commission, 'Draft Articles on Responsibility of States for Internationally Wrongful Acts, with commentaries' (2001) *Yearbook of the International Commission* Vol II, Art 10, para 5.

[167] ie Danzig, Cracow, Trieste, the United Nations, the World Health Organization, the European Commission of the Danube.

[168] Examples include Canada, the United States, Switzerland, and the Commonwealth of Australia. See above n 83, 37, 43.

[169] *Reparations for injuries suffered in the services of the United Nations*, above n 20, 179.

[170] 'The Status of Rebels under the 1977 Geneva Protocol on Non-International Armed Conflicts' above n 6, 423. See also, *The Law of Internal Armed Conflict* above n 22, 53.

[171] 'Binding Armed Opposition Groups' above n 6, 377.

[172] 'The Status of Rebels under the 1977 Geneva Protocol on Non-International Armed Conflicts' above n 6, 423. Emphasis in original.

[173] 'Binding Armed Opposition Groups' above n 6, 377.

[174] See eg 'The applicability of international humanitarian law to organized armed groups' above n 6, 458.

applies to all subjects of international law, it does not necessarily do so in a uniform manner. In particular, and in light of the *pacta tertiis* rule's basis in state sovereignty and equality, it must be asked whether this custom between states exists equally as between states and non-state actors; '[t]he customary rule may be limited *ratione personae*.'[175]

The very raison d'etre for the international law provisions codifying the *pacta tertiis* principle is to ensure that states may not be bound against their will:[176] such considerations simply do not arise with respect to non-state actors. As stated in the *Bank for International Settlements* arbitration, while the Bank may be an international legal person:

> [T]he Bank is wrong in assuming that this statement means that it has 'sovereign powers' or that acts, such as the recall of shares, fall in the category of *acta jure imperii*. While states have sovereign powers, an international actor does not, *qua* international actor and by virtue of that status, have sovereignty.[177]

Thus, while an armed group may legitimately possess international legal personality, this 'is not the same thing as saying that it is a State, which it certainly is not, or that its legal personality and rights and duties are the same as those of a State.'[178] It is this distinguished international legal personality of armed groups which calls into question the applicability of the *pacta tertiis* rule: while the 'fundamental principle' of the sovereign equality of states generally prevents states from being bound against their will,[179] this simply does not apply to armed groups. Indeed, Cassese has acknowledged this point, explicitly stating that the principle of the sovereign equality of states is inapplicable with respect to 'in particular, insurgents, peoples represented by liberation movements, and international organizations'.[180] This claim is supported by reference to state practice: states have consistently imposed obligations on non-state international persons, absent the consent of such entities; a reality made possible by states' position as 'full' subjects of international law.[181]

It should be noted that while the *pacta tertiis* principle does not require armed groups' consent to be bound, it does not preclude groups being bound in this way. Unilateral declarations may result in legal obligations,[182]

[175] 'Binding Armed Opposition Groups' above n 6, 377.

[176] See above Ch 4 section III.A.1.

[177] *Reineccius et al v Bank for International Settlements*, Permanent Court of Arbitration, 22 November 2002, para 123.

[178] *Reparations for injuries suffered in the services of the United Nations*, above n 20, 179. This judgment referred to International Organisations; however, it is presented that the reasoning is equally applicable to the current context.

[179] Albeit with the exceptions detailed above. See Ch 4 section III.B.1.

[180] Above n 15, 64.

[181] See above Ch 4 section III.B.3.

[182] *Nuclear Test Case (New Zealand v France)*, Judgment, International Court of Justice, 20 December 1974, 47–51.

and there are clear practical benefits associated with such declarations, including a potentially greater 'engagement' by the group with international law.

(iv) Practical Issues Relating to Armed Group Consent

A final practical issue opposing adherence to the third party consent theory must be highlighted. If the consent of armed groups is required in order for the rules of international humanitarian law to become applicable, this would result in the possibility that such groups could refuse consent, removing their acts from any regulatory, or indeed punitive, framework.[183] Furthermore, and as a result of the transient nature of armed groups, any expression of consent would necessarily occur in an ad hoc manner, varying 'from conflict to conflict, armed opposition group to armed opposition group and treaty to treaty.'[184] It would be impossible to know in advance whether armed groups would be subject to legal regulation, and the attribution of legal obligations may only take place in the middle, or at the end, of the conflict (if at all). Switzerland warned against precisely this situation during the common Article 3 drafting process:

> [T]his Article [has] significance only if the *de jure* government was bound in advance by the Convention. If the two Parties to the conflict had to declare themselves bound, the Article would become useless, and would be nothing more than a recommendation.[185]

Ultimately, by granting a free will with respect to any international obligations, the third party consent theory treats armed groups as state-like entities, possessing elements of sovereignty, equality, and independence. This seems impossible to reconcile with states' concerns during the common Article 3 drafting process.[186]

IV. THE PRESCRIPTIVE JURISDICTION/LEGISLATIVE JURISDICTION THEORY

The doctrine of legislative jurisdiction[187] is the second of the two dominant theories explaining the application of international law obligations

[183] See 'Binding Armed Opposition Groups' above n 6, 378.

[184] ibid, 379.

[185] 'Final Record of the Diplomatic Conference of Geneva of 1949', Vol II Section B, Switzerland, 47.

[186] See eg GIAD Draper, *The Red Cross Conventions* (London, Stevens & Sons, 1958) 17.

[187] It is noted that—as explained in this section—on the international plane legislative jurisdiction is equivalent to prescriptive jurisdiction. As such, the term prescriptive jurisdiction will be principally utilised herein. However, it must be highlighted that legislative jurisdiction remains the term most often employed in the literature.

to armed opposition groups, and is supported by perhaps the majority of writers.[188] First proposed by the Greek delegate in Geneva,[189] the American law principle of legislative jurisdiction holds that the federal state has jurisdiction to legislate with respect to a specific area within a federated state and any entities therein;[190] ie it has the authority to 'apply its law to create or affect legal interests.'[191] While this principle may be based in American law, it has a direct equivalent on the international legal plane, namely the principle of prescriptive jurisdiction.[192] This principle is primarily applied on the basis of territory and holds, for example, that a state may 'pass binding legislation applicable to persons and entities in the territory of the State.'[193] Prescriptive territorial jurisdiction is regarded as the 'quintessence of sovereignty',[194] and one of the strongest jurisdictional bases in international law; Brownlie, for example, has referred to it as 'the best foundation for the law'.[195] In explaining the attribution of international humanitarian law obligations to armed groups the *Commentary on the Additional Protocols* also adopts this principle: 'the commitment made by a State not only applies to the government but also to any established authorities and private individuals within the national territory of that State and certain obligations are therefore imposed upon them.'[196] It is noted that a state's prescriptive jurisdiction is also accepted as including the right to legislate vis-à-vis its nationals (prescriptive nationality jurisdiction), an authority derived from the fact of state sovereignty.[197]

Surprisingly, given the controversy surrounding Article 3 in general, relatively little attention was paid to the legal difficulty involved in binding a non-state entity during the drafting process,[198] and it must be concluded that 'there was no agreement at the Diplomatic Conference as to

[188] 'The applicability of international humanitarian law to organized armed groups' above n 6, 445; *International Law and the Use of Force by National Liberation Movements* above n 12, 51; *The Law of Internal Armed Conflict* above n 22, 53–54; Yves Sandov, Christophe Swinarski and Brun Zimmermann (eds), *Commentary on the Additional Protocols of 8 June 1977 to the Geneva Conventions of 12 August 1949* (The Hague, Martinus Nijhoff, 1987) 1345; 'Binding Armed Opposition Groups' above n 6, 381.

[189] 'Final Record of the Diplomatic Conference of Geneva of 1949', Vol II Section B, Greece, 94.

[190] See further, *Report of the Interdepartmental Committee for the Study of Jurisdiction over Federal Areas within the States, Part II: A text of the law of legislative jurisdiction*, June 1957. Available at http://constitution.org/juris/fjur/2fj1-2.htm.

[191] Willis LM Reese, 'Legislative Jurisdiction' (1978) 78 *Columbia Law Review* 1587.

[192] Ronald Roxburgh (ed), *Oppenheim's International Law, vol 1*, 3rd edn (London, Longmans, 1920) 238, para 144; above n 15, 49.

[193] Above n 15, 49.

[194] ibid, 49.

[195] Above n 56, 299.

[196] *Commentary on the Additional Protocols of 8 June 1977 to the Geneva Conventions of 12 August 1949* above n 188, 1345.

[197] Above n 54, 459.

[198] Above n 186, 17.

exactly how armed opposition groups were bound.'[199] Nonetheless, limited support for the prescriptive jurisdiction theory may be derived from the statements of certain states, notably Greece, and the US. In discussing draft common Article 3, Greece referred to the principle of prescriptive nationality jurisdiction:

> Insurgents and even bandits were obviously nationals of some State, and were thereby bound by the obligations undertaken by the latter; since practically all civilized States would sign the Conventions which were being drawn up, it therefore followed that, subject to exceptions, any insurgent or bandit would be a national of a Signatory State, and would *ipso facto* be bound by the Convention.[200]

Similarly, albeit slightly ambiguously, the US 'observed that the legal government would be the only signatory of the Conventions, and the dissidents would be parties bound by its obligations'.[201] Despite the lack of clarity, however, it must be presumed that the legal basis underpinning the application of international humanitarian law to non-state armed groups is prescriptive jurisdiction.[202] Indeed, the final text of common Article 3 itself may be read as implying application on the basis of prescriptive territorial jurisdiction; the text holds that, '[i]n the case of armed conflict not of an international character occurring *in the territory* of one of the High Contracting Parties'. Reference is not made, for example, to 'cases of armed conflict not of an international character involving the *nationals* of a High Contracting Party', or to 'cases of armed conflict not of an international character to which all parties have *consented* to be bound'.

Based on the statement made by Greece in Geneva,[203] it has been proposed that the legislative jurisdiction theory applies only to nationals of a state.[204] If interpreted as such, this theory would not provide a satisfactory explanation for the attribution of international law obligations to armed groups, as it would fail 'to explain why IHL [International Humanitarian Law] treaty rules are binding in a situation in which an organized armed group is (also) composed of foreign nationals from a state that has not ratified the respective treaty.'[205] However, a state's prescriptive

[199] 'Binding Armed Opposition Groups' above n 6, 383.

[200] 'Final Record of the Diplomatic Conference of Geneva of 1949', Vol II Section B, Greece, 94.

[201] ibid, United States, 79.

[202] The other theories presented herein fail to adequately explain the statement. For example, consent is not mentioned, discussion of customary law is premature, and so on.

[203] See 'Final Record of the Diplomatic Conference of Geneva of 1949', Vol II Section B, Greece, 94.

[204] In relation to the claim that legislative jurisdiction relates exclusively to a state's authority over its nationals see *The Law of Internal Armed Conflict* above n 22, 53.

[205] 'The applicability of international humanitarian law to organized armed groups' above n 6, 448. Kleffner also notes further difficulties with respect to the concept of nationality. See ibid, 448–49.

jurisdiction includes both prescriptive national jurisdiction and prescriptive territorial jurisdiction.[206] In the above example, any foreign fighters would be bound, first and foremost, on the basis of prescriptive territorial jurisdiction.[207] Any such criticisms are thus effectively addressed by reference to the fact that the principle of prescriptive jurisdiction applies on the basis of both territoriality and nationality, and by the plain meaning of the text of common Article 3 itself.

A. Acts of State Bind a State *Qua* State

It is important to note that, when referring to a state as a subject of international law, what is meant is the state itself, not the government or any other state agent.[208] Any international obligation entered into by a state binds the state *qua* state. In this sense, international law does not look within the state, rather, from an external perspective, the state is regarded as an enduring entity and internal changes are shielded from international eyes. For example, new governments remain bound by previous acts of the state, irrespective of whether they came to power consequent to a peaceful democratic transfer of authority or a violent revolutionary process.[209] Indeed, this holds true despite the fact that a new government may entirely reject the basis of the state, as happened, for example, with the Russian revolution in 1917, or the Cuban revolution in 1959. Ultimately, other states have a right to the continued observance of any agreement.[210] The fact that the state's authority is challenged thus has no effect on the binding force of an international treaty, and, 'in this regard, the laws of war function like any other treaty.'[211] Consequently, 'since treaties are made on behalf of the State, and bind the State as a whole, all treaties already in existence when an insurrection breaks out are necessarily binding on the insurgent community'.[212] Interestingly, the application of prescriptive

[206] This is analogous to legislative jurisdiction which refers to the authority to legislate with respect to an area (ie territory) and the entities therein (ie nationals).

[207] Prescriptive national jurisdiction may be relevant should an armed group based in state A conduct operations in state B. However, in this situation, state B's territorial jurisdiction remains primarily relevant.

[208] Above n 83, 668.

[209] See eg 'Fourth Report on State Responsibility, by Mr Robert Ago, Special Rapporteur—The internationally wrongful act of the State, source of international responsibility (continued)' (1972) *Yearbook of International Law Commission* Vol II, UN Doc A/Cn.4/264, 131. See also, 'Arbitration between Great Britain and Costa Rica, Opinion and Award of William H Taft, Sole Arbitrator' (1924) 18 *American Journal of International Law*, 152.

[210] Above n 83, 676.

[211] 'Binding Armed Opposition Groups' above n 6, 382.

[212] Above n 83, 676. Of course, this presumes that the relevant international treaty is capable of binding the 'insurgent community' in question.

jurisdiction in this sense treats insurgents as somewhat equivalent to the 'legitimate' government: both are bound by previous acts of state to which they did not consent.[213]

B. Prescriptive Jurisdiction and the Intent to Bind Requirement

As with the third party consent theory, the actual application of international rights and duties is dependent upon the intent of the drafters. The importance of intent has been previously addressed and will not be repeated herein,[214] suffice to note that 'there is virtual unanimity among international lawyers that, at the very least, intent is one of the main determinants of international rights and obligations.'[215] With respect to common Article 3, the intention to bind armed groups is unambiguously expressed within the text itself: '[i]n the case of armed conflict not of an international character occurring in the territory of one of the High Contracting Parties, *each Party to the conflict shall be bound* to apply, as a minimum, the following provisions'.[216] As noted by Moir, this provision 'was obviously intended to create duties and rights for both States *and* insurgents.'[217] This conclusion is further supported by reference to the discussion at Geneva,[218] including, for example, concerns regarding the 'difficulty' in applying the Conventions—or parts thereof—to armed groups.[219]

While the phrase 'each Party to the conflict' does not appear in the text of Additional Protocol II, Article 1 states that the Protocol 'develops and supplements Article 3 common to the Geneva Conventions of 12 August 1949 without modifying its existing conditions of application'.[220] On the basis of this provision:

> [T]he conclusion is inescapable that Protocol II was destined by its authors to operate for rebels. It would indeed be absurd to contend that Article 3 gives rights and imposes obligations on rebels, while Protocol II—which is but an elaboration of that article—refuses to make itself available to them.[221]

[213] See eg Jonathan Somer, 'Jungle justice: passing sentence on the equality of belligerents in non-international armed conflict' (2007) 89 *International Review of the Red Cross* 661.

[214] For a more detailed discussion of the intent requirement, see above Ch 4 section III.A(ii).

[215] *The Concept of Treaty in International Law* above n 88, 68.

[216] Emphasis added.

[217] *The Law of Internal Armed Conflict* above n 22, 53.

[218] See eg 'Final Record of the Diplomatic Conference of Geneva of 1949', Vol II Section B, UK, 10; 'Final Record of the Diplomatic Conference of Geneva of 1949', Vol II Section B, Norway, 11; 'Final Record of the Diplomatic Conference of Geneva of 1949', Vol II Section B, Spain, 11.

[219] See above n 186, 14.

[220] Art 1, Additional Protocol II.

[221] 'The Status of Rebels under the 1977 Geneva Protocol on Non-International Armed Conflicts' above n 6, 424.

This conclusion is confirmed by reference to the drafting history. For example, Argentina stated that 'the entire philosophy of the provisions of common Article 3, whether explicitly reaffirmed or not, is included in the Protocol. It is implicit that the same applies to the basic sovereign principle that the obligations of the Protocol are equally binding on both Parties to the conflict'.[222] Similarly, Belgium stated that 'the obligations of the Protocol are equally binding on both Parties to the conflict',[223] while in 1975, during the very early stages of the drafting process, the USSR stated that, if draft Article 22 was accepted, 'it would impose an obligation not only on Governments but on those who, for various reasons, were engaged in movements against Governments.'[224] It is evident, both from the plain text of the provisions and the *traveaux preparatoires*,[225] that common Article 3 and Additional Protocol II were intended to apply equally to all parties to a non-international armed conflict; indeed, this equal application was seen as a 'sovereign principle'.[226]

C. Addressing the International v Domestic Law Obligations Critique

The principal critique of the legislative/prescriptive jurisdiction theory was advanced by Cassese,[227] who argued that this theory:

> [I]s plainly based on a misconception of the relationship between international and domestic law. Indisputedly, in most States international treaties become part of domestic law upon ratification, but they then bind individuals and State authorities *qua* domestic law, and indeed benefit from all the judicial guarantees provided for by that legal system. However, what is at stake in the present case is not whether rebels are subjects of domestic law, but their legal standing in *international* law—their status vis-a-vis both the lawful Government and third States and the international community at large.[228]

[222] 'Official Records of the Diplomatic Conference on the Reaffirmation and Development of International Humanitarian Law Applicable in Armed Conflicts (Geneva 1974–1977)' Vol VII, CDDH/SR 49, Argentina, 76.

[223] ibid, Annex, 76.

[224] ibid, USSR, 314.

[225] See especially, 'The Status of Rebels under the 1977 Geneva Protocol on Non-International Armed Conflicts' above n 6.

[226] 'Official Records of the Diplomatic Conference on the Reaffirmation and Development of International Humanitarian Law Applicable in Armed Conflicts (Geneva 1974–1977)' Vol VII, CDDH/SR.49, Argentina, 76.

[227] 'The Status of Rebels under the 1977 Geneva Protocol on Non-International Armed Conflicts' above n 6.

[228] ibid, 429.

A related line of criticism notes the existence of two types of systems: monist and dualist.[229] Within monist systems international treaties become part of domestic law immediately upon ratification. However, in dualist systems, a further act of implementation vis-à-vis domestic law is required, giving rise to the danger that 'the effectiveness of the treaty rules "may be eviscerated" if they are not transformed into domestic law.'[230]

Clearly, should armed groups be bound by domestic law and not international law—a consequence of the prescriptive jurisdiction theory according to Cassese—this would negate the very purpose of the relevant international humanitarian law provisions. These were intended to offer protection beyond the national authorities by ensuring the international supervision of non-international armed conflicts. As explained by Klabbers:

> The problem, as the Commentary to the First Convention makes abundantly clear, was that governments would tend to consider their adversaries in domestic strife as common criminals, *'vulgaires criminels'*, for this reason, the application of humanitarian standards should be taken away from those national authorities.[231]

However, the national v international law obligations critique is based on the conception that international treaties cannot impose direct international obligations on non-state entities; ie that non-state entities will be bound only by national and not international law. As will be shown, this conception does not hold true in the modern international legal order.

(i) The Impact of Evolutionary Developments in International Law

The dominant conception in the pre-United Nations era was that international law could not address non-state actors: these entities were considered to be subjects of national law—and not international law—and as such, subject to states' exclusive domestic jurisdiction. For instance, in *Jurisdiction of the Courts of Danzig* the Permanent Court of International Justice expressed the principle that international law cannot impose direct obligations on non-state entities: 'according to a well-established principle of international law, the *Beamtenabkommen*, being an international agreement, cannot, as such, create direct rights and obligations for private

[229] Jan Klabbers, '(I Can't Get No) Recognition: Subjects Doctrine and the Emergence of Non-State Actors' in Andrea Bianchi (ed), *Non-State Actors and International Law* (Farnham, Ashgate, 2009) 44.

[230] 'Binding Armed Opposition Groups' above n 6, 384.

[231] Above n 229, 44.

individuals.'[232] Consequently, when a state chose to make an international claim on behalf of one of its nationals, it was not regarded as giving effect to any right of the national, but rather to its own sovereign right: '[b]y taking up the case of one of its subjects and by resorting to diplomatic action or international judicial proceedings on his behalf, a State is in reality asserting its own rights—its right to ensure, in the person of its subjects, respect for the rules of international law.'[233] Thus, while a state could enter into an international agreement relating to a non-state actor, any effects of the agreement were regarded as binding on the entity *qua* domestic and not international law.

However, Sivakumaran notes that the *Jurisdiction of the Courts of Danzig* case, while upholding the presumption against the direct attribution of rights, contained a caveat that such rights or obligations could be directly attributed if the contracting Parties so intended.[234] According to the Court:

> [T]he very object of an international agreement, according to the intention of the contracting Parties, may be the adoption by the Parties of some definite rules creating individual rights and obligations and enforceable by the national courts.[235]

In this regard, the Court held the intention of the parties to be decisive.[236] While it is unclear that direct international rights were envisaged in this instance—noting in particular the 'enforceable by the national courts' provision—it is clear that the Permanent Court of International Justice held that international agreements could apply directly at the national level on the basis of the parties' intent, irrespective of any act of transformation.[237]

Developments since the advent of the United Nations era have confirmed that international agreements can in fact create direct international rights and obligations vis-à-vis non-state entities.[238] Principle I of the 'Principles of International Law Recognized in the Charter of the Nüremberg Tribunal and in the Judgment of the Tribunal' states that: '[a]ny person who commits an act which constitutes a crime under international law is responsible

[232] *Jurisdiction of the Courts of Danzig (Pecuniary Claims of Danzig Railway Officials Who Have Passed into the Polish Service against the Polish Railways Administration)*, Advisory Opinion, Permanent Court of International Justice, 3 March 1928, 17.

[233] *The Mavrommatis Palestine Concessions*, Judgment, Permanent Court of International Justice, 30 August 1924, 12.

[234] 'Binding Armed Opposition Groups' above n 6, 384.

[235] *Jurisdiction of the Courts of Danzig (Pecuniary Claims of Danzig Railway Officials Who Have Passed into the Polish Service against the Polish Railways Administration)*, above n 232, 17–18.

[236] ibid, 18.

[237] ibid, 26; 'Binding Armed Opposition Groups' above n 6, 384.

[238] See *Reparations for injuries suffered in the services of the United Nations*, above n 20.

therefor and liable to punishment.'[239] According to the *Commentary* to the Principles prepared by the International Law Commission:

> The general rule underlying Principle 1 is that international law may impose duties on individuals directly without any interposition of national law. The findings of the Tribunal were very definite on the question whether rules of international law may apply to individuals. 'That international law imposes duties and liabilities upon individuals as well as upon States', said the judgment of the Tribunal, 'has long been recognized'.[240]

That international law could create direct international obligations was clearly expressed in both the Principles, and by the Tribunal. This was subsequently confirmed—on the same basis—by the International Law Commission in the 1956 Draft Code of Offences against the Peace and Security of Mankind,[241] and the 1996 Draft Code of Crimes against the Peace and Security of Mankind.[242] As stated in the commentary to the 1996 Draft Code: 'the prohibition of such types of behaviour and their punishability *are a direct consequence of international law.*'[243] This position was authoritatively upheld by the International Court of Justice in the *LaGrand* and *Avena* cases. These cases related to, inter alia, Article 36(1)(b) of the Vienna Convention on Consular Relations, which holds that:

> [I]f he so requests, the competent authorities of the receiving State shall, without delay, inform the consular post of the sending State if, within its consular district, a national of that State is arrested or committed to prison or to custody pending trial or is detained in any other manner ... The said authorities shall inform the person concerned without delay of his rights under this subparagraph.[244]

At issue, was whether this provision created direct individual rights or merely individual rights derivate of the rights of states. The Court was unambiguous in its conclusion: '[t]he clarity of the provisions, viewed in their context, admits of no doubt ... the Court concludes that Article 36, paragraph 1, creates individual rights ... These rights were violated in the present case.'[245] That the Vienna Convention created individual rights—distinct from those of the state—was upheld in the *Avena* judgment.[246]

[239] Principle 1, Principles of International Law Recognized in the Charter of the Nürnberg Tribunal and in the Judgment of the Tribunal (1950).

[240] 'Principles of International Law recognized in the Charter of ther Nürnberg Tribunal and in the Judgment of the Tribunal, with commentaries' (1950) *Yearbook of the International Law Commission*, vol II, 374, para 99.

[241] Art 1, Draft Code of Offences against the Peace and Security of Mankind (1956).

[242] Art 1, Draft Code of Crimes against the Peace and Security of Mankind (1996).

[243] 'Draft Code of Crimes against the Peace and Security of Mankind, with commentaries' (1996) *Yearbook of the International Law Commission*, vol II, 17. Emphasis added.

[244] Art 36(1)(b), Vienna Convention on Consular Relations, Vienna, 24 April 1963.

[245] *LaGrand Case (Germany v United States of America)*, above n 87, para 77.

[246] *Avena and Other Mexican Nationals (Mexico v United States of America)*, Judgment, International Court of Justice, 31 March 2004, para 40.

Interestingly, and in a development from the *Mavrommatis* decision discussed above, the Court confirmed that a state could make a claim directly on behalf of an individual, as well as in its own right;[247] it is no longer true that in the eyes of the relevant international tribunal, 'the state is sole claimant'.[248] It is thus evident that international law can establish direct international rights and obligations vis-à-vis non-state actors. It is no longer true that non-state actors are regulated exclusively by means of domestic law.

D. Issues Relating to Armed Groups' Lack of Participation or Consent to be Bound

A final criticism of the prescriptive jurisdiction theory, and one frequently made in academic writings,[249] is founded on armed groups' lack of participation in the development of the law and the fact that, unlike the third party consent theory, there is no requirement that armed groups agree to be bound by any obligations arising under international law. It is believed that armed groups will refuse to be bound by rules to which they did not consent, particularly as such rules may arise consequent to an act of the very state they are fighting against. In this respect the examples of Colombia and Vietnam are often given. During the Vietnam War the National Liberation Front of South Vietnam refused to be bound by international treaties ratified by the government, 'asserting that they were not bound by the actions of a government whose legal authority they did not respect.'[250] Similarly, Human Rights Watch reported that in Colombia, 'guerrillas argued in repeated interviews … that although they support humanitarian standards in theory, they do not accept Protocol II since it was not negotiated directly with them.'[251] This point of view is summarised by Kleffner:

> [I]t does not come as a surprise when an organized armed group rejects an explanation that draws on the fact that the very state against whom that organized armed group is fighting has accepted a given rule of IHL. Indeed, the very fact that an organized armed group is a party to an armed conflict against the

[247] ibid, para 40.

[248] *The Mavrommatis Palestine Concessions*, above n 233, 12.

[249] See eg Antonio Cassese, 'The Status of Rebels under the 1977 Geneva Conventions on Non-International Armed Conflicts' (1981) 30 *International and Comparative Law Quarterly*, 429; 'The applicability of international humanitarian law to organized armed groups' above n 6, 446.

[250] David P Forsythe, 'Legal Management of Internal War: The 1977 Protocol on Non-International Armed Conflicts' (1978) 72 *American Journal of International Law* 2, 292.

[251] Chapter II, Human Rights Watch, 'War Without Quarter: Colombia and International Humanitarian Law' (1998), www.hrw.org/legacy/reports/reports98/colombia/.

> central government of a state suggests very strongly that it does not recognize even the most basic laws of that state, which seek to perpetuate the central government's monopoly on the use of force by criminalizing any challenge to that monopoly. The equation of members of an organized armed group with 'ordinary citizens', who can reasonably be assumed to be at least receptive to the suggestion that they are bound by the legal rules that the state has accepted or issued, appears to be somewhat strained, if not entirely neglecting the reality of organized armed groups as challengers to the monopoly of force that states arrogate for themselves.[252]

However, this assumption does not necessarily reflect the reality of armed groups' opposition to international humanitarian law. Bangerter, a former ICRC Advisor for Dialogue with Armed Groups, recently stated that: '[t]his reluctance to accept IHL as a law not negotiated by armed groups seems quite logical to Western people with a legal training, but is only rarely maintained by today's armed groups. Those who have issues with IHL as such have different reasons.'[253] Importantly, he further noted that:

> [T]he idea that armed groups have an issue with IHL because they have not contributed to its formulation and cannot ratify it seems wrong if we consider their discourse. Nowadays this idea is consistently articulated by armed groups only in Colombia, and even there the reality is quite complex.[254]

As evidence of this complexity, Bangerter highlighted how FARC would often reject the applicability of international humanitarian law, while noting—often in the same document—that they had incorporated international humanitarian law into their own code of conduct.[255] Sassoli also supports this conclusion:

> In the 1970s, several guerrilla movements declared that they would not feel bound by new rules of IHL which they could not participate in developing. Today, in my experience, armed groups are more concerned that the law applies to them equally and that it is realistic than that they may contribute to its development.[256]

There exist numerous examples of armed groups who have expressed a willingness to apply international humanitarian law,[257] including the

[252] 'The applicability of international humanitarian law to organized armed groups' above n 6, 446.

[253] Olivier Bangerter, 'Reasons why armed groups choose to respect international humanitarian law or not' (2011) 93 *International Review of the Red Cross* 882, 28, fn 110.

[254] ibid, 28.

[255] ibid, 29.

[256] 'Taking Armed Groups Seriously' above n 65, 21.

[257] See generally, Olivier Bangerter, 'Internal Control: Codes of Conduct within Insurgent Armed Groups' (2012) Small Arms Survey Occasional Paper No 31; Sandesh Sivakumaran, *The Law of Non-International Armed Conflict* (Oxford, OUP, 2012).

Algeria National Liberation Front,[258] the Kosovo Liberation Army,[259] the Free Libya Army,[260] and the Huthis in Yemen.[261] Evidently, the practical consequences often associated with armed groups' lack of consent are questionable.

Ultimately, armed groups' status as non-state actors means that they may be legitimately subject to international law rights and obligations irrespective of their consent. This conclusion is consistent with the law's humanitarian imperative, particularly when one considers that the obvious consequence of requiring a group's consent is that they can choose to operate in a legal vacuum. Indeed, states themselves have often proved unwilling to apply international humanitarian law: it seems unrealistic to assume that armed groups would act differently. Switzerland's statement during the common Article 3 drafting process seems pertinent: '[i]f the two Parties to the conflict had to declare themselves bound, the Article would become useless, and would be nothing more than a recommendation.'[262] This is not to undermine the significant issues that arise in relation to armed groups' refusal to comply with international humanitarian law, but rather to suggest that the causes may lie elsewhere.[263]

V. CONCLUSION

The requirement that non-state armed groups must indicate their consent as a precondition for the application of international law has been discussed and rejected. This requirement fails to acknowledge the differentiated international legal personality of non-state armed groups and the erosion of the absolute nature of the *pacta tertiis* principle, while granting an exaggerated status to armed groups that is inconsistent with their position within the international legal system. This is not to imply that the consent of armed groups should not be sought, such 'buy-in' can have evident practical benefits. Rather, it is to state that, as a matter of international law, consent is not required.

[258] Above n 250, 274.

[259] Human Rights Watch, 'Under Orders: War Crimes in Kosovo' (2001) 102.

[260] Sandesh Sivakumaran, 'Lessons for the law of armed conflict from commitments of armed groups: identification of legitimate targets and prisoners of war' (2011) 93 *International Review of the Red Cross* 882, 8.

[261] 'Internal Control: Codes of Conduct within Insurgent Armed Groups' above n 257, 6.

[262] 'Final Record of the Diplomatic Conference of Geneva of 1949', Vol II Section B, Switzerland, 47.

[263] See generally, above n 253.

The customary law, general principles, and prescriptive jurisdiction theories all provide a sound legal basis for the application of international law rights and obligations to armed opposition groups. However, despite their legal validity, the customary law and general principles theories are subject to certain limitations: they apply only to groups with an already established international legal personality and are restricted to a subset of the potentially applicable international law. Accordingly, the prescriptive jurisdiction theory most effectively explains the legal basis underpinning the initial application of treaty-based international law rights and obligations to armed opposition groups, establishing that states may legislate at the international level with respect to any entities subject to their nationality or territorial jurisdiction. This theory has a firm basis in international law, state practice, and case law, and is reflective of the reality of the contemporary international legal order. Importantly from states' perspectives, unlike the other theories, '[t]he legislative jurisdiction approach treats armed opposition groups as entities subordinate to states.'[264] As noted, the essential requirement vis-à-vis the prescriptive jurisdiction theory is that the drafters intended the relevant treaty to bind non-state third parties. This intent is widely, if not universally, accepted with respect to common Article 3 and Additional Protocol II, and the prescriptive jurisdiction theory thus offers a coherent explanation for the binding force of international humanitarian law with respect to armed opposition groups.

Significantly, the prescriptive jurisdiction theory—and the now proven non-applicability of the consent requirement—provides a coherent basis for the future application of international treaty law to non-state actors in general. Clarity regarding the application of international humanitarian law to armed groups paves the way for the direct application of other treaties to armed groups, and non-state actors generally, for example, establishing a legal basis for the future application of international human rights law treaty regulation to armed groups engaged in armed conflict. Given the increasing role of non-state actors in international life, this is an important basis for extending the rule of international law and ensuring that it remains capable of responding to the realities of international life.

The application of international law on the basis of the customary law, general principles, or legislative jurisdiction theories will satisfy the actual possession criterion identified in relation to international legal personality. As noted, however, the applicability of each of these theories is dependent upon the direct application of international treaty law, and as it stands few international treaties directly address armed opposition groups. A notable exception does exist with respect to armed groups recognised

[264] 'Binding Armed Opposition Groups' above n 6, 394.

as a party to a non-international armed conflict.[265] In such situations the applicable international treaty law includes:[266] Article 3 common to the four Geneva Conventions of 1949, and Additional Protocol II to the Geneva Conventions,[267] the Optional Protocol to the Convention on the Rights of the Child on the Involvement of Children in Armed Conflict,[268] and the Hague Convention for the Protection of Cultural Property in the Event of an Armed Conflict.[269]

However, the international legal personality of armed groups bound on the basis of the above theories will only persist while the relevant treaty remains applicable: with respect to those treaties which currently directly address non-state armed groups, this is restricted to the duration of the groups' classification as a party to an armed conflict.[270] This temporal conditionality associated with a group's international legal personality may lead to a number of potentially problematic situations. For instance, a situation may transition in and out of non-international armed conflict consequent to a cycle of ceasefire followed by renewed hostilities:[271] the group's international legal personality may be extinguished during these lulls.[272] Equally, an armed group may satisfy the organisation criterion, but not engage in hostilities (or engage only in sporadic or low level hostilities, which fail to satisfy the intensity criteria),[273] perhaps in the early stages of a situation which will later escalate to one of non-international armed conflict,[274] or following the end of the armed conflict.[275] In each of these

[265] A number of other non-state entities are also subject to direct international rights or obligations consequent to the application of international treaty law. See eg, Art 36, Vienna Convention on Consular Relations; Art 1, Convention on the Prevention and Punishment of the Crime of Genocide; Art 1, International Convention on the Suppression and Punishment of the Crime of Apartheid; Art 1, Rome Statute of the International Criminal Court. Treaties establishing International Organisations will necessarily contain obligations with respect to the International Organisation in question, and the UN Charter is an example in this regard.

[266] See further *The Law of Non-International Armed Conflict* above n 257, 236–38.

[267] Additional Protocol I is also relevant vis-à-vis those non-state groups falling under the provisions of Art 1(4).

[268] Controversy exists in this regard. See below Ch 6 section I.

[269] Convention for the Protection of Cultural Property in the Event of Armed Conflict (adopted 14 May 1954, entered into force 7 August 1956) 249 UNTS 240.

[270] Individual members of an armed group remain directly bound by international criminal law beyond the duration of the conflict, and may, for example, be held accountable with respect to the commission of war crimes.

[271] See eg *Prosecutor v Tadic*, Decision on the Defence Motion for Interlocutory Appeal on Jurisdiction, above n 33, para 70.

[272] Groups which might fall into this category include Hezbollah (in relation to hostilities with Israel), the Forces Nouvelles, and the FDLR.

[273] For instance, in 2012 the ICC Prosecutor considered that although the Urabeños satisfied the organisational criteria, the level of violence vis-à-vis the group and the state did not satisfy the non-international armed conflict threshold. International Criminal Court, The Office of the Prosecutor, 'Report on Preliminary Examination Activities' (2013) para 129.

[274] Drug gangs such as the Zetas in Mexico may fall into this category.

[275] 'Report of the Internaitonal Commission of Inquiry on Libya', UN Doc A/HRC/19/68, 8 March 2012, para 36.

instances, which may or may not involve elements of territorial control, a group may exert significant influence over a population—to the exclusion of the state—but remain outside the scope of the international law of armed conflict.[276]

This presents a significant problem with respect to both the regulation of armed group activity and the relevance of international law: a potentially large number of armed groups may exert a significant influence over civilians and territory while remaining beyond the scope of international regulation.[277] This will result in the existence of a legal vacuum wherein civilians are denied the protection of international law and armed groups are, in effect, granted complete freedom of action. None of the above-mentioned principles of attribution are capable of responding to this situation. However, the de facto control theory may provide a basis for the application of international law to non-state armed groups not addressed by existing international treaty law, and therefore not possessing international legal personality on this basis. This theory is discussed in greater detail in the next chapter.

[276] The precise criteria regulating the end of non-international armed conflicts are unclear. For instance, a non-international armed conflict may also end should the hostilities drop below the intensity threshold associated with the establishment of non-international armed conflict. This raises the possibility that a situation could cycle in and out of non-international armed conflict, based on fluctuations in the intensity of fighting.

[277] For instance, this could potentially include groups such as the LTTE, FARC, POLISARIO, the MILF, the NPA, the SPLM/A, Hezbollah, the FDLR, the Forces Nouvelles, the Urabeños, and a number of nascent insurgencies.

5

The De Facto Control Theory and the International Regulation of Armed Groups in the Absence of Directly Applicable International Treaty Law

IT HAS BEEN established that non-state armed groups may be directly bound by international treaty law, thereby satisfying the 'actual possession' criterion necessary for the possession of international legal personality.[1] However, the establishment of international legal personality on this basis is currently restricted to armed groups party to a non-international armed conflict, and only persists for the duration of that conflict. A large number of armed groups will therefore be excluded from international regulation.[2] The de facto control theory offers a potential solution in this regard, as it may provide a basis for the application of international law to armed groups who do not possess international legal personality, ie in the absence of directly applicable international treaty law. This theory of attribution is discussed in the opening section of this chapter.

Significantly, the de facto control theory may also be used to determine the extent of the law applicable to armed groups. As noted, armed groups whose international legal personality is established following the direct application of international treaty law will be bound by that treaty and the applicable customary international law. The de facto control theory, however, may provide a basis for the application of additional rules of international law, such as those related to environmental law or international human rights law. The application of international law on this basis applies both to armed groups whose personality is established consequent to the direct application of treaty law, and to those armed groups whose

[1] See above, Ch 2 section IV. Armed groups must also satisfy the independence and capacity criteria. With respect to those international humanitarian law treaties which currently bind non-state armed groups, satisfaction of these criteria is contained within the threshold of application for the treaties themselves.

[2] See further above Ch 4 section V.

legal personality is established consequent to the de facto control theory itself; this is discussed in section II of this chapter. Finally, if an armed group is to be bound by the de facto control theory, it must exist independently; this is also an essential criterion for the acquisition of international legal personality. The circumstances under which an armed group may establish an independent existence are discussed in section III, in relation both to armed groups party to a non-international armed conflict and to armed groups existing outside this framework.

I. THE DE FACTO CONTROL THEORY

The de facto control theory applies international law to non-state entities on the basis of exclusive control exercised over a specific territory.[3] The decisive element is thus that the entity exists—and has established effective control—in an area beyond the reach of the de jure authority,[4] thereby generating a legal vacuum.[5] De facto entities are regarded as 'independent entities that exist side-by-side with the established authorities'[6] and exercise 'effective sovereignty'.[7] While such situations will often arise in the context of armed conflict, this is not always the case, and the de facto control theory applies equally to entities that are party to a non-international armed conflict and to those that are not.[8] Entities addressed by the de facto control theory will satisfy the 'actual possession' criterion and must be recognised as possessing international legal personality.[9] However, as a result of their transient nature, de facto entities are regarded as provisional subjects of international law,[10] and their subject-specific competence is

[3] See Jochen A Frowein, 'De Facto Regime' in *Max Planck Encyclopaedia of Public International Law*, para 3; Jean S Pictet (ed), *Commentary: III Geneva Convention Relative to the Treatment of Prisoners of War* (Geneva, International Committee of the Red Cross, 1960) 37; JK Kleffner, 'The applicability of international humanitarian law to organized armed groups' (2011) 93 *International Review of the Red Cross* 452; Sandesh Sivakumaran, 'Binding Armed Opposition Groups' (2006) 55 *International and Comparative Law Quarterly* 379.

[4] See eg 'Arbitration between Great Britain and Costa Rica, Opinion and Award of William H Taft, Sole Arbitrator' (1924) 18 *American Journal of International Law* 154.

[5] See generally Philip Brown, 'The Legal Effects of Recognition' (1950) 44 *American Journal of International Law* 630.

[6] Liesbeth Zegveld, *The Accountability of Armed Opposition Groups in International Law* (Cambridge, CUP, 2002) 15.

[7] *Commentary: III Geneva Convention Relative to the Treatment of Prisoners of War* above n 3 at 37.

[8] Michael Schoiswohl, '*De Facto* Regimes and Human Rights Obligations—The Twilight Zone of Public International Law?' (2001) 6 *Austrian Review of International and European Law* 50.

[9] See eg 'De Facto Regime' above n 3, para 3. See also, 'Third Report on the Law of Treaties by Mr GG Fitzmaurice, Special Rapporteur' (1958) *Yearbook of the International Law Commission*, Vol II, 32.

[10] 'Fourth Report on State responsibility, by Mr Roberto Ago, Special Rapporteur—The internationally wrongful act of the State, sources of international responsibility' (1972) *Yearbook of the International Law Commission*, Vol II, 130.

restricted.[11] Thus, while they will be subject to international rights and obligations, de facto entities are not equivalent to states, and cannot, for example, exercise sovereign rights, such as the lawful ceding of territory under their control to another international subject.[12]

In 1910 Judge Constantineau explained the de facto theory in its broad form as follows:

> The de facto doctrine is a rule or principle of law which, in the first place, justifies the recognition of the authority of governments established and maintained by persons who have usurped the sovereign authority of the State, and assert themselves by force and arms against the lawful government; secondly, which recognizes the existence of, and protects from collateral attack, public or private bodies corporate, which, though irregularly or illegally organized, yet, under color of law, openly exercise the powers and functions of regularly created bodies; and, thirdly, which imparts validity to the official acts of persons who, under color of right or authority, hold office under the aforementioned governments or bodies, or exercise lawfully existing offices of whatever nature, in which the public or third persons are interested, where the performance of such official acts is for the benefit of the public or third persons, and not for their own personal advantage.[13]

A key element in the de facto control theory is the principle of effectiveness and the desire to maintain the rule of international law.[14] The focus is not on pre-existing legal formulations, but rather on the factual circumstances of the situation at hand:[15] international law as a realistic legal system takes into account the factual situation, and transforms it into a legal reality. It is important to note that the de facto control theory concerns itself solely with responding to the reality of the situation and does not legitimise the entity in question.[16] As stated by the Canadian Supreme Court, '[t]he application of the de facto doctrine is, however, limited to validating acts which are taken under invalid authority: it does not validate the authority under which the acts took place.'[17] In this sense the de facto control theory may be thought of as resembling the distinction in public international law between *jus ad bellum* and *jus in bello*.[18]

[11] H Lauterpacht, 'Recognition of Insurgents as a De Facto Government' (1939) 3 *Modern Law Review* 1, 9.

[12] EH Riedel, 'Recognition of Belligerency' in R Bernhardt (ed), *Encyclopedia of Public International Law, Vol 4* (North-Holland, Elsevier, 2000).

[13] Albert Constantineau, *A Treatise on the De Facto Doctrine* (Rochester, The Lawyers Co-operative Publishing Company, 1910) para 1.

[14] See further: *Cyprus v Turkey* App No 25781/94 (ECtHR, 10 May 2001), para 91.

[15] 'The applicability of international humanitarian law to organized armed groups' above n 3, 453.

[16] See eg, International Law Commission, 'Draft Articles on Responsibility of States for Internationally Wrongful Acts, with commentaries' (2001) *Yearbook of the International Commission* Vol II, 51.

[17] *Re Manitoba Language Rights* [1985] 1 SCR 721, para 80.

[18] ie the authority of the entity is subject to international regulation (*jus in bello*), without commenting on the validity of the authority itself (*jus ad bellum*).

This section will discuss the role of the principle of effectiveness and the importance attributed to avoiding a legal vacuum, before examining the de facto control theory in international and national case law. First, however, it is beneficial to clarify some issues relating to recognition in order to avoid any potential confusion. It is also noted that this section is concerned with entities exercising effective control over a portion of a state's territory, as distinct from those de facto entities which have succeeded in gaining control of a state but who nonetheless remain classified as de facto entities.[19]

A. Overcoming Confusion Relating to Recognition De Jure or De Facto

The de facto control theory should not be confused with the concept of recognition de jure or de facto. The de facto control theory concerns the application of international law to entities exercising exclusive control of a specific territory. Recognition de jure or de facto, however, is a separate concept used to refer to the form of recognition which a state may choose to extend to an entity.[20] states traditionally extended recognition de jure to an entity considered to represent the state, and recognition de facto to an entity which, although exercising territorial control, could not (yet) be considered to represent the state on the international plane; recognition de facto was thus seen as a less absolute form of recognition.[21] During the Spanish civil war, for example, the United Kingdom recognised the Republicans as the de jure government, while extending recognition de facto to the Nationalist forces of General Franco.[22] As recognition de facto also entails certain—although not necessarily equivalent—legal consequences, the distinction between recognition de facto and the de facto control theory may be likened in some respects to the distinction between the constitutive and declarative approaches to statehood respectively.

[19] Examples of such entities may include the Soviet government which took control of Russia in 1917, but was not recognised as the de jure government by the United Kingdom until 1924. Similar was the initial refusal by the United States to recognise the People's Republic of China.

[20] Charles Cochran, 'De Facto and De Jure Recognition: Is There a Difference?' (1968) 62 *American Journal of International Law* 457.

[21] See above n 11, 9. See further James Crawford, *Brownlie's Principles of Public International Law*, 8th edn (Oxford, OUP, 2012) 153; *Banco de Bilbao v Rey; Banco de Bilbao v Sancha* [1938] 2 All ER 253, 260; *The Arantzazu Mendi* [1939] 1 All ER 719, 722.

[22] *Banco de Bilbao v Rey; Banco de Bilbao v Sancha* above n 21, 260.

B. Must De Facto Entities be Recognised?

This raises the question of whether de facto entities must be recognised in order to render the de facto control theory applicable? Previously, states extended recognition de facto as a matter of routine. For example, the United Kingdom formally recognised the USSR as the de facto government in Russia in 1921,[23] and Italy as the de facto government in Abyssinia (Ethiopia),[24] while the United States similarly recognised the Carranza government as the de facto government in Mexico in 1915.[25] National courts have subsequently relied on this recognition in reaching judgments.[26] For instance, in *Bank of Ethiopia v National Bank of Egypt and Liguori* the court held that:

> Where ... his Majesty's Government has recognized a *de facto* government, there is, as it appears to me, no ground for suggesting that the *de jure* monarch's theoretical rights (for *ex hypothesi* he has no practical power of enforcing them) can be taken into account in any way in any of his Majesty's courts.[27]

However, while these cases involved the formal recognition of a de facto entity—supporting an argument for a recognition-based approach—courts have not definitively required such recognition. For example, in *Hesperides Hotels Ltd v Aegean Turkish Holidays Ltd* the UK Court of Appeal stated that 'English courts could recognise the laws or acts of a body which was in effective control of a territory even though that body had not been recognised by Her Majesty's Government de jure or de facto.'[28] The European Court of Human Rights has similarly recognised the responsibilities of the de facto TRNC regime in Northern Cyprus, despite a lack of recognition by members of the European Union.[29] Equally, the courts of the United States have held that legal consequences may be attributed to a de facto entity, absent recognition, as held in *Banque de France v Equitable Trust Co*:

> [T]here has now developed what I think will be generally regarded as the rule here. It holds to the principle that the refusal of the political department to

[23] *Luther v Sagor* (1921) 3 KB 532.

[24] *Bank of Ethiopia v National Bank of Egypt and Liguori*, Great Britain: High Court of Justice Chancery Division, 11 May 1937, in (1937) 31 *American Journal of International Law* 744.

[25] *Oetjen v Central Leather Co* (1918) 246 US 297.

[26] See eg *The Arantzazu Mendi* above n 21; *Banco de Bilbao v Rey; Banco de Bilbao v Sancha* above n 21; *Luther v Sagor* above n 23.

[27] *Bank of Ethiopia v National Bank of Egypt and Liguori*, above n 24, 746.

[28] *Hesperides Hotels Ltd and another v Aegean Turkish Holidays Ltd* [1978] 1 All ER 277, 278.

[29] *Protopapa v Turkey* App No 16084/90 (ECtHR, 24 February 2009), para 60; *Demopoulos and others v Turkey, Admissibility* App Nos 46113.99, 3843/02, 13751/02, 13466/03, 10200/04, 14163/04, 19993/04, 21819/04 (ECtHR, 1 March 2010), para 89.

> recognize a government should not be allowed to affect private rights which may depend upon proving the existing conditions in such state.[30]

As noted in *Kadic v Karadzic* 'an unrecognised state is not a judicial nullity',[31] and '[a]ny government, however violent and wrongful in its origin, must be considered a de facto government if it was in the full and actual exercise of sovereignty over a territory and people large enough for a nation.'[32] A similar factual approach is evident in the International Criminal Tribunal for the former Yugoslavia's Rules of Procedure and Evidence,[33] while the Foreign Relations Law of the United States, Third Restatement does not require recognition by other states.[34] In this regard, it is further noted that the practice of recognising governments, or de facto entities, has died out in recent years; the UK, for instance, formally abolished this policy in 1980.[35]

It must be concluded that recognition of a de facto entity is not required in order to render the de facto control theory applicable.[36] Rather, it is the factual situation which is decisive.[37] Indeed, in the *Namibia* Advisory Opinion, the International Court of Justice explicitly declared that states were under a legal obligation not to recognise the government,[38] but nonetheless declared that certain acts of that government must be regarded as valid, in particular acts such as 'the registration of births, deaths and marriages, the effects of which can be ignored only to the detriment of the inhabitants of the Territory.'[39] This conclusion was reiterated and reinforced by the European Court of Human Rights, 'despite having been invited to do so by the Secretary-General of the United Nations, the International Court resolutely rejected the approach refusing any effect to unlawful de facto regimes.'[40]

[30] *Banque de France v Equitable Trust Co* (1929) 33 F 2d 202, 21 March 1929, District Court, SD New York, 206.

[31] *Kadic v Karadzic*, 70 F 3rd 232 (2nd Cir 1995) 244.

[32] ibid, 244. Disregarding state recognition.

[33] The definition of a state therein includes: '(iii) a self-proclaimed entity de facto exercising governmental functions, whether recognised as a State or not'. Rules of Procedure and Evidence, International Criminal Tribunal for the former Yugoslavia, IT/32/Rev 46, 20 October 2011.

[34] Quoted in *Kadic v Karadzic*, above n 31, 244.

[35] 'De Facto Regime' above n 3, para 2.

[36] However, as with statehood (see above) in exceptional circumstances recognition may be decisive in the absence of clear satisfaction of the facts. See Paola Gaeta, 'The Dayton Agreements and International Law' (1996) 7 *European Journal of International Law* 158.

[37] See eg, *Legal Consequences for States of the Continued Presence of South Africa in Namibia (South West Africa) Notwithstanding Security Council Resolution 276 (1970)*, Advisory Opinion, International Court of Justice, 21 June 1971, para 54.

[38] ibid, para 119.

[39] ibid, para 125.

[40] Referring to the *Namibia* opinion. *Cyprus v Turkey*, above n 14, para 94.

C. The Motivation Underlying the De Facto Control Theory

The de facto control theory is grounded in the principle of effectiveness:[41] it is the reality of the concerned entity's effective control, and in particular the displacement of state authority—ie the establishment of a legal vacuum—which forces the entity onto the international plane and demands the direct attribution of international law rights and obligations. As such, the de facto control theory may appropriately be regarded as an 'agency of necessity',[42] and as a response to the needs of the international community and the requirements of international life.[43] As explained by the European Court of Human Rights in *Cyprus v Turkey*:

> Life goes on in the territory concerned for its inhabitants. That life must be made tolerable and be protected by the *de facto* authorities, including their courts; and, in the very interest of the inhabitants, the acts of these authorities related thereto cannot be simply ignored by third States or by international institutions, especially courts, including this one. To hold otherwise would amount to stripping the inhabitants of the territory of all their rights whenever they are discussed in an international context, which would amount to depriving them even of the minimum standard of rights to which they are entitled.[44]

Ultimately, if international law is 'to be coherent and meaningful [it cannot] be either static or blind to concrete factual circumstances.'[45] This conclusion was endorsed by the International Court of Justice in its *Namibia* Advisory Opinion—albeit in the context of state activity—where the court held that, '[p]hysical control of a territory, and not sovereignty or legitimacy of title, is the basis of State liability for acts affecting other States.'[46]

D. Further Examples in Support of the De Facto Control Theory

A number of further examples in support for the de facto control theory—UN Commissions of Inquiry, the law of state responsibility, and to a lesser extent states' extraterritorial human rights obligations—will now be briefly addressed. A number of UN Commissions of Inquiry have

[41] In relation to the principle of effectiveness, see Antonio Cassese, *International Law*, 2nd edn (Oxford, OUP, 2005) 12–13.

[42] Above n 16, 49.

[43] Paraphrasing *Reparations for injuries suffered in the services of the United Nations*, Advisory Opinion, International Court of Justice, 11 April 1949, 178.

[44] *Cyprus v Turkey*, above n 14, para 96.

[45] *Demopoulos and others v Turkey*, above n 29, para 85.

[46] *Legal Consequences for States of the Continued Presence of South Africa in Namibia (South West Africa) Notwithstanding Security Council Resolution 276 (1970)*, above n 37, para 54. Without legitimate title, control is by definition de facto control.

established the international legal obligations applicable to non-state armed groups on the basis of the de facto control theory.[47] For instance, the Report of the Secretary-General's Panel of Experts on Accountability in Sri Lanka held that:

> With respect to the LTTE, although non-state actors cannot formally become party to a human rights treaty, it is now increasingly accepted that non-state groups exercising de facto control over a part of a State's territory must respect fundamental human rights of persons in that territory. Various organs of the United Nations, including the Security Council, have repeatedly demanded that such actors respect human rights law.[48]

A similar finding was made in relation to the situation in Libya,[49] while the UN Commission of Inquiry on Syria has also reported on human rights violations committed by non-state anti-Government forces,[50] although no mention of the de facto control theory was made. Equally, recent UN reports on the protection of civilians in Afghanistan have stated that:

> While non-State actors in Afghanistan, including non-State armed groups, cannot formally become parties to international human rights law treaties, international human rights law increasingly recognizes that where non-State actors, such as the Taliban, exercise de facto control over territory, they are bound by international human rights obligations.[51]

Significantly, the law of state responsibility also establishes that a state may not be held responsible for the acts of a de facto authority, unless negligence on the part of the state can be proved. In *GL Solis (USA) v United Mexican States* it was held that: 'It is a well-established principle of international law that no government can be held responsible for the act of rebellious bodies of men committed in violation of its authority, where it is itself guilty of no breach of good faith, or of no negligence in suppressing

[47] See Andrew Clapham, 'Focusing on Armed Non-State Actors' in Andrew Clapham and Paola Gaeta (eds), *The Oxford Handbook of International Law in Armed Conflict* (Oxford, OUP, 2014) 793–99.

[48] 'Report of the Secretary-General's Panel of Experts on Accountability in Sri Lanka', 31 March 2011, para 188.

[49] 'Report of the International Commission of Inquiry to investigate all alleged violations of international human rights law in the Libyan Arab Jamahiriya', UN Doc A/HRC/17/44, 1 June 2011, para 72.

[50] 'Report of the independent international commission of inquiry on the Syrian Arab Republic', UN Doc A/HRC/22/59, 5 February 2013. See also, 'Report of the independent international commission of inquiry on the Syrian Arab Republic', UN Doc A/HRC/19/69, 22 February 2012, para 106; United Nations Mission in the Republic of South Sudan (UNMISS), 'Conflict in South Sudan: A Human Rights Report', 8 May 2014, para 18.

[51] United Nations Assistance Mission in Afghanistan and UN Office of the High Commissioner for Human Rights, *Afghanistan Annual Report 2011: Protection of Civilians in Armed Conflict* (2012) iv. See also, United Nations Assistance Mission in Afghanistan & UN Office of the High Commissioner for Human Rights, *Afghanistan Annual Report 2014: Protection of Civilians in Armed Conflict* (2015) 98.

insurrection.'[52] This finding has been repeated in numerous arbitration awards,[53] and was codified in the International Law Commission's Draft Articles on the Responsibility of States for Internationally Wrongful Acts.[54] In such situations, if direct international obligations are not imposed on the de facto authority this will result in a legal vacuum.

The *Commentary* to the Third Geneva Convention presents a variation of the de facto control theory when explaining the attribution of international humanitarian law to armed groups: 'if the responsible authority at [its] head exercises effective sovereignty, it is bound by the very fact that it *claims* to represent the country, or part of the country.'[55] However, this emphasis on motivation is not a suitable basis for legal obligation. As noted by Sivakumaran, '[i]f an armed opposition group claims to represent the country and is defeated some two days later, would it really make sense for it to have been subject to the rules governing internal armed conflict by reason of its claim to represent the state?'[56] Equally, it is far from certain that armed groups will in fact claim to represent the state, or a part thereof.[57] For example, armed groups may simply wish to establish an autonomous existence to facilitate the group's operations, while equally 'the aim in many conflicts may be rather to create a new State, and to bind insurgents on this basis in such circumstances would be absurd.'[58]

E. The De Facto Control Theory and the Implied Mandate

The de facto control theory holds that non-state entities may be subject to international regulation should they exercise exclusive control over a specific territory, thereby establishing themselves as a de facto authority.[59] In order for the rule of international law to be maintained in such a situation the legal vacuum generated by the existence of the de facto entity must be filled, and so certain acts of the de facto authority must be acknowledged

52 *GL Solis (USA) v United Mexican States*, 3 October 1928, Reports of International Arbitral Awards, Vol IV, 361.

53 See eg *Sambiaggio Case (of a general nature)* 1903 Reports of International Arbitral Awards, Vol X; *Bolivar Railway Case (on merits)*, (1903) Reports of International Arbitral Awards, Vol IX. See further, 'Fourth Report on State responsibility, by Mr. Roberto Ago, Special Rapporteur—The internationally wrongful act of the State, sources of international responsibility' (1972) *Yearbook of the International Law Commission*, Vol II, 132.

54 See above n 16, 49–50.

55 *Commentary: III Geneva Convention Relative to the Treatment of Prisoners of War* above n 3, 37. Emphasis added.

56 'Binding Armed Opposition Groups' above n 3, 380.

57 'The applicability of international humanitarian law to organized armed groups' above n 3, 453.

58 Lindsay Moir, *The Law of Internal Armed Conflict* (Cambridge, CUP, 2002) 56.

59 See above Ch 5 section I.

and given legal validity; 'it follows from the very fact that no other power has authority over them that they [de facto entities] must have a certain status in international relations'.[60] The need to ensure this status,[61] and to avoid a legal vacuum, is a consistent theme throughout the case law. For example, in the *Arantzazu Mendi* case it was held that:

> [T]he law, based on the reality of facts material to the particular case, must regard as having the essentials of sovereignty a government in effective administrative control over the territory in question and not subordinate to any other government, *because their decrees are the only legal authority which governs the area to which the subject matter of the dispute belongs.*[62]

Similarly, in *United States v Rice* it was held that where the state cannot extend 'protection or allegiance or sovereignty, there can be no claim to obedience'[63] and so the authority—and law—of the de facto ruler must be acknowledged. This acknowledgement takes the form of what is referred to in the case law as an implied mandate:[64] acts of a de facto authority which are required for the maintenance of civil life must be regarded as legitimate—on the basis of their sole authority, and the necessity of avoiding a legal vacuum—while acts undertaken directly against the state—for example, in furtherance of a rebellion—are invalid. This doctrine was explained by the United States Supreme Court in *Texas v White*:

> [A]cts necessary to peace and good order among citizens, such for example, as acts sanctioning and protecting marriage and the domestic relations, governing the course of descents, regulating the conveyance and transfer of property, real and personal, and providing remedies for injuries to person and estate, and other similar acts, which would be valid if emanating from a lawful government must be regarded in general as valid when proceeding from an actual, though unlawful, government, and that acts in furtherance or support of rebellion against the United States, or intended to defeat the just rights of citizens, and other acts of like nature, must, in general, be regarded as invalid and void.[65]

[60] Martin Schoiswohl, *Status and (Human Rights) Obligations of Non-Recognized* De Facto *Regimes in International Law: The Case of 'Somaliland'* (The Hague, Martinus Nijhoff, 2004) 209, quoting Mosler, 'Subjects of International law'.

[61] The status referred to equates to cognition by the international legal order.

[62] Bucknill J in *The Arantzazu Mendi*, Probate Divorce and Admiralty Division, 17 June 1938. Quoted in Herbert W Briggs, 'De Facto and De Jure Recognition: The Arantzazu Mendi' (1939) 33 *American Journal of International Law* 695. Emphasis added.

[63] *United States v Rice* (1819) 17 US 246, 254.

[64] See eg *Samuel Oguebie v Odunwoke*, Supreme Court of Nigeria, SC 467/1975, 19 April 1973.

[65] *Texas v White* (1869) 74 US 700, 733.

Subsequently, in *Horn v Lockhart*, the same court stated:

> The existence of a state of insurrection and war did not loosen the bonds of society, or do away with civil government or the regular administration of the laws. Order was to be preserved, police regulations maintained, crime prosecuted, property protected, contracts enforced, marriages celebrated, estates settled, and the transfer and descent of property regulated precisely as in time of peace. No one that we are aware of seriously questions the validity of judicial or legislative acts of the insurrectionary states touching these and kindred subjects where they were not hostile in their purpose or mode of enforcement to the authority of the national government and did not impair the rights of citizens under the Constitution.[66]

This doctrine has been adopted by other courts,[67] including the International Court of Justice, albeit in the context of state and not armed group conduct.[68] It is apparent that certain acts of a de facto entity are recognised as legitimate both in the interest of the individuals subject to that entity's authority, and in the interests of the international community itself. This recognition necessarily results in cognition of the de facto entity as an 'active participant' of the international legal order, and under such circumstances the application of international law is both necessary and appropriate: if the acts of a de facto entity are to be recognised as effective on the international plane, it follows that the entity must be subject to international regulation.[69] Significantly, the application of international law on this basis satisfies the 'actual possession' criterion, thereby establishing the de facto authority's international legal personality.[70] As an international legal person, a de facto authority is bound by customary international law.[71] The application of other elements of international law is discussed further below.[72]

[66] *Horn v Lockhart* (1873) 84 US 570, 581.

[67] *Samuel Oguebie v Odunwoke*, above n 64; *Hesperides Hotels Ltd and another v Aegean Turkish Holidays Ltd* above n 28, 283; *Banque de France v Equitable Trust Co* above n 30, 205. This doctrine has also been applied with respect to de facto administrations established by states.

[68] See *Legal Consequences for States of the Continued Presence of South Africa in Namibia (South West Africa) Notwithstanding Security Council Resolution 276 (1970)*, above n 37, para 125. See further *Loizidou v Turkey* App No 15318/89 (ECtHR, 18 December 1996), para 45.

[69] If the armed group in question does not possess a pre-existing international legal personality (arising from the application of treaty-based international law), the necessity-based application of international law will satisfy the 'actual possession' criterion thereby establishing the international legal personality of an independent armed group.

[70] The threshold for recognition as a de facto authority includes satisfaction of the capacity and independence criteria.

[71] See Ch 4 section I.

[72] See Ch 5 section II.

F. Application of the De Facto Control Theory to Entities Existing Below the De Facto Authority Threshold

The traditionally accepted threshold associated with de facto authorities is high,[73] typically requiring control of territory and some form of administration.[74] However, analysis of the justifications underpinning the extension of international regulation to de facto entities indicates that, under appropriate conditions, these factors are equally relevant with respect to non-state actors falling below this threshold. The application of international law to such non-state armed groups is premised on the existence of a legal vacuum. By existing independently of the territorial state, these entities have forced themselves onto the international plane, necessitating that their actions be regulated.

In this regard it is significant to recall that states have consistently refused to accept responsibility for the acts of insurgent entities ostensibly subject to their territorial jurisdiction, but in fact existing beyond their authority.[75] In the *Sambiaggio* arbitration it was held that states could not be held responsible for the acts of revolutionary entities, inter alia because '[t]he revolutionists are beyond governmental control, and the Government can not be held responsible for injuries committed by those who have escaped its restraint.'[76] Equally, as stated in *GL Solis (USA) v United Mexican States*: '[i]t is a well-established principle of international law that no government can be held responsible for the act of rebellious bodies of men committed in violation of its authority, where it is itself guilty of no breach of good faith, or of no negligence in suppressing insurrection.'[77] The principle of non-responsibility vis-à-vis the acts of insurgent entities 'rests upon the ground that the latter have withdrawn themselves by force of arms from the control and jurisdiction of the sovereign, putting it out of his power, so long as they make their resistance effectual, to extend this protection within the hostile territory to either strangers or his own subjects'.[78]

Equally, the law of state responsibility also specifies that all acts of an ultimately successful insurrectionary movement—ie from the moment of

[73] See eg above n 62, 207; *George W Hopkins (USA) v United Mexican States*, 31 March 1926, Reports of International Arbitral Awards, Vol IV, 45; 'Arbitration between Great Britain and Costa Rica, Opinion and Award of William H Taft, Sole Arbitrator' above n 4, 154.

[74] See eg Edwin M Borchard, 'The Unrecognized Government in American Courts' (1932) 26 *American Journal of International Law* 263. See also, *Thorington v Smith* (1868) 75 US 1, 9.

[75] See eg 'Fourth Report on State Responsibility, by Mr Robert Ago, Special Rapporteur—The internationally wrongful act of the State, source of international responsibility (continued)' (1972) *Yearbook of International Law Commission* Vol II, UN Doc A/Cn.4/264, 136; See also ibid, 132. See further, above Ch 5 section I.D.

[76] *Sambiaggio Case (of a general nature)* above n 53, 513.

[77] *GL Solis (USA) v United Mexican states*, above n 52, 361.

[78] *Sambiaggio Case (of a general nature)* above n 53, 513.

the insurrection's inception—are considered to be acts of state, capable of giving rise to international responsibility: '[t]he situation requires that acts committed during the struggle for power by the apparatus of the insurrectional movement should be attributable to the state, *alongside acts of the then established Government*.'[79] By accepting the existence of a parallel authority in this manner, the law of state responsibility accepts that international obligations can be directly imposed on a non-state armed group—including those existing below the de facto authority threshold—concurrent to the imposition of obligations on the territorial state.

That states will not, and cannot, be held responsible for the actions of de facto entities existing beyond their control confirms the necessity of directly subjecting the armed groups themselves to the rule of international law, so that they may be held to account and a legal vacuum avoided.[80] This principle was stated by the British Secretary of State for Foreign Affairs in 1861 with respect to an unrecognised de facto government: 'Her Majesty's Government hold it to be an undoubted principle of international law, that when the persons or the property of the subjects or citizens of a state are injured by a de facto government, the state so aggrieved has a right to claim from the de facto government redress and reparation.'[81] While the above examples relate to situations of conflict—withdrawing from the state's control and jurisdiction by force of arms—it is equally possible that non-state actors may establish an independent existence outside armed conflict; potential examples include Boko Haram in northern Nigeria prior to May 2013,[82] the Urabeños in Colombia,[83] various armed groups operating in Libya following the end of the armed conflict in 2011,[84] the Provisional Irish Republican Army ('IRA') in Northern Ireland during the

[79] Above n 16, 51. Emphasis added.

[80] See eg above n 16, 52.

[81] 'Fourth Report on State Responsibility, by Mr Robert Ago, Special Rapporteur—The internationally wrongful act of the State, source of international responsibility (continued)' (1972) *Yearbook of International Law Commission* Vol II, UN Doc A/Cn.4/264, 139. It is noted that this statement was made at a time when recognition of belligerency and the legal ramifications thereof enjoyed a prominent role in the international legal order.

[82] For instance, the Office of the Prosecutor of the International Common Court concluded that Boko Haram may have committed crimes against humanity in northern Nigeria, but (at the time) did not consider that the situation amounted to one of non-international armed conflict. International Criminal Court, Office of the Prosecutor, 'Report on Preliminary Examination Activities', November 2012, paras 89–90.

[83] International Criminal Court, The Office of the Prosecutor, 'Report on Preliminary Examination Activities' (2013) para 129.

[84] 'Report of the International Commission of Inquiry on Libya', UN Doc A/HRC/19/68, 8 March 2012, para 36.

1980s,[85] corporations which exert influence over the state in which they operate,[86] or drug gangs which run areas 'off limits' to state authorities.[87]

Of course, states are often reluctant to acknowledge the existence of an entity beyond their control, inter alia as they do not wish to acknowledge any limitations of their authority. However, if unrecognised entities are not acknowledged by international law this will result in an effective status superior to that of states. While states enjoy extensive freedom of action on the international plane, their actions remain constrained by the requirements of international law.[88] Unrecognised entities, on the other hand, are not subject to any international regulation, and as such are granted complete impunity and freedom of action, resulting in greater freedom of action than states. Accordingly, while states may perceive a political interest in leaving unrecognised entities unregulated, this may actually undermine both their own position on the international plane, as well as the effectiveness of international law.

It is concluded that armed groups existing below the threshold traditionally associated with de facto authorities may be bound consequent to the necessity-based application of international law. However, in order for international law to apply on this basis it is essential that the armed group fulfil two criteria: it must have the capacity to possess international obligations and it must exist independently.[89] The independence criterion is particularly significant as it is this factor which results in the existence of a legal vacuum, providing the justification for the application of the de facto control theory. It is recalled that if an entity is subject to the exclusive authority of another legal person it is the personality of the superior authority which is more appropriately relevant to the international legal order. As such, the 'classic'[90] definition of independence in the context of statehood—'the state has over it no other authority than that of international law'[91]—may be applied to non-state actors in general, and armed

[85] Although not recognised by the UK, it is generally accepted that a non-international armed conflict existed in Northern Ireland. However, the duration of this conflict is generally understood as limited to 1971–74. See Steven Haines, 'Northern Ireland' in Elizabeth Wilmshurst (ed), *International Law and the Classification of Conflicts* (Oxford, OUP, 2012) 124–27.

[86] David Smith, 'WikiLeaks cables: Shell's grip on Nigerian State revealed', *The Guardian* (London, 8 December 2010).

[87] Sven Peterke, 'Urban Insurgency, "Drug War" and International Humanitarian Law: The Case of Rio de Janeiro' (2010) 1 *International Humanitarian Legal Studies* 166.

[88] *Customs Regime between Germany and Austria (Protocol of March 19th, 1931)*, Separate Opinion of Judge Anzilotti, Permanent Court of International Justice, 5 September 1931, para 81.

[89] See further above Ch 2 section IV.

[90] James R Crawford, *The Creation of States in International Law*, 2nd edn (Oxford, OUP, 2006) 65.

[91] *Customs Regime between Germany and Austria (Protocol of March 19th, 1931)*, Separate Opinion of Judge Anzilotti, Permanent Court of International Justice, 5 September 1931, para 81.

opposition groups in particular. The means by which an armed group's independent existence may be established is discussed further below.[92]

II. LEGAL OBLIGATIONS ARISING CONSEQUENT TO THE DE FACTO CONTROL THEORY

Having established that non-state armed groups may be subject to international legal regulation on the basis of the de facto control theory, the specific law applicable must now be determined. This may also be determined in light of the de facto control theory, with respect both to groups directly bound by existing international treaty law and to groups initially bound on the basis of the de facto control theory itself. As customary international law applies to all international legal persons,[93] this body of law is clearly applicable: any form of international regulation will constitute active cognition of an entity, thereby fulfilling the actual possession criterion of international legal personality.[94]

However, the question also arises as to whether a non-state actor should be bound by other elements of international law, such as the international treaty obligations of the state in which it is active. The reasoning underpinning the application of the de facto control doctrine appears equally applicable when answering this question.[95] As this doctrine is premised on the displacement of state authority and a desire to avoid the resultant legal vacuum, it seems appropriate that armed groups also be bound by the international obligations of the displaced state, thereby ensuring consistency with respect to the application of international law. Similarly, if individuals enjoy specific treaty-based rights or protections vis-à-vis the state, it seems appropriate that these remain protected vis-à-vis an entity that has imposed its own authority in lieu of the state.[96]

In determining which treaty obligations of the displaced state will bind a non-state armed group, it is noted that certain treaties apply to a specific territory, and therefore remain applicable even in the event of state succession:[97] if these treaties are capable of binding a new state, they must

[92] See below Ch 5 section III.A.

[93] See above Ch 4 section I.

[94] It is recalled that the capacity to possess international rights or obligations and independence are prerequisite criteria with respect to the necessity-based application of international law.

[95] See above Ch 5 section I.

[96] The requirement that armed groups consent to be bound by such obligations has been discussed, and dismissed as not legally necessary. See above Ch 4 section III.B(iii).

[97] The concept of acquired rights is also relevant. See *Questions relating to Settlers of German Origin in Poland*, Advisory Opinion, Permanent Court of International Justice, 10 September 1923, para 86. See also, Anthony Cullen and Steven Wheatley, 'The Human Rights of Individuals in De Facto Regimes under the European Convention on Human Rights' (2013) 13 *Human Rights Law Review* 721–23.

also bind a non-state armed group.[98] For instance, localised treaties—relating to issues such as demilitarisation, transit, and the delimitation of boundaries—have a territory-specific application, and in order to ensure the preservation of international stability these treaties are not affected by state succession.[99] Article 12 of the Vienna Convention on Succession of States in respect of Treaties holds that state succession shall not affect: 'obligations relating to the use of any territory, or to restrictions upon its use, established by a treaty for the benefit of any territory of a foreign state and considered as attaching to the territories in question';[100] this principle is considered to form part of customary international law.[101]

International human rights law treaties are also regarded as establishing rules in relation to the population of a specific territory. In his Separate Opinion in *Application of the Genocide Convention*, Judge Shahabuddeen proposed that the humanitarian nature of a treaty, coupled with its object and purpose, supports a construction that would treat successor states as parties.[102] In this regard Cassese has identified the emergence of a general rule whereby a successor state remains bound by the international human rights law treaty obligations applicable to a territory:[103] 'what matters is that individuals should continue to be protected even after a change of sovereignty over a particular territory.'[104] In General Comment 26 the Human Rights Committee stated that:

> The rights enshrined in the Covenant belong to the people living in the territory of the State party. The Human Rights Committee has consistently taken the view, as evidenced by its long-standing practice, that once the people are accorded the protection of the rights under the Covenant, such protection devolves with territory and continues to belong to them, notwithstanding change in government of the State party, including dismemberment in more than one State or State succession or any subsequent action of the State party designed to divest them of the rights guaranteed by the Covenant.[105]

98 Concerns related to state sovereignty etc do not apply to non-state armed groups.

99 See generally *Brownlie's Principles of Public International Law* above n 21, 439–40; above n 41, 78.

100 Art 12, Vienna Convention on Succession of States in respect of Treaties (adopted 23 August 1978, entered into force 6 November 1996) 1946 UNTS 3.

101 *Case Concerning the Gabcikovo-Nagymaros Project (Hungary/Slovakia)*, Judgment, International Court of Justice, 25 September 1997, para 123.

102 *Application of the Convention on the Prevention and Punishment of the Crime of Genocide (Bosnia and Herzegovina v Serbia and Montenegro)*, Separate Opinion of Judge Shahabuddeen, Preliminary Objections, International Court of Justice, 11 July 1996, 43–46.

103 See further, 'Binding Armed Opposition Groups' above n 3, 379–80.

104 Above n 42, 79. However, according to Brownlie's, 'Recent state practice indicates that successor states will often accept human rights and arms control agreements of their predecessors, although this is arguably contingent on the successor state's consent rather than a rule of automatic succession.' *Brownlie's Principles of Public International Law* above n 21, 440.

105 Human Rights Committee, 'General Comment 26: Continuity of Obligations', UN Doc CCPR/C/21/Rev.1/Add.8/Rev.1, 12 August 1997, para 4.

Multilateral treaties similarly establish 'a comprehensive code of rules or standards for [a] particular subject-matter'[106] and on this basis are also regarded as remaining applicable in the event of state succession.[107] Accordingly, it seems appropriate that any non-state actor that has displaced the authority of the state should remain bound by that state's international treaty obligations in relation to multilateral treaties, localised treaties, and international human rights law treaties. This conclusion remains valid even if continuity with respect to international human rights law treaties is considered to be an option available to states and not an obligation.[108] In this regard two factors differentiate the situation with respect to states from that of non-state armed groups. First, as discussed previously, the *pacta tertiis* rule (requiring an expression of consent to be bound by an international obligation) is not applicable to non-state armed groups.[109] Second, certain international human rights law obligations are obligations *erga omnes*.[110] As such, and '[i]n view of the importance of the rights involved, all states can be held to have a legal interest in their protection'.[111] There is thus a pressing need to redress the legal vacuum generated in relation to these obligations consequent to the displacement of state authority. This legal imperative, and the inapplicability of the *pacta tertiis* rule, indicate that the international human rights law treaty obligations of the state must remain applicable, and must therefore bind the non-state armed group. Indeed, this is in the interests of both the affected population, whose rights will continue to be protected, and the international community as a whole, whose legal interest in the continued performance of the relevant international obligations is satisfied.

In this regard it is significant to refer by analogy to the law of belligerent occupation, which also involves the displacement of the territorial state's authority,[112] and similarly requires that 'the laws in force in the country' be respected.[113] The ICRC *Commentary* states that this provision enshrines a

[106] *Brownlie's Principles of Public International Law* above n 21, 440.

[107] Accordingly, it may be argued that armed groups should be bound by all applicable multilateral standard-setting conventions, such as those relating to the environment. See for example, DP O'Connell, *State succession in municipal law and international law* (Cambridge, CUP, 1967) 212–29.

[108] *Brownlie's Principles of Public International Law* above n 21, 440.

[109] See above Ch 4 section III.B.3.

[110] *Barcelona Traction, Light and Power Company, Limited*, Judgment, International Court of Justice, 5 February 1970, para 34. See further, *Juridical Condition and Rights of Undocumented Migrants*, Advisory Opinion, Inter-American Court of Human Rights, OC-18/03, 17 September 2003, para 109; Human Rights Committee, General Comment 31, 'The Nature of the General Legal Obligation Imposed on States Parties to the Covenant', UN Doc CCPR/C/21/Rev.1/Add.13, 26 May 2004, para 2.

[111] *Barcelona Traction, Light and Power Company, Limited*, above n 110, 33.

[112] The law of belligerent occupation is relevant herein as analogy, it is not proposed to apply occupation law direct to non-state armed groups.

[113] Art 43, Hague Regulations 1907. Art 64 of the Fourth Geneva Convention 1949 builds on this provision.

'basic principle' of occupation law, namely that 'the continuity of the legal system applies to the whole of the law (civil law and penal law) in the occupied territory.'[114] As with the motivation underpinning the implied mandate, these occupation law measures are established consequent to an obligation to ensure public order and 'social functions [and] ordinary transactions which constitute daily life',[115] so that the rights of the population are not affected by a change in governing authority.[116]

However, in the situations under consideration only a portion of the state's authority is displaced. As such, the state's continuing international legal personality must be acknowledged, and an armed group cannot assume all of the international treaty obligations binding the territorial state. For example, the territorial state will still be able to fulfil certain obligations, such as bilateral trade agreements, while equally it does not seem reasonable or appropriate to subject armed groups to certain other obligations of the state, such as those concerning political cooperation, intelligence sharing, research assistance, and so on.

To summarise, it is submitted that non-state entities that are bound by the de facto control theory must be bound by both the obligations arising under customary international law, and the international treaty law specifically applicable to the territory in question, such as international human rights law treaties. This conclusion is particularly significant, given the uncertainty surrounding the content of customary international law: the application of treaty law will result in much-needed clarity regarding the nature and extent of the non-state entity's obligations.[117] Of course, armed groups will also be bound by any directly applicable international treaty law, such as international humanitarian law if they are party to a non-international armed conflict. The circumstances under which a non-state armed group may establish an independent existence—generating the circumstances required for the application of the de facto control theory—must now be examined.

[114] Jean S Pictet (ed), *Commentary: IV Geneva Convention Relative to the Protection of Civilian Persons in Time of War* (Geneva, International Committee of the Red Cross, 1958) 335.

[115] Edmund Schwenk, 'Legislative Power of the Military Occupation Under Article 43, Hague Regulations' (1944–45) 54 *Yale Law Journal* 398. See Art 43 Hague Regulations; Yoram Dinstein, *The International Law of Belligerent Occupation* (Cambridge, CUP, 2009) 89.

[116] It is noted that debate exists as to whether the Occupying Power is bound by its own human rights obligations, or those of the occupied state. However, for present purposes it is noted that under current international law an armed group cannot become party to a human rights treaty, and therefore will not have an independent source of human rights obligations. See further Noam Lubell, 'Human rights obligations in military occupation' (2012) 94 *International Review of the Red Cross* 334–37.

[117] However, a non-state entity—such as an armed group or transnational corporation—may operate across state borders, possibly in the absence of a specific territory which can be considered to be its base of operations. In such instances, due to the fluidity of the situation, it may be difficult to determine what body of international treaty law to apply.

III. ESTABLISHING AN ARMED GROUP'S INDEPENDENT EXISTENCE

A non-state entity must be regarded as existing independently when the state cannot reasonably subject that entity to its will: at this point the authority of the state has been displaced and the non-state entity exists independently of any superior authority.[118] A state's ability to reasonably impose its will is defined as the ability to subject a non-state entity to state authority using the state's normal internal rule of law mechanisms, such as legislation, the police force, the judiciary, and so on.[119] Applying this definition, should an armed group seize control of a building in the capital city, taking a number of hostages, the armed group will have clearly moved beyond the immediate control of the state—as evidenced, inter alia, by the blatant violation of state law—and so the question is whether the state can reasonably impose its will. It is submitted that although the use of armed force may be necessary, the normal mechanisms of the state are nonetheless capable of responding to situations such as these, and so the state must be regarded as reasonably able to impose its will.[120] However, if an armed group establishes exclusive control over a territory and maintains this control despite efforts by the state to reclaim the territory, then the state must be regarded as unable to reasonably impose its will.[121] Equally, should a state's attempts to impose its authority on an armed group result in a situation of non-international armed conflict, this will clearly indicate a

[118] This requirement establishes that state authority must be actively displaced. It is not sufficient that a non-state actor assumes responsibilities of the state, if the state acquiesces to this role. For example, a state may allow customary or religious dispute resolution mechanisms or courts to operate as an alternative to the national judicial system. The question of whether a powerful transnational corporation can be regarded as existing beyond the state's ability to reasonably impose its will poses an interesting question. For example, a transnational corporation (TNC) may have offices in the capital city of the state, and be registered in accordance with the state's national law. However, it is possible that the financial power of the TNC may effectively preclude state efforts to impose its will, either because the state is concerned regarding potential loss of investment, employment, and so on, or as a result of corruption.

[119] A derogation under international human rights law may be indicative of a state's inability to reasonably impose its will, but in and of itself, this is not determinative. While resort to a derogation is exceptional, it nonetheless remains a legal tool available to the state.

[120] An example in this regard is the October 2002 takeover of the Dubrovka theatre in Moscow by Chechen separatists, which included the seizure of a large number of hostages. Although the separatists were heavily armed, and included 18 suicide bombers, the operation to retake the theatre was nonetheless conducted through the lens of a law enforcement operation. See *Finogenov and others v Russia* App Nos 18299/03 and 27311/03 (ECtHR, 20 December 2011).

[121] Examples in this regard might include the drug gangs exercising control over certain territory in Mexico, or the PKK in Turkey. See eg, 'Mexican vigilantes drive out religious drug carter from gang-held city', *The Guardian* (London, 9 February 2014); Ed Vulliamy, 'The Zetas: Gangster Kings of Their Own Brutal Narco-State', *The Guardian* (London, 14 November 2009); International Crisis Group, 'Turkey: Ending the PKK Insurgency' (2011).

state's inability to reasonably impose its will: the state's response will have moved beyond normal rule of law mechanisms, as evidenced by satisfaction of the intensity criterion.[122] It is possible that, owing to resource constraints or other factors, a state may not attempt to—or may not persist in attempting to—subject an armed group to its control. In this situation, the state must be regarded as unable to impose its will, and the armed group will have established an independent existence. This situation is, however, distinguished from one wherein the state delegates control to an armed group, in which case the group may not be regarded as independent.[123]

This test of an armed group's independent existence is based upon the traditional international law approach to insurgency, and the graded evolution from rebellion to insurgency and then belligerency.[124] Rebellion was regulated solely by the domestic legal system, ie the state was deemed capable of reasonably imposing its will, while insurgency and belligerency were subject to intervention by the international legal order.[125] Rebellion was regarded as a situation of internal violence involving either a sporadic challenge to state authority, or a short-lived insurrection which could be suppressed 'by normal procedures of internal security'.[126] The defining marker of rebellion was thus that the normal mechanisms of the state—notably the police force—could be utilised in order to induce the relevant entity to respect the domestic legal order.[127] It was only when the normal state mechanisms proved insufficient, for example, when sustained military intervention was required, that a situation would graduate from rebellion to insurgency necessitating some form of international regulation:[128]

> [W]hen the insurrection became so widespread that it *could not be contained by the state's civil administration*, then it was customary … for the government and foreign states 'to make an admission of insurgency'. This 'was an acknowledg-

[122] See above Ch 3 section III.A.

[123] 'Since the 13 April 2007 peace agreement, the government, aware of its army's weakness, has authorised the [UFDR] rebel group to maintain security in both Vakaga and Haute-Kotto prefectures.' International Crisis Group, 'Central African Republic: Keeping the Dialogue Alive' (Report) (2010) 13.

[124] See eg Richard Falk, 'Janus Tormented: The International Law of Internal War' in James N Rosenau (ed), *International Aspects of Civil Strife* (Princeton NJ, Princeton University Press, 1964) 197.

[125] See eg Heather A Wilson, *International Law and the Use of Force by National Liberation Movements* (Oxford, Clarendon Press, 1988) 23. See further, Sandesh Sivakumaran, *The Law of Non-International Armed Conflict* (Oxford, OUP, 2012) 9–10; above n 41, 124–31.

[126] Above n 124, 197. See also, *The Law of Non-International Armed Conflict* above n 125, 9.

[127] See eg Rogier Bartels, 'Timelines, borderlines and conflicts: The historical evolution of the legal divide between international and non-international armed conflicts' (2009) 91 *International Review of the Red Cross* 48–49. See also above n 124, 197.

[128] See eg above n 124, 197.

> ment of the fact that an organized uprising for political ends involving the use of armed force *and temporarily beyond the control of the civil authorities'* was taking place.[129]

The contemporary law of non-international armed conflict evidences a similar approach, whereby international legal intervention is necessitated on the basis of a state's inability to resolve a situation by recourse to normal law enforcement mechanisms. As with states of rebellion, situations of internal disturbances and tensions are today deemed to fall below the threshold of application for non-international armed conflict,[130] and so are not subject to explicit international regulation.[131] The ICRC considers such situations to be characterised by recourse to the police forces—potentially supported by the armed forces—to restore law and order.[132] During the Article 3 drafting process states held that the common Article 3 threshold 'did not include "a mere riot or disturbances caused by bandits", situations of "disorder, anarchy or brigandage", an "uprising", or "mere strife".'[133] As such, it has been stated that when determining the common Article 3 threshold of application, inter alia, a 'point to be considered is whether the legally constituted government has been compelled to have recourse to the regular armed forces'.[134] Similarly, during the Additional Protocol II drafting process the Netherlands stated that the:

> [D]raft Protocol II would not be applicable in situations of conflict that were being dealt with by police forces using normal police methods and equipment, but that it would become applicable as soon as the authorities were forced to seek substantial assistance from military units or to hand full responsibility for dealing with the conflict over to the armed forces.[135]

[129] Hilaire McCoubrey and Nigel D White, *International Organizations and Civil Wars* (Aldershot, Dartmouth, 1995) 6. Emphasis added.

[130] See eg *The Law of Non-International Armed Conflict* above n 125, 162.

[131] Of course, such situations remain regulated by the 'normal' international obligations of the state, such as those arising under international human rights law.

[132] See Yves Sandov, Christophe Swinarski and Brun Zimmermann (eds), *Commentary on the Additional Protocols of 8 June 1977 to the Geneva Conventions of 12 August 1949* (The Hague, Martinus Nijhoff, 1987) paras 4475–78. As internal disturbances are considered to be a step below non-international armed conflict it is noted that at the higher end of the internal disturbance spectrum armed forces approximate to that consistent with the non-international armed conflict intensity criterion may be deployed.

[133] See *The Law of Non-International Armed Conflict* above n 125, 162, referring to the Report of the Joint Committee to the Plenary of the Assembly, France, Norway and various unnamed delegations respectively.

[134] David A Elder, 'The Historical Background of Common Article 3 to the Geneva Conventions of 1949' (1979) 11 *Case Western Reserve Journal of International Law* 52. See also, GIAD Draper, *The Red Cross Conventions* (London, Stevens & Sons, 1958) 15–16.

[135] Official Records of the Diplomatic Conference on the Reaffirmation and Development of International Humanitarian Law Applicable in Armed Conflicts (Geneva 1974–1977), Vol VIII, 222, para 39 (Netherlands). However, as noted above armed forces may be used in situations of internal disturbance and tension, and so 'while a useful indicia, use of the armed forces cannot be determinative'. *The Law of Non-International Armed Conflict* above n 125, 169.

Indeed, the very existence of a non-international armed conflict 'presupposes that a certain set of men have gone temporarily or permanently beyond the power of the authorities'.[136] The legal reality of this independence is confirmed in the law of state responsibility which holds that the state is not responsible for the acts of insurgents,[137] and by the fact that an armed group party to a non-international armed conflict exists as a separate subject of international law.[138] Accordingly, it is concluded that international regulation is required when a state cannot reasonably impose its will on a non-state entity. In such situations, the entity in question must be regarded as having established an independent existence: it is not subject to the exclusive authority of any superior entity.

A state's inability to reasonably impose its authority may be demonstrated in one of two ways. First, when a non-state entity becomes party to a non-international armed conflict and second, outside armed conflict, when a non-state entity displaces state authority.[139]

Before proceeding, however, two issues must be addressed. First, it must be clarified that it is the displacement of state authority—effectively withdrawing from the state's control and jurisdiction—that is at issue and not merely the evasion of state authority. An evasion of state authority occurs when the state has the potential to reasonably impose its will, but is temporarily unable to do so. For example, if an armed group commits a series of robberies and then goes 'on the run', it may be said that they are evading—and not displacing—state authority. The state can reasonably impose its will using the normal mechanisms of the state, but these mechanisms have yet to catch up with the group: once this occurs, the gang will be dealt with using the state's normal procedures, such as extradition, arrest, prosecution, and so on. Indeed, such evasion is an inevitable component of any rule of law system. This situation is distinct from one whereby the state attempts to subject a group to its authority, but cannot reasonably do so. For example, in Mexico the state attempted to bring

[136] *Sambiaggio Case (of a general nature)* above n 53, 513.

[137] In addition to those sources referred to above in Ch 4 section III.B(ii), see 'Fourth Report on State Responsibility, by Mr Robert Ago, Special Rapporteur—The internationally wrongful act of the State, source of international responsibility (continued)' (1972) *Yearbook of International Law Commission* Vol II, UN Doc A/Cn.4/264, para 162.

[138] ibid, 129.

[139] It is highlighted that, outside armed conflict, the displacement of state authority may nonetheless occur in the context of violence. For instance, an armed group may have displaced state authority during a non-international armed conflict which has subsided (this may be the case with respect to the Tuareg region of northern Mali), the displacement of state authority may occur in the context of a weakened state (this may be the case with respect to certain armed groups active in Libya following the end of the 2011 armed conflict), or displacement may have evolved over time (perhaps in the context of criminality) resulting in a situation where the state's attempt to impose its authority is met with violence. This may be the case, for example, in relation to certain favelas in Rio de Janeiro, or perhaps the Tivoli Gardens in Kingston, Jamaica.

areas subject to the control of a number of different drug gangs back under its control and deployed significant military resources to achieve this aim. Despite these efforts, however, the state was unable to effectively impose its authority on a number of these groups.[140]

Second, an armed group cannot be considered independent if a third state is responsible for the conduct of the armed group. The International Court of Justice has established that this situation occurs when the relationship between the armed group and the third state is one of 'complete dependence'.[141] In this situation the armed group is not considered to be an independent entity, but is instead regarded as a de facto organ of the third state. However, this situation must be distinguished from one where a third state exercises effective control over certain acts of the armed group, such that the third state is internationally responsible for those acts. In this scenario the armed group maintains an independent existence vis-à-vis its other activities—at least partially—and is not considered to be an organ of the third state.[142] Accordingly, an armed group may be considered independent as long as it is not completely dependent on a third state.

A. Establishing an Armed Group's Independent Existence Outside Armed Conflict

Turning to the displacement of state authority in situations outside non-international armed conflict, it is recalled that 'effective government' is a central criterion of independence with respect to the establishment of statehood, and that in this regard international law defines territory by reference to the extent of government power exercised, or capable of being exercised, with respect to a specific territory and population.[143] Reflecting this understanding, the ICRC Commentary to Additional Protocol II negatively defines territory 'controlled' by an armed group as 'that which escapes the control of the government armed forces'.[144] Accordingly, it is submitted that when an armed group displaces a state's ability to exercise

[140] See Nick Miroff and William Booth, 'Mexico's drug war is, a stalemate as Calderon's presidency ends', *Washington Post* (Washington, 27 November 2012); 'Q&A: Mexico's drug-related violence', *BBC News* (London, 25 November 2013).

[141] *Case Concerning Military and Paramilitary Activities in and Against Nicaragua (Nicaragua v United States of America)*, Merits, Judgment, International Court of Justice, 27 June 1986, paras 109–10; *Case Concerning Application of the Convention on the Prevention and Punishment of the Crime of Genocide (Bosnia and Herzegovina v Serbia and Montenegro)*, above n 102, para 392.

[142] *Case Concerning Application of the Convention on the Prevention and Punishment of the Crime of Genocide (Bosnia and Herzegovina v Serbia and Montenegro)*, above n 102, para 393.

[143] Above n 92, 56.

[144] Above n 134, para 1353. See also *Prosecutor v Jean-Paul Akayesu*, Judgment, Trial Chamber, International Criminal Tribunal for Rwanda, 2 September 1998, para 626.

effective governmental authority, it must be regarded as having established an independent existence. This displacement of state authority most clearly occurs when an armed group exercises control over a territory or population.[145]

Determining whether an armed group exerts a level of control sufficient to establish an independent existence is relatively straightforward when a group exerts stable territorial control,[146] to the effective exclusion of state armed forces.[147] For example, in India the Naxalites have established de facto control over certain districts and, despite the deployment of significant resources, the state has been unable to reasonably impose its will.[148] Similarly, although at a less comprehensive level of control, in the first half of 2013 Boko Haram seized control of at least 10 local government districts and displaced state authority in Borno state in northern Nigeria.[149] The state's inability to reasonably impose its will is demonstrated by the fact that the May 2013 offensive intended to displace Boko Haram necessitated the involvement of 'several thousand' members of the armed forces supported by fighter jets and helicopter gunships.[150]

[145] States are widely regarded as being subject to extraterritorial human rights obligations when exercising effective control over a territory. See by analogy, *Case Concerning Armed Activities on the Territory of the Congo (Democratic Republic of the Congo v Uganda)*, Judgment, International Court of Justice, 19 December 2005, paras 216–20, *Loizidou v Turkey*, above n 68.

[146] Control over territory alone is insufficient to warrant international regulation. For example, an armed group may control a remote uninhabited area of the state. This situation will remain a domestic issue—the armed group is not engaging in any acts of international concern—unless the group violates international law (for example through environmental destruction) thereby necessitating international intervention. Of course, this situation changes if the territory is inhabited, as the armed group then constitutes the relevant authority with respect to the inhabitants internationally protected rights. See further below Ch 5 section III.A(i).

[147] See eg *The Law of Non-International Armed Conflict* above n 125, 187.

[148] 'The government has deployed thousands of federal paramilitary police, such as the Central Reserve Police Force (CRPF) and the Border Security Force (BSF), to support state police forces. It has resisted calls to deploy the army, although the army has provided training in guerrilla warfare to these forces. In 2008 the government created the Commando Battalions for Resolute Action ("COBRA"). COBRA consists of 10 battalions (approximately 10,000 troops) of special forces trained and equipped for counterinsurgency and jungle-warfare operations. It operates as part of the CRPF.' Human Rights Watch, 'Between Two Sets of Guns: Attacks on Civil Society Activists in India's Maoist Conflict' (2012) 14.

[149] Nigerian President Goodluck Jonathan is reported as stating in May 2103 that Boko Haram had 'taken over' parts of north-eastern Nigeria; see 'Nigeria begins offensive against Islamist sect', *France 24* (Paris, 17 May 2013). See also, '"Massive" troop deployment in Nigeria', *Al Jazeera English* (Doha, 16 May 2013). Indicative of the absence of state authority, in villages subject to their control, Boko Haram replaced the Nigerian flag with the group's black flag, see Will Ross, 'Nigeria's army gunning for Boko Haram', *BBC News* (London, 7 June 2013).

[150] 'Nigerian forces target Boko Haram strongholds', *Al Jazeera English* (Doha, 17 May 2013). It is noted that this offensive may haver marked the transition to non-international armed conflict. See also, International Criminal Court, The Office of the Prosecutor, 'Report on Preliminary Examination Activities' (2013) para 218.

Other contemporary examples include the control exercised by drug cartels—such as the Knights Templar—over certain areas of Mexico.[151]

However, determining the independent existence of an armed group exercising less established, or indeed less traditional, levels of control is more difficult, particularly as the control exerted by armed groups may take a number of markedly different forms. For instance, in Nepal the state exerted control over certain areas by day while the CPN-M ruled by night,[152] while in southern Thailand the BRN-C (National Revolution Front-Coordinate) exerted control over the local population—and conducted armed patrols—without exercising stable territorial control.[153] In Rio de Janeiro, gangs such as the Red Command or the Third Pure Command exert exclusive control over a significant number of the city's shantytowns, or favelas,[154] and armed gang members patrol the streets.[155] It is reported that the control exercised by these groups 'has stabilised to such levels that it is not even challenged by the State',[156] and that: '[t]he state is almost completely absent in the favelas. The drug gangs impose their own system of justice, law and order, and taxation—all by force of arms.'[157] Similarly, in Northern Ireland the IRA engaged in 'community policing'—including the execution of suspected collaborators[158]—and

[151] 'Mexican vigilantes drive out religious drug carter from gang-held city', *The Guardian* (Manchester, 9 February 2014).

[152] 'The RNA [Nepalese armed forces] could take most positions by day, and the Maoists could return, night. "Control" is a relative term in the many remote areas where there is little administration to assume.' International Crisis Group, 'Nepal Backgrounder: Ceasefire—Soft Landing or Strategic Pause?' (2003) 13.

[153] '… they [*pejuang kemerdekaan patani*] now control everything in this area. Sometimes you can even see their patrol units—armed with AK-47s—going around the village in broad daylight. Many village chiefs have been put in power with their consent and served as their puppets.' Witness interview, Human Rights Watch, 'No One is Safe: Insurgent Attacks on Civilians in Thailand's Southern Border Provinces' (2007) 21.

[154] For example, it is reported that in 2005 'the Red Command were thought to control more than half of Rio de Janeiro's most violent areas, though this fell to under 40 percent by 2008'. See 'Red Command' *InSight Crime*, www.insightcrime.org/groups-brazil/comando-vermelho.

[155] 'Visible expression of the drug factions' takeover are the so-called "soldiers"—children and teenagers who, equipped with AK-47, M-16 and grenades, patrol through housing structures.' Above n 87, 166.

[156] Above n 87, 166.

[157] Jon Lee Anderson, 'Gangland: Who controls the streets of Rio de Janeiro', *The New Yorker* (New York, 5 October 2009) 50. State access to favelas is sporadic, and only possible through reliance on militarised means involving armoured vehicles and ironclad helicopters. While equally, it is noted that despite being subject to a number of outstanding arrest warrants, Fernandinho—a leader of the Third Pure Command—'lives openly in Morro de Dende, essentially hiding in plain sight', see Jon Lee Anderson, 'Gangland: Who controls the streets of Rio de Janeiro', *The New Yorker* (New York, 5 October 2009) 49.

[158] Kevin Toolis, 'Informer: The Life and Death of an I.R.A. Man', *New York Times* (New York, 3 February 1991).

were turned to by the local community for dispute resolution, despite the fact that British forces exerted effective control over the territory.[159] In these situations, although the armed groups exert an—often significant—level of control, it is unclear whether this is sufficient to constitute the effective displacement of state authority.

In order to address these varied forms of control, and to determine whether the level of control exercised is sufficient to displace state authority, it is appropriate that the concept of control be interpreted in a flexible manner. Continuous exclusive control over a territory or population—although decisive—should not be the sole indicator with respect to the displacement of state authority. Rather, an armed group's ability to exercise control to the exclusion of the state must also be regarded as relevant. In this regard it is the activity made possible by the exercise of control, and not the precise contours of the control itself, that is determinative.[160] Indeed, from an individual's perspective it is the armed group's ability to act that has a decisive impact on their lives: returning to the 'state by day, armed group by night' example, the fact that the state is present during the day is not the only relevant factor; equally critical is the armed group's ability to return and exert influence by night.

Accordingly, it is submitted that in uncertain situations—ie situations outside armed conflict where control over a territory or population is exercised but is not exclusive—the displacement of state authority may be demonstrated by the ability to conduct certain activity in relation to that territory or population, coupled with the state's inability to reasonably impose its will. Of course, this activity must warrant international regulation, and it is submitted that the commission of internationally prohibited acts satisfies this requirement.[161] By violating prohibitions of international concern, in the absence of an effective superior authority capable of ensuring the armed group's respect for international law, an armed group contributes to the generation of a legal vacuum. In such circumstances, the armed group forces itself onto the international plane, justifying the

[159] See generally, Steven Haines, 'Northern Ireland' in Elizabeth Wilmshurst (ed), *International Law and the Classification of Conflicts* (Oxford, OUP, 2012).

[160] Reference may be made to the territorial control requirement specified in Art I Additional Protocol II which may be interpreted in a qualitative manner, dependent upon the activity made possible by the control exercised. See *The Law of Non-International Armed Conflict* above n 125, 186. See also, Sylvie Junod, 'Additional Protocol II: History and Scope' (1984) 33 *American University Law Review* 37; *Prosecutor v Akayesu*, Judgment, Trial Chamber, International Criminal Tribunal for Rwanda, Case No ICTR-96-4-T, 2 September 1998, para 626.

[161] The phrase 'violations of international law' is deliberately not used here as, this point, armed groups are not subject to obligations under international law and therefore cannot commit violations as such; issue, however, are certain acts which would be regarded as violations of international law if committed by a state.

application of international law in accordance with the de facto control theory.[162]

(i) Control Over a Territory or Population Demonstrated by the Ability to Commit Certain Acts

The specific internationally prohibited acts capable of giving rise to the application of the de facto control theory must be determined. It is submitted that such acts must be of concern to the international community as a whole, and must therefore be distinguished from acts of primarily domestic concern, such as individual instances of theft, fraud, or murder.[163] Two principal categories of acts may be identified: crimes against humanity (which can be committed outside armed conflict) and violations of obligations *erga omnes*. Crimes against humanity are recognised as international crimes,[164] while obligations *erga omnes* are obligations owed to the international community as a whole,[165] and '[i]n view of the importance of the rights involved, all states can be held to have a legal interest in their protection'.[166] When the state is unable to ensure respect for international law in relation to these prohibitions, the international legal order must intervene and subject the armed group themselves to direct international regulation.[167] Indeed, Cassese notes that a right to ensure obligations *erga omnes* may be exercised 'on behalf of the international community'[168] in order to 'safeguard fundamental values of that community'.[169]

With respect to the specific content of *erga omnes* obligations, in *Barcelona Traction* the International Court of Justice specified that such obligations include the prohibition of acts of aggression and genocide, as well as obligations derived 'from the principles and rules concerning the basic rights of the human person, including protection from slavery and racial discrimination.'[170] Subsequent opinions of the Court have confirmed the

[162] See above Ch 5 section I.

[163] These acts may also constitute violations of international human rights law. For instance, murder is a crime under domestic law and a violation of the right to life. The precise circumstances in which acts of murder may give rise to international legal intervention are discussed further below.

[164] See eg, Art 7, Statute of the International Criminal Court.

[165] See above n 16, 33.

[166] *Barcelona Traction, Light and Power Company, Limited*, above n 110, para 33.

[167] The Draft Articles on State Responsibility for Internationally Wrongful Acts require that States shall 'cooperate to bring to an end through lawful means' (Art 41) any serious breach 'of an obligation arising under a peremptory norm of international law' (Art 40).

[168] Above n 41, 16. Emphasis in original omitted.

[169] ibid, 16. Emphasis in original omitted.

[170] *Barcelona Traction, Light and Power Company, Limited*, above n 110, para 34.

erga omnes nature of obligations relating to the prohibition of genocide,[171] respect for the right to self-determination,[172] and relevant obligations determined by international humanitarian law.[173] With respect to human rights in particular, the Human Rights Committee has stated that, with respect to:

> the obligations of States Parties towards individuals as the right-holders under the Covenant, every State Party has a legal interest in the performance by every other State Party of its obligations. This follows from the fact that the 'rules concerning the basic rights of the human person' are *erga omnes* obligations and that, as indicated in the fourth preambular paragraph of the Covenant, there is a United Nations Charter obligation to promote universal respect for, and observance of, human rights and fundamental freedoms.[174]

Similarly, the Inter-American Court of Human Rights has noted that the 'general obligation to respect and ensure the exercise of rights has an *erga omnes* character'.[175] The International Tribunal for the Law of the Sea has also held that 'obligations relating to preservation of the environment of the high seas'[176] are *erga omnes* in character. Those obligations *erga omnes* most relevant for present purposes are likely to be the obligations arising under international human rights law, and obligations related to the protection of the environment. The precise scope of those international human rights law obligations constituting *erga omnes* obligations is unclear. However, it is suggested that these obligations should be regarded as including, as a minimum, those contained in the International Covenant on Civil and Political Rights and the International Covenant on Economic, Social and Cultural Rights.

In order to necessitate international legal intervention, it is necessary to distinguish acts warranting international intervention from acts which—although they infringe upon human rights protections—are more appropriately of domestic concern. In this regard it is perhaps appropriate that the commission of internationally prohibited acts occur on a large-scale

[171] *Case Concerning Application of the Convention on the Prevention and Punishment of the Crime of Genocide (Bosnia and Herzegovina v Yugoslavia)*, Preliminary Objections, International Court of Justice, 11 July 1996, para 31.

[172] *Case Concerning East Timor (Portugal v Australia)*, Judgment, International Court of Justice, 30 June 1995, para 29.

[173] *Legal Consequences for States of the Continued Presence of South Africa in Namibia (South West Africa) Notwithstanding Security Council Resolution 276 (1970)*, above n 37, para 199

[174] General Comment 31 above n 110, para 2. See also, Art 1, International Law Institute, 'The Protection of Human Rights and the Principle of Non-Intervention in Internal Affairs of States' (1989) 63 *Institut de Droit International Annuaire* 338. Cassese notes that this Resolution authoritatively restates and spells out existing customary laws, above n 41, 17, fn 3.

[175] *Juridical Condition and Rights of Undocumented Migrants*, above n 110, para 109.

[176] *Responsibilities and Obligations of States Sponsoring Persons and Entities with respect to Activities in the Area*, Advisory Opinion, Seabed Disputes Chamber of the International Tribunal for the Law of the Sea, Case No 17, 1 February 2011, para 180.

basis. This threshold is proximate to the 'widespread' requirement associated with crimes against humanity,[177] although the underlying elements are distinct. For instance, while the crime against humanity of persecution involves 'the intentional and severe deprivation of fundamental rights contrary to international law',[178] this must be perpetrated on the basis 'of the identity of the group or collectivity'.[179] However, it is submitted that in order to implicate the de facto control theory, the large-scale violation of individuals' human rights alone is sufficient, ie irrespective of persecutory intent.

In determining whether state authority has been displaced, the time-scale associated with the commission of internationally prohibited acts (ie their protracted nature) is also relevant. A one-off incident cannot be regarded as a conclusive indicator of a state's inability to reasonably impose its will. However, should such acts extend over time, the state's inability to effectively bring the situation under control would indicate that its authority has been displaced. An entity's protracted commission of internationally prohibited acts to which the state is unable to respond clearly calls into question the state's ability to govern effectively, indicating that the armed group responsible for the acts exists independently, beyond state control. In evaluating this temporal requirement, analogy may be made to the requirement of 'protracted armed violence' associated with the non-international armed conflict threshold of application.[180] While this criterion is primarily understood as relating to the intensity of the violence,[181] the *Boskoski* Trial Chamber has noted that 'care is needed not to lose sight of the requirement of protracted armed violence in the case of an internal armed conflict, when assessing the intensity of the conflict',[182] and that this requirement 'adds a temporal element to the definition of armed conflict.'[183] Similarly, the *Kordic* Appeals Chamber held that '[t]he requirement of protracted fighting is significant in excluding mere cases of civil unrest or *single acts* of terrorism',[184] while the Statute of the International

[177] Art 7(1), Statute of the International Criminal Court.

[178] ibid, Art 7(2)(g).

[179] ibid, Art 7(2)(g).

[180] *Prosecutor v Tadic*, Decision on the Defence Motion for Interlocutory Appeal on Jurisdiction, Appeals Chamber, International Criminal Tribunal for the former Yugoslavia, 2 October 1995, para 70.

[181] See eg *Prosecutor v Haradinaj*, Judgment, Trial Chamber, International Criminal Tribunal for the former Yugoslavia, Case No IT-04-84-T, 3 April 2008, para 49; Dapo Akande, 'Classification of Armed Conflicts: Relevant Legal Concepts' in Elizabeth Wilmshurst (ed), *International Law and the Classification of Conflicts* (Oxford, OUP, 2012) 52–54; *The Law of Non-International Armed Conflict* above n 125, 167–70.

[182] *Prosecutor v Boskoski & Tarculovski*, Judgment, Trial Chamber, International Criminal Tribunal for the former Yugoslavia, Case No IT-04-82-T, 10 July 2008, para 175.

[183] ibid, para 186.

[184] Emphasis added.

Criminal Court specifies that non-international armed conflict does not include 'internal disturbances and tensions, such as riots, isolated and sporadic acts of violence or other acts of a similar nature.'[185] Significantly, the protracted element does not 'require that hostilities be carried out in a sustained or continuous manner'[186] and so this criterion must be understood in relation to the entire period of hostilities.[187] For present purposes, given the focus on establishing a non-state entity's independent existence, the temporal element must play a key role:[188] it demonstrates a state's inability to subject an armed group to its authority.[189]

However, while the protracted commission of internationally prohibited acts is indicative vis-à-vis a state's inability to reasonably impose its will, it is not necessarily decisive: at issue is the distinction between evasion and displacement of state authority referred to above. It is possible that an individual or entity may commit internationally prohibited acts and subsequently evade the authority of the state; this is a possibility inherent in any rule of law system, and does not necessarily necessitate international intervention. For instance, it is foreseeable that a group, such as a 'hit squad' associated with a drug gang, might consistently carry out murders (implicating the right to life) over a protracted period of time. Typically, however, the state will retain the ability to reasonably subject that group to its authority using the normal mechanisms of the state; in such a situation the group would more appropriately be considered as evading state authority (being on the run) rather than displacing state authority.

The question is, at what point does the situation move beyond evasion of state authority to constitute the displacement of that authority? There is no easy answer to this question. It is recalled, however, that the commission of internationally prohibited acts is regarded as indicative of control over

[185] Art 8(2)(d), Statute of the International Criminal Court.

[186] Anthony Cullen, *The Concept of Non-International Armed Conflict in International Humanitarian Law* (Cambridge, CUP, 2010) 128.

[187] Of course, this timeframe cannot be stretched beyond that which is reasonable, and while continuous acts may not be required they must be temporally related. See by analogy, Noam Lubell, *Extraterritorial Use of Force Against Non-State Actors* (Oxford, OUP, 2010) 112–21.

[188] This is distinct from the question of the application of international humanitarian law. See ibid, 105–06.

[189] It is recalled that a single incident cannot be decisive with respect to the displacement of state authority, and that as such, determining the displacement of state authority on the basis of the protracted commission of violations is distinguished from the intensity criterion associated with the non-international armed conflict threshold which may be satisfied consequent to the commission of a single large-scale incident. Equally, while a lag in the classification of a situation as one of non-international armed conflict may be problematic, this concern is not as pressing herein as an entity will inevitably take time to establish an independent existence. It is possible that responsibility could apply retroactively once independence is established, similar to the case of an insurgent group assuming control of a state. See Draft Articles on State Responsibility for Internationally Wrongful Acts, UNGA Res A/56/49(Vol.1)/Corr.4, Art 10(1).

a territory or population, and not demonstrative of independence in and of itself. This evaluation will therefore be applied to situations wherein an armed group exercises elements of control over a territory or population, but it is unclear whether this control displaces the authority of the state to an extent necessitating international intervention.[190] For instance, should the hit squad referred to above operate from an area that is 'off-limits' to the state,[191] and it is this factor which facilitates the continued commission of internationally prohibited acts, then this may indicate that the state cannot reasonably impose its will. Similar to the question of statehood,[192] or satisfaction of the criteria associated with the non-international armed conflict threshold,[193] this question will ultimately have to be decided on a case-by-case basis with reference to the facts and circumstances particular to each individual situation.[194]

To summarise, an armed group may demonstrate its independent existence through the effective displacement of state authority. This requirement will be satisfied should an armed group become a party to a non-international armed conflict. Outside armed conflict, an armed group may demonstrate the displacement of state authority—and thus the establishment of an independent existence—through the exercise of control over a territory or population. This is most clearly demonstrated through the exercise of exclusive territorial control. In less certain situations where control is exercised but is not exclusive, an independent existence may be demonstrated by the commission of internationally prohibited acts coupled with the state's inability to reasonably impose its will. Factors relevant in this regard include: whether the acts were committed on a large-scale basis, the temporal frame of the armed group's activity, and the exercise of elements of 'traditional' control over either territory or a population.

[190] The examples given above are recalled, see Ch 5 section III.A.

[191] A pertinent example may be the *favelas* in Rio de Janeiro referred to above. See above n 87, 166.

[192] See above Ch 3 section I.

[193] See eg 'Classification of Armed Conflicts: Relevant Legal Concepts' above n 181, 50; Jelena Pejic, 'Status of Armed Conflicts' in Elizabeth Wilmshurst and Susan Breau (eds), *Perspectives on the ICRC Study on Customary International Humanitarian Law* (Cambridge, CUP, 2007) 85; 'Official Records of the Diplomatic Conference on the Reaffirmation and Development of International Humanitarian Law Applicable in Armed Conflicts (Geneva 1974–1977)' Vol VIII, 230.

[194] The motivation of the non-state entity is irrelevant: it is the factual situation that is decisive. See eg *Prosecutor v Boskoski & Tarculovski*, above n 182, para 185. See also, 'Classification of Armed Conflicts: Relevant Legal Concepts' above n 181, 52; Sylvain Vite, 'Typology of armed conflicts in international humanitarian law: legal concepts and actual situations' (2009) 91 *International Review of the Red Cross* 78.

IV. CONCLUSION: INDEPENDENT ARMED GROUPS AS A VERTICAL AUTHORITY

This chapter has established that non-state armed groups may be subject to international regulation on the basis of the de facto control theory. This conclusion is significant in that international law is applied in response to the factual reality of a particular situation. Accordingly, the de facto control theory establishes that non-state armed groups may be bound by international law in the absence of direct international treaty regulation. The application of international law on this basis satisfies the 'actual possession' criterion necessary for international legal personality.[195]

The de facto control theory may also be used to determine the extent of the applicable international law, in relation both to groups with a pre-existing international legal personality and groups whose legal personality is established consequent to the de facto control theory itself. In addition to being bound by customary international law,[196] and any directly applicable international law, an armed group will also be bound by the law specifically applicable to the territory or population in question. This law may include localised treaties, international environmental law, or international human rights law.[197]

Importantly, by making the attribution of international law dependent upon the displacement of state authority, the de facto control theory treats the non-state armed group in question as a vertical authority. In doing so the established hierarchy of international legal regulation is maintained. At issue is not an innovative approach to the legal regulation of non-state actors, but rather a modification of the traditional vertical means of application in response to the reality of the situation. Importantly, as the rights and obligations contained in the relevant international treaties will continue to be applied in their intended manner, this construction may circumvent potential *ratione personae* restrictions: the specific circumstances of the situation at hand necessitates that the entity addressed by the law is different, but this entity fulfils the role anticipated by the drafters, and exerts similar elements of control and authority.[198] In this regard it is significant that when adopting the UN Declaration against Torture, the General

[195] Satisfaction of the independence criterion is a prerequisite for application of the de facto control theory, and armed groups must also satisfy the capacity criterion, demonstrated by the existence of a responsible command. See above Ch 3 section III.C.

[196] On the basis of their international legal personality.

[197] The application of these bodies of law, and potential *ratione personae* restrictions are discussed over the coming paragraphs, and further in Ch 6 section III.

[198] For instance, the Islamic State is estimated as expending resources at a level proximate to that of the Iraqi government before it was displaced. Richard Barrett, 'The Islamic State', The Soufan Group, November 2014, 46.

Assembly noted that the Declaration constituted a 'guideline for all States *and other entities exercising effective power.*'[199] As highlighted by Rodley:

> The emphasized words capture precisely the spirit of both the conceptual scope of human rights and the rationale behind the international law approach to them. It conveys the reality of the human rights equation: the individual at the mercy of a government *or of another power over whose actions the government is impotent*.[200]

In *Elmi v Australia* the Committee against Torture held that a non-state actor—in this case one of the warring factions in Somalia—should be regarded as a vertical authority, in light of the specific circumstances of the situation, which included the absence of a central government, and the factions' establishment of quasi-governmental institutions. The Committee concluded that: 'the members of those factions can fall, for the purposes of the application of the Convention, within the phrase "public officials or other persons acting in an official capacity" contained in article 1.'[201] Similarly, in *R v Zardad*—a case involving the prosecution of a member of a non-state armed group for acts of torture—the Court held that:

> [W]hat needs to be looked at is the reality of any particular situation. Is there sufficient evidence that Hezb-I-Islami had a sufficient degree of organisation, a sufficient degree of actual control of an area and that it exercised the type of functions which a government or governmental organisation would exercise? It seems to me that I have to take care not to impose Western ideas of an appropriate structure for government, but to be sensitive to the fact that in countries such as Afghanistan different types of structure may exist, but which may legitimately come within the ambit of an authority which wields power sufficient to constitute an official body.[202]

The appropriateness of considering an armed group that cannot be reasonably subject to the authority of the state as a vertical authority is underlined by reference to *Thorington v Smith*.[203] Here, the US Supreme Court confirmed that the reality of a situation may require that individuals subject to the authority of an armed group obey that authority. In the case at hand the court held that the effective control exercised by the armed group 'made obedience to its authority, in civil and local matters,

[199] UN General Assembly Resolution 3452 (XXX), 9 December 1975. Emphasis added.

[200] Nigel S Rodley, 'Can Armed Opposition Groups Violate Human Rights?' in Kathleen E Mahoney and Paul Mahoney (eds), *Human Rights in the Twenty-first Century: A Global Challenge* (The Hague, Martinus Nijhoff Publishers, 1993) 313. Emphasis added. It is noted that the emphasised text reflects the requirement that the state be unable to reasonably impose its will, as elaborated upon above in Ch 5 section III.

[201] *Sadiq Shek Elmi v Australia*, Committee against Torture, Communication No 120/1998, UN Doc CAT/C/22/D/120/1998, 14 May 1999, para 6.5.

[202] *R v Zardad*, Central Criminal Court, Case No T22037676, 7 April 2004, para 33. Emphasis added.

[203] *Thorington v Smith* above n 74, 1.

not only a necessity but a duty. Without such obedience, civil order was impossible.'[204] Accordingly, armed groups who exercise control over an area or population, in circumstances under which the state cannot reasonably impose its will, should be regarded as a vertical authority.[205] Such groups need not engage in government-like functions;[206] rather, it is the ability to exert unregulated authority which necessitates international regulation.

To allow armed groups to exert unregulated authority undermines the effectiveness of the rule of international law, and, in effect, strips the affected individuals of their internationally recognised rights, depriving them of even the minimum rights to which they are entitled.[207] Returning to the justifications underpinning the implied mandate doctrine, there would appear to be no reasonable basis for precluding the doctrines' application to non-state armed groups who fail to qualify as de facto regimes, but who nonetheless exercise control over a territory or population. Life continues for the affected individuals regardless of the nature of the entity to whose authority they are subject.[208] By subjecting armed groups to the requirements of international law the international legal order can respond to the demands of international life through the articulation of clear standards regulating the conduct of such armed groups, in the interests of the civilian population subject to their authority.[209] Indeed, this eventuality appears to have been anticipated to a certain extent by the European Court of Human Rights:

> In certain circumstances, a court belonging to the judicial system of an entity not recognised under international law may be regarded as a tribunal 'established by law' provided that it forms part of a judicial system operating on a 'constitutional and legal basis' reflecting a judicial tradition compatible with the Convention, *in order to enable individuals to enjoy the Convention guarantees*[210]

While understandably controversial vis-à-vis any traditional understanding of the state-centric international system, recent developments in international law—and in particular the recognition of non-state international legal persons and the emergence of international human rights law—mean

[204] ibid, 10–11. Emphasis added.

[205] See eg, *Prosecutor v Delalic, Mucic, Delic and Landzo*, Appeals Chamber, International Criminal Tribunal for the former Yugoslavia, Case No IT-96-21-A, 20 February 2001, para 193.

[206] Indeed, such a requirement could facilitate armed group circumvention of responsibility were they to ignore the needs of the population subject to their control.

[207] *Cyprus v Turkey*, above n 14, para 96.

[208] See *Horn v Lockhart* above n 66, 581.

[209] See above, Ch 5 section II.

[210] *Ilascu and Others v Moldova and Russia*, Judgment, European Court of Human Rights, Application No 48787/99, 8 July 2004, para 460. Emphasis added.

that international law is now capable of responding to the changed reality of international life. The proposed approach acknowledges this changed reality, in order to facilitate the effective regulation of the modern international order. The fact that non-state armed groups are subject to international regulation will necessarily result in the validation of certain of their acts. This is necessitated by the factual situation and is not equivalent to validating the armed group itself.[211] Having established that non-state armed groups may be bound by certain international treaty obligations of the territorial state including, in principle, international human rights law, the potential application of this body of law to non-state armed groups must now be addressed.

[211] See eg *Re Manitoba Language Rights*, above n 17, para 80; *Cyprus v Turkey*, above n 14, para 92.

Part II

Can Armed Groups be Bound by International Human Rights Law?

6

The Application of International Human Rights Law to Armed Groups

HAVING ESTABLISHED THAT international human rights law can in principle apply to non-state armed groups consequent to the de facto control theory, the possibility that the application of this body of law may be restricted *ratione personae* must be addressed. It is widely accepted that international human rights law treaties exclusively regulate the relationship between states and the individuals subject to their jurisdiction.[1] At the time of their drafting this construction was appropriate, as it accurately reflected the most effective means of protecting human rights in practice. This is not the case today. Armed groups, and non-state actors generally, exert increasing influence over individuals and civilian populations, often to the exclusion of state authority.[2] It does not seem reasonable that affected individuals should be denied the protections of international human rights law solely because the entity to whose authority they are subject is not a state.

This conclusion is particularly pertinent given human rights' foundation in the inherent dignity of the human person.[3] A focus on human rights as an expression of human dignity was evident during the drafting

[1] Nigel S Rodley, 'Can Armed Opposition Groups Violate Human Rights?' in Kathleen E Mahoney and Paul Mahoney (eds), *Human Rights in the Twenty-first Century: A Global Challenge* (The Hague, Martinus Nijhoff Publishers, 1993) 308. See further, language utilised in Art 2(1) International Covenant on Civil and Political Rights; Art 2(1) International Covenant on Economic, Social and Cultural Rights; Art 1 European Convention on Human Rights; Art 2(1) Convention on the Rights of the Child (adopted 20 November 1989, entered into force 2 September 1990) 1577 UNTS 3.

[2] See, further above Ch 1 section I. See also, Celia Wells and Juanita Elias, 'Catching the Conscience of the King: Corporate Players on the International Stage' in Philip Alston (ed), *Non-State Actors and Human Rights* (Oxford, OUP, 2005) 147.

[3] See further, Andrew Clapham, *Human Rights Obligations of Non-State Actors* (Oxford, OUP, 2006) 533–48; Chris Jochnick, 'Confronting the Impunity of Non-State Actors: New Fields for the Promotion of Human Rights' (1999) 21 *Human Rights Quarterly* 60–61; Christopher McCrudden, 'Human Dignity and Judicial Interpretation of Human Rights' (2008) 19 *European Journal of International Law* 669.

of the Universal Declaration of Human Rights.[4] The draft preamble prepared by the United Kingdom stated that: '[t]he Declaration of Human Rights sets forth the rights and freedoms which are essential to the highest expression of human dignity',[5] while similarly the first proposal submitted by the Committee of the Preamble recognised 'in the following solemn Declaration the rights and freedoms which, being essential for the dignity and worth of the human person, should form a common standard of achievement for all nations'.[6] The final text of the Universal Declaration of Human Rights notes that 'recognition of the inherent dignity and of the equal and inalienable rights of all members of the human family is the foundation of freedom, justice and peace in the world',[7] while Article 1 affirms that '[a]ll human beings are born free and equal in dignity and rights.'[8] This sentiment is reflected in both the International Covenant on Civil and Political Rights, and the International Covenant on Economic, Social and Cultural Rights, which 'recognize' that the rights enshrined in the Covenants 'derive from the inherent dignity of the human person.'[9] Similarly, in 1993, the Vienna Declaration and Programme of Action adopted by the World Conference on Human Rights recognised and affirmed 'that all human rights derive from the dignity and worth inherent in the human person'.[10] Emphasising the centrality of dignity, the Trial Chamber of the International Criminal Tribunal for the former Yugoslavia held that:

> It is unquestionable that the prohibition of acts constituting outrages upon personal dignity safeguards an important value. Indeed, it is difficult to conceive of a more important value than that of respect for human personality. It can be said that the entire edifice of international human rights law, and of the evolution of international humanitarian law, rests on this founding principle.[11]

[4] See, 'Summary of the Fiftieth Meeting', Commission on Human Rights, Third Session, UN Doc E/CN.4/SR.50, 4 June 1948; 'Report of the Credentials Committee', 139th Plenary Meeting, UN Doc A/PV.139, 23 September 1948.

[5] UK Draft Preamble to the International Declaration of Human Rights, E/CN.4/124. See also, 'Lebanon: Suggested Preamble for the Draft International Declaration on Human Rights', Commission on Human Rights, Third Session, UN Doc E/CN.4/132, 14 June 1949.

[6] 'Committee on the Preamble', Commission on Human Rights, Third Session, UN Doc E/CN.4/138, 15 June 1948.

[7] Preamble, para 1, Universal Declaration of Human Rights.

[8] Art 1, Universal Declaration of Human Rights. See also, General Assembly Resolution 290 (IV) 'Essentials of Peace', 1 December 1949.

[9] Preamble, para 3, International Covenant on Civil and Political Rights; Preamble, para 3, International Covenant on Economic, Social and Cultural Rights. For further references to dignity in international human rights law treaties see, inter alia, the Convention Against Torture and Other Cruel, Inhuman or Degrading Treatment or Punishment and the Convention on the Rights of the Child.

[10] Vienna Declaration and Programme of Action, adopted by the World Conference on Human Rights, Vienna, 25 June 1993, Preamble.

[11] *Prosecutor v Zlatko Aleksovski*, Judgment, Trial Chamber, International Criminal Tribunal for the former Yugoslavia, Case No IT-95-14/1-T, 25 June 1999, para 54. See also, *Prosecutor v*

In this light, establishing a distinction between state and non-state armed group authorities in relation to the attribution of human rights obligations purely on the basis of their distinct status seems inconsistent with the motivation underpinning human rights protection:[12]

> Once one accepts the proposition that human rights are ultimately concerned with the protection of human dignity and that assaults on that dignity have to be prevented, remedied, and punished, there is little room left for arguments about the state or non-state character of the assailant.[13]

Indeed, the Inter-American Court of Human Rights has held that the attributes inherent to an individual's human dignity 'make them possessors of fundamental rights that may not be disregarded and which are, consequently, superior to the power of the State'.[14] Accordingly, in order to ensure the effectiveness of human rights protection it is not only appropriate but necessary that international human rights law regulates the relationship between individuals and the authority to which they are subject, in this instance armed groups.[15] The alternative is not only the negation of individuals' rights, but also the acceptance of a legal vacuum. Today, this proposition enjoys increasing support.[16] For example, a number of UN bodies have held that certain armed groups are bound by international human rights law,[17] while a number of states also appear to have endorsed this position, 'at least when the conflict has been taking place for a certain duration and reached a certain intensity.'[18] However, the legal basis underpinning the application of international human rights

Furundzija, Judgment, Trial Chamber, International Criminal Tribunal for the former Yugoslavia, Case No IT-95-17/1-T, 10 December 1998, para 183.

[12] Referring to discussion on para 2 to the preamble of the ICCPR, in the Commission on Human Rights see MJ Bossuyt, *Guide to the 'Travaux Preparatoires' of the International Covenant on Civil and Political Rights* (The Hague, Martinus Nijhoff, 1987) 6. See further, Antonio Cassese, *International Law*, 2nd edn (Oxford, OUP, 2005) 397.

[13] *Human Rights Obligations of Non-State Actors* above n 3, 534.

[14] *Juridical Condition and Rights of Undocumented Migrants*, Advisory Opinion, Inter-American Court of Human Rights, OC-18/03, 17 September 2003, para 73; 'Human Dignity and Judicial Interpretation of Human Rights' above n 3, 677.

[15] In this regard the classification of an armed group as a vertical authority is recalled. See above, Ch 5 section IV.

[16] See generally, *Human Rights Obligations of Non-State Actors* above n 3; Philip Alston (ed), *Non-State Actors and Human Rights* (Oxford, OUP, 2005).

[17] See, for example, 'Report of the Secretary-General's Panel of Experts on Accountability in Sri Lanka', 31 March 2011, para 188; 'Report of the International Commission of Inquiry to investigate all alleged violations of international human rights law in the Libyan Arab Jamahiriya', UN Doc A/HRC/17/44, 1 June 2011, para 72; 'Report of the independent international commission of inquiry on the Syrian Arab Republic', UN Doc A/HRC/22/59, 5 February 2013.

[18] Sandesh Sivakumaran, *The Law of Non-International Armed Conflict* (Oxford, OUP, 2012) 97. In this regard Sivakumaran refers to El Salvador, Guatemala, Liberia, Nepal, Papua New Guinea, the Philippines, Sierra Leone and Sudan.

law to armed opposition groups—or other non-state actors—has not been effectively established. Before proceeding further, however, the possibility that certain international human rights law treaties establish direct obligations vis-à-vis armed groups must be addressed.

I. INTERNATIONAL HUMAN RIGHTS LAW TREATIES THAT DIRECTLY ADDRESS ARMED GROUPS

It has been suggested that certain international human rights law treaties directly bind non-state armed groups.[19] Reference in this regard may be made to the Optional Protocol to the Convention on the Rights of the Child on the involvement of children in armed conflict,[20] the African Union Convention for the Protection and Assistance of Internally Displaced Persons in Africa (Kampala Convention),[21] and—to a lesser extent—the International Convention for the Protection of All Persons from Enforced Disappearance.[22]

Article 4(1) of the Optional Protocol to the Convention on the Rights of the Child states that: '[a]rmed groups that are distinct from the armed forces of a State should not, under any circumstances, recruit or use in hostilities persons under the age of 18 years.' Debate exists as to whether this provision subjects armed groups to direct obligations under international law. Typically, when used in UN treaties, the word 'shall' is used to denote a binding obligation, while the word 'should' denotes a recommendation, or 'soft-law' provision.[23] In this regard it is significant that the provisions of the Optional Protocol addressed to states use the word 'shall'. However, Clapham argues that the inclusion of the phrase '*under any circumstances*' clearly indicates that the drafters intended to create a binding obligation, allowing no exception. In this sense, 'should' may be interpreted as referring to an obligation imposed on a third party, ie entities—such as armed groups—not involved in the treaty-making

[19] See, Andrew Clapham, 'Focusing on Armed Non-State Actors' in Andrew Clapham and Paola Gaeta (eds), *The Oxford Handbook of International Law in Armed Conflict* (Oxford, OUP, 2014) 790–92; *Human Rights Obligations of Non-State Actors* above n 3, 75.

[20] Optional Protocol to the Convention on the Rights of the Child on the involvement of children in armed conflict (adopted 25 May 2000, entered into force 12 February 2002) 2173 UNTS 222.

[21] African Union Convention for the Protection and Assistance of Internally Displaced Persons in Africa (Kampala Convention) (adopted 23 October 2009, entered into force 6 December 2012).

[22] International Convention for the Protection of All Persons from Enforced Disappearance (adopted 20 December 2006, entered into force 23 December 2010) 2716 UNTS 3.

[23] Paul C Szasz, 'General Law Making Processes' in Christopher C Joyner (ed), *The United Nations and International Law* (Cambridge, CUP/ASIL, 1997) 32–33.

process.[24] On this reading, the Optional Protocol may be interpreted as establishing direct obligations vis-à-vis armed groups.

The Kampala Convention is less ambiguous. Article 2(e) states that one of the objectives of the Convention is to '[p]rovide for the respective obligations, responsibilities and roles of armed groups, non-state actors and other relevant actors, including civil society organizations, with respect to the prevention of internal displacement and protection of, and assistance to, internally displaced persons'. In this regard, Article 7(5) states that armed groups are prohibited from:

(a) Carrying out arbitrary displacement;
(b) Hampering the provision of protection and assistance to internally displaced persons under any circumstances;
(c) Denying internally displaced persons the right to live in satisfactory conditions of dignity, security, sanitation, food, water, health and shelter; and separating members of the same family;
(d) Restriction the freedom of movement of internally displaced persons within and outside their areas of residence;
(e) Recruiting children or requiring or permitting them to take part in hostilities under any circumstances;
(f) Forcibly recruiting persons, kidnapping, abduction or hostage taking, engaging in sexual slavery and trafficking in persons especially women and children;
(g) Impeding humanitarian assistance and passage of all relief consignments, equipment and personnel to internally displaced persons;
(h) Attacking or otherwise harming humanitarian personnel and resources or other materials deployed for the assistance or benefit of internally displaced persons and shall not destroy, confiscate or divert such materials, and
(i) Violating the civilian and humanitarian character of the places where internally displaced persons are sheltered and shall not infiltrate such places.

The drafters' intent to bind armed groups seems clear.[25]

The International Convention for the Protection of All Persons from Enforced Disappearance does not create direct obligations for armed groups. Rather, Article 3 requires states to 'take appropriate measures to investigate acts defined in article 2 [enforced disappearances by state agents] committed by persons or groups of persons acting without the authorization, support or acquiescence of the State and to bring those responsible to justice.' Interestingly, Clapham notes that the accountability provisions contained in Articles 30 and 31 are not limited to enforced disappearances carried out by state agents, and the 'Committee could therefore find itself

[24] *Human Rights Obligations of Non-State Actors* above n 3, 75.
[25] Art 1(e) of the Convention defines armed groups as: 'dissident armed forces or other organized armed groups that are distinct from the armed forces of the state.'

dealing with complaints concerning "a disappeared person" where the principal perpetrators were members of an armed group.'[26] However, while the Committee may find itself investigating the activities of armed groups, the text of the Convention appears to indicate that it will be the state's response to this activity that concerns the Committee.[27]

It is accepted that international human rights law treaties can directly bind armed groups, and the legal basis underpinning this application is discussed in detail in Chapter 4. Indeed, the Kampala Convention is a clear example in this regard. However, although important, the obligations established by existing treaties are exceedingly narrow, even if the Optional Protocol to the Convention on the Rights of the Child is included. As such, these treaties, and the obligations they establish, are of relatively limited relevance to the vast majority of individuals affected by the activities of armed groups. They do not address the legal vacuum created by the displacement of state authority and they do not provide for the protection of affected individuals' essential human rights. Accordingly, it must be established whether the broader provisions of international human rights law—as established in the core international human rights law treaties, for example—can apply to armed groups.

II. THE *DRITTWIRKUNG* AND HORIZONTAL EFFECT THEORIES

The *Drittwirkung*[28] ('third-party effect') and horizontal effect[29] theories provide a legal basis for the regulation of both the relationship between the state and the individual (the traditional vertical effect), and the relationship between individuals themselves (the horizontal, or third-party effect).[30] In *Juridical Condition and Rights of Undocumented Migrants* the

[26] 'Focusing on Armed Non-State Actors' above n 19, 791.

[27] However, it is emphasised that, as argued in this monograph, certain armed groups may be directly bound by international human rights law, and may, accordingly, be subject to the prohibition of enforced disappearances in their own right.

[28] '*Drittwirkung* is taken to mean that provisions apply not only between the State and the individual but also in the legal relations between private parties.' Nicola Jagers, *Corporate Human Rights Obligations: in Search of Accountability* (Cambridge, Intersentia, 2002) 37.

[29] The vertical and horizontal theories 'refer to whether constitutional rights regulate only the conduct of governmental actors in their dealings with private individuals (vertical) or also relations between private individuals (horizontal).' Stephen Gardbaum, 'The "Horizontal Effect" of Constitutional Rights' (2003–2004) 102 *Michigan Law Review* 388.

[30] This refers to both legal and natural persons. See further, Andrew Clapham, 'The "Drittwirkung" of the Convention' in RStJ Macdonald, F Matscher and H Petzold (eds), *The European System for the Protection of Human Rights* (The Hague, Martinus Nijhoff, 1993); Andrew Drzemczewski, 'The European Human Rights Convention and Relations between Private Parties' (1979) 26 *Netherlands International Law Review*; above n 28, 36–40; John H Knox, 'Horizontal Human Rights Law' (2008) 102 *American Journal of International Law*.

Inter-American Court of Human Rights referred to the *Drittwirkung* theory:

> [T]he obligation to respect human rights between individuals should be taken into consideration. That is, the positive obligation of the State to ensure the effectiveness of the protected human rights gives rise to effects in relation to third parties (erga omnes). This obligation has been developed in legal writings, and particularly by the Drittwirkung theory, according to which fundamental rights must be respected by both the public authorities and by individuals with regard to other individuals.[31]

On this basis the Court concluded that 'the obligation to respect and ensure human rights, which normally has effects on the relations between the State and the individuals subject to its jurisdiction, also has effects on relations between individuals.'[32] It is reported that this approach has been adopted 'to varying degrees … in Ireland, Canada, Germany, South Africa, and the European Union'.[33] However, the *Drittwirkung* and horizontal effect theories apply to traditional and normally functioning national structures, with the state at the apex.[34] For instance, it has been noted that the European Convention on Human Rights may create indirect obligations for individuals, 'in that it may oblige the legislature or the courts to protect individuals from one another'.[35] Thus, while private persons may have human rights obligations vis-à-vis other private persons, these are regulated by the state and addressed before state courts.[36]

The context considered herein is significantly different: armed opposition groups, by their very nature, exist beyond the effective control of the state, and the nature of the relationship between armed groups and the individuals subject to their influence is substantively different than that typically considered under the *Drittwirkung* and horizontal effects theories.[37] Armed opposition groups occupy a position of authority vis-à-vis the individuals subject to their influence, and are themselves beyond

[31] *Juridical Condition and Rights of Undocumented Migrants*, above n 14, para 140.

[32] *ibid*, para 146.

[33] Above n 29, 388.

[34] See, eg August Reinisch, 'The Changing International Legal Framework for Dealing with Non-State Actors' in Philip Alston (ed), *Non-State Actors and Human Rights* (Oxford, OUP, 2005) 70.

[35] 'The European Human Rights Convention and Relations between Private Parties' above n 30, 176.

[36] See above n 28, 37. In this sense, the horizontal effects theory may be considered as an extension of the obligation to protect. See Ida Elisabeth Koch, 'Dichotomies, Trichotomies or Waves of Duties?' (2005) 5 *Human Rights Law Review* 94.

[37] For example, the horizontal effects theory may addresses issues such as the application of human rights law to an individual's claim of privacy versus a magazine's freedom of expression. See, *Douglas v Northern and Shell Plc* [2000] EWCA Civ 353, paras 129, 133, 137.

the authority of the state.[38] In such situations of unregulated influence what is at issue is not the horizontal effect of human rights obligations, but the vertical effect: the armed group is in a position of vertical authority and the traditional authority structure is maintained.[39]

III. OVERCOMING *RATIONE PERSONAE* RESTRICTIONS

The drafters of international human rights treaties such as the International Covenant on Civil and Political Rights and the International Covenant on Economic, Social, and Cultural Rights explicitly sought to bind states, regulating the relationship between states and the individuals subject to their jurisdiction.[40] This is clear from the text of the relevant treaties. For example, Article 2 of the International Covenant on Civil and Political Rights states that: '[*e*]*ach State Party* to the present Covenant undertakes to respect and to ensure to all individuals within its territory and subject to its jurisdiction the rights recognized in the present Covenant', while Article 2 of the International Covenant on Economic, Social and Cultural Rights similarly addresses '[*e*]*ach State Party*'.[41] When interpreting the application of these treaties, the law on treaty interpretation requires that '[a] treaty shall be interpreted in good faith in accordance with the ordinary meaning to be given to the terms of the treaty in their context and in the light of its object and purpose.'[42] Prima facie, it would thus appear that the application of international human rights law treaties is restricted, *ratione personae*, to states. In this regard it is noted that, at the time of drafting, states were the dominant actors of concern on the international plane, both from the perspective of international law and in relation to the reality of international affairs.

In the intervening years, however, global changes have significantly altered the international reality.[43] This situation—wherein the reality of the international context changes subsequent to the adoption of a specific treaty—is not uncommon, and in such circumstances the need for reinterpretation of the relevant international treaty has been acknowledged in international case law. In the *Reparations* Advisory Opinion, the International Court of Justice noted that '[t]hroughout its history, the development of international law has been influenced by the requirements of

[38] Thus rendering it impractical—if not impossible—to bring a claim against the armed group before the domestic courts of the state.
[39] See above Ch 5 section IV.
[40] 'Can Armed Opposition Groups Violate Human Rights?' above n 1, 308.
[41] Emphasis added.
[42] Art 31(1) Vienna Convention on the Law of Treaties.
[43] See, for instance, above Ch 1 section V.

international life'.[44] The Court accordingly confirmed that although not explicitly specified in the Charter, in order for the UN to achieve its goals, 'the attribution of international personality is indispensable.'[45] The Court further recognised certain implied powers of the United Nations, despite the fact that these powers were not explicitly specified in the international treaty establishing the organisation's competence: '[u]nder international law, the Organization must be deemed to have those powers which, though not expressly provided in the Charter, are conferred upon it by necessary implication as being essential to the performance of its duties.'[46] In *Legal Consequences for States of the Continued Presence of South Africa in Namibia (South West Africa) Notwithstanding Security Council Resolution 276 (1970)*, the Court applied this evolutionary principle specifically to treaty interpretation:[47]

> Mindful as it is of the primary necessity of interpreting an instrument in accordance with the intentions of the parties at the time of its conclusion, the Court is bound to take into account the fact that the concepts embodied in Article 22 of the Covenant—'the strenuous conditions of the modern world' and 'the well-being and development' of the peoples concerned—were not static, but were by definition evolutionary, as also, therefore, was the concept of the 'sacred trust'.[48]

The Court thus held that, when viewing the institutions of 1919, it was required to:

> [T]ake into consideration the changes which have occurred in the supervening half-century, and its interpretation cannot remain unaffected by the subsequent development of law, through the Charter of the United Nations and by way of customary law. Moreover, an international instrument has to be interpreted and applied within the framework of the entire legal system prevailing at the time of the interpretation.[49]

[44] *Reparations for injuries suffered in the services of the United Nations*, Advisory Opinion, International Court of Justice, 11 April 1949, 178

[45] ibid, 178

[46] ibid, 182–83.

[47] This case involved a discussion of the mandate system established by Art 22 of the Covenant of the League of Nations. Art 22(1) states that: 'To those colonies and territories which as a consequence of the late war have ceased to be under the sovereignty of the States which formerly governed them and which are inhabited by peoples not yet able to stand by themselves under the strenuous conditions of the modern world, there should be applied the principle that the well-being and development of such peoples form a sacred trust of civilisation and that securities for the performance of this trust should be embodied in this Covenant.'

[48] *Legal Consequences for States of the Continued Presence of South Africa in Namibia (South West Africa) Notwithstanding Security Council Resolution 276 (1970)*, Advisory Opinion, International Court of Justice, 21 June 1971, para 53.

[49] ibid, para 53.

It is this approach which is applied: the relevant international human rights law treaties are interpreted and applied in light of the reality of the contemporary international legal order.[50] As such, the importance attributed to protecting individuals' rights in the contemporary international legal system,[51] and the fact that international human rights law obligations are now recognised as constituting obligations *erga omnes*, must be acknowledged.[52] That said, it is acknowledged that treaty interpretation must be subject to limits: a treaty cannot be interpreted beyond breaking point. However, this is not at issue herein. As noted, a radical rethink of international human rights law is not proposed. Rather, international human rights law is applied consequent to the existence of a legal vacuum and binds entities filling the role of a vertical authority. In such circumstances, the effectiveness of international law, and the effective protection of individuals' human rights, demands that the authority of an armed group be recognised and regulated. Importantly, the treaties are applied both in the same vertical manner envisioned by the drafters, and for the same purpose, namely the regulation of the relationship between individuals and the authority to which they are subject.

IV. REMAINING CONSISTENT WITH THE 'OBJECT AND PURPOSE' OF HUMAN RIGHTS TREATIES

The application of international human rights law on this basis is consistent with the 'object and purpose' of international human rights law treaties.[53] These treaties establish direct international rights vis-à-vis individuals,[54] and it is the nature of these rights which gives rise to a 'special characteristic', differentiating human rights treaties from other international instruments.[55] In this regard it is recalled that obligations arising under international human rights law are considered to be obligations *erga*

[50] See eg *Yakye Aza v Paraguay*, Judgment, Inter-American Court of Human Rights, 17 June 2005, para 125.

[51] See for example, *Juridical Condition and Rights of Undocumented Migrants*, above n 14, para 73.

[52] This is discussed further above in Ch 5 section III.A(i) and below in Ch 6 section IV.

[53] See Art 31(1), Vienna Convention on the Law of Treaties.

[54] Confirming the possibility that international treaties may create direct international rights, see *LaGrand (Germany v United States of America)*, Judgment, International Court of Justice, 27 June 2001, para 77.

[55] See, eg, *Loizidou v Turkey* App No 15318/89 (ECtHR, 18 December 1996), para 43; *Behrami and Behrmai v France, Saramati v France, Germany and Norway* App Nos 71412/01, 78166/01 (ECtHR, 2 May 2007), para 122.

omnes.[56] As discussed above,[57] the special nature of human rights law treaties has been underlined by the Human Rights Committee when interpreting the International Covenant on Civil and Political Rights: '[t]he rights enshrined in the Covenant belong to the people living in the territory of the State party.'[58] These rights are considered to be invested in the population and to devolve with the territory, and the Human Rights Committee has held that they may override the established non-transmission rule associated with international treaties and a change in sovereignty.[59] The International Court of Justice has also addressed the distinct nature of 'humanitarian' treaties,[60] holding that such treaties are objective and not contractual in nature. Referring to the Genocide Convention, the Court held that:

> In such a convention the contracting States do not have any interests of their own; they merely have, one and all, a common interest, namely, the accomplishment of those high purposes which are the *raison d'etre* of the convention. Consequently, in a convention of this type one cannot speak of individual advantages or disadvantages to States, or of the maintenance of a perfect contractual balance between rights and duties. The high ideals which inspired the Convention provide, by virtue of the common will of the parties, the foundation and measure of all its provisions.[61]

The Inter-American Court of Human Rights reached a similar conclusion, holding that the object and purpose of human rights treaties 'is the protection of the basic rights of individual human beings'.[62] Accordingly, states are held to 'submit themselves to a legal order within which they, for the common good, assume various obligations, not in relation to other States, but towards all individuals within their jurisdiction.'[63] Similar findings have been made by the European Commission of Human Rights,[64] and the European Court of Human Rights.[65]

[56] See, discussion above Ch 5 section III.A(i).

[57] See, above Ch 1 section V.

[58] Human Rights Committee, General Comment 26, 'Continuity of Obligations', UN Doc CCPR/C/21/Rev.1/Add.8/Rev.1, 12 August 1997, para 4. See further, *Guide to the 'Travaux Preparatoires' of the International Covenant on Civil and Political Rights* above n 12, 6.

[59] General Comment 26, above n 58, para 4. See further, James Crawford, *Brownlie's Principles of Public International Law*, 8th edn (Oxford, OUP, 2012) 440.

[60] The phrase 'humanitarian treaties' is understood as referring to international human rights law and international humanitarian law treaties.

[61] *Reservations to the Convention on the Prevention and Punishment of the Crime of Genocide*, Advisory Opinion, International Court of Justice, 28 May 1951, p 23.

[62] *The Effect of Reservations on the Entry Into Force of the American Convention on Human Rights (Arts 74 and 75)*, Advisory Opinion, Inter-American Court of Human Rights, 24 September 1982, para 29.

[63] ibid, para 29.

[64] *Austria v Italy* App No 788/60 (ECtHR, 11 January 1961), para 19.

[65] *Blecic v Croatia* App No 59532/00 (ECtHR, 8 March 2006), para 90.

The importance attributed to international human rights law treaties necessitates that they be applied in all situations: they are intended to protect the individual.[66] In keeping with their object and purpose, it seems appropriate that international human rights law treaties be interpreted so as to allow their continued application when the authority of the state has been displaced by that of a non-state armed group. As stated by the European Court of Human Rights, 'the object and purpose of the Convention as an instrument for the protection of individual human beings requires that its provisions be interpreted and applied so as to make its safeguards practical and effective.'[67] The alternative is the negation of individuals' 'inalienable' human rights, and the perpetuation of a legal vacuum to which international law is incapable of effectively responding.

V. INTERNATIONAL HUMAN RIGHTS LAW AND THE IMPLIED MANDATE

Today, the application of international human rights law must be regarded as a central component of the implied mandate, as understood in the context of the de facto control theory. It is recalled that the acts of a de facto entity will be treated as valid if undertaken in the best interests of the individuals subject to the de facto authority.[68] Today there exists overwhelming international support regarding the fundamental importance of human rights to the international order.[69] For example, paragraph 4 of the Vienna Declaration and Programme of Action,[70] which was endorsed without a vote by the UN General Assembly,[71] states that:

> The promotion and protection of all human rights and fundamental freedoms must be considered as a priority objective of the United Nations in accordance with its purposes and principles, in particular the purpose of international

[66] See further, *Demopoulos and others v Turkey* App Nos 46113.99, 3843/02, 13751/02, 13466/03, 10200/04, 14163/04, 19993/04, 21819/04 (ECtHR, 1 March 2010), para 96.

[67] *Loizidou v Turkey (Preliminary Objections)* App No 15318/89 (ECtHR, 23 March 1995), para 70. See further, *Ilhan v Turkey* App No 22277/93 (ECtHR, 27 June 2000), para 73; *McCann and Others v United Kingdom* App No 18984/91 (ECtHR, 27 September 1995), para 146.

[68] See, eg, *Texas v White* (1869) 74 US 700, 733; *Legal Consequences for States of the Continued Presence of South Africa in Namibia (South West Africa) Notwithstanding Security Council Resolution 276 (1970)*, above n 48, para 125. See further, above Ch 5 section I.E.

[69] See, in general, 'Characteristics of International Human Rights Law' in *Human Rights Obligations of Non-State Actors* above n 3, 85–108.

[70] Vienna Declaration and Programme of Action, adopted by the World Conference on Human Rights, Vienna, 25 June 1993.

[71] A/Res/48/121, UN General Assembly, 14 February 1994, para 2.

> cooperation. In the framework of these purposes and principles, the promotion and protection of all human rights is a legitimate concern of the international community.[72]

Applying the standard elaborated by the International Court of Justice: to deprive individuals subject to the authority of a de facto entity of the protections of international human rights law would unequivocally be 'to the detriment of the inhabitants of the [t]erritory.'[73] Equally, if certain acts of a de facto entity are to be recognised as valid under international law, the acts of that entity must be subject to international recognition. With respect to those acts that impact upon individuals this regulation must include international human rights law. In this regard the European Court of Human Rights noted that:

> [T]he International Court's Advisory Opinion, read in conjunction with the pleadings and the explanations given by some of that court's members, shows clearly that, in situations similar to those arising in the present case, the obligation to disregard acts of *de facto* entities is far from absolute. Life goes on in the territory concerned for its inhabitants. That life must be made tolerable and be protected by the *de facto* authorities, including their courts' and, in the very interest of the inhabitants, the acts of these authorities related thereto cannot be simply ignored by third States or by international institutions, especially courts, including this one. To hold otherwise would amount to stripping the inhabitants of the territory of all their rights whenever they are discussed in an international context, which would amount to depriving them even of the minimum standard of rights to which they are entitled.[74]

VI. SUMMARY

The application of international law to non-state armed groups on the basis of the de facto control theory must include the attribution of international human rights law obligations. Developments in the contemporary international legal order demand that international human rights law treaties be reinterpreted so that they may bind non-state armed groups who have displaced the authority of the state. In such situations the group has, in effect, substituted their own authority for that of the state and the vertical application of international human rights law is maintained. Importantly, this reinterpretation is consistent with both the object and purpose of international human rights law, and the importance attributed to the

[72] Vienna Declaration and Programme of Action, adopted by the World Conference on Human Rights, Vienna, 25 June 1993, para 4.

[73] *Legal Consequences for States of the Continued Presence of South Africa in Namibia (South West Africa) Notwithstanding Security Council Resolution 276 (1970)*, above n 48, para 125.

[74] *Cyprus v Turkey* App No 25781/94 (ECtHR, 10 May 2001), para 96.

protection of individuals' human rights. While at first glance this proposition may appear novel, it is, on reflection, no more novel than the application in 1949 of common Article 3 to armed groups,[75] and the subsequent application of customary international humanitarian law to such entities.[76] Indeed, it is driven by the same imperative: to ensure the international regulation of situations which cannot be left to the exclusive jurisdiction of the state. Of course, this is not to propose the demise of the state.[77] states remain the dominant actors on the international plane, and any attempt to subject armed groups to international human rights law obligations must remain cognisant of this fact.[78] Thus, any human rights law obligations imposed on armed groups must not detract from, or negate, states' own obligations.[79] This is discussed further in Chapter 7.

It may be argued that the attribution of international human rights law obligations to armed opposition groups constitutes an unwarranted interference with the territorial state's sovereignty, and should not be permissible on this basis.[80] It is beyond question that such attribution denotes a limitation of the territorial state's authority. Indeed, it is precisely this reality which underpins the application of the de facto control theory: in order to be bound by international law an armed group must have displaced state authority. However, the application of international law to armed groups on this basis does not affect the state's sovereign claim over the territory,[81] and to preclude acknowledgement of armed group obligations on the basis of interference with this sovereignty would be inconsistent with the principle of effectiveness. It is widely accepted that a state cannot be held liable for the acts of an insurgent group on the basis that such groups exist beyond the control of the state, despite the fact that the acts concerned occurred within the sovereign territory of the state.[82]

[75] See, eg GIAD Draper, *The Red Cross Conventions* (London, Stevens & Sons, 1958) 17.

[76] *Case concerning military and paramilitary activities in and against Nicaragua (Nicaragua v United States of America)*, Merits, International Court of Justice, 27 June 1986, para 218.

[77] See, eg Philip Alston, 'The "Not-a-Cat" Syndrome: Can the International Human Rights Regime Accommodate Non-State Actors?' in Philip Alston (ed), *Non-State Actors and Human Rights* (Oxford, OUP, 2005) 4.

[78] See, eg 'Horizontal Human Rights Law' above n 30, 20.

[79] For example, the potential human rights obligations of armed groups must be formulated in such a way that they cannot be used by states as an excuse not to fulfil their own obligations.

[80] With respect to the impact of extraterritorial human rights obligations on sovereignty, see Marko Milanovic, *Extraterritorial Application of Human Rights Treaties: Law, Principles, and Policy* (Oxford, OUP, 2011) 58–62.

[81] *Ilascu and Others v Moldova and Russia* App No 48787/99 (ECtHR, 8 July 2004), para 313.

[82] See further, International Law Commission, 'Draft Articles on Responsibility of States for Internationally Wrongful Acts, with commentaries' (2001) *Yearbook of the International Commission* Vol II, 50.

In the *Namibia* Advisory Opinion, the International Court of Justice clearly stated that '[p]hysical control of a territory, and not sovereignty or legitimacy of title, is the basis of State liability for acts affecting other States.'[83] Restrictions with respect to sovereignty were confirmed in *United States v Rice*, where it was held that the laws of the United States could not apply to the inhabitants of US territory which had come under the control of the British government: 'where there is no protection or allegiance or sovereignty, there can be no claim to obedience.'[84] It is clear that limitations on states' authority are recognised with respect to areas beyond the effective authority of the state, regardless of the legitimacy of the state's title to that area. Accordingly, international law acknowledges the effective exercise of authority by an entity other than the territorial state—in this instance a non-state armed group—without affecting the legality of the territorial state's title.[85] This is evident, for example, with respect to the law of belligerent occupation,[86] and the extraterritorial application of international human rights law.[87]

[83] *Legal Consequences for States of the Continued Presence of South Africa in Namibia (South West Africa) Notwithstanding Security Council Resolution 276 (1970)*, above n 48, para 54.
[84] *United States v Rice* (1819) 17 US 246, 254.
[85] See, eg *Ilascu and Others v Moldova and Russia*, above n 81, paras 312–13.
[86] See, eg Yoram Dinstein, *The International Law of Belligerent Occupation* (Cambridge, CUP, 2009) 49.
[87] See, eg Marko Milanovic, *Extraterritorial Application of Human Rights Treaties: Law, Principles, and Policy* (Oxford, OUP, 2011) 107.

7

The Gradated Application of International Human Rights Law Obligations

HAVING ESTABLISHED THAT non-state armed groups may be bound by international human rights law under certain conditions,[1] the precise scope and content of the imposed obligations must now be determined. In doing so, it is imperative that the application of international law be responsive to the needs of the affected populations and realistic vis-à-vis the capability of the relevant armed group. As a general rule, armed opposition groups do not possess resources equivalent to those of states, and it is evident that not all armed groups will have the ability to, inter alia, provide free primary education,[2] guarantee the right to a fair trial,[3] protect against employers' infringement of the right to join trade unions,[4] or provide social security.[5] Subjecting armed groups to obligations that they are incapable of fulfilling will not only contradict the principle of effectiveness,[6] but it may also affect groups' perceptions in relation to the credibility of international law itself, undermining respect for other binding obligations.[7] Accordingly, a solution must be found whereby the obligations imposed are responsive to both the reality of the situation and the reality of the armed group in question. The alternative is an 'all or nothing' approach, whereby obligations are only imposed on those groups with the ability to ensure the full spectrum of human rights, thereby excluding the vast majority of armed groups from any obligations. Of course, if the law is to be effective, and to move from theory into practical application, armed groups must be made

[1] Namely the displacement of state authority either during or outside armed conflict. See above, Chs 5 and 6.

[2] Art 13, International Covenant on Economic, Social and Cultural Rights.

[3] Art 10, International Covenant on Civil and Political Rights.

[4] Art 22, International Covenant on Civil and Political Rights.

[5] Art 9, International Covenant on Economic, Social and Cultural Rights.

[6] Thereby undermining the law's ability to respond to the realities of international life.

[7] See, eg Marco Sassoli, 'Should the obligations of states and armed groups under international humanitarian law really be equal?' (2011) 882 *International Review of the Red Cross* 429.

aware of their obligations. Possibilities in this regard are discussed in section II of this chapter.

I. DETERMINING THE CONTENT OF ARMED GROUPS' INTERNATIONAL HUMAN RIGHTS LAW OBLIGATIONS

In determining the content of armed groups' international human rights law obligations, states' extraterritorial human rights obligations may provide an appropriate analogy.[8] Similar to the situation vis-à-vis the attribution of human rights obligations to non-state armed groups, states' extraterritorial obligations arise only in 'exceptional circumstances',[9] in response to the reality of the control exercised,[10] and in an area typically subject to the jurisdiction of a sovereign state.

International and regional case law has confirmed that states are subject to extraterritorial human rights obligations consequent to either the exercise of effective control over an area, or on the basis of 'state agent authority'.[11] When a state exerts effective control over an area outside its national territory—whether as a result of lawful or unlawful activity[12]—then that area is considered to fall within the state's jurisdiction for the purposes of international human rights law.[13] Effective territorial control

[8] States are also subject to extraterritorial obligations in the field of economic, social and cultural rights. However, there exists uncertainty regarding the content of these rights, and it is primarily—although not exclusively—extraterritorial civil and political rights that are discussed herein. With respect to economic, social and cultural rights, see further Malcolm Langford, Wouter Vandenhole, Martin Scheinin and Willem van Genugten (eds), *Global Justice, State Duties: The Extraterritorial Scope of Economic, Social and Cultural Rights in International Law* (Cambridge, CUP, 2013).

[9] *Catan and Others v Moldova and Russia*, Judgment, European Court of Human Rights, Application Nos 43370/04, 8252/05 and 18484/06, 19 October 2012, para 105.

[10] See, eg ibid, para 105.

[11] See *Al-Skeini v The United Kingdom* App No 55721/07 (ECtHR, 7 July 2011), paras 133–40. Similar standards have been utilised by other courts. In *The Wall* and *DRC v Uganda* the International Court of Justice established states' extraterritorial jurisdiction on the basis of territorial control, while an approach similar to the state agent authority appears to have been used by the Inter-American Commission on Human Rights in *Alejandre and Others v Cuba*, and by the Human Rights Committee in *De Salidia Lopez v Uruguay*. See *Legal Consequences of the Construction of a Wall in the Occupied Palestinian Territory*, Advisory Opinion, International Court of Justice, 9 July 2004, paras 111–13; *Case Concerning Armed Activities on the Territory of the Congo (Democratic Republic of the Congo v Uganda)* Judgment, International Court of Justice, 19 December 2005, paras 216–17; *Alejandre Jr and Others v Cuba*, Inter-American Commission on Human Rights, Case No 11.589, Report No 86/99, September 29 1999, para 23; *Delia Saldia de Lopez v Uruguay*, Human Rights Committee, Communication No 52/1979, UN Doc CCPR/C/OP/1, 29 July 1981, para 12.1. Certain states reject the extraterritorial application of international human rights law treaties such as the International Covenant on Civil and Political Rights. However, this has been rejected by both the International Court of Justice and the Human Rights Committee.

[12] *Ilascu and Others v Moldova and Russia* App No 48787/99 (ECtHR, 8 July 2004), para 314.

[13] *Legal Consequences of the Construction of a Wall in the Occupied Palestinian Territory*, above n 11, para 112; *Al-Skeini and Others v The United Kingdom*, above n 11, para 138.

is typically established on the basis of military control,[14] but '[o]ther factors may also be relevant, such as the extent to which [the state's] military and economic and political support for the local subordinate regime provides it with influence and control over the region'.[15] For example, jurisdiction may be established consequent to a state's decisive influence vis-à-vis a local administration.[16] Both the International Court of Justice and the European Court of Human Rights have held that in situations of effective territorial control,[17] 'the entire range of substantive rights'[18] is applicable.[19]

However, as noted by the Inter-American Commission on Human Rights in *Alejandre Jr and Others v Cuba*, in certain instances jurisdiction can also 'refer to extraterritorial actions, when the person is present in the territory of a state but subject to the control of another state, generally through the actions of that state's agents abroad.'[20] Accordingly, the 'state agent authority' approach engages a state's jurisdiction when the actions of a state's agents bring an individual or group of individuals under the authority of that state.[21] In this regard it is not control over territory that is decisive, but rather the ability to exercise control vis-à-vis an individual's rights.[22] In contrast to the territorial control approach, and consequent to the state agent's reduced level of influence, only those rights relevant to the specific situation at hand are engaged:

> [W]henever the State through its agents exercises control and authority over an individual, and thus jurisdiction, the State is under an obligation under Article 1 to secure to that individual the rights and freedoms under Section 1 of the Convention that are relevant to the situation of that individual. In this sense, therefore, the Convention rights can be 'divided and tailored'.[23]

[14] *Loizidou v Turkey* App No 15312/89 (ECtHR, 18 December 1996), para 56.

[15] *Catan and Others v Moldova and Russia*, above n 9, para 107.

[16] See eg *Ilascu and Others v Moldova and Russia*, above n 12, para 394.

[17] The level of control exercised is typically extensive. For example, in *The Wall* and *DRC v Uganda* control was exercised on the basis of belligerent occupation, while in *Ilascu v Moldova and Russia* control was established based on the extent of influence exerted over a local subordinate regime.

[18] *Cyprus v Turkey* App No 25781/94 (ECtHR, 10 May 2001), para 77.

[19] See *Legal Consequences of the Construction of a Wall in the Occupied Palestinian Territory*, above n 11, paras 111–12; *Case Concerning Armed Activities on the Territory of the Congo (Democratic Republic of the Congo v Uganda)* above n 11, para 217.

[20] *Alejandre Jr and Others v Cuba*, above n 11, para 23.

[21] See eg *Al-Skeini and Others v The United Kingdom*, above n 11, para 137; *Delia Saldia de Lopez v Uruguay*, above n 11, para 12.1.

[22] See Noam Lubell, *Extraterritorial Use of Force Against Non-State Actors* (Oxford, OUP, 2010) 223–24. See further Rick Lawson, 'Life after Bankovic: On the Extraterritorial Application of the European Convention on Human Rights' in Fons Coomans and Menno T Kamminga (eds), *Extraterritorial Application of Human Rights Treaties* (Cambridge, Intersentia, 2004) 104.

[23] *Al-Skeini and Others v The United Kingdom*, above n 11, para 137.

Significantly, the state agent authority approach provides an alternative to the 'all or nothing' attribution of international human rights law obligations. In order to respond most effectively to the situation at hand, the obligation imposed on states may be tailored to the situation at hand.

However, while the territorial control and state agent authority approaches may be utilised to establish whether a state's human rights obligations are applicable to instances of extraterritorial activity, the unique circumstances under which extraterritorial obligations arise mean that these obligations cannot typically be applied in a manner directly equivalent to territorial obligations, and so the specific content of individual obligations must be determined. If, for example, a state acting extraterritorially is subject to an obligation in relation to the right to health—for instance if state agents have detained a fighter—does this include responsibilities related to the provision of mental health care?[24] Similarly, if the extraterritorial state has established effective control over an area—ie by means of belligerent occupation—is the state required to realise the right to the highest attainable standard of health by providing a level of health care equivalent to that existing in its own territory?[25]

In order to address issues such as these a contextual approach has been advanced whereby the specific obligations applicable, and their substantive content, are determined in relation to the context at hand:[26] this approach acknowledges that it may not be possible for a state to protect all rights in any given situation, but ensures that states are under an obligation to protect those rights which are subject to their control.[27] For example, should a state detain an individual during an extraterritorial operation, inter alia, the prohibition on arbitrary detention, and the prohibition on torture, or cruel, inhuman or degrading treatment will be immediately relevant,[28] while if the detention continues for a number of hours positive obligations concerning the right to food will become relevant,[29] as might positive obligations concerning the right to health if the detainee was injured during the operation.[30] However, although the state will be required to provide appropriate health care, given the context, it is not required to ensure all aspects of the detainee's right to the highest

[24] The provision of health care to detainees is an obligation; withholding such treatment may constitute cruel, inhuman or degrading treatment. See *Keenan v United Kingdom* App No 27229/95 (ECtHR, 3 April 2001), para 111.

[25] See further, Noam Lubell, 'Human rights obligations in military occupation' (2012) 94 *International Review of the Red Cross* 329–34.

[26] 'Life after Bankovic' above n 22, 105; above n 25, 323–29; *Extraterritorial Use of Force against Non-State Actors* above n 22, 227–31.

[27] See eg above n 25, 323.

[28] Art 9 International Covenant on Civil and Political Rights, and Art 7 International Covenant on Civil and Political Rights respectively.

[29] Art 11 International Covenant on Civil and Political Rights

[30] Art 12 International Covenant on Civil and Political Rights.

achievable standard of mental and physical health, or the detainee's right to join a trade union.[31]

Although not referred to explicitly, a contextual approach can be identified in international and regional case law. With respect to the territorial control approach, although the entire range of rights may be applicable in principle,[32] the content of these rights must necessarily be adapted in light of the specific context. For example, when the level of territorial control exercised constitutes military occupation, the content of any human rights obligations must necessarily be determined in light of the law of belligerent occupation. Further context-dependent modifications may also be necessitated. In *The Wall* Advisory Opinion, the International Court of Justice held that Israel was subject to extensive human rights obligations arising from its military occupation of the West Bank and the Gaza Strip. However, the content of these obligations was modified consequent to the peculiarities of the context: as certain powers had been transferred to the Palestinian Authority, Israel was not required to ensure the rights related to these powers but was instead subject to an obligation not to raise any obstacle vis-à-vis their protection.[33] Regarding the state agent authority approach, which applies at less extensive levels of control, the European Court of Human Rights in *Al-Skeini* held that, in a given context, only those rights 'that are relevant to the situation of that individual'[34] are engaged.[35] For instance, it must be presumed that, having established that Cuba had placed the occupants of the 'Brothers to the Rescue' aircraft under its authority,[36] the Inter-American Commission on Human Rights in *Alejandro v Cuba* only envisaged Cuban responsibility vis-à-vis those rights—such as the right to life—that were within Cuba's power to affect.[37]

The contextual approach defines a general principle of application, while allowing specific obligations to be determined in relation to the case at hand, thereby ensuring that the law can respond to all situations. This flexibility facilitates maximum human rights protection, while imposing obligations on states commensurate to their ability to fulfil them.[38] The alternative is the establishment of precise laws which may not adequately respond to specific situations and which therefore risk either allowing entities to evade responsibilities, or subjecting entities to obligations

[31] Example given in *Extraterritorial Use of Force against Non-State Actors* above n 22, 228.

[32] See *Cyprus v Turkey*, above n 18, para 77.

[33] *Legal Consequences of the Construction of a Wall in the Occupied Palestinian Territory*, above n 11, para 112.

[34] *Al-Skeini and Others v The United Kingdom*, above n 11, para 137.

[35] See further 'Life after Bankovic' above n 22, 105.

[36] *Alejandre Jr v Cuba*, above n 11, para 25. In this case a Cuban air force MiG-29 targeted and destroyed a civilian light aircraft operated by an organisation called 'Brothers to the Rescue'. The incident took place in international airspace.

[37] See eg, ibid, para 45.

[38] See 'Life after Bankovic' above n 22, 105; above n 25, 323.

which they are incapable of fulfilling in a given context.[39] Ultimately, as noted by Lubell: '[t]he likeliest route to achieving protection of human rights wherever possible is to have a general principle determining the applicability of international human rights law, while allowing for a case-by-case approach that takes the context into account when determining the precise content of the obligation.'[40]

A. A Contextual Approach to Armed Group Obligations

Returning to the international human rights obligations of non-state armed groups, utilisation of a context-dependent approach similar to that outlined above seems appropriate in light of the significant organisational and resource differential between armed groups, and between armed groups and states.[41] International human rights law must be capable of responding to different situations, and it does not seem appropriate that just because an armed group cannot guarantee all human rights, it should not be required to guarantee any. Indeed, the justifications underpinning the contextual approach as applied to states seem equally applicable in relation to armed group obligations. Thus, while the entire spectrum of international human rights law is potentially applicable to armed groups with international legal personality,[42] the applicability and content of each individual obligation must be determined on a context-dependent basis.[43]

[39] See eg above n 25, 324; *Extraterritorial Use of Force against Non-State Actors* above n 22, 227–31.

[40] This statement was made with respect to instances of belligerent occupation, however, it is submitted that this is equally relevant to more general situations. See above n 25, 324.

[41] The context-dependent balancing of obligations between the state and an armed group is similar, in certain respects, to the principle of common but differentiated responsibilities associated with international environmental law. This principle holds that the risks associated with damage to the environment are shared by all states, and so protection of the environment is a common responsibility. However, responsibilities are considered differentiated in that not all states can, or should, contribute equally. For example, states which have undergone industrialisation may have greater responsibilities than states which have not, on the basis of, inter alia, past contribution to environmental degradation. However, the common but differentiated responsibility principle does not establish a mechanism by which to differentiate responsibility, and is thus of limited utility. With respect to common but differentiated responsibilities, see further Christopher D Stone, 'Common but Differentiated Responsibilities in International Law' (2004) 98 *American Journal of International Law*; Lavanya Rajamani, 'The Principle of Common but Differentiated Responsibility and the Balance of Commitments under the Climate Regime' (2000) 9 *Review of European, Comparative & International Environmental Law*; Paul G Harris, 'Common but Differentiated Responsibility: The Kyoto Protocol and United States Policy' (1999) 7 *New York University Environmental Law Journal*.

[42] Consequent to satisfaction of the necessary independence and independent will criteria. The body of applicable international law is discussed above in Ch 5 section II.

[43] A context-dependent approach to human rights obligations is not novel; indeed, this is the basis underlying the progressive realisation clause associated with the International Covenant on Economic, Social and Cultural Rights. See broadly, above n 25, 324.

For instance, while it may be reasonable to subject states to immediate obligations vis-à-vis the entire range of rights under certain conditions—for example, on establishment of a belligerent occupation—given the significant disparity in available resources, infrastructure, and so on, it is not necessarily feasible to subject armed groups to directly equivalent obligations. An armed group may not have the resources available to immediately satisfy the entire spectrum of applicable international obligations, and so a process of gradual—but concrete—development may be more appropriate. For instance, in Sri Lanka, although the LTTE began to exert territorial control during the 1980s, it was only later, as the organisation developed and control stabilised, that it felt able to further develop certain elements of its service provision,[44] such as the rule of law.[45] As stated by Mr E Pararajasinham, former head of the LTTE judicial division:

> In the beginning we were a guerrilla organisation, engaging in hit and run tactics against the Sri Lankan armed forces. We had no stable control over large territories or populations. Therefore we neither had the resources nor the environment to set up and run a proper judicial system. But in 1993, as soon as we were in control of most of the north, our leadership established the Tamil Eelam Judiciary and College of Law.[46]

This gradual or gradated development of armed group capacity and service provision is evident in other situations, such as with respect to the EPLF in Eritrea,[47] the SPLM/A in Sudan,[48] and the Islamic State.[49]

[44] See eg 'In the 1980s, before the establishment of a separate judicial system, the LTTE set up village mediation boards, comprised of retired civil servants, school teachers and other local intellectuals. However, these turned out to be highly problematic and created much tension in society, not the least because of the lack of a legal code as a basis for adjudication and a lack of training and judicial competence. Therefore, *as LTTE attained increased organisational capacity and territorial control,* the village mediation boards were dismantled and a Tamil Eelam judiciary, a legal code and a college of law were established' in Kristian Stokke, 'Building the Tamil Eelam State: emerging state institutions and forms of governance in LTTE-controlled areas in Sri Lanka' (2006) 27 *Third World Quarterly* 6, 1027. Emphasis added.

[45] 'Therefore we as a liberation movement had to come up with an expeditious solution to prevent the collapse of the social order in the northeast while creating structures that would reflect the Sovereign Will of our people. So in the beginning we established mediation boards (Inakka Saphai) at the village level. These functioned from 1984–1992.' 'Thamil Eelam judiciary said a basis for rebuilding northeast', *TamilNet* (30 October 2003).

[46] 'Thamil Eelam judiciary said a basis for rebuilding northeast', *TamilNet* (30 October 2003). Of course, it is noted that the question remains as to whether the LTTE initially lacked the ability, or the will, to develop service provision.

[47] See generally, David Pool, *From Guerrillas to Government: The Eritrean People's Liberation Front* (Athens, Ohio University Press, 2001).

[48] See eg Adam Branch and Zachariah Cherian Mampilly, 'Winning the war, but losing the peace? The dilemma of SPLM/A civil administration and the tasks ahead' (2005) 43 *Journal of Modern African Studies*; Monyluak Alor Kuol, 'Administration of Justice in the (SPLA/M) Liberated Areas: Court Cases in War-Torn Southern Sudan' (1997) Refugee Studies Programme, University of Oxford.

[49] Charles C Caris and Samuel Reynolds, 'ISIS Governance in Syria', Middle East Security Report 22, Institute for the Study of War, July 2014, 14.

Of course, a careful distinction must be made between an armed group's ability to satisfy an obligation and its willingness to do so, and a lack of will cannot be used as a means of evading responsibility. Returning to the above-mentioned LTTE example, care must be taken to verify that the group did in fact lack the resources necessary to establish a judicial system, and to ensure that this was not merely a claim made by the organisation.

A context-dependent approach to armed group obligations is facilitated by states' continuing obligations with respect to the entirety of state territory,[50] including in those areas where the state's effective authority has been displaced.[51] Thus, while an armed group may be responsible for only a limited number of rights in any given context, the state's continuing obligations with respect to the entirety of the territory avoids a vacuum in protection vis-à-vis the remaining rights. The result is a 'division' of human rights obligations between the territorial state and the armed group.[52] The concept of shared or joint responsibility is not new to international law.[53] The European Court of Human Rights has addressed scenarios similar to that proposed herein—whereby two entities are internationally responsible for the same obligation—on a number of occasions.[54] In *Ilascu and others*, Moldova and Russia exercised de jure and de facto control respectively over Transdniestria, and both states were found to be responsible for violations of Articles 3 and 5 of the European Convention with respect to the same incidents.[55] The European Court held that Russia's responsibility was engaged by virtue of the effective authority—or at the very least decisive influence—exercised over the MRT regime in Transdniestria,[56] and Moldova's responsibility was engaged by virtue of its continuing de jure territorial jurisdiction:[57] while both shared responsibility vis-à-vis the rights in question, the content of their obligations differed. Similarly, in *MSS v Belgium and Others* both Belgium and Greece were held responsible under Article 3 of the European Convention in relation to the same

[50] See *Ilascu and Others v Moldova and Russia*, above n 12, para 313.

[51] ibid, para 312.

[52] See eg Andrew Clapham, 'Non-State Actors' in David Moeckli, Sangeeta Shah and Sandesh Sivakumaran (eds), *International Human Rights Law* (Oxford, OUP, 2010) 563; Wouter Vandenhole and Wolfgang Benedek, 'Extraterritorial Human Rights Obligations and the North-South Divide' in Malcolm Langford, Wouter Vandenhole, Martin Scheinin and Willem van Genugten (eds), *Global Justice, State Duties: The Extraterritorial Scope of Economic, Social and Cultural Rights in International Law* (Cambridge, CUP, 2013).

[53] See eg Andre Nollkaemper and Dov Jacobs, 'Shared Responsibility in International Law: A Conceptual Framework' (2013) 34 *Michigan Journal of International Law* 379–80.

[54] At issue herein is what is referred to as independent responsibility, as distinct from shared responsibility.

[55] *Ilascu and Others v Moldova and Russia*, above n 12, 454, 464.

[56] ibid, para 394.

[57] ibid, para 335.

incident, Belgium for exposing the applicant 'to conditions of detention and living conditions that amounted to degrading treatment',[58] and Greece for carrying out the actual treatment.[59] Again, while both states shared obligations with respect to the same right, the content of their obligations differed.

At first glance the division of obligations between a state and an armed group may seem difficult to achieve. However, actual cooperation between the state and a non-state armed group is possible. For instance, in Waziristan the state and the Pakistani Taliban coordinated vis-à-vis the operation of the local government,[60] in Syria, opposition forces and the government negotiated to ensure humanitarian access to Homs and other areas,[61] while in Senegal 'state health teams, accompanied by ICRC staff, vaccinated people in areas controlled by armed groups'.[62] That noted, it is important to highlight that the division of responsibility does not necessarily require active cooperation between the state and the armed group: while responsibility for protection of the right in question is shared, the state and armed group are subject to independent obligations, and the content of their respective obligations is distinct. In a number of situations, maintaining the pre-existing status quo will be sufficient,[63] and this occurs frequently in practice. Returning to the Sri Lanka example, schools and hospitals in LTTE-controlled areas continued to be staffed by government-paid employees, with the transfer of salaries facilitated by the use of a dedicated bank in Kilinochichi.[64] Similarly, the Islamic State has established authority over certain institutions previously run by the state—such as oil and gas installations—but the wages of the workers continued to be paid by the governments in Damascus and Baghdad.[65] In other situations, state services may continue to be provided in areas affected by armed group activity.[66]

[58] *MSS v Belgium* App No 30696/09 (ECtHR, 21 January 2011), para 367.

[59] ibid, para 264.

[60] International Crisis Group, 'Pakistan's Tribal Areas: Appeasing the Militants' (2006) 22.

[61] In this instance the UN acted as an intermediary.

[62] International Committee of the Red Cross, *Annual Report 2014* (2015) 107.

[63] ie in a manner similar to the *status quo ante bellum* requirement associated with occupation law. This is discussed further below in Ch 7 section I.D(i)(a)).

[64] 'A first hand report from LTTE-controlled territory in Sri Lanka', *World Socialist Web Site* (27 April 2001); above n 44, 1030. See also, Zachariah Cherian Mampilly, *Rebel Rulers: Insurgent Governance and Civilian Life during War* (Ithaca NY, Cornell University Press, 2011) 112.

[65] Sarah Birke, 'How ISIS Rules', NYRblog, *The New York Review of Books*, 1 August 2015.

[66] Examples in this regard include the continued provision of state services in areas affected by the BRN-C in Southern Thailand, by Hezbollah in Southern Lebanon, by the CPN-M in Nepal, or by the IRA in Northern Ireland.

B. Determining the Context-Dependent Content of Obligations: The Respect, Protect and Fulfil Framework

Having established that a contextual approach to the obligations imposed on non-state actors is appropriate, a means of determining the content of the imposed obligations must now be established. The respect, protect, fulfil framework is proposed as a useful tool in this regard.[67] This framework was developed in light of the 'progressive realisation' clause associated with economic, social and cultural rights, and is itself cognisant of capacity, providing a framework for the resource-dependent realisation of human rights.[68] Significantly, however, this framework is not restricted to economic, social and cultural rights, but is equally applicable to civil and political rights.[69]

The respect, protect, fulfil framework imposes three interdependent levels of obligations.[70] The obligation to respect is a negative obligation, requiring an authority to refrain from any activity that will result in a violation of international human rights law. The obligation to protect is a positive obligation, requiring an authority to ensure that third parties do not violate individuals' human rights. This obligation is composed of a preventive obligation, typically satisfied through the enactment of legislation but requiring action in certain instances, and a remedial obligation to provide a remedy in the event of a violation.[71] The obligation to fulfil is also a positive obligation, requiring that measures be undertaken to secure the realisation of human rights standards. It consists of three elements: first, the obligation to fulfil (facilitate) requires 'positive measures to assist

[67] See Andrew Clapham, *Human Rights Obligations of Non-State Actors* (Oxford, OUP, 2006) 230; Nicola Jagers, *Corporate Human Rights Obligations: in Search of Accountability* (Cambridge, Intersentia, 2002) 78; *Extraterritorial Use of Force against Non-State Actors* above n 22, 228–31.

[68] See eg Committee on Economic, Social and Cultural Rights, General Comment 14, 'The right to the highest attainable standard of health (article 12 of the International Covenant on Economic, Social and Cultural Rights)', UN Doc E/C.12/2000/4, 11 August 2000, para 30; Asbjorn Eide, 'Adequate Standard of Living' in Daniel Moeckli, Sangeeta Shah and Sandesh Sivakumaran (eds), *International Human Rights Law* (Oxford, OUP, 2010) 252–53.

[69] *The Social and Economic Rights Action Center and the Center for Economic and Social Rights v Nigeria*, Decision, African Commission on Human and Peoples' Rights, Communication No 155/96, 13–27 October 2001, para 44; Marco Odello and Francesco Seatzu, *The UN Committee on Economic, Social and Cultural Rights: The Law, Process and Practice* (Abingdon, Routledge, 2013) 242.

[70] See further, 'Report on the right to adequate food as a human right submitted by Mr Asbjorn Eide, Special Rapporteur', Commission on Human Rights, UN Doc No. E/CN.4/Sub.2/1987/23, 7 July 1987; Committee on Economic, Social and Cultural Rights, General Comment 13, 'The right to education (article 13 of the Covenant)', UN Doc E/C.12/1999/10, 8 December 1999, para 46; Frederic Megret, 'Nature of Obligations' in Daniel Moeckli, Sangeeta Shah and Sandesh Sivakumaran (eds), *International Human Rights Law* (Oxford, OUP, 2010) 130–31.

[71] General Comment 14 above n 68, para 35; Tawhida Ahmed and Israel de Jesus Butler, 'The European Union and Human Rights: An International Law Perspective' (2006) 17 *European Journal of International Law* 797.

individuals and communities to enjoy the right' in question;[72] second, the obligation to fulfil (provide) requires that an authority directly ensure the provision of a right, 'when individuals or a group are unable, for reasons beyond their control, to realize that right themselves by the means at their disposal';[73] and third, the obligation to fulfil (promote) requires the provision of, inter alia, appropriate education with respect to the right in question.[74]

It is important to note that the obligations to respect, protect, and fulfil are not distinct obligations but rather are complementary components of the overall international human rights law obligation. With respect to the prohibition of torture, for example, the obligation to respect requires that states refrain from engaging in acts of torture, while the obligation to fulfil requires, inter alia, that states implement appropriate legislation and conduct the necessary training of state authorities to give effect to this right. Similarly, in the event of a famine, a state's obligation with respect to the right to food may require that it: does not take any measures that will prevent an individual's access to food (obligation to respect),[75] provide security against bandits who are looting or destroying crops (obligation to protect),[76] provide direct food aid to the extent possible (obligation to fulfil (provide)),[77] and facilitate third parties—such as International Organisations or non-governmental organisations—in ensuring the immediate provision of humanitarian relief (obligation to fulfil (facilitate)).[78]

Applying the respect, protect, fulfil framework to non-state actors accommodates the application of the entire spectrum of international human rights law obligations while ensuring that the substantive content of each obligation is determined in a manner appropriate to the context. This framework is not applied in the traditional manner. Rather, it is adapted to provide a structure for the regulated application of gradated obligations. As discussed above, this framework involves a division of responsibility between the state and the armed group.[79] In keeping with established international law, the state retains the overall responsibility for securing human rights obligations within the national territory.[80]

[72] Committee on Economic, Social and Cultural Rights, General Comment 15, 'The right to water (arts 11 and 12 of the International Covenant on Economic, Social and Cultural Rights)', UN Doc E/C.12/2002/11, 20 January 2003, para 25.

[73] General Comment 14 above n 68, para 37.

[74] See eg ibid, fn 23. See also, General Comment 15, above n 72, para 25.

[75] See Committee on Economic, Social and Cultural Rights, General Comment 12, 'The right to adequate food (art 11)', UN Doc E/C.12/1999/5, 12 May 1999, para 15.

[76] See eg ibid, para 15.

[77] See eg ibid, para 15; General Comment 14 above n 68, para 33.

[78] See eg General Comment 12, above n 75, para 15; General Comment 14 above n 68, para 33.

[79] See above, Ch 7 section I.B. This issue is also discussed in greater detail below, see Ch 7 section I.F.

[80] *Ilascu and Others v Moldova and Russia*, above n 12, paras 312–13.

However, the content of states' obligations must be determined in relation to the context, and so the reality of armed group control—including the extent to which state authority has been displaced—and any obligations imposed on armed groups must be taken into consideration.[81] For example, it may not be possible for the state to satisfy the obligation to fulfil (provide) in areas subject to the exclusive control of an armed group, and so the content of the state's obligation to fulfil must be modified accordingly, perhaps focusing upon the obligation to fulfil (facilitate). At the same time, armed groups are subject to gradated obligations, dependent upon the extent to which state authority has been displaced. As a starting point, all armed groups are subject to the obligation to respect: as a negative obligation this is capable of being fulfilled by all armed groups. As an armed group displaces state authority to an increasing extent it will become bound by the obligation to fulfil, while the obligation to protect—implicating as it does the maintenance of the rule of law and the administration of justice[82]—should appropriately become applicable when an armed group establishes itself as the sole authority with respect to a specific territory and population. This shared responsibility between a state and an armed group ensures that states cannot evade responsibility vis-à-vis their human rights obligations by claiming that responsibility has passed on to armed groups. The specific content of each obligation will now be addressed in greater detail.[83]

C. The Obligation to Respect

The obligation to respect is a negative obligation requiring that no action be undertaken that undermines or negates individuals' rights under international human rights law. As this obligation 'can be fulfilled by an authority simply refraining from action',[84] its fulfilment is dependent upon an entity's ability to control its agents, an essential criterion vis-à-vis recognition as an international legal person.[85] All international legal

[81] This will be of particular relevance vis-à-vis the obligation to fulfil. See below Ch 7 section I.D.

[82] See below Ch 7 section I.E.

[83] The literature refers to the 'respect, protect, and fulfil framework'. However, for present purposes, first the obligation to respect, then fulfil, and finally protect are addressed. This is based on armed groups' capacity to satisfy each obligation, and the conclusion that the obligation to protect will apply only to armed groups, an advanced stage of insurgency, who have displaced state authority and exercise control over territory and population. This is not the case vis-à-vis the obligations to respect and fulfil, which apply to armed groups, less advanced levels.

[84] 'The European Union and Human Rights' above n 71, 796.

[85] See above, Ch 2 section IV.E.

persons are therefore capable of fulfilling the obligation to respect and this obligation must be regarded as binding all international legal persons, at all times:[86] it constitutes the lowest rung of obligation arising under international human rights law.[87]

In *The Social and Economic Rights Action Center and the Center for Economic and Social Rights v Nigeria*, the African Commission on Human and People's Rights held that 'the obligation to respect entails that the state should refrain from interfering in the enjoyment of all fundamental rights; it should respect right-holders, their freedoms, autonomy, resources, and liberty of their action.'[88] Regarding the right to water, the Committee on Economic, Social and Cultural rights has noted that '[t]he obligation to *respect* requires that States parties refrain from interfering directly or indirectly with the enjoyment of the right to water'.[89] This obligation includes, for example, refraining from any action that denies or limits equal access to adequate water, refraining from illegally polluting water, and refraining from limiting access to, or destroying, water infrastructure as a punitive measure.[90] With respect to freedom of expression, the European Court of Human Rights has held that 'there is little scope … for restrictions on political speech or on debate on matters of public interest',[91] while equally the obligation to respect precludes actions that will, inter alia, interfere with individuals' right to a fair trial, or the right to freedom of movement.[92] Applied to armed groups, the obligation to respect may require, for instance, that armed groups allow government teachers or medical staff to continue to work, or that groups refrain from interfering with humanitarian relief activities.

The international human rights law obligation to respect is similar to the rules on the conduct of hostilities established under the law of armed conflict applicable to both international and non-international armed conflicts. These rules are primarily negative, requiring that parties to an armed conflict refrain from undertaking certain actions.[93] For example, the law of armed conflict prohibits armed groups from directly targeting

[86] See eg Chris Jochnick, 'Confronting the Impunity of Non-State Actors: New Fields for the Promotion of Human Rights' (1999) 21 *Human Rights Quarterly*, 78.

[87] Philip Alston and Gerard Quinn, 'The Nature and Scope of States Parties' Obligations under the International Covenant on Economic, Social and Cultural Rights' (1987) 9 *Human Rights Quarterly* 2, 184.

[88] *The Social and Economic Rights Action Center and the Center for Economic and Social Rights v Nigeria*, above n 69, para 45.

[89] General Comment 15, above n 72, para 21.

[90] ibid, para 21.

[91] *Erdogdu and Ince v Turkey* App Nos 25067/94, 25068/94 (ECtHR, 8 July 1999), para 50.

[92] ie, through the illegitimate imposition of curfews, or the denial of habeas corpus rights.

[93] Not all rules on the conduct of hostilities are negative. For example, the obligation to take all feasible precautions in attack, and the obligation to take all feasible measures to verify that a target is a military objective contain positive elements. Nonetheless, the overall point remains valid.

civilians,[94] civilian objects,[95] medical personnel,[96] medical units,[97] or objects indispensable to the survival of the civilian population such as foodstuffs, agricultural areas, water supplies and water infrastructure, crops, and livestock.[98] Refraining from attacking such targets may be regarded as equivalent to satisfying the obligation to respect the right to life, the right to adequate housing, the right to the highest attainable standard of health, and so on. Similarly, the obligations contained in common Article 3(1) to the four Geneva Conventions of 1949, which relate to, inter alia, the prohibition on torture and fair trial rights, are all negative obligations.

The correlation between obligations arising under international human rights law and the law of armed conflict has been noted by both the Human Rights Committee and the Committee on Economic, Social and Cultural Rights. General Comment 15 on the right to water states that:

> [D]uring armed conflicts, emergency situations and natural disasters, the right to water embraces those obligations by which States parties are bound under international humanitarian law. This includes protection of objects indispensable for survival of the civilian population, including drinking water installations and supplies and irrigation works, protection of the natural environment against widespread, long-term and severe damage and ensuring that civilians, internees and prisoners have access to adequate water.[99]

Equally, General Comment 14 on the right to the highest attainable standard of health notes that the obligation to respect prohibits states 'from limiting access to health as a punitive measure, e.g. during armed conflicts in violation of international humanitarian law',[100] while in General Comment 29 the Human Rights Committee notes the correlation between fair trial rights under international human rights law and international humanitarian law.[101] The rules on the conduct of hostilities apply from the moment an armed group qualifies as a party to an armed conflict, underlining the appropriateness of applying the obligation to respect to

[94] Art 13(2), Additional Protocol II to the Geneva Conventions. See also, Rule 1, Jean-Marie Henckaerts and Louise Doswald-Beck, *Customary International Humanitarian Law, Vol 1: Rules* (Geneva, International Committee of the Red Cross/CUP, 2005).

[95] Rule 7, *Customary International Humanitarian Law, Vol 1: Rules* above n 94. See also, Art 8(2)(e)(xii) Statute of the International Criminal Court.

[96] Art 9, Additional Protocol II to the Geneva Conventions. See also, Rule 25, *Customary International Humanitarian Law, Vol 1: Rules* above n 94.

[97] Art 11, Additional Protocol II to the Geneva Conventions. See also, Rules 28 and 29, *Customary International Humanitarian Law, Vol 1: Rules* above n 94.

[98] Art 14, Additional Protocol II to the Geneva Conventions. See also, Rule 54, *Customary International Humanitarian Law, Vol 1: Rules* above n 94.

[99] General Comment 15, above n 72, para 22.

[100] General Comment 14 above n 68, para 34.

[101] Human Rights Committee, General Comment 29, 'States of Emergency (article 4)', UN Doc CCPR/C/21/Rev.1/Add.11, 31 August 2001, para 16.

all entities bound by international human rights law, at all times. Interestingly, this correlation between the law of armed conflict and international human rights law may also facilitate awareness-raising amongst armed groups with respect to their human rights obligations, as it is possible that appropriate training may be incorporated into existing dissemination activities.[102]

As the obligation to respect is negative, it may be fulfilled by both states and armed groups simultaneously, and so the issue of divided responsibility does not arise. However, it is noted that fulfilment of the obligation to respect may be problematic in certain exceptional situations. With respect to the right to health, for instance, while it seems reasonable to expect armed groups to satisfy the obligation to ensure non-discriminatory access to available health services, the obligation to respect also prohibits armed groups from marketing unsafe drugs.[103] Prima facie, this may seem reasonable, yet it is not always certain that an armed group will know whether certain drugs are unsafe, or have the resources necessary to make this determination.[104] Accordingly, while the obligation to respect is applicable to all international legal persons, in certain situations the precise content of this obligation may need to be determined in relation to the specific context at hand.

D. The Obligation to Fulfil

The obligation to fulfil is intended to achieve the full realisation of the human right in question, and to ensure that it is effective in reality.[105] As such, satisfaction of the obligation to fulfil requires positive action, including 'appropriate legislative, administrative, budgetary, judicial, promotional and other measures'[106] necessary for the full realisation of the right. A starting point may be the adoption of legislation intended to ensure the implementation of international obligations. For example, in dualist systems the international obligation may need to be incorporated into domestic legislation to be effective. However, in and of itself, the enactment of legislation is insufficient: it would be meaningless to implement legislation in relation to the prohibition on torture without,

[102] See below, Ch 7 section II.

[103] See General Comment 14 above n 68, para 34.

[104] For instance, an armed group may overrun a medical depot containing drugs which were being used as part of a limited clinical trial, or which contained drugs that were subsequently recalled.

[105] See eg Olivier de Schutter, *International Human Rights Law: Cases, Materials, Commentary* (Cambridge, CUP, 2010) 465. *The Social and Economic Rights Action Center and the Center for Economic and Social Rights v Nigeria*, above n 69, para 47.

[106] General Comment 14 above n 68, para 33.

inter alia, training state agents appropriately and ensuring accountability in the event of a violation. Similarly, legislation guaranteeing each individual's right to a house will be ineffective without measures to ensure that there is sufficient housing available.[107] As held by the Inter-American Court of Human Rights: '[t]he obligation to ensure the free and full exercise of human rights is not fulfilled by the existence of a legal system designed to make it possible to comply with this obligation—it also requires the government to conduct itself so as to effectively ensure the free and full exercise of human rights.'[108] Satisfaction of the obligation to fulfil therefore requires that the right in question be monitored and, if required, positive actions—such as the development of a plan of action or direct provision[109]—must be undertaken.[110]

As noted above, the obligation to fulfil is composed of three elements, the obligation to fulfil (facilitate), the obligation to fulfil (provide), and the obligation to fulfil (promote).[111] The obligation to facilitate requires that the relevant authority undertake 'positive measures to assist individuals and communities to enjoy the right'[112] in question. With respect to the right to food, the Committee on Economic, Social and Cultural Rights noted that this obligation requires that the state 'pro-actively engage in activities intended to strengthen people's access to and utilization of' the necessary resources and means to ensure the right.[113] At issue, therefore, is not direct provision, but rather ensuring access to the means necessary to realise the relevant right.[114] For instance, the right to participate in public affairs requires that '[p]ositive measures should be taken to overcome specific difficulties, such as illiteracy, language barriers, poverty or impediments to freedom of movement which prevent persons entitled to vote from exercising their rights effectively'.[115] Similarly, the imposition of fees that de facto prevent an individual's access to justice may result in a violation of the obligation to facilitate the right to a fair trial and equal access to a court.[116] In this regard the Human Rights Committee noted that 'a rigid

[107] Example given in: Matthew CR Craven, *The International Covenant on Economic, Social, and Cultural Rights: A Perspective on its Development* (Oxford, Clarendon Press, 1995) 126.

[108] *Velasquez-Rodriquez v Honduras*, Judgment (Merits), Inter-American Court of Human Rights, 29 July 1988, para 167.

[109] See eg General Comment 15, above n 72, para 26; *International Human Rights Law: Cases, Materials, Commentary* above n 105, 465.

[110] *International Human Rights Law: Cases, Materials, Commentary* above n 105, 465.

[111] For convenience these will be referred to simply as the obligations to facilitate, provide, and promote.

[112] General Comment 13, above n 70, para 47.

[113] General Comment 12, above n 75, para 15.

[114] For instance, instead of directly providing food aid, a state may be required to facilitate access to employment, information on food production techniques, and so on.

[115] Human Rights Committee, General Comment 25, 'Participation in Public Affairs and the Right to Vote', UN Doc CCPR/C/21/Rev.1/Add.7, 12 July 1996, para 12.

[116] See eg *Lindon v Australia*, Decision, Human Rights Committee, Communication No 646/1995, UN Doc CCPR/C/64/D/646/1995, 20 October 1998, para 6.4.

duty under law to award costs to a winning party without consideration of the implications thereof or without providing legal aid may have a deterrent effect on the ability of persons to pursue the vindication of their rights under the Covenant in proceedings available to them'.[117]

The obligation to provide requires that when individuals or a group are unable to realise a right themselves, for reasons beyond their control, the relevant authority must directly provide that right.[118] For example, '[t]he availability or absence of legal assistance often determines whether or not a person can access the relevant proceedings or participate in them in a meaningful way'[119] and so the right to a fair trial requires that the state provide access to free-of-charge defence counsel where necessary.[120] Similarly, the right to adequate housing may necessitate that states 'establish housing subsidies for those unable to obtain affordable housing',[121] and the right to health requires the provision of safe drinking water, basic sanitation and adequate housing conditions, or immunisation programmes.[122]

The relationship between the obligation to facilitate and the obligation to provide is illustrated by reference to the *Grootboom* case before the Constitutional Court of South Africa:

> [T]here is a difference between the position of those who can afford to pay for housing, even if it is only basic though adequate housing, and those who cannot. For those who can afford to pay for adequate housing, the state's primary obligation lies in unlocking the system, providing access to housing stock and a legislative framework to facilitate self-built houses through planning laws and access to finance. Issues of development and social welfare are raised in respect of those who cannot afford to provide themselves with housing.[123]

For those individuals with the requisite resources, 'unlocking the system'—implicating the obligation to facilitate—is sufficient. However, for those without the requisite resources,[124] the provision of housing

[117] Human Rights Committee, General Comment No 32, 'Article 14: Right to equality before courts and tribunals and to a fair trial', UN Doc CCPR/C/GC/32, 23 August 2007, para 11. See also, *Aarela and Nakkalajarvi v Finland*, Views, Human Rights Committee, Communication No 779/1997, UN Doc CCPR/C/73/D/779/1997, 24 October 2001, para 7.4.

[118] General Comment 14 above n 68, para 37.

[119] General Comment No 32, above n 117, para 10.

[120] Art 14(d) ICCPR. See also General Comment No 32, above n 117, para 10.

[121] Committee on Economic, Social and Cultural Rights, General Comment 4, 'The right to adequate housing (Art 11(1) of the Covenant)', UN Doc E/1991/23, 14 December 1991, para 8(c).

[122] General Comment 14 above n 68, para 36. See further *World Organisation Against Torture, Lawyers' Committee for Human Rights, Jehovah Witnesses, Inter-African Union for Human Rights v Zaire*, Decision, African Commission on Human and Peoples' Rights, Communication No 25/89, 47/90, 56/91, 100/93, 4 April 1996, para 47.

[123] *Government of the Republic of South Africa and others v Grootboom and others*, Judgment, Constitutional Court of South Africa, Case CCT 11/00, 4 October 2000, para 36.

[124] ie for those without the ability to realise the right through the means at their disposal.

through social welfare—implicating the obligation to provide—is necessitated.

The obligation to promote requires that efforts be undertaken to provide the education necessary for the realisation of certain rights. For example, the equality of rights between women and men requires that states 'furnish appropriate information on those aspects of tradition, history, cultural practices and religious attitudes which jeopardise, or may jeopardise',[125] the right. Similarly, the right to health requires education in relation to healthy lifestyles or harmful traditional practices, or research into factors favouring positive health results,[126] while the right to water may require education vis-à-vis hygienic water usage.[127]

(i) The Obligation to Fulfil and Armed Groups

As an armed group displaces the state's authority to an increasing extent, it must become subject to the obligation to fulfil. Initially, it is likely that the obligation to facilitate will be most immediately relevant, given the reduced resources required to satisfy this obligation when compared to the obligation to provide. For example, if there are food shortages in an area subject to an armed group's control and the group does not have the ability to provide direct food aid (obligation to provide), then the obligation to facilitate will require that the group ensure, inter alia, the rights to life, food, and health by actively facilitating the provision of humanitarian relief provided by the state or third party organisations.[128] This may require positive measures, such as contacting the state or third party organisation so that they make take the appropriate action,[129] or—if the situation demands—coordinating their activities.[130] In this instance, merely satisfying the obligation to respect would be insufficient, as it would be incapable of ensuring the human rights of the affected population. As the resources available to an armed group increase, it may be in a position to satisfy the obligation to provide. Depending on the situation, an armed group may satisfy this obligation through the provision of health

[125] Human Rights Committee, General Comment 28, 'Equality of rights between men and women (article 3)', UN Doc CCPR/C/21/Rev.1/Add.10, 29 March 2000, para 5.

[126] General Comment 14 above n 68, para 37.

[127] General Comment 15, above n 72, para 25.

[128] The obligation to facilitate may require that the armed group initiate contact with the relevant relief provider. It is possible that this obligation may also require that a group develop capacity in order to fulfil its obligation under international human rights law. For example, the group may be required to coordinate third party activities necessitating the establishment of a dedicated organ or liaison.

[129] For instance, in Mali, the MNLA informed the ICRC of wounded soldiers' whereabouts and conditions. International Committee of the Red Cross, *Annual Report 2014* (2015) 171.

[130] Coordination may be necessary to avoid overlap in service provision and to ensure equal access. For example, in Sri Lanka the LTTE established a Planning and Development Secretariat to ensure centralised planning and coordination. Above n 44, 1034.

services to the local population,[131] or through the provision of free-of-charge defence counsel;[132] in the above example, the obligation to provide would be satisfied through the provision of direct food aid by the armed group. However, it is important to note that the obligation to provide does not always require extensive resources, and in certain situations it may be easier to ensure than the obligation to facilitate. For instance, the provision of food or water to detainees is arguably within the capability of any armed group with the capacity to detain, given that the group will have to provide such necessities to its own personnel, and direct provision removes the need to liaise with a third party. Equally the provision of medical assistance may not require advanced capacity or resources in all situations: allowing affected individuals access to an armed group's doctor or health care facilities—such as a mobile clinic—may be sufficient.[133]

Prima facie, the obligation to promote appears to require significant resources. For example, the right to health requires that an armed group 'undertake actions that create, maintain and restore the health of the population',[134] necessitating activities such as the development and distribution of educational materials. Similarly, the right to equality between men and women requires education and awareness raising vis-à-vis potentially discriminatory historical, cultural, religious, or traditional attitudes or practices.[135] However, a number of armed groups do engage in some form of outreach activity,[136] and so, with access to appropriate information and resources—perhaps provided by organisations such as the Office of the High Commissioner for Human Rights or the World Health Organization[137]—fulfilment of this obligation may be possible.[138] A number

[131] For instance, in Colombia the FARC provide a variety of health services to the local population. Garry Leech, 'Farc rebel group in peace talks: Is Colombia's 50-year war about to end' *The Independent* (London, 21 July 2013); 'Colombia rebel army brings healthcare to the jungle', Al Jazeera English, 31 May 2011, www.youtube.com/watch?v=1hxkoiZVJRQ.

[132] It appears that the FMLN in El Salvador provided defence counsel. Sandesh Sivakumaran, 'Courts of Armed Opposition Groups: Fair Trials or Summary Justice' (2009) 7 *Journal of International Criminal Justice*, 492.

[133] For instance, in Eritrea the EPLF established a system of 'barefoot doctors'. Above n 47, 100. See also, Ernesto 'Che' Guevara, *Guerrilla Warfare* (USA, BN Publishing, 2007) 73.

[134] General Comment 14 above n 68, para 37.

[135] General Comment 28, above n 125, para 5.

[136] For example, Human Rights Watch note with respect to the Naxalites in India that: 'The movement's ideology is propagated through village meetings, community groups, and theater performances. Indoctrination is done through public meetings, speeches, and in schools.' Human Rights Watch, 'Between Two Sets of Guns: Attacks on Civil Society Activists in India's Maoist Conflict' (2012) 12–13.

[137] It is noted that organisations routinely engage with armed groups. For example, Geneva Call work with armed groups to sign 'Deeds of Commitment', Child Soldiers International and their partner organisations work directly with armed groups to advocate for an end to the use of child soldiers, while the ICRC train members of armed groups on the requirements of international humanitarian law.

[138] Indeed, it may be in the best interest of an armed group to provide such information to civilian populations subject to their authority. For example, Giap notes that '[w]e had

of specific issues relating to armed groups and the obligation to fulfil must now be addressed, namely the progressive realisation of economic, social and cultural rights, the possibility that armed groups may be required to develop their organisational capacity, and third party assistance with respect to the realisation of rights.

(a) The Progressive Realisation of Economic, Social, and Cultural Rights

The 'progressive realisation' requirement associated with economic, social and cultural rights holds that—in order to be reflective of, and responsive to, the reality of a particular situation[139]—steps towards the full realisation of a right may be taken over time.[140] While in principle certain armed groups should have the potential to fulfil this obligation, it is submitted that its application should be restricted to armed groups that have displaced state authority and exercise exclusive control over a territory and population:[141] below this point the state will have the principal responsibility to ensure the relevant right,[142] while the armed group will lack both the authority to engage in long-term measures vis-à-vis the affected population,[143] and the stability necessary to implement any such measures. In this regard it is important that, in applying the obligation of progressive realisation, the impermanence of armed group control and such group's lack of sovereignty be acknowledged. Any long-term plan undertaken by the armed group must be cognisant of the territorial state's continuing sovereignty. It therefore seems appropriate that armed group activity be evaluated by analogy to the *status quo ante bellum* requirement established by the law of belligerent occupation.[144] This provision is intended to preserve a territory's unique tapestry of laws, customs and culture, while ensuring its continuing independent viability, thereby acknowledging the temporary nature of occupation and the occupants' lack of sovereignty.[145]

to mobilize the masses for the resistance while trying to satisfy their immediate interest in improving their living conditions'. Vo Nguyen Giap, *The Military Art of People's War: Selected Writings of General Vo Nguyen Giap* (Russell Stetler (ed), New York, Monthly Review Press, 1970) 103.

139 See Committee on Economic, Social and Cultural Rights, General Comment 3, 'The nature of States parties' obligations (Art 2 Para 1 of the Covenant)', UN Doc E/1991/23, 14 December 1990, para 9.

140 However, certain steps must be taken immediately. See eg General Comment 15, above n 72, para 17.

141 This is discussed further in the context of the legislative authority of armed groups. See below Ch 8 section I.A(iv).

142 This does not result in a legal lacuna: an armed group's obligation to fulfil (facilitate) will require that it allow the state to take measures towards progressive realisation.

143 See further below, Ch 8 section I.A(iv).

144 See eg Marco Sassoli, 'Legislation and Maintenance of Public Order and Civil Life by Occupying Powers' (2005) 16 *European Journal of International Law*, 661.

145 See Art 43 Hague Regulations; Art 64 Geneva Convention IV. See inter alia, Marco A Sassoli and Antoine A Bouvier, *How Does Law Protect in War? Cases, Documents and Teaching*

The principle of progressive realisation is regarded as entailing a strong presumption against the permissibility of retrogressive measures.[146] As such, if deliberately retrogressive measures are undertaken,[147] the responsible authority must prove that they were introduced only after careful consideration of all alternatives, and that they are justified 'by reference to the totality of the rights provided for in the Covenant in the context of the full use of the State party's maximum available resources.'[148] The principle of non-retrogression is particularly important when considering the obligations placed on armed groups. For example, an armed group may wish to demonstrate its authority, or perpetuate its ideology, by replacing government employees with armed group-appointed doctors or teachers.[149] If this results in a regression with respect to the right in question, it must be considered impermissible, as in this instance the obligation to fulfil is better realised by facilitating the continued work of government employees.[150] Of course, in certain situations it may be impossible for an armed group to maintain the status quo, and a context-dependent approach must acknowledge this reality. For instance, if state employees refuse to work under the authority of the armed group, then their replacement may not only be justified but necessary to ensure continued protection of the right, to the extent possible.

(b) The Development of Armed Group Capacity

In certain scenarios, the positive obligations imposed in relation to the obligation to fulfil may require that an armed group respond to a situation through the development of its organisational capacity:[151] international human rights law cannot allow armed groups to avoid obligations—resulting in a violation of individuals' rights—by failing to develop in

Materials on Contemporary Practice in International Humanitarian Law, Vol 1, 2nd edn (Geneva, ICRC, 2006) 186; Conor McCarthy, 'The Paradox of the International Law of Military Occupation: Sovereignty and the Reformation of Iraq' (2005) 10 *Journal of Conflict & Security Law* 43.

[146] See eg *Miranda Cortez v El Salvador*, Decision, Inter-American Commission on Human Rights, Case 12.249, 20 March 2009, para 105; General Comment 15, above n 72, para 19.

[147] Of course, it is noted that a situation in which an armed group displaces state authority may itself contribute to a certain retrogression vis-à-vis rights protection. However, this may be an unavoidable result of the situation, and should not affect international regulation of the resultant situation.

[148] General Comment 14 above n 68, para 32.

[149] For example, in El Salvador the UN Observer Mission reported that the 'FMLN Political and Diplomatic Commission informed ONUSAL that no government employees may enter the conflict zones because government activities are not permitted there.' Second report of the United Nations Observer Mission in El Salvador, UN Doc A/46/658, S/23222, 15 November 1991, para 78.

[150] See further below, Ch 7 section I.F.

[151] In a certain sense this may be regarded as a form of internal progressive realisation, whereby an armed group may be required to take steps to develop its own capacity in order to better ensure individuals' rights.

accordance with the reality of a situation.[152] Of course, to be effective any such requirement must be realistic, and an armed group cannot be expected to develop beyond its ability to do so. For example, if an armed group exerts exclusive or near-exclusive control of an area whose inhabitants require humanitarian relief, satisfaction of the obligation to fulfil may reasonably require that the armed group develop the capacity necessary to ensure that the work of third party humanitarian organisations is facilitated by the armed group[153]—ie through the provision of safe-passage documents, or the identification of areas or communities in need of particular assistance—or to coordinate the provision of humanitarian relief by third parties, perhaps necessitating the creation of a dedicated liaison organ.[154] It is recalled that the ability to conduct such activities is closely related to the capacity criterion associated with the international legal personality test. This criterion requires that a non-state entity have the ability to impose its will on its members, indicating an organisational structure conducive to cooperation and coordination with third parties.[155]

(c) The Role of Third Party Assistance

The possibility that armed groups may turn to third party organisations in order to satisfy the obligation to fulfil is anticipated—vis-à-vis state activity—in Article 2(1) of the International Covenant on Economic, Social and Cultural Rights. In General Comment 3, the Committee on Economic, Social and Cultural Rights noted that 'the phrase "to the maximum of its available resources" was intended by the drafters of the Covenant to refer to both the resources existing within a state and those available from the international community through international cooperation and assistance.'[156] Similar resource constraints suggest that the 'general understanding'[157] that the realisation of economic, social and cultural rights in developing countries may be dependent—at least to a certain

[152] See the example given above in relation to the LTTE's gradual development of rule of law infrastructure, in above Ch 7 section I.A.

[153] This occurs routinely in practice. See for example, International Crisis Group, 'Cote d'Ivoire: "The War Is Not Yet Over"' (2003) 15; Human Rights Watch, 'War Without Quarter: Colombia and International Humanitarian Law' (1998); 'Sudan: ICRC facilitates handover of five soldiers in Darfur', ICRC News Release (4 December 2013).

[154] For example, in Syria the Al Nusrah Front established the 'Sharia Committee for the Eastern Region' which, inter alia, oversaw humanitarian aid. Bill Roggio, 'Al Nusrah Front poised to take over last major city on Euphrates River', *The Long War Journal* (13 March 2013). In Sudan, the SPLA established the Sudan Relief and Rehabilitation Association. Monyluak Alor Kuol, 'Administration of Justice in the (SPLA/M) Liberated Areas: Court Cases in War-Torn Southern Sudan' (1997) Refugee Studies Programme, University of Oxford, 47.

[155] See above Ch 2 section IV.B.

[156] General Comment 3, above n 139, para 13.

[157] Above n 107, 144.

extent—on international assistance should be regarded as equally applicable in relation to areas subject to armed group control.[158]

In General Comment 3 the Committee on Economic, Social and Cultural Rights emphasised the role of third states, noting that 'in the absence of an active programme of international assistance and cooperation on the part of all those states that are in a position to undertake one, the full realization of economic, social and cultural rights will remain an unfulfilled aspiration in many countries.'[159] The law of non-international armed conflict also recognises the importance of international or third party assistance. Article 18(1) Additional Protocol II states that relief actions shall be undertaken by organisations such as the ICRC, '[i]f the civilian population is suffering undue hardship owing to a lack of the supplies essential for its survival, such as food stuffs and medical supplies',[160] and this provision is reflected in customary international humanitarian law.[161] In practice a large number of International Organisations and non-governmental organisations work to provide services and to facilitate development in areas subject to the control or influence of armed groups.[162] It is noted, however, that dependent on the group in question, third party assistance may conflict with counter-terrorism legislation in certain states.[163]

(d) Summary

Satisfaction of the overall obligation to fulfil requires a balancing of the obligations to facilitate, provide and promote. As with states, the means by which a particular right is fulfilled is left to the discretion of the armed group.[164] In certain situations it may be permissible for an armed group to satisfy the obligation to fulfil solely by means of the obligation to facilitate, thereby reducing the resource constraints placed upon the group. In and of itself this is not problematic. However, if at any point an armed group can better ensure the realisation of a right by means of the obligation to provide or a combination of the obligations to provide and facilitate, then mere reliance on the obligation to facilitate may violate the armed group's obligations under international human rights law. The obligations to facilitate and provide are means of ensuring satisfaction of the overall right in

[158] See generally ibid, 144.
[159] General Comment 3, above n 139, para 14.
[160] Article 18(1) Additional Protocol II.
[161] See Rules 55 and 56, *Customary International Humanitarian Law, Vol 1: Rules* above n 94.
[162] Examples include the UN Office for the Coordination of Humanitarian Affairs ('OCHA'), ICRC, Doctors Without Borders ('MSF'), Oxfam, ActionAid, and Islamic Relief.
[163] *Holder v Humanitarian Law Project*, Supreme Court of the United States, No 08-1498, 21 June 2010.
[164] See eg *Government of the Republic of South Africa and others v Grootboom and others*, above n 123, para 41; *Soobramoney v Minister of Health (Kwazulu-Natal)*, Judgment, Constitutional Court of South Africa, Case CCT 32/97, 27 November 1997, para 29.

question and cannot be abused in order to abdicate responsibility: if an armed group does not, or cannot, satisfy the obligation to provide, it must satisfy the obligation to facilitate, and vice versa.[165] Ultimately, armed group activity in relation to the obligation to fulfil must be evaluated in a manner similar to that of states, taking into account the resources available to the armed group and the needs of the population.[166]

E. The Obligation to Protect

The obligation to protect requires that efforts be undertaken to protect against the violation of individuals' rights by third parties such as individuals, corporations, or other entities,[167] including armed groups.[168] It consists of a preventive component involving the establishment of criminal or administrative sanctions, and a remedial component requiring an effective investigation and the establishment of a remedy.[169] Under certain conditions further positive measures may be necessitated to prevent third parties from interfering—either directly or indirectly—with individual rights;[170] these may involve, for example, preventive measures required to protect the right to life,[171] measures to ensure equal access to services provided by third parties,[172] or measures to prevent other infringements such as pollution or the inequitable extraction of resources.[173] Importantly, the obligation to protect is determined on the basis of 'reasonableness' and will vary according to the circumstances of any particular situation.[174] For instance, in *Osman v United Kingdom*, the European Court of Human Rights held that in order to show a violation of the state's obligation to protect with respect to the actions of a third party,

[165] This is not to imply that the obligation to fulfil may be satisfied through facilitation in all instances; certain situations may require a combination of facilitation and provision.

[166] In this regard the existence of minimum core obligations is recalled. See below Ch 8 sections I.B(iii) and II.B).

[167] See eg *The Social and Economic Rights Action Center and the Center for Economic and Social Rights v Nigeria*, above n 69, para 57; General Comment 15, above n 72, para 23.

[168] For instance, the state must take reasonable measures to protect against the activities of armed groups.

[169] 'The European Union and Human Rights' above n 71, 797; *The Social and Economic Rights Action Center and the Center for Economic and Social Rights v Nigeria*, above n 69, para 61.

[170] Committee on Economic, Social and Cultural Rights, General Comment 16, 'The equal right of men and women to the enjoyment of all economic, social and cultural rights (art 3 of the International Covenant on Economic, Social and Cultural Rights)', UN Doc E/C.12/2005/4, 11 August 2005, para 19.

[171] *Osman v United Kingdom*, Judgment, European Court of Human Rights, App No 87/1997/871/1083, 28 October 1998, para 115; *Keenan v United Kingdom*, above n 24, para 89.

[172] General Comment 14 above n 68, para 35.

[173] General Comment 15, above n 72, para 23.

[174] *International Human Rights Law: Cases, Materials, Commentary* above n 105, 389.

an applicant must 'show that the authorities did not do all that could be reasonably expected of them to avoid a real and immediate risk to life which they have or ought to have knowledge.'[175]

From the above it is apparent that the obligation to protect relates to the maintenance of public order and the rule of law: in order to protect against third party violations an appropriate regulatory framework must be established against which individuals and groups can evaluate their actions, and remedial measures—potentially including prosecution and detention—must be put in place to address any violation. Distinct from the obligations to respect and fulfil, which relate to activity undertaken by armed groups on behalf of third parties, the obligation to protect requires that armed groups regulate the activities of, and impose obligations on, these same third party actors; i.e. in order to protect the right to life or the right to property, armed groups may be required to undertake policing activities and to detain and prosecute suspected individuals. As such, the obligation to protect requires active involvement in the life of the community.

Applying the preventive component of the obligation to protect to armed groups will require that armed groups issue decrees regulating activity in areas subject to their authority,[176] necessitating a certain level of sophistication with respect to internal and external communications, and raising questions vis-à-vis armed groups' legislative authority.[177] The remedial element of the obligation to protect, and the enforcement of armed group regulations—potentially by means of prosecution and detention—also implicates armed groups' legislative authority and raises a number of additional human rights concerns. For example, the prohibition of arbitrary detention establishes specific safeguards which armed groups will be required to adhere to, including the requirements that detention be on grounds established by law,[178] and that detainees be brought before a court to challenge the legality of their detention.[179] Similarly, the right to a fair trial establishes detailed requirements in relation to the trial process, including the right 'to a fair and public hearing by a competent, independent and impartial tribunal established by law';[180] the right to adequate time and facilities for the preparation of a defence and consultation with counsel;[181] the right to free-of-charge legal assistance;[182] and the right to

[175] *Osman v United Kingdom*, above n 171, para 116.

[176] Of course, such decrees may generate human rights implications with respect to their enforcement.

[177] This issue is discussed in greater detail below, see Ch 8 section I.A.4.

[178] International Covenant on Civil and Political Rights, Art 9(1).

[179] ibid, Art 9(4).

[180] ibid, Art 14(1).

[181] ibid, Art 14(3)(b).

[182] ibid, Art 14(3)(d).

an interpreter.[183] Imposing the obligation to protect on armed groups who do not possess the ability to ensure all related human rights obligations risks encouraging violations of international human rights law.

In order to fulfil the obligation to protect, armed groups must possess legislative authority vis-à-vis the affected population. This is necessary if an armed group is to intervene in the life of the community, through the promulgation of laws or regulations, or the prosecution and detention of individuals. Accordingly, it is necessary that application of the obligation to protect to armed groups be restricted to those groups who have displaced state authority and exercise exclusive control over a territory and population.[184]

F. The Territorial State's Obligations

International human rights law subjects states to an obligation to respect, protect, and ensure human rights in relation to the entire national territory of the state and the individuals therein.[185] Significantly, the European Court of Human Rights has established that this obligation persists 'even where the exercise of the state's authority is limited in part of its territory'.[186] In *Catan and Others v Moldova and Russia*, a case involving the existence of the de facto MRT regime in the Transdniestria region of Moldova, the Court held that:

> Although Moldova has no effective control over the acts of the 'MRT' in Transdniestria, the fact that the region is recognised under public international law as part of Moldova's territory gives rise to an obligation, under Article 1 of the Convention, to use all legal and diplomatic means available to it to continue to guarantee the enjoyment of the rights and freedoms defined in the Convention to those living there.[187]

Accordingly, in situations where a non-state armed group exerts control, the territorial state is subject to a positive obligation 'to take all the appropriate measures still within its power to take'[188] to fulfil its obligations under international human rights law. Such measures have been held to include, 'diplomatic, economic, judicial, or other measures' that are themselves in accordance with the requirements of international law.[189] The division of human rights responsibilities between the territorial state and

[183] ibid, Art 14(3)(f).
[184] This issue is discussed further below, see Ch 8 section I.A(iv).
[185] See eg International Covenant on Civil and Political Rights, Art 2(1).
[186] *Ilascu and Others v Moldova and Russia*, above n 12, para 313.
[187] *Catan and Others v Moldova and Russia*, above n 9, para 110.
[188] *Ilascu and Others v Moldova and Russia*, above n 12, para 313.
[189] ibid, para 331.

an armed group must be regarded as falling within the scope of states' positive obligations. Referring to the above-quoted decision in *Ilascu and Others v Moldova and Russia*, the division of responsibility is an 'appropriate measure' intended to ensure the overall protection of human rights. Importantly this measure is context-dependent, ensuring that any obligation imposed on the state is 'within its power to take'.[190]

States are subject to the primary obligation to respect and ensure respect for international human rights law, and states' positive obligations in this regard must be presumed applicable at all times, with respect to the entirety of the national territory. Accordingly, the content of states' obligations will only be modified to the extent that an armed group, or other non-state actor, displaces state authority. This proposition respects state primacy with respect to its national territory, while ensuring that a state cannot absolve itself of its human rights obligations by claiming that the obligation has passed to the non-state actor, or that the non-state actor did not cooperate: the state is subject to a pressing obligation to do all that can reasonably be expected of it. states must therefore continue to provide government services in areas subject to the influence of armed groups, to the extent possible, or if they are unable to do so, to facilitate third party assistance. In practice, the territorial state often facilitates the work of aid agencies, such as the ICRC, MSF, or UN OCHA, which provide services in areas under armed group control.[191] Applying this to an example scenario, it is possible that in response to armed group attacks on police forces and other rule of law institutions the state may suspend operation of the court system and the provision of policing services.[192] Provided that the government's reaction to the situation is reasonable, this will not result in a violation of the state's continuing obligation. However, were the government to prevent hospital or teaching staff from working this may be unreasonable vis-à-vis the state's continuing obligations,[193] if these personnel were not targeted, threatened or otherwise affected by the attacks.

Returning to the respect, protect, fulfil framework, it is highlighted that these obligations are applicable at all times—although their content may be altered dependent upon the context[194]—and that the content of the

[190] ibid, para 313.

[191] See eg International Committee of the Red Cross, 'Syria: Civilians in besieged areas in urgent need of relief', Operational Update, 24 July 2013; International Committee of the Red Cross, 'DR Congo: Situation still very precarious in east of country', Operational Update, 21 June 2013.

[192] Police forces may have to withdraw to barracks at night, for example, or local courts may have to relocate to more secure cities.

[193] With respect to the right to health, and the right to education, for example.

[194] It is recalled that the obligation to respect is not context-dependent and, as with armed groups, this obligation therefore binds the state at all times.

state's obligations with respect to territory outside its exclusive control must be subject to a requirement of reasonableness:

> In determining the scope of a State's positive obligations, regard must be had to the fair balance that has to be struck between the general interest and the interests of the individual, the diversity of situations obtaining in Contracting States and the choices which must be made in terms of priorities and resources. Nor must these obligations be interpreted in such a way as to impose an impossible or disproportionate burden.[195]

Accordingly, any analysis of the context must acknowledge the acts of the relevant armed group. For example, a state cannot remain subject to an obligation to provide in relation to the right to food if an armed group continuously attacks relief convoys: under the circumstances the state's fulfilment of this obligation is not reasonable. However, the state does remain subject to the obligation to facilitate, requiring that it allow a third party organisation to undertake the necessary direct provision. In this regard it is recalled that a state 'must endeavour, with all the legal and diplomatic means available to its *vis-à-vis foreign States and international organisations*, to continue to guarantee the enjoyment of the rights and freedoms defined in the Convention.'[196] Of course, this assumes that the armed group satisfies its obligation to fulfil by cooperating with a third party organisation. If it fails to do so, it is the armed group that is responsible for the resultant violation of international human rights law, presuming that the state took all appropriate measures within its power to take.[197]

II. ENSURING THAT ARMED GROUPS ARE AWARE OF THEIR INTERNATIONAL OBLIGATIONS

Having established that armed groups may be bound by international human rights law, and having developed a context-dependent means of determining the resultant obligations, a final practical issue must now be addressed: how can non-state armed groups be made aware of their international obligations? This is an essential issue. If armed groups are unaware of their obligations, any developments in international law will be largely irrelevant with respect to the day-to-day lives of civilians affected by armed group activities.[198]

[195] *Ilascu and Others v Moldova and Russia,* above n 12, para 332.

[196] ibid, para 333. Emphasis added.

[197] In non-international armed conflict States are subject to an obligation to facilitate humanitarian access. See Art 18 AP II, Rule 55, *Customary International Humanitarian Law, Vol 1: Rules* above n 94.

[198] It is recalled that the application of certain of the obligations imposed on armed groups, and in particular, positive obligations such as the obligation to fulfil (facilitate), have been conditioned upon the group being aware of their obligations, and having had contact with an external actor.

It is submitted that an approach similar to that of the International Committee of the Red Cross should be adopted, whereby efforts are made to actively engage armed groups in a humanitarian dialogue so that the rules of international humanitarian law—or in this case international human rights law—may be effectively disseminated. Importantly, from a practical perspective, it appears that a significant number of armed groups are receptive to such engagement. The International Committee of the Red Cross routinely engages in dialogue and training with a large number of armed groups and in 2014, for instance, the organisation maintained relations with over 200 armed groups operating in approximately 50 different contexts.[199] A number of other organisations also engage in international law dialogue with armed groups. For example, Human Rights Watch has engaged, inter alia, with the Huthi rebels in Yemen,[200] the FARC in Colombia,[201] and the Free Syrian Army,[202] while similarly the United Nations (or its agencies, such as the United Nations Children's Fund (UNICEF)) has engaged in dialogue with armed groups in, *inter alia*, Sudan,[203] the Philippines,[204] and El Salvador.[205] The non-governmental organisation Geneva Call also engages in innovative—and to date highly successful—dialogue with armed groups, encouraging them to sign 'Deeds of Commitment' pledging to respect various aspects of international law. For example, Geneva Call has secured the signature of 43 armed groups to a 'Deed of Commitment' banning the use of anti-personnel land mines.[206]

[199] International Committee of the Red Cross, *Annual Report 2014* (2015) 94. See further, 'Keynote address by Jacques Forster, Vice-President of the ICRC', First Meeting of Signatories to Geneva Call's Deed of Commitment, October 31—November 1 2004, Geneva, Switzerland.

[200] Human Rights Watch, 'All Quiet on the Northern Front?' (2010) 34.

[201] See Human Rights Watch, 'War Without Quarter: Colombia and International Humanitarian Law' (1998).

[202] Human Rights Watch, 'Syria: End Opposition Use of Torture, Executions', 17 September 2012.

[203] See for example,'SPLM/OLS Agreement on Ground Rules' signed by the head of the UN's Operation Lifeline Sudan southern sector and John Garang, Commander-in-Chief of the Sudan People's Liberation Movement/Army. A similar agreement was subsequently signed between Operation Lifeline Sudan and the South Sudan Independence Movement (SSIM/A) and the SPLM-United. See Mark Bradbury, Nicholas Leader and Kate Mackintosh, 'The "Agreement on Ground Rules" in South Sudan', Humanitarian Policy Group Report 4, Overseas Development Institute, March 2000.

[204] See 'Action Plan between the Moro Islamic Liberation Front (MILF) and the United Nations in the Philippines regarding the Issue of Recruitment and Use of Child Soldiers in the Armed Conflict in Mindanao', 1 August 2009.

[205] See for example, 'FMLN provided the Mission with a set of criteria which it applies in taking prisoners and in the treatment of prisoners. FMLN prisoners may be its own combatants who have violated the rules of international law; informers or individuals who have infiltrated its ranks; members of the armed forces captured in combat; or members of the civilian population who have committed ordinary crimes in conflict zones.' 'First Report of the United Nations Observer Mission in El Salvador', UN Doc A/45/1055, 16 September 1991, section 38.

[206] Further information available at www.genevacall.org/what-we-do/landmine-ban/.

With respect to gender issues, the organisation has engaged in dialogue with over 20 armed groups, securing the signature of seven to the related 'Deed of Commitment',[207] while similarly, negotiations have been undertaken with over 20 armed groups and nine signatures secured in relation to children in armed conflict.[208] Given the level of existing engagement, there appears to be no conceptual difficulty in extending such activity to include obligations arising under international human rights law.

Of course, in certain situations security concerns may mean that direct engagement with armed groups is not immediately possible. However, limited engagement may still occur, and for example, it may be possible to engage with civilian populations generally, or individuals who are connected to, or exert influence over, armed groups. The International Committee of the Red Cross adopted this approach in Afghanistan, engaging in dialogue with 'local religious/community leaders with influence over armed groups'[209] when it could not directly reach the groups themselves. Similarly, in Rio de Janeiro the International Committee of the Red Cross established a community outreach programme in order to build trust and raise awareness of the organisation, prior to establishing contact with specific armed groups.[210]

As is evident from the above, a number of different organisations may potentially engage in international law dialogue with armed groups. However, in order to be effective at a global level—and to address potential state concerns in relation to such activity legitimising armed groups or interfering in sovereign affairs—it is perhaps preferable that a well-known international organisation take on this role. Although any proposal in this regard would necessarily require further discussion and negotiation, including a potential modification of the relevant organisation's mandate, it would appear that an organisation such as the Office of the High Commissioner for Human Rights is well placed to systematically engage with armed groups vis-à-vis their obligations under international human rights law.

III. CONCLUSION

As previously established, armed groups may be bound by international human rights law obligations.[211] However, it is apparent that, in general,

[207] Further information available at www.genevacall.org/what-we-do/gender-issues/.

[208] Further information available at www.genevacall.org/what-we-do/child-protection/.

[209] International Committee of the Red Cross, *Annual Report 2012* (2013) 240.

[210] Robert Muggah and Oliver Jutersonke, 'Rethinking Stabilization and Humanitarian Action in "Fragile Cities"' in Benjamin Perrin (ed), *Modern Warfare: Armed Groups, Private Militaries, Humanitarian Organizations, and the Law* (Vancouver, UBC Press, 2012) 320–21.

[211] Either consequent to the de facto control theory, or potentially, vis-à-vis the creation of international treaty law.

armed groups will not possess the ability to immediately secure the full realisation of these obligations. Indeed, given the significant resource differences between states and armed groups, and the reality within which armed group activity occurs, in many instances it would be unrealistic to expect them to do so. As such, a context-dependent approach is advocated whereby responsibility for the overall obligation is divided between the state and the armed group on the basis of the specific situation at hand, and in particular the extent of control exercised by an armed group. This approach ensures that international law is capable of responding to any given situation, and that obligations imposed on armed groups are realistic, and capable of being fulfilled.

In determining the context-dependent content of an armed group's individual obligations, it is submitted that an adaptation of the respect, protect, fulfil framework may be adopted. This framework allows for the resource-dependent realisation of human rights, whereby the content of individual obligations is determined based on the reality of any given situation. Application of this framework to armed groups centres upon a context-dependent division of responsibility between the armed group and the state: it is this division of responsibility which ensures the overall protection of human rights, including in situations wherein a right cannot be secured by one party acting individually. However, states' primary obligations vis-à-vis the realisation of human rights in its territory must be acknowledged. As such, state obligations may only be modified consequent to an armed group's demonstrable interference with state authority.

Of course, if the application of international human rights law obligations to non-state armed groups is to be effective in practice, it is essential that armed groups be made aware of their obligations. A number of possibilities in this regard have been discussed, and it is submitted that an International Organisation—such as the Office of the High Commissioner for Human Rights (OHCHR)—may be best placed to fulfil this role. Certain specific rights will now be analysed, in order to determine how the context-specific approach can work in practice.

Part III

Testing the Application of International Human Rights Law to Armed Groups in Practice

8

Prosecution, Detention, and Satisfaction of the Right to Health by Armed Groups

UTILISING THE CONTEXT-DEPENDENT approach developed in Chapter 7, Part III examines *how* specific human rights obligations can be applied to armed groups in practice. First addressed are issues relating to the rule of law and the administration of justice, focusing on the convening of courts and detention by armed groups, both of which implicate an armed group's legislative authority. These services are key elements in the protection of human rights, have a significant impact on the affected population, and will form a key element of any imposed human rights obligation. Furthermore, armed groups operating at all levels of sophistication typically provide some form of rule of law and administration of justice system. Indeed, establishing a police force or court system is often one of the first activities of an armed group.[1] International obligations imposed on armed groups in relation to respecting and protecting the right to health are then discussed. The provision of health care has been chosen for several reasons. First, it is an essential element in ensuring the wellbeing of a population, particularly during conflict situations. Second, it is a resource intensive service that may require interaction with the territorial state or other third parties. Third, the provision of health care is a core socio-economic right, and discussion in this regard can offer insight into how armed groups may ensure resource intensive economic, social and cultural rights more generally. Each individual section addresses the legal content of the obligation in question as well as practical issues arising from its application to non-state armed groups.

[1] Zachariah Cherian Mampilly, *Rebel Rulers. Insurgent Governance and Civilian Life during War* (Ithaca NY, Cornell University Press, 2011) 63. See, eg Richard Barrett, 'The Islamic State', The Soufan Group, November 2014, 35.

I. ARMED GROUP PROSECUTION AND DETENTION

Prosecution and detention are central components of any rule of law system, and are considered essential to the protection of human rights.[2] However, while activity in this area was once the exclusive preserve of states—with international rights and obligations oriented accordingly—today, non-state armed groups regularly convene trials and detain individuals, often at state-like levels of sophistication.[3] In Cote d'Ivoire, for example, the FAFN undertook extensive detention operations utilising the pre-existing state infrastructure,[4] in Sri Lanka the LTTE established a judicial system involving six district courts, two high courts, and an appeal court,[5] while the Islamic State has established both a police force and a hierarchical court system.[6] Further examples at less well-established levels include: the CPN-M in Nepal and the Afghan Taliban who created judicial systems parallel to those of the state that were often regarded as preferable to state institutions by the local population;[7] the National Movement for the Liberation of Azawad (MNLA) in Mali, which detained both civilians and members of the Malian armed forces;[8] and both the IRA

[2] See generally, James Crawford, *Brownlie's Principles of Public International Law*, 8th edn (Oxford, OUP, 2012) 668.

[3] For example, the Naxalites in India established a system of people's courts (see Arundhati Roy, 'Walking with the Comrades', *Outlook India* (29 March 2010); Human Rights Watch, '"Being Neutral is Our Biggest Crime": Government, Vigilante, and Naxalite Abuses in India's Chhattisgarh State' (2008) 113); the GAM in Indonesia convene councils at village, sub-district, and district level (see Human Rights Watch, 'Indonesia: The War in Aceh' (2001) 22); the Mahdi movement in Iraq established a network of arbitration committees (see International Crisis Group, 'Iraq's Muqtada Al-Sadr: Spoiler or Stabiliser?' (2006) 20; International Crisis Group, 'Iraq's Civil War, the Sadrists and the Surge' (2008) 7); and the Syrian opposition have established courts that continue to apply the Syrian criminal law system (see Human Rights Watch, 'Syria: End Opposition Use of Torture, Executions', 17 September 2012, 3). See also, 'In the first decade of the twenty-first century alone, and among many others, the Communist Party-Maoists (CPN-M) in Nepal, the Liberation Tigers of Tamil Eelam (LTTE) in Sri Lanka, the Taliban in Afghanistan, the Forces Armees Fore Nouvelles (FAFN) in Cote d'Ivoire, the Sudanese People's Liberation Army/Movement in Sudan, and the Fuerzas Armadas Revolucionarias de Colombia (FARC) and the Ejercito de Liberacion Nacional (ELN) in Colombia have all, and on multiple occasions, deprived people of their liberty'. David Tuck, 'Detention by armed groups: overcoming challenges to humanitarian action' (2011) 93 *International Review of the Red Cross* 761.

[4] 'Detention by armed groups' above n 3, 761–62.

[5] 'Thamil Eelam judiciary said a basis for rebuilding northeast', *TamilNet* (30 October 2003). See also, Sandesh Sivakumaran, 'Courts of Armed Opposition Groups: Fair Trials or Summary Justice' (2009) 7 *Journal of International Criminal Justice* 494.

[6] Charles C Caris and Samuel Reynolds, 'ISIS Governance in Syria', Middle East Security Report 22, Institute for the Study of War, July 2014, 18; Rahmeem Salman and Oliver Holmes, 'Islamic State creates Police Force in Northwest Iraq', *Reuters*, 21 September 2014.

[7] See eg Office of the High Commissioner for Human Rights in Nepal, 'Human rights abuses by the CPN-M, Summary of Concerns', September 2006, 4; Tim McGirk, 'Behind the Taliban's Resurgence in Afghanistan', *TIME* (16 September 2009).

[8] See 'Mali: New Abuses by Tuareg Rebels, Soldiers', Human Rights Watch (7 June 2013); 'Mali: ICRC visits detainees in the north', News Release, International Committee of the Red Cross (31 July 2012).

in Ireland and 'Basque Homeland and Freedom' ('ETA') in Spain which detained individuals in the absence of established territorial control,[9] with the IRA apparently conducting courts martial in accordance with established internal procedures.[10]

Given the centrality of the rule of law and the administration of justice to the protection of human rights, it is essential that the international law applicable to instances of armed group prosecution and detention be determined. This is a complex issue: in addition to states' concerns vis-à-vis an extension of sovereign activity to non-state actors, instances of detention and prosecution by armed groups raise concerns in relation to the inherent vulnerability of detained individuals, and consequent to the uncertain and diverse nature of armed groups themselves: ie are armed groups capable of conducting fair trials or detaining individuals in accordance with international standards? The concern is that, rather than contributing to the protection of individuals' human rights, armed group courts may instead add 'a veneer of legality to what would better be termed vigilantism'.[11] This section examines issues relating first to prosecution by armed groups, and second to detention by armed groups. Both of these subsections evaluate the relevant procedural guarantees, before looking at issues concerning what armed groups can prosecute (and under what conditions) and who armed groups can detain (and when).

A. Issues Relating to Prosecution by Armed Groups

A large number of armed groups establish courts and conduct prosecutions, trying members of their own forces, the 'enemy', and members of the civilian population.[12] This section examines what international obligations and procedural guarantees regulate the conduct of armed groups in this regard. Three specific scenarios are then addressed in order to determine whether a legal basis for prosecution exists: first, prosecutions related to violations of international humanitarian law;[13] second, prosecutions related to group-specific issues, such as internal discipline, treason or collaboration;[14] and third, the prosecution of non-conflict related issues,

[9] 'IRA kidnappers release industrialist', *BBC News* (London, 7 November 1975); Elizabeth Nash, 'Hostage freed by Eta after 341 days', *The Independent* (London, 15 April 1996).

[10] See 'The I.R.A. Court Martial Procedure' in The Irish Republic Army, 'The Green Book' (Book II).

[11] Speaking in the context of Communist Party of the Philippines/New People's Army/National Democratic Front ('CPP'/'NPA'/'NDF') people's courts, 'Report of the Special Rapporteur on extrajudicial, summary or arbitrary executions, Philip Alston', Mission to Philippines, UN Doc A/HRC/8/3/Add.2, 16 April 2008, para 32.

[12] See generally above Ch 1 section I.

[13] Necessarily such prosecutions may only occur in the context of an armed conflict.

[14] Prosecutions in this regard may occur both during, and outside, armed conflict.

such as offences relating to the maintenance of the rule of law and public order.[15]

(i) Procedural Guarantees Regulating Armed Group Courts

The principal guarantees relevant to the operation of armed group courts are the prohibition of retroactive criminal laws, the requirement that a court be independent and impartial, and the requirement of adequate time and means for a defence;[16] issues relating to public trials and the ability to call witnesses will also be discussed. This section analyses both international human rights law and international humanitarian law, although international human rights law is of principal concern.[17]

(a) The Prohibition on Retroactive Criminal Laws

The prohibition on retroactive criminal laws (the principle of *nullum crimen sine lege*) is considered non-derogable under international human rights law,[18] and is also codified in Art 6(2)(c) of Additional Protocol II, which adopts the wording of Art 15 of the International Covenant on Civil and Political Rights. This rule establishes that:

> No one shall be held guilty of any criminal offence on account of any act or omission which did not constitute a criminal offence, under national or international law, at the time when it was committed. Nor shall a heavier penalty be imposed than the one that was applicable at the time when the criminal offence was committed. If, subsequent to the commission of the offence, provision is made by law for the imposition of the lighter penalty, the offender shall benefit thereby.[19]

The Nowak *Commentary* to the International Covenant on Civil and Political Rights notes that this rule establishes a general duty 'to define precisely by law all *criminal offences* in the interest of *legal certainty*'.[20] As such,

[15] Prosecutions in this regard may occur both during, and outside, armed conflict.

[16] These issues have been identified on the basis of the core requirements common to both international humanitarian law and international human rights law, as codified in, inter alia, Arts 14 and 15 of the International Covenant on Civil and Political Rights, common Art 3 to the Geneva Conventions of 1949, and Art 6 Additional Protocol II.

[17] The law of non-international armed conflict draws heavily on international human rights law with respect to procedural guarantees. See for example, Rule 100, Jean-Marie Henckaerts and Louise Doswald-Beck, *Customary International Humanitarian Law, Vol 1: Rules* (Geneva, International Committee of the Red Cross/CUP, 2005).

[18] See Art 4(2) International Covenant on Civil and Political Rights, Art 15(2) European Convention on Human Rights, Art 27(2) American Convention on Human Rights.

[19] Art 15(1) International Covenant on Civil and Political Rights; Art 6(2)(c) Additional Protocol II.

[20] Manfred Nowak, *UN Covenant on Civil and Political Rights: CCPR Commentary*, 2nd edn (Kehl am rhein, NP Engel, 2005) 360.

it is imperative that the law be sufficiently clear so as to allow individuals to regulate their conduct.[21]

The *nullum crimen sine lege* principle is particularly relevant when considering non-state armed groups: it is foreseeable that uncertainty may arise among members of the civilian population vis-à-vis laws promulgated by armed groups, making it difficult for them to regulate their conduct.[22] As noted in the Additional Protocol II *Commentary*, '[t]he possible co-existence of two sorts of national legislation, namely, that of the State and that of the insurgents, makes the concept of national law rather complicated in this context.'[23] However, the coexistence of state law and armed group law need not be problematic, and similar situations of overlapping laws exist in practice. For instance, both federal and state law are applicable within each constituent state of a federal state, while the applicable state law will differ amongst each individual state.[24] A number of different options are available to armed groups seeking to address *nullum crimen sine lege* concerns. For instance, armed groups may apply state law, pre-existing customary or religious law, or effectively announce the promulgation of new laws or an entirely new penal code. The practice of armed groups in this regard is discussed in greater detail below.[25]

(b) Independence and Impartiality

Both international human rights law,[26] and international humanitarian law,[27] require that courts be independent and impartial.[28] In General

[21] See eg *Muller and others v Switzerland* App No 10737/84 (ECtHR, 24 May 1988), para 29.

[22] For instance, civilians may be unaware of the existence of laws promulgated by an armed group, or may be unsure whether to adhere to state law or to the law of the armed group.

[23] Yves Sandov, Christophe Swinarski and Brun Zimmermann (eds), *Commentary on the Additional Protocols of 8 June 1977 to the Geneva Conventions of 12 August 1949* (The Hague, Martinus Nijhoff, 1987) para 4605.

[24] The examples of the United States and Switzerland are pertinent in this regard.

[25] See below, Ch 8 section I.A(iv)(b).

[26] See for example, Art 14(1) International Covenant on Civil and Political Rights; Art 6 European Convention on Human Rights; Art 8 American Convention on Human Rights; Art 26 of the African Charter on Human and Peoples' Rights.

[27] See common Art 3(1)(d); Art 6(2) Additional Protocol II. See also above n 23, para 4597; Sandesh Sivakumaran, *The Law of Non-International Armed Conflict* (Oxford, OUP, 2012) 307.

[28] It is noted that international humanitarian law refers to a 'court', while international human rights law refers to a 'tribunal'. However, it appears that the distinction is minimal and that both terms refer to similar bodies. International humanitarian law requires that a court exhibit the essential guarantees of independence and impartiality, while the European Court of Human Rights has held that 'a "tribunal" is characterised in the substantive sense of the term by its judicial function', and the Human Rights Committee has specified that the term tribunal 'denotes a body, regardless of its denomination, that is established by law, is independent of the executive and legislative branches of government or enjoys in specific cases judicial independence in deciding legal matters in proceedings that are judicial in nature'. *Belilos v Switzerland* App No 10328/83 (ECtHR, 29 April 1988), para 64; Human Rights Committee, General Comment No 32, 'Article 14: Right to equality before courts and tribunals and to a fair trial', UN Doc CCPR/C/GC/32, 23 August 2007, para 18.

Comment 32, the Human Rights Committee confirmed the non-derogable nature of this requirement, stating that '[t]he requirement of competence, independence and impartiality ... is an absolute right that is not subject to any exception.'[29] Independence primarily relates to the institutional independence of the court,[30] and in particular, independence from interference by other branches of the government[31]—or, for present purposes, the armed group—as well as procedures relating to the appointment and security of tenure of judges.[32] For example, in *Bryan v United Kingdom* the European Court of Human Rights held that:

> [I]n order to establish whether a tribunal can be considered as 'independent', regard must be had, inter alia, to the manner of appointment of its members and to their term of office, to the existence of guarantees against outside pressures and to the question whether the body presents an appearance of independence.[33]

The impartiality requirement primarily concerns the judges themselves: 'judges must not harbour preconceptions about the matter put before them, and ... must not act in ways that promote the interests of one of the parties.'[34] Importantly, a tribunal must appear to be impartial to a 'reasonable observer'.[35]

A first question to be addressed is whether military courts are, in and of themselves, incompatible with the independence and impartiality requirements. This is pertinent in relation to armed groups, as it is likely that armed group courts will be internal to the group and be the only judicial structure available.[36] With respect to international armed conflict, the law of belligerent occupation explicitly allows for both the establishment of military courts and the prosecution of civilians before such courts.[37] Article 66 of the fourth Geneva Convention states: '[i]n case of a breach of the penal provisions promulgated by it by virtue of the second paragraph

[29] General Comment No 32, above n 28, para 19.

[30] See further, *Basic Principles on the Independence of the Judiciary*, adopted by the Seventh United Nations Congress on the Prevention of Crime and the Treatment of Offenders held at Milan from 26 August to 6 September 1985, endorsed by General Assembly resolutions 40/32 of 29 November 1985 and 40/146 of 13 December 1985.

[31] See eg General Comment No 32, above n 28, para 19.

[32] See ibid, para 19.

[33] *Bryan v United Kingdom* App No 19178/91 (ECtHR, 22 November 1995), para 37. See also, *Langborger v Sweden* App No 11179/84, 22 June 1989, para 32; *Molero Coca v Peru*, Report, Inter-American Commission on Human Rights, Case 11.182, 13 April 2000, para 127.

[34] *Karttunen v Finland*, Views, Human Rights Committee, Communication No 387/1989, UN Doc. CCPR/C/46/D/387/1989, para 7.2. See further, General Comment No 32, above n 28, para 21.

[35] General Comment No 32, above n 28, para 21.

[36] Examples in this regard include the FMLN, FARC, and the Shining Path. Of course, a possible exception are groups at advanced levels of organisational development, with the courts established by the LTTE or SPLM/A being cases on point.

[37] See eg Sharon Weill, 'The Judicial Arm of the Occupation: The Israeli Military Courts in the Occupied Territories' (2007) 89 *International Review of the Red Cross* 403.

of Article 64 the Occupying Power may hand over the accused to its properly constituted, non-political military courts, on condition that the said courts sit in the occupied country.'[38] Significantly, given the present focus, the law of non-international armed conflict is silent on the issue.[39]

In contrast, the case law of regional human rights bodies has repeatedly found elements of military court systems—in particular links to the executive—to be in violation of human rights law obligations.[40] However, none of these cases concluded that military courts are inherently incompatible with the requirements of international human rights law,[41] and it is noted that military court systems in both the United Kingdom and Canada have been restructured to comply with international human rights law requirements following adverse judicial decisions.[42] Ultimately, it must be concluded that military courts' compliance with international human rights law is not prima facie precluded, either during, or outside, armed conflict.[43] However, outside armed conflict there does appear to be an emerging trend that seeks to prohibit the trial of civilians before military courts.[44]

As such, it must be determined whether armed group courts should be considered equivalent to military courts, as this may preclude the trial of civilians by armed groups. In this regard, one significant factor differentiates judicial systems established by armed groups from states' systems: within a state's domestic system a separate judicial apparatus with jurisdiction over civilians will exist,[45] and so the prosecution of civilians before a military court will typically be an exception to the jurisdiction of these courts. This factor does not apply straightforwardly to armed

[38] Art 66 Fourth Geneva Convention.

[39] For example, Art 6 Additional Protocol II does not mention whether courts may be military courts, requiring only that they be independent and impartial.

[40] See eg *Media Rights Agenda v Nigeria*, Decision, African Commission on Human and Peoples' Rights, Communication No 224/98, 2000, para 61; *Salinas Sedo v Peru*, Inter-American Commission on Human Rights, Report No 27/94, Case No 11.084, 30 September 1994; *Sahiner v Turkey* App No 29279/95 (ECtHR, 25 September 2001), para 41.

[41] See Rule 100, above n 17. See also, *Morris v United Kingdom* App No 38784/97 (ECtHR, 26 February 2002), para 59; Louise Doswald-Beck, *Human Rights in Times of Conflict and Terrorism* (Oxford, OUP, 2011) 340.

[42] See *Findlay v United Kingdom* App No 22107/93 (ECtHR, 25 February 1997); *R v Genereux*, Supreme Court of Canada [1992] 1 SCR 259.

[43] See General Comment No 32, above n 28, para 22. See further, Human Rights Committee, General Comment No 13 'Equality before the courts and tribunals and the right to a fair and public hearing by a competent, independent and impartial tribunal established by law', UN Doc HR1/GEN/1/Rev 1, para 4.

[44] See eg *Zambrano Velez v Ecuador*, Judgment, Inter-American Court of Human Rights, 4 July 2007, para 66. See also, *Castillo Petruzzi et al*, Judgment, Inter-American Court of Human Rights, Ser C No 52, 30 May 1999, para 128; Human Rights Committee, Concluding Observations on Lebanon, UN Doc CCPR/C/79/Add.78, 1 April 1997, para 14.

[45] See eg *Media Rights Agenda v Nigeria*, above n 40, para 62, referring to the African Commission's Resolution on the Right to Fair Trial and Legal Assistance in Africa.

groups, who—in the majority of instances—do not have a distinct parallel judicial wing with jurisdiction over civilians.[46] Accordingly, should courts established by armed groups comply with the requirements of international human rights law, the trial of civilians before such courts must be regarded as permissible in principle. Indeed, this may constitute the closest achievable replication of a state's civilian court structure,[47] and one that is potentially capable of ensuring defendants' rights. Of course, if an armed group does possess a distinct civilian system—as was the case with respect to the LTTE in Sri Lanka—this should be used to try civilians.

In practice, however, the requirement that courts be independent and impartial may present a number of difficulties for armed groups. In particular, it is noted that unlike state armed forces, armed groups do not typically exist within an overall governance structure based upon the principle of the separation of powers, which in and of itself facilitates adherence to the structural elements of the independence requirement.[48] While in certain instances the 'party may control the gun',[49] the political and combat wings of armed groups are often intertwined, and distinct legislative, executive, and judicial structures may not exist. In this regard, a number of international human rights law requirements that may pose difficulties with respect to armed group compliance can be identified.

First, in *Cyprus v Turkey*, the European Court of Human Rights held that the 'close structural links between the executive power and the military officers serving on the "TRNC" military courts'[50] meant that individuals appearing before the court 'could legitimately fear that they lacked independence and impartiality.'[51] This implies that courts established by armed groups should not have structural links to the armed group command structure (equivalent to the executive branch in the context of state armed forces).[52] Second, and in an extension of the absence of structural links requirement, the authority responsible for convening a court must

[46] As noted above, at high levels of development there may be exceptions to this statement, and the court systems established by the LTTE and the SPLM/A are examples in this regard.

[47] In this sense the armed group structure may be regarded as a microcosm of a state's structure. Thus, although the court may exist within the structure of the armed group, if it is, inter alia, independent of the armed group's command structure (ie the 'executive'), this may be sufficient vis-à-vis the requirements of international human rights law.

[48] Of course, certain armed groups do establish a distinction between their armed and political wings. For instance, a distinction exists between the political leadership of the Hamas movement and its armed wing, the *Izz ad-Din al-Qassam* Brigades. Similarly, Maoist-style groups, such as the CPN-M, the Naxalites, and the NPA, have established distinctions between the political and armed wings of the groups, operating under the principle that 'the party controls the gun'.

[49] This is a feature of Maoist guerrilla doctrine.

[50] *Cyprus v Turkey* App No 25781/94 (ECtHR, 10 May 2001), para 358.

[51] ibid, para 358.

[52] See eg *R v Genereux*, above n 42, 261–62.

not be in such a position that it also plays a central role in the courts martial,[53] or has the authority to appoint the members of the court.[54] In *Findlay v United Kingdom* the European Court of Human Rights held that:

> In order to maintain confidence in the independence and impartiality of the court, appearances may be of importance. Since all the members of the court martial which decided Mr Findlay's case *were subordinate in rank to the convening officer* and *fell within his chain of command*, Mr Findlay's doubts about the tribunal's independence and impartiality could be objectively justified.[55]

Accordingly, if members of a court convened by an armed group are subordinate to the convening authority, and subject to the same chain of command, then objective doubts as to the court's independence and impartiality may be justified.[56] Finally, in the *Durand and Ugarte Case*, the Inter-American Court of Human Rights held that, as the members of the military tribunal were at the same time members of the armed forces on active duty, 'they were unable to issue an independent and impartial judgment.'[57] A similar finding was made by the European Court of Human Rights which held that as one of the judges of the Izmir National Security Court was a military judge—and so subject to military discipline and assessment procedures[58]—the court might 'be unduly influenced by considerations which had nothing to do with the nature of the case.'[59] International human rights law thus requires that members of the armed group who sit on courts cannot be 'active service' members of the armed group, as this may affect their judgment.

Evidently, compliance with the requirements of international human rights law will have implications with respect to an armed group's organisational structure, perhaps necessitating the existence of a unit outside the armed group's chain of command, from which judges are drawn.[60] The organisational sophistication required to satisfy these requirements will inevitably be beyond the capability of a number of armed groups. For example, although Jemaah Islamiyah has a separate disciplinary council (*majelis hisbah*), its members are appointed by the *amir* (overall commander), and subject to his control.[61] However, satisfaction of these

[53] *Findlay v United Kingdom*, above n 42, paras 74–80. See also, *Hood v United Kingdom* App No 27267/95 ECtHR, 18 February 1999), paras 76–78; *Coyne v United Kingdom* App No 25942/94 (ECtHR, 24 September 1997), paras 56–58.

[54] *R v Genereux*, above n 42, 263.

[55] *Findlay v United Kingdom*, above n 42, para 76. Emphasis added.

[56] See eg *Sramek v Austria* App No 8790/79 (ECtHR, 22 October 1984), para 42.

[57] *Durand and Ugarte Case*, Judgment, Inter-American Court of Human Rights, Ser C No 68 (2000), 16 August 2000, para 126.

[58] *Incal v Turkey* App No 41/1997/825/1031 (ECtHR, 9 June 1998), para 68.

[59] ibid, para 72.

[60] To ensure independence from the armed group's command structure (ie the executive).

[61] International Crisis Group, 'Jemaah Islamiyah in South East Asia: Damaged but Still Dangerous' (2003) 11.

requirements by other armed groups may be possible. In Nepal, for example, the CPN-M reportedly established a court system involving distinct organs for investigation, prosecution, and decision-making,[62] and in Sri Lanka the LTTE developed an advanced, state-like, judicial apparatus.[63] At less developed levels of sophistication it is possible that 'people's courts', or similar bodies, may satisfy the independence and impartiality requirement. In India the Naxalites established a system of people's courts which are convened by the local Naxalite committee with cases decided by the local population.[64] In Iraq, the Mahdi movement established a rule of law system with arbitration committees composed of tribal chiefs,[65] while in Indonesia, GAM convened councils at the village, sub-district, or district levels, presided over by an Islamic judge.[66] It is also possible that traditional or religious courts may continue to operate in areas subject to armed group control, while an armed group may also permit the continued operation of state courts.[67]

In analysing armed group courts' compliance with the requirements of international human rights law it is noted that state judicial systems around the world operate in accordance with different standards and rules. Accordingly, it is submitted that it is respect for the content of the relevant rights that is important: ie, is a trial generally free and fair? In this regard the complexity of the case at hand will be an important factor. In Nepal it was noted that a large proportion of cases addressed by CPN-M courts concerned issues relating to 'minor disputes over land, money, and familial relationships',[68] and in the majority of instances, these cases, and others such as theft or assault, may be addressed in a relatively straightforward manner by the courts. As such, it is feasible that an armed group may operate, or facilitate the operation of, a court system that is capable of effectively maintaining law and order and addressing routine crimes, but which cannot cope with more complex cases.[69] In this situation, a court's

[62] 'Courts of Armed Opposition Groups' above n 5, 493. The extent to which these organs may be considered independent is, however, unclear. Equally, in the Gaza Strip a state-like court system operates largely independently of the armed wing of the Hamas movement. However, it is noted that uncertainty exists regarding Hamas' classification as a non-state actor. While Hamas is not internationally recognised as the legitimate government of Palestine, the movement did win a majority in the 2005 legislative elections, and although this term of office has expired, there have been no subsequent elections.

[63] 'Courts of Armed Opposition Groups' above n 5, 494.

[64] See 'Walking with the Comrades' above n 3; '"Being Neutral is Our Biggest Crime"' above n 3, 113.

[65] 'Iraq's Muqtada Al-Sadr' above n 3, 20; 'Iraq's Civil War, the Sadrists and the Surge' above n 3, 7.

[66] 'Indonesia: The War in Aceh' above n 3, 10, 35.

[67] See further below Ch 8 section I.A(iv)(b)).

[68] 'Courts of Armed Opposition Groups' above n 5, 492–93. See 'Nepal: Judged by the people', *The Economist* (5 October 2006).

[69] For instance, complex cases involving state infrastructural projects, or white collar crime.

inability to effectively address all crimes does not mean that it should be precluded from addressing those cases within its capacity to adjudicate effectively. Of course, the inverse is also true, and a court incapable of delivering an international human rights law-compliant judgment with respect to a specific case should not do so.[70] Interestingly, in a number of instances it has been reported that individuals have regarded armed group courts as preferable to those of the state, seeing them as fairer and less corrupt.[71]

(c) Adequate Time and Means for the Preparation of a Defence

An accused's right to 'all necessary rights and means of defence'[72] is established under both the international humanitarian law of non-international armed conflict, and international human rights law.[73] Underlining its significance, the Human Rights Committee has noted that this right 'is an important element of the guarantee of a fair trial and an application of the principle of equality of arms.'[74] In determining the content of the right, the International Committee of the Red Cross' Customary International Humanitarian Law Study specifies that an adequate defence must include: the right to defend oneself or be assisted by a lawyer of one's own choosing; the right to free legal assistance if the interests of justice so require; the right to sufficient time and facilities to prepare a defence; and the right of the accused to communicate freely with counsel.[75] A proposal submitted by Costa Rica during the drafting of the Elements of Crimes of the International Criminal Court also includes: 'the right to be tried without undue delay; the right to present and examine witnesses; and the right to an interpreter.'[76] These requirements, established in relation to armed conflict, broadly mirror those of international human rights law, as codified in Article 14 of the International Covenant on Civil and Political Rights.[77] The right to legal assistance may determine 'whether or not a person can

[70] In situations such as these, presumably involving complex crimes, it is possible that the accused may be released on bail and the trial postponed to a later date.

[71] See eg Office of the High Commissioner for Human Rights in Nepal, 'Human rights abuses by the CPN-M, Summary of Concerns', September 2006, 4; 'Behind the Taliban's Resurgence in Afghanistan' above n 7; Michael Weiss and Hassan Hassan, *ISIS: Inside the Army of Terror* (New York, Regan Arts, 2015) 223–24.

[72] Art 6(2)(a) Additional Protocol II.

[73] See Art 6(2)(a) Additional Protocol II, and Art 14(3)(b) International Covenant on Civil and Political Rights.

[74] General Comment No 32, above n 28, para 32.

[75] Rule 100, above n 17.

[76] Proposal submitted by Costa Rica, Hungary and Switzerland on Art 8 para 2(c) of the Rome Statute of the International Criminal Court, Doc No PCNICC/1999/WGEC/DP.10.

[77] See Manfred Nowak, *UN Covenant on Civil and Political Rights: CCPR Commentary* (Kehl am rhein, NP Engel, 1993) 258.

access the relevant proceedings or participate in them in a meaningful way',[78] and so—dependent upon the circumstances of the case—this may be an essential component of an adequate defence.[79] Ultimately, however, while all of these factors are potentially relevant, a determination as to what constitutes 'adequate' time and means must be made on a case-by-case basis,[80] and will be dependent upon the complexity of the case.[81]

The obligation to provide adequate time and means for defence may pose practical difficulties for armed groups, particularly in relation to access to a lawyer and adequate facilities. At first glance, it may appear that fulfilment of this obligation may only be achieved when an armed group exerts stable control over territory:[82] under such circumstances security-related time constraints will presumably be avoided,[83] and detainees may be kept in a stationary location, in close proximity to the court, with appropriate facilities made available for the preparation of the defence. For instance, in Sri Lanka the LTTE operated a state-like court system within the area subject to its control,[84] and it is reasonable to expect that groups at this level of sophistication and who exercise territorial control have the ability to fulfil this obligation.[85] However, a complex judicial system is not a prerequisite to satisfaction of the obligation, and it is possible that adequate means of defence may be made available at less developed levels of sophistication,[86] including if the group is mobile.[87]

Of course, the complexity of the case will be a factor potentially necessitating access to legal advice or further time for the preparation of the defence, thereby placing an increased burden on the armed group.[88] Conflict realities—or an area's level of development—may also frustrate access to a lawyer in certain situations. For example, in El Salvador 'the FMLN observed that there could be no requirement that the defence counsel

[78] General Comment No 32, above n 28, para 10.

[79] International human rights law also requires that the defendant has access to all documents and other evidence. See General Comment No 32, above n 28, para 33.

[80] *Alrick Thomas v Jamaica*, Views, Human Rights Committee, Communication No 272/1988, UN Doc CCPR/C/44/d/272/1988, 31 March 1992, para 11.4.

[81] See eg African Commission on Human and People's Rights, 'Principles and Guidelines on the Right to a Fair Trial and Legal Assistance in Africa', SOC/OS(XXX)247, 14.

[82] See discussion in *The Law of Non-International Armed Conflict* above n 27, 309.

[83] Noting that an armed group that does not exercise stable territorial control may have to relocate frequently and may be subject to routine harassment, and so on.

[84] 'Thamil Eelam judiciary said a basis for rebuilding northeast' above n 5.

[85] Other possible examples in this regard include the CPN-M in Nepal.

[86] Examples in this regard include FARC in Colombia, and the Naxalites in India.

[87] See James E Bond, 'Application of the Law of War to Internal Conflicts' (1973) 3 *Georgia Journal of International and Comparative Law* 375. Of course, certain practical issues may arise in such situations and, for example, a detainee may need to move with the court in order to facilitate access to the necessary facilities.

[88] For example, access to a large number of case-related documents may be required, necessitating time and facilities to review them.

be a licensed attorney if there were no licensed attorneys in the region.'[89] Instead, the FMLN proposed that defence counsel should be selected on the basis of their conduct and ethical principles.[90] This proposal seems hard to reconcile with the widely accepted understanding of the judicial process, although, it is noted that non-lawyers do engage in the judicial process, particularly in traditional justice mechanisms, with the *Gacaca* courts in Rwanda providing a prominent contemporary example wherein non-lawyers were appointed as judges.[91] At a minimum, it is submitted that in order to preserve the requirement of equality of arms, both defence and prosecution counsel must be trained to an equivalent standard.

The right to call witnesses—considered to be one of the 'essential rights and means of defence'[92]—may also prove problematic in the context of courts convened by armed groups, as defence witnesses may be situated in 'enemy' territory, or may be reluctant to appear before the court, fearing either reprisals by the state or consequences from the armed group. However, although international human rights law guarantees a defendant's right 'to obtain the attendance and examination of witnesses on his behalf under the same conditions as witnesses against him',[93] this is not listed as a non-derogable right, either in Article 4(2) of the International Covenant on Civil and Political Rights or in the expanded list of non-derogable provisions detailed in General Comment 29,[94] and is considered to be a qualified right.[95] In this regard the Inter-American Commission on Human Rights has noted that:

> Potentially derogable protections may include, for example, the right to a public trial and a defendant's right to examine or have examined witnesses against him or her, where limitations on these rights are necessary to ensure the safety of judges, lawyers, witnesses or others involved in the administration of justice.[96]

Of course, if this right is to be derogated from, it remains essential that this derogation does not interfere with the fundamental principles

[89] Quoted in 'Courts of Armed Opposition Groups' above n 5, 492.

[90] ibid, 492.

[91] See William A Schabas, 'Genocide Trials and *Gacaca* Courts' (2005) 3 *Journal of International Criminal Justice*, 887. However, it is noted that these courts' compliance with international standards is strongly contested. See for example Jacques Fierens, '*Gacaca* Courts: Between Fantasy and Reality' (2005) 3 *Journal of International Criminal Justice* 910; Paul Christoph Bornkamm, *Rwanda's Gacaca Courts: Between Retribution and Reparation* (Oxford, OUP, 2012) 111, 117.

[92] Above n 23, para 4602. See also, General Comment No 32, above n 28, para 39.

[93] Art 14(3)(e) International Covenant on Civil and Political Rights.

[94] See Human Rights Committee, 'General Comment No 29: States of Emergency (Article 4)', UN Doc CCPR/C/21/Rev.1/Add.11, 31 August 2001.

[95] See eg above n 77, 261.

[96] 'Report of the Inter-American Commission on Human Rights on Terrorism and Human Rights (Executive Summary and Recommendations)', Inter-American Commission on Human Rights, OEA/Ser.G CP/CAJP-2126/04, 13 February 2004, para 20.

of a fair trial.[97] In this regard, if witnesses do appear before the court, a defendant must have the ability to examine them, including the ability to examine 'witnesses on his behalf under the same conditions as witnesses against him'.[98] There appears to be no valid reason for interfering with this right in the context of armed group courts, and to do so would violate the principle of equality of arms, interfering with the overall right to a fair trial.[99]

(d) Public Trials

International human rights law establishes the right to 'a fair and public hearing',[100] and this is also a feature of the law of international armed conflict.[101] There is no equivalent provision in the treaty-based law of non-international armed conflict, although—as with other international human rights law provisions relating to a fair trial—the International Committee of the Red Cross' Customary International Humanitarian Law Study concluded that it does form part of the applicable customary international law.[102] In General Comment 32 the Human Rights Committee held that, '[t]he publicity of hearings ensures the transparency of proceedings and provides an important safeguard for the interest of the individual and of society at large'.[103] However, international human rights law does anticipate that the public may be legitimately excluded from a trial for a number of different reasons, including public order and national security.[104] The requirement that judgments be pronounced publicly is, however, absolute:[105] '[e]ven in cases in which the public is excluded from the trial, the judgment, including the essential findings, evidence and legal reasoning must be made public'.[106]

Certain factors may prevent an armed group from holding a trial in public. For example, a trial may be conducted in an area not subject to the exclusive control of the armed group, and in this situation public notice regarding a trial may prompt an attack by state forces. In such situations a limitation on the right to a public hearing may be justified on

[97] Above n 94, para 11.

[98] Art 14(3)(e) International Covenant on Civil and Political Rights.

[99] See eg above n 77, 262.

[100] Art 14(1) International Covenant on Civil and Political Rights. See also, Art 6(1) European Convention on Human Rights; Art 8(5) American Convention on Human Rights.

[101] See Art 105(5) Second Geneva Convention, Art 74(1) Fourth Geneva Convention.

[102] Rule 100, above n 17.

[103] General Comment No 32, above n 28, para 28. See also above n 77, 249.

[104] Art 14(1) International Covenant on Civil and Political Rights.

[105] Above n 77, 252; *Luciano Weinberger Weisz and Ismael Weinberger v Uruguay*, Views, Human Rights Committee, Communication No 28/1978, UN Doc CCPR/C/11/D/28/1978, 29 October 1980, para 16; General Comment No 32, above n 28, para 29.

[106] General Comment No 32, above n 28, para 29.

the basis of security considerations, and potentially also in the interests of the participants' safety.[107] However, while the public may be excluded, the judgment must still be pronounced publicly.[108] This should not pose insurmountable difficulties for armed groups in practice;[109] security considerations associated with the physical location of the trial do not apply, and the availability and accessibility of communications technology facilitates public dissemination.[110] In fact, publishing judgments may be in the strategic interest of an armed group, as it demonstrates the armed group's displacement of state authority.[111] Of course, the possibility of excluding the public applies only in limited circumstances, and where possible, all trials should be held in public. For example, when an armed group exerts stable territorial control it is difficult to envisage justifications for not holding public trials.[112]

(e) The Death Penalty

The issue of the death penalty is also relevant. The Human Rights Committee has stated that, '[i]n cases of trials leading to the imposition of the death penalty scrupulous respect of the guarantees of fair trial is particularly important',[113] and the imposition of a death sentence on the basis of a trial which did not adhere to the requirements of the International Covenant on Civil and Political Rights has been held to constitute a violation of the right to life.[114] In situations of non-international armed conflict, such conduct amounts to a war crime.[115] Given the stringent requirements

[107] See eg above n 96, para 20.

[108] See eg above n 77, 251–52.

[109] All judgments must be reasoned. See *Little v Jamaica*, Decision, Human Rights Committee, Communication No 283/1988, UN Doc CCPR/C/43/D/283/1988, 1 November 1991, para 8.5.

[110] For example, an M23 fighter in the Democratic Republic of Congo noted that communications technology is 'essential in modern war' and carried a modified wireless router to ensure access to the Internet. See Anjan Sundaram, 'The Things They Carried: The Congolese Rebel', *Foreign Policy* (4 March 2013). A number of other groups also have facebook or twitter accounts, as well as active Internet presences. For example, Jund al Islam took credit for suicide car bomb attacks in the Sinai in a statement released to 'jihadist' Internet forums (see David Barnett, 'Jund al Islam claims credit for Sinai suicide car bomb attacks', *The Long War Journal* (12 September 2013)) while similarly the Al Nusrah Front in Syria released a statement claiming responsibility for attacks in the province of Homs on 10 September 2013 (see Bill Roggio, 'Al Nusrah Front, Ahrar al Sham attack Syrian villages', *The Long War Journal* (17 September 2013)).

[111] Bruce Hoffman, 'The Use of the Internet by Islamic Extremists', Testimony presented to the House Select Committee on Intelligence, 4 May 2006.

[112] Although this does not preclude the possibility that certain components of a trial may be conducted *in camera*.

[113] General Comment No 32, above n 28, para 59.

[114] *Osbourne Wright and Eric Harvey v Jamaica*, Views, Human Rights Committee, Communication No 459/1991, UN Doc CCPR/C/55/D/459/1991, 27 October 1995, para 10.6.

[115] See Art 8(2)(c)(iv) Statute of the International Criminal Court.

associated with death penalty cases, and the growing movement towards abolition of the death penalty more broadly,[116] an absolute prohibition on the issuance of death sentences by armed groups may be appropriate. At a minimum, armed groups should not be allowed to impose death sentences in states where the death penalty has been abolished.[117]

Having established the relevant procedural guarantees, the specific crimes that armed groups may prosecute must now be determined. Three categories of crime are addressed: violations of the law of armed conflict, group-specific crimes established in accordance with the law of an armed group, and non-conflict-related crimes.

(ii) Can an Armed Group Prosecute Violations of the Law of Armed Conflict?

The specific crimes that may be legitimately prosecuted before armed group courts remain to be determined. In this regard it is submitted that if international humanitarian law regulates the operation of courts, it stands to reason that, as a minimum, this is for the purpose of ensuring respect for international humanitarian law.[118] The decision of the International Criminal Tribunal for the former Yugoslavia in *Hadzihasanovic* is relevant to this conclusion: referring to Article 6 Additional Protocol II, the Trial Chamber noted that '[t]he primary aim of this provision is to provide guarantees that a person who is charged with violations of international humanitarian law in internal armed conflicts will receive a fair trial and not be sentenced without such a fair trial.'[119] It must be concluded that the court regarded the prosecution of international humanitarian law violations as legitimate.

Indeed, armed groups may be subject to an obligation to prosecute war crimes committed by their members. The principle of command responsibility holds that:[120] '[c]ommanders and other superiors are criminally responsible for war crimes committed by their subordinates' if they 'did not take all necessary and reasonable measures … to punish the persons

[116] See for instance, UNGA Res 62/149, UNGA Res 63/168, UNGA Res 65/206.

[117] With respect to the law of belligerent occupation, see eg Yoram Dinstein, *The International Law of Belligerent Occupation* (Cambridge, CUP, 2009) 143–44.

[118] See eg Art 1 common to the four Geneva Conventions of 1949. Discussion in this regard is necessarily restricted to armed groups party to a non-international armed conflict.

[119] *Prosecutor v Enver Hadzihasanovic, Mehmed Alagic, Amir Kubura*, Decision on Joint Challenge to Jurisdiction, Trial Chamber, International Criminal Tribunal for the former Yugoslavia, Case No IT-01-47-PT, 12 November 2002, para 162.

[120] The application of the principle of command responsibility to non-international armed conflict was confirmed by the Appeals Chamber of the International Criminal Tribunal for the former Yugoslavia in *Hadzihasanovic* (see *Prosecutor v Enver Hadzihasanovic, Mehmed Alagic, Amir Kubura*, Decision on Interlocutory Appeal Challenging Jurisdiction in Relation to Command Responsibility, Appeals Chamber, International Criminal Tribunal for the former Yugoslavia, Case No IT-01-47-AR72, 16 July 2003, para 31).

responsible.'[121] While a commander may discharge his responsibility by reporting an incident to the appropriate authority, in order to be effective, overall responsibility must remain with the armed group.[122] As war crimes give rise to individual criminal responsibility, the obligation to prosecute cannot be satisfied by means of a purely disciplinary process,[123] and so armed groups may be required to establish courts in order to prosecute suspected war crimes committed by members of the armed group. In such situations the armed group is the only entity realistically capable of conducting prosecutions, raising the possibility of a vacuum in accountability should they fail to do so. This conclusion is somewhat problematic, however, given that armed groups may not have the capacity to conduct fair trials. As the passing of sentences by a court failing to offer the essential guarantees of independence and impartiality is itself a war crime,[124] commanders whose forces are suspected of committing war crimes, but whose armed group does not have the capacity to conduct fair trials, are placed in a difficult position vis-à-vis the obligation to prevent and punish. It is possible that armed groups may pass such suspects over to an international criminal tribunal or third state, although this proposal is not straightforward, given that third states may not have jurisdiction and that the crimes may not be of sufficient severity to warrant intervention by an international tribunal.[125] It is also possible that the armed group could pass suspects over to the state for prosecution. However, this would appear to be an unreasonable requirement, given the reality of the situation, and the transfer of detainees on this basis might be regarded by group members as an act of treason.

In seeking to address this situation a number of possibilities may be identified. First, an armed group may be required to develop the capacity to conduct the required fair trials. However, while this may be the most desirable outcome, it appears unlikely that the expenditure of resources

[121] Rule 153, above n 17.

[122] In terms of individual responsibility, responsibility will remain with the commander's commander etc.

[123] Other violations of international humanitarian law may be dealt with by means of an internal disciplinary process, and that this, in fact, constitutes an element of the responsible command requirement. See eg, above n 23, para 4463. See also, Anthony Cullen, *The Concept of Non-International Armed Conflict in International Humanitarian Law* (Cambridge, CUP, 2010) 151. However, internal disciplinary measures not involving criminal prosecution are not relevant herein.

[124] See Art 147 Fourth Geneva Convention; Art 8(2)(a)(vi) Statute of the International Criminal Court.

[125] See eg Art 5(1) of the Statute of the International Criminal Court. The use of universal jurisdiction by third states is also typically restricted in a number of ways, for instance, crimes giving rise to universal jurisdiction are often restricted to grave breaches of the Geneva Conventions or torture, and there is often a requirement that the suspect be a resident of the third State. See further, 'FIDH-REDRESS Update on Universal Jurisdiction: Fighting Impunity Worldwide' (2009).

in this area will be regarded as a priority by an armed group actively engaged in armed conflict, noting in particular the extensive resources that are often required to conduct effective war crimes trials. Second, it may be possible for an armed group to develop the capacity to try the underlying offences of the war crime in question, such as murder or torture, while avoiding the extra capacity requirements associated with prosecuting certain international crimes. While this may not be sufficient with respect to the requirement that international crimes be prosecuted as international crimes, it may be sufficient to demonstrate that the conduct in question is not acceptable, and to satisfy the requirements of command responsibility, noting that the international crime can be prosecuted at a later date if necessary. Third, it is possible that the suspect may be subject to internal disciplinary procedures, potentially including demotion, removal from a position of command, or discharge from the group. This approach has the benefit of clearly censuring the conduct and establishing a deterrent—provided that the sanction is sufficiently severe—and the required prosecution may be deferred until such time as it is possible.[126] However, regardless of the practicalities involved, it must be concluded that a legal basis for the prosecution of international humanitarian law violations exists.

This leads to the question of whether armed groups may also prosecute violations of the law of armed conflict committed by individuals external to the group, namely members of opposition forces or members of the civilian population. In *Nicaragua*, the International Court of Justice held that the obligation 'to respect and to ensure respect' for the Geneva Conventions 'in all circumstances' constitutes a general principle of international law.[127] As the punishment of violations is regarded as one of the most effective means of securing respect for the law,[128] the obligation to ensure respect may provide a legal basis for armed group prosecutions of violations of the law of armed conflict committed by non-members.[129]

[126] It seems appropriate that any evidence or case files be preserved; both to facilitate a future prosecution and to clearly demonstrate that the group does in fact intend to prosecute in the future.

[127] *Case Concerning Military and Paramilitary Activities In and Against Nicaragua (Nicaragua v United States of America)*, Merits, International Court of Justice, 27 June 1986, para 220; See further, Rule 138, above n 17; Restating *Decision on Defence Motion to Summon Witnesses*, 3 February 1999, in *Prosecutor v Kupreskic et al*, Decision on Evidence of the Good Character of the Accused and the Defence of *Tu Quoque*, Trial Chamber, International Criminal Tribunal for the former Yugoslavia, Case No IT-95-16, 17 February 1999.

[128] See eg Marco Sassoli, 'Legislation and Maintenance of Public Order and Civil Life by Occupying Powers' (2005) 16 *European Journal of International Law* 665; *Prosecutor v Jean-Pierre Bemba Gombo*, Decision Pursuant to Art 61(7)(a) and (b) of the Rome Statue on the Charges of the Prosecutor Against Jean-Pierre Bemba Gombo, Pre-Trial Chamber, International Criminal Court, Case No ICC-01/05-01/08, 15 June 2009, para 501.

[129] See Liesbeth Zegveld, *The Accountability of Armed Opposition Groups in International Law* (Cambridge, CUP, 2002) 67.

Indeed if this possibility were precluded, there exists a real danger that a 'frustrated demand for justice' could lead to the summary execution of suspects.[130]

However, similar problems to those discussed above arise should the armed group lack the capacity to conduct fair trials. In particular, it is likely that suspected war crimes committed by individuals external to an armed group will have targeted group members or their constituent community, and so transferring such individuals for prosecution may prove unacceptable;[131] even if this is not the case, transferring individuals to the state may not be acceptable on an ideological basis. It is possible that suspects may be detained pending trial, while the group develops the required capacity. However, the uncertainty inherent in this proposal raises real concerns in relation to indefinite detention. Alternatively, if the suspect is an enemy fighter, a potential solution may be internment for the duration of the conflict—justified on the basis of military necessity[132]—at which point it is hoped that an effective investigation and, if appropriate, prosecution, may be conducted. Detention on the same basis may not be possible with respect to suspects who are not fighters, given the absence of a military necessity based justification. If there is sufficient evidence to indicate that a suspect is likely to commit future violations, then preventive detention may be possible, although use of this measure is necessarily subject to strict procedural guarantees, including judicial review.[133] Given the continued relevance of the 'established by law' requirement, it is likely that preventive imprisonment may only be utilised by armed groups with legislative authority, thereby restricting its application.[134]

(iii) Can an Armed Group Prosecute Group-Specific Crimes Established under the Law of the Armed Group?

This section addresses whether armed groups can prosecute crimes established under the law of the armed group that relate to 'group-specific'

[130] For instance, in Mexico it was reported that vigilante groups detained suspected members of drug gangs and handed them over to the police for prosecution, but that these individuals were released a short time later. In response to this apparent lack of action, the vigilante groups stated that 'we decided not to detain anyone anymore'. Stephanie McCrummen, 'In Mexico, self defense groups battle a cartel', *The Washington Post* (Washington, 10 September 2013).

[131] If an armed group captures a member of the state's armed forces suspected of committing a war crime (for instance the wilful killing of civilians associated with the armed group), but lacks the capacity to conduct a prosecution, is it reasonable to expect the armed group to turn this individual over to the state?

[132] For further discussion in this regard, see below, Ch 8 section I.B(ii)(a)).

[133] Procedural guarantees relating to detention are discussed further below, see Ch 8 section I.B(i).

[134] See discussion below, Ch 8 section I.B(ii)(b)).

issues such as breaches of internal regulations or treason. The phrase group-specific is used to highlight that these crimes are defined by armed groups for their own purposes; such crimes are therefore distinguished from those related to violations of the law of armed conflict, as discussed above, and those relating to the rule of law more generally—which may be in the 'best interests' of the affected population—as discussed below.[135] This section is relevant to situations occurring both during, and outside, armed conflict.

Members of armed groups are typically required to adhere to internal regulations in order to ensure the effective organisation and operation of the group.[136] Such regulations are considered to be the concrete expression of a group's will, and a signal to 'group members that prohibited conduct will not be tolerated',[137] thereby ensuring order and contributing to the prevention of future egressions. Internal regulations are often enacted on the basis of publicised internal rules,[138] and may be enforced by means of a courts martial procedure.[139] Common disciplinary measures include the issuance of a warning, demotion, extra duty, dismissal from the group, and so on, although they may also include 'imprisonment and corporal punishment, including capital punishment'.[140] It is also possible

[135] See Ch 8 section I.A(iv). The distinction vis-à-vis group-specific crimes is necessitated on the basis that the issues addressed in this section do not necessarily relate to the regulation of the civilian population, large.

[136] It is noted that this section relates to prosecution by armed groups, and so only those internal regulations relating to criminal charges are of concern. Furthermore, it is highlighted that in the context of non-international armed conflict, the requirement of responsible command includes the ability to ensure respect for international humanitarian law, and this requirement is typically satisfied by means of an internal discipline mechanism. The promulgation of internal rules is widely regarded as a means of controlling fighters and maintaining the effectiveness of the military-like structures. Olivier Bangerter, 'Internal Control: Codes of Conduct within Insurgent Armed Groups' (2012) Small Arms Survey Occasional Paper No 31, 1.

[137] Anne-Marie La Rosa and Carolin Wuerzner, 'Armed groups, sanctions and the implementation of international humanitarian law' (2008) 90 *International Review of the Red Cross* 334.

[138] Disciplinary codes have also been established by the KLA, the FARC, the RUF, the African National Congress (ANC), the Chin National Front (CNF), the Forces pour la Defense de la Democratie, the Nicaraguan Democratic Force (FDN) in Nicaragua, the Karen National Liberation Army, the Sudan Liberation Movement-Unity leadership; the SPLM/A, and the Zomi Re-unification Organisation. See for example: *Prosecutor v Haradinaj*, International Criminal Tribunal for the former Yugoslavia, IT-04-84-T, 3 April 2008, para 69; International Crisis Group, 'Ending Colombia's FARC Conflict: Dealing the Right Card', March 2009, 3, fn 15; *Prosecutor v Sesay, Kallon and Gbao,* Trial Chamber, Special Court for Sierra Leone, Case No SCSL-04-15-T, 2 March 2009), para 706; 'Courts of Armed Opposition Groups' above n 5, 494; above n 136, 26.

[139] See for instance, 'The IRA Court Martial Procedure' in Irish Republican Army, *The Green Book (Book I and II)*.

[140] Above n 137, 334. For example, a former member of Al-Shabab reported the execution of an attempted deserter. See Peter Taylor, 'On the trail of al-Shabab's Kenyan recruitment 'pipeline', *BBC News* (London, 29 September 2013).

that armed groups may prosecute individuals—whether members of the armed group or not—for other group-defined crimes such as treason or collaboration. Armed group codes of conduct often include a prohibition of treason,[141] and, for example, this was criminalised in the penal code promulgated by the LTTE.[142] Any law promulgated by an armed group must satisfy the 'established by law' requirement,[143] and so must have a basis in either domestic law or international law. As the domestic law of the state will not provide a legal basis for the law of a non-state armed group, to satisfy this requirement a legal basis for group specific laws must exist under international law.

In situations of non-international armed conflict, international humanitarian law requires that an armed group be organised.[144] This criterion is regarded as including the ability to fulfil obligations arising under international humanitarian law—typically by means of a controlling authority exercising internal discipline—and a legal basis for the prosecution of violations of international humanitarian law by armed groups has already been established.[145] Beyond this, however, it is uncertain whether international humanitarian law provides a legal basis for an armed group's internal regulations, ie those issues not amounting to violations of international humanitarian law. Indeed, while international humanitarian law requires that armed groups be organised, this is a requirement related to the threshold of application of international humanitarian law. Presuming the intensity criterion is satisfied, if an armed group is sufficiently organised international humanitarian law becomes applicable, if it is not then international humanitarian law cannot apply. Accordingly, it is difficult to view international humanitarian law as establishing an obligation that armed groups be organised, thereby providing a legal basis for the imposition of measures related to internal discipline; rather, organisation is a requirement related to the threshold of application. It is possible that the maintenance of internal discipline may be justified on the basis of military necessity, given the centrality of discipline to the conduct of effective military operations. However, the validity of extending the concept of military necessity in this manner seems difficult to uphold,[146] and any such laws

[141] Above n 136, 15.

[142] Kristian Stokke, 'Building the Tamil Eelam State: emerging state institutions and forms of governance in LTTE-controlled areas in Sri Lanka' (2006) 27 *Third World Quarterly* 6, 1037.

[143] See Art 14(1), International Covenant on Civil and Political Rights.

[144] *Prosecutor v Tadic*, Decision on the Defence Motion for Interlocutory Appeal on Jurisdiction, Appeals Chamber, International Criminal Tribunal for the former Yugoslavia, 2 October 1995, para 70.

[145] See further, above Ch 8 section I.A(ii).

[146] For example, this appears inconsistent with the concept of military necessity established in Art 51 Additional Protocol I, which refers to 'the concrete and direct military advantage anticipated'.

would raise serious difficulties vis-à-vis the principle of *nullum crimen sine lege*.

Outside armed conflict, legislative authority is regarded as a central component of state sovereignty and is prima facie held exclusively by the state.[147] As such, it is difficult to envisage an extension of legislative authority to non-sovereign non-state armed groups. This conclusion is reinforced by reference to the *nullem crimen sine lege* principle codified in Article 15 of the International Covenant on Civil and Political Rights. If the laws of two conflicting authorities (the state and the non-state armed group) were regarded as valid in the same territory, it would be exceptionally difficult for an individual to regulate their conduct. The crime of treason is a case on point: the law of the state would prohibit collaboration with the armed group, while the law of the armed group would prohibit collaboration with the state, resulting in a patently unworkable situation. Accordingly, it must be concluded that there is no legal basis regulating an armed group's promulgation of group-specific laws, such as internal regulations. The only possible exception is when the armed group has displaced the authority of the state, and exercises exclusive control over a territory and population. This issue is discussed further in the next section.

(iv) Can Armed Groups Prosecute Non-Conflict-Related Crimes?

The final question to be addressed in this section is whether armed groups may prosecute non-conflict-related crimes, namely those relating to maintenance of the rule of law and public order. This is particularly important given that 'the establishment of a force capable of policing the population, followed by a broader judicial mechanism to regulate disputes, [is] often the first step taken by any rebel group'.[148] In situations of non-international armed conflict,[149] international humanitarian law regulation is expressly limited to instances of detention and prosecution that are 'related to the armed conflict',[150] and thus to issues such as those concerning the treatment of prisoners, the conduct of hostilities, and so on. The *Commentary* to Article 5 Additional Protocol II makes clear that 'there must be a link between the situation of conflict and the deprivation of liberty … prisoners held under normal rules of criminal law are not covered by this provision'.[151] International humanitarian law evidently does not establish a legal basis for the regulation of the population by armed groups, and it is noted that regulation of the civilian population

147 Above n 2, 447.
148 See *Rebel Rulers* above n 1, 63.
149 See inter alia, Arts 5 and 6 Additional Protocol II.
150 Arts 5(1) and 6(1) Additional Protocol II.
151 Above n 23, para 4568.

for non-conflict-related reasons cannot reasonably be justified on the basis of military necessity.[152] Outside situations of armed conflict, the exclusive authority of the state with respect to legislative authority has already been noted, and the conclusion must be that armed group regulation of the civilian population is prohibited.

However, it is possible that an exception may exist in situations where an armed group has established itself as the sole authority with respect to a specific territory and population, either during or outside armed conflict. In such situations, the best interests of the population may be served by allowing armed groups to maintain public order so that individuals can be protected from any negative effects resulting from a breakdown in the rule of law.[153] Indeed, the obligation to protect requires that measures be taken to protect the population at large from third party violations, and as noted above, such measures include the promulgation of legislation and accountability in the event of a violation.[154] As the authority of the state has been effectively displaced there exists a legal lacuna, and states' concerns regarding sovereignty and a dilution of their exclusive legislative authority must be 'balanced against the counterweight provided by [armed group] courts to the disorder and chaos that would otherwise reign in the territory under armed group control.'[155] The potential impact of a breakdown in the rule of law vis-à-vis the interests of the civilian population is highlighted by reference to two different situations. In a 2006 report that noted the commission of grave human rights violations and prevalent impunity in Cote d'Ivoire, the UN Secretary-General stated that he was 'deeply concerned by the absence of a system for the administration of justice in areas under the control of the Forces nouvelles',[156] while on the other hand, in Qandil, Iraq, the PKK ensured order in areas subject to their exclusive control, prompting the statement that: '[i]t is a place without government, yet also without disorder.'[157] Similarly, the chaos evident along the front lines in the conflict in Sierra Leone may be distinguished from the relative order in RUF base areas where elements

[152] See eg Deborah Casalin, 'Taking prisoners: reviewing the international humanitarian law grounds for deprivation of liberty by armed opposition groups' (2011) 93 *International Review of the Red Cross* 13.

[153] '[W]here an armed group maintains effective territorial control for extended periods, such as in Sri Lanka and Cote d'Ivoire', the local population may require that the armed group 'provide protection from criminality'. 'Detention by armed groups' above n 3, 772–74. See also, Stefan Trechsel, 'Why Must Trials Be Fair?' (1997) 31 *Israel Law Review* 100.

[154] See above, Ch 7 section I.E. It is noted that in the situations under consideration the state is unable to fulfil its obligation to protect as its authority has been displaced.

[155] *The Law of Non-International Armed Conflict* above n 27, 559.

[156] 'Report of the Secretary-General on children and armed conflict in Cote d'Ivoire', UN Doc S/2006/835, 25 October 2006, para 51.

[157] Namo Abdulla, 'A Kurdish Village Governed by None', *New York Times* (New York, 24 August 2010).

of the rule of law were enforced.[158] Interestingly, in a number of different situations, civilian populations have responded positively to an armed group's imposition of public order, seeing this as preferable to corrupt or chaotic systems. This appears to apply irrespective of the population's opinion of the group, and has been noted in relation to groups as diverse as, inter alia, the Islamic State in Syria and Iraq,[159] Al Shabaab in Somalia,[160] and the Huthis in Yemen.[161]

As discussed in detail previously, the de facto control theory recognises the legitimacy of those acts of a non-state authority which are required for the maintenance of civil life.[162] The logic underpinning this theory is described in the *Arantzazu Mendi* ruling:

> [T]he law, based on the reality of facts material to the particular case, must regard as having the essentials of sovereignty a government in effective administrative control over the territory in question and not subordinate to any other government, *because their decrees are the only legal authority which governs the area to which the subject matter of the dispute belongs.*[163]

International law thus establishes a legal basis for certain acts of an armed group in situations where the authority of the state has been displaced and replaced by that of the armed group. Necessarily this requires a determination with respect to those acts of an armed group that may be considered valid; ie what acts are necessary to ensure 'peace and order among citizens'?[164] Answering this question may be facilitated by analogy to the law of belligerent occupation.[165]

(a) The Law of Belligerent Occupation and the Maintenance of Public Life

Occupation law regulates a situation similar to that involving the exercise of de facto authority, wherein the authority of the territorial state has been displaced, but its sovereign claim over the territory remains.

[158] ie RUF personnel who abused civilians were punished in order to secure the loyalty of civilians. See above n 136, 40; *Prosecutor v Sesay, Kallon and Gbao*, above n 138, para 712.

[159] *ISIS: Inside the Army of Terror* above n 71, 223–24; Sarah Birke, 'How ISIS Rules', NYRblog, *The New York Review of Books*, 1 August 2015.

[160] International Crisis Group, 'Somalia: Al-Shabaab—It Will Be a Long War' (2014) 8, 15.

[161] International Crisis Group, 'The Huthis: From Saada to Sanaa' (2014) 6.

[162] See above, Ch 5 section I.E.

[163] Bucknill J in *The Arantzazu Mendi*, Probate Divorce and Admiralty Division, 17 June 1938. Quoted in Herbert W Briggs, 'De Facto and De Jure Recognition: The Arantzazu Mendi' (1939) 33 *American Journal of International Law* 695.

[164] *Texas v White*, (1869) 74 US 700, 733.

[165] It is not proposed that occupation law be applied directly to non-state actors. Rather, given occupation law's exceptional nature, the existence of laws intended to ensure the best interests of the occupied population, and the requirement that the sovereignty of the displaced authority be respected, it is proposed that this body of law may provide an appropriate analogy against which the conduct of non-state actors may be evaluated.

The law of occupation requires that an Occupying Power 'take all measures in his power to restore, and ensure, as far as possible, public order and safety,[166] while respecting, unless absolutely prevented, the laws in force in the country.'[167] This obligation is based on logic similar to that underpinning the de facto control theory, namely a desire to avoid a breakdown of the rule of law, and 'to protect the civilian population from a meaningful decline in orderly life'.[168] Importantly, this rule acknowledges the de facto and temporary nature of control, inter alia, by ensuring respect for the displaced sovereign,[169] a pertinent requirement when considering the regulation of non-state armed groups.

With respect to the scope of an occupant's legislative authority, the public order and public life requirement 'enjoins the Occupying Power not to sit idly by when law and order in the occupied territory are in jeopardy, even if its personnel are not at risk and its facilities are not encroached upon.'[170] The Occupying Power is accordingly authorised to enact legislation 'to maintain the orderly government of the territory'.[171] This may extend to a number of spheres, including 'child welfare, labour, food, hygiene and public health'.[172] Under certain circumstances,[173] quite extensive legislative changes are anticipated, in order 'to ensure that societal needs in the occupied territory do not remain too long in a legal limbo',[174] and 'to allow for the normal development of the occupied territory.'[175] Such situations may impose 'at least some positive obligations to take action in favour of growth and development in the occupied territory'.[176]

[166] 'Public order and safety' is considered to be an inaccurate translation of the authoritative French text which refers to *'l'ordre et la vie publics'* (public order and public life). See above n 117, 89; Yutaka Arai-Takahashi, *The Law of Occupation: Continuity and Change of International Humanitarian Law, and its Interaction with International Human Rights Law* (The Hague, Martinus Nijhoff, 2009) 96.

[167] Art 43 Hague Regulations.

[168] Above n 117, 92. See also, 'Legislation and Maintenance of Public Order and Civil Life by Occupying Powers' above n 128, 678,

[169] Above n 117, 49.

[170] ibid, 92.

[171] Art 64(3) Fourth Geneva Convention.

[172] Jean S Pictet (ed), *Commentary: IV Geneva Convention Relative to the Protection of Civilian Persons in Time of War* (Geneva, International Committee of the Red Cross, 1958) 337. See further, 'Legislation and Maintenance of Public Order and Civil Life by Occupying Powers' above n 128, 678.

[173] Such as instances of prolonged or semi-prolonged occupation, see above n 117, 116. Of course, such measures must be tightly regulated in order to ensure that they are, in fact, in the best interests of the occupied population and are not actually intended to further the interests of the Occupying Power, or to facilitate annexation, for example.

[174] ibid, 117; See further, Adam Roberts 'Prolonged Military Occupation: The Israeli-occupied Territories since 1967' (1990) 84 *American Journal of International Law*.

[175] Vaios Koutroulis, 'The application of international humanitarian law and international human rights law in situations of prolonged occupation: only a matter of time?' (2012) 94 *International Review of the Red Cross* 179.

[176] ibid, 183.

For example, legislation may be required not only to ensure the minimum core obligations associated with economic, social and cultural rights but also to address 'the long-term strategic aspects of fulfilling the population's rights.'[177] The majority of commentators support the view that an Occupying Power may be subject to an obligation to enact legislation to ensure public order and public life,[178] and in *United States v List* the United States Military Tribunal at Nuremberg held that:

> The status of an occupant of the territory of the enemy having been achieved, international law places the responsibility upon the commanding general of preserving order, punishing crime, and protecting lives and property within the occupied territory. His power in accomplishing these ends is as great as his responsibility.[179]

However, it must be emphasised that while an occupant may make certain changes to the laws of an occupied territory, the general rule is that the Occupying Power must respect 'the laws in force in the country',[180] and any changes must be in the interests of the occupied population. This is based on the understanding that occupation is a temporary phenomenon that does not affect the displaced sovereign's legitimacy of title,[181] and so efforts must be taken in order to preserve a territory's unique tapestry of laws, customs and culture, while ensuring its continuing independent viability.[182] This maxim seems equally appropriate in situations where an armed group has displaced the authority of the state;[183] while the acts of the armed group may be subject to international regulation in response to the reality of the situation, the armed group does not gain legitimacy of title, and the displaced state retains overall sovereignty.[184]

[177] Noam Lubell, 'Human rights obligations in military occupation' (2012) 94 *International Review of the Red Cross* 333. See further, *Jamayat Askan Alma'Almun Althaunia Almahduda Almasaulia, Lawfully registered Cooperative in regional Command of Judea and Samaria v Commander of IDF Forces in the Judea and Samaria region—the Superior Planning Council for the Judea and Samaria Region*, Supreme Court of Israel, Case No HCJ 393/82, 12 December 1983, para 26. Quoted in above n 175, 180.

[178] *The Law of Occupation: Continuity and Change of International Humanitarian Law, and its Interaction with International Human Rights Law* above n 166, 100.

[179] *United States of America v Wilhelm List et al*, United States Military Tribunal, 19 February 1948, 1244–45.

[180] Art 43 Hague Regulations. See also, Art 64 fourth Geneva Convention. See further, 'Legislation and Maintenance of Public Order and Civil Life by Occupying Powers' above n 128, 661.

[181] Art 4, Additional Protocol I.

[182] See inter alia, Marco A Sassoli and Antoine A Bouvier, *How Does Law Protect in War? Cases, Documents and Teaching Materials on Contemporary Practice in International Humanitarian Law, Vol 1*, 2nd edn (Geneva, ICRC, 2006) 186 and Conor McCarthy, 'The Paradox of the International Law of Military Occupation: Sovereignty and the Reformation of Iraq' (2005) 10 *Journal of Conflict & Security Law*, 43.

[183] See eg above n 129, 71.

[184] It is recalled that the implied mandate recognises acts undertaken in the best interests of the population, while regarding as illegitimate those acts 'in furtherance of rebellion'.

(b) Armed Groups and the Maintenance of Public Order

There are two alternatives open to an armed group endeavouring to maintain public order and the effective administration of justice in conformity with the requirements of international human rights law: an armed group may either utilise the existing law of the state, or promulgate new laws. Use of the existing laws of the state has clear benefits with respect to the *nullum crimen sine lege* principle: the requirement of non-retroactivity should not be an issue, and the concerned population will be aware of the law and can regulate their behaviour accordingly. Importantly, the use of existing state laws may also have benefits from a capacity perspective as armed groups will not be required to develop and promulgate new laws or a new legal code, and a network of appropriately qualified professionals—such as lawyers, judges, and police officers—should be available. While it might be presumed that armed opposition groups will be reluctant to apply the law of the state for political reasons—ie given their opposition to the authority of the state—armed group use of state law does actually occur in practice. For example, in Syria it has been reported that certain opposition forces applied Syrian criminal law,[185] while in Libya the National Transitional Council applied the Libyan Criminal Code to regulate the detention of fighters.[186]

Armed groups may also utilise existing alternatives to state law, such as religious law, or local customary law. Returning to Syria, the Al Nusrah Front is reported as applying *Shari'a* law in areas subject to its control,[187] as are other opposition groups,[188] and the use of Islamic law by armed groups to settle disputes has also been reported, inter alia, in Indonesia,[189] the Lebanon (with respect to civil disputes),[190] and Iraq.[191]

185 'Syria: End Opposition Use of Torture, Executions' above n 3, 3.

186 'Procedure on detaining or capturing people' in National Transitional Council/Free Libyan Army, Frontline Manual, 2011.

187 The Al Nusrah Front are reported as having established a 'Sharia Committee for the Eastern Region' for this purpose. See 'Al Nusrah Front poised to take over last major city on Euphrates River' above n 110.

188 'Syria: End Opposition Use of Torture, Executions' above n 3, 3.

189 'A second consequence [of the breakdown of courts] is the emergence of makeshift courts at the village level, presided over by a *qazi*, or Islamic judge, sometimes selected by GAM, to deal with petty theft and local disputes'. 'Indonesia: The War in Aceh' above n 3, 35.

190 'Another Council subordinate to the Shura and tasked with managing activities of the group is the Judicial Council, staffed by religious authorities this represents Hezbollah's reliance on Shari'a in the area in which it governs. These judges rule on violations of religious law as well as on civil disputes between members and between those in Hezbollah governed communities'. Michael T Kindt, 'Hezbollah: A State within a State' in Michael T Kindt, Jerrold M Post, and Barry R Schneider (eds), *The World's Most Threatening Terrorist Networks and Criminal Gangs* (London, Palgrave Macmillan, 2009) 133.

191 'In the absence of a functioning public judicial system, Mohammed Fartousi, al-Sadr's agent in Sadr city, used his Hikma mosque to establish rudimentary personal status courts. Al-Sadr's *wakils*, or agents, distributed vests to traffic wardens emblazoned with the words "*hawza* police"'. International Crisis Group, 'Iraq's Shiites Under Occupation' (2003) 17.

Regarding local customary law,[192] SPLA courts operating in Sudan in the 1980s applied 'the customary law which was in force before the establishment of SPLA authority'.[193] Of course, it is also possible that armed groups may use a combination of the above mechanisms. For instance, in Somalia, the Rahanweyn Resistance Army and the Lower Shabelle Administration both adopted 'modifications of the post-independence judicial structures, including courts of first instance applying secular laws for penal and commercial cases, and *shari'a* law for private civil matters',[194] while in Somaliland the government utilised the former state law augmented with a new juvenile code, and applied traditional law in more rural areas.[195] Of course, any mechanism adopted by armed group courts must comply with the requirements discussed above.[196]

Armed groups may also promulgate new laws in areas subject to their control. For instance, in Nepal the CPN-M established a 'wartime and transitional' public legal code which addressed civil and criminal provisions.[197] Similarly, in Sri Lanka the LTTE established the Tamil Eelam Penal and Civil Codes, which were based on a mix of Sri Lankan, Indian and British law,[198] while in Myanmar the Karen National Union (KNU) 'has passed laws and acts for civilians, the organization and the military to follow'.[199] The establishment of a new legal system will necessarily require significant capacity on the part of an armed group, and it is noted that the above examples related to armed groups in an advanced stage of insurgency. However, it is also possible that an armed group may promulgate laws supplementary to the existing law of the state, in a manner

[192] Used here, this phrase refers to local customary law, as distinct from customary international law.

[193] 'All state laws were irrelevant in SPLA areas except the customary laws'. Monyluak Alor Kuol, 'Administration of Justice in the (SPLA/M) Liberated Areas: Court Cases in War-Torn Southern Sudan' (1997) Refugee Studies Programme, University of Oxford, 12.

[194] Andre Le Sage, 'Stateless Justice in Somalia: Formal and Informal Rule of Law Initiatives' (Centre for Humanitarian Dialogue, 2005) 49.

[195] 'Somaliland' in *In Their Words: Perspectives of Armed Non-State Actors on the Protection of Children from the Effects of Armed Conflict* (Geneva, Geneva Call, 2010) 30.

[196] See above, Ch 8 section I.A(i).

[197] Jonathan Somer, 'Jungle justice: passing sentence on the equality of belligerents in non-international armed conflict' (2007) 89 *International Review of the Red Cross* 681.

[198] Mr E Pararajasingham, head of the LTTE Judicial Division, stated that: 'Distinguished Tamil jurists, legal experts and leading lawyers studied the British, Indian and Sri Lankan criminal justice systems before formulating the Tamil Eelam Penal Code'. 'Thamil Eelam judiciary said a basis for rebuilding northeast' above n 5.

[199] 'Karen National Union (KNU)' in *In Their Words: Perspectives of Armed Non-State Actors on the Protection of Children from the Effects of Armed Conflict* (Geneva, Geneva Call, 2010) 21. During the war of independence in Ireland the IRA created a separate legal system and court structure, see David Foxton, *Revolutionary Lawyers: Sinn Fein and Crown Courts in Ireland and Britain 1916–1923* (Dublin, Four Courts Press, 2008) 187–97.

similar to regulations issued by an Occupying Power, thereby avoiding the need to establish an entirely new legal code.[200]

This practice demonstrate that a number of alternatives exist with respect to the administration of justice in areas subject to armed group control, and it is highlighted that the adoption of pre-existing systems for the administration of justice, and the associated infrastructure, may ease the burden imposed on an armed group. Interestingly, such systems may be used as a stage in the gradual development of a rule of law system. For example, while customary law was initially applied by SPLA courts, in 1994 the New Sudan Penal Code was established which 'specified the criminal law applicable in "SPLM/SPLA controlled areas".'[201] Similarly, while the LTTE initially utilised mediation boards in areas subject to their control, these were later replaced by a court system applying the LTTE Penal and Civil Codes.[202]

To summarise, when an armed group has displaced the authority of the state and established exclusive control, international law must respond to the reality of the situation and subject the acts of the armed group to international regulation. Necessarily, this requires that certain acts of the armed group be regarded as valid.[203] In particular, when an armed group has established exclusive stable control over both a population and territory it must be allowed to undertake acts necessary to maintain law and order in the area subject to its exclusive control. In determining the legitimacy of acts undertaken by an armed group in this regard, the law of belligerent occupation may provide an appropriate analogy.

(c) An Obligation to Maintain Public Order?

Having established that armed groups may regulate the civilian population in certain circumstances, it remains to be determined whether they are required to do so. In the situations under consideration herein it is the existence of a legal vacuum that gives rise to the necessity-based application of international law. Given this underpinning, it seems appropriate that armed groups be required to maintain public order, thereby ensuring the protection of individuals' rights, and the obligations to protect and fulfil established under international human rights law are highlighted in

[200] The example of Somaliland is recalled, wherein the pre-existing law of the state was supplemented with a new juvenile code. See above n 195, 30.

[201] *The Law of Non-International Armed Conflict* above n 27, 554.

[202] 'Thamil Eelam judiciary said a basis for rebuilding northeast' above n 5.

[203] This conclusion necessarily implicates state sovereignty. However, such interference is justified consequent to the exceptional nature of the situation, which includes the displacement of state authority.

this regard.[204] It is recalled that, in a number of diverse situations, civilian populations have responded positively to armed groups' imposition of public order.[205] This is not to suggest that the imposition of public order by armed groups is an ideal solution, but it does highlight the perceived desirability associated with avoiding a breakdown in the rule of law.

Of course, any public order obligation must be carefully considered given the importance of the relevant international human rights law guarantees, and the ability of armed groups to comply with them.[206] It is noted that the equivalent obligation under the law of belligerent occupation is 'an obligation not of result but of conduct.'[207] Accordingly, the obligation itself may be best approached on the basis of progressive realisation: while armed groups are subject to an immediate obligation to maintain public order,[208] they are also required to progressively develop their capability, on the basis of available resources, in order to better secure the needs and rights of those subject to their authority.

Initially, an obligation to maintain public order may require that an armed group conduct patrols and intervene to settle disputes. However, over time the group may be required to engage in, or to facilitate, governmental functions in order to ensure the orderly running of the area and to prevent stagnation.[209] The important factor is that the population's needs and rights are ensured, and in this regard the respect, protect, fulfil framework is relevant. For example, an armed group may fulfil obligations relating to the maintenance of public order by allowing members of the state judiciary and police force to continue work (obligation to facilitate). Continuing the occupation law analogy, it is noted that this possibility exists under the law of belligerent occupation. Article 54 of the Fourth Geneva Convention requires, inter alia, that '[t]he Occupying Power may not alter the status of public officials or judges in the occupied territories'.[210] This provision is intended 'to enable [the public officials] to continue carrying out the duties of their office as in the past',[211] and the Occupying Power

[204] See above, Ch 7 sections I.D and I.E. The necessity of maintaining public order is highlighted by reference to the law of belligerent occupation. See Art 43 Hague Regulations. The consequences of failing to ensure this obligation were graphically demonstrated in the early stages of the occupation of Iraq in 2003.

[205] *ISIS: Inside the Army of Terror* above n 71, 223–24; 'How ISIS Rules' above n 159; above n 160, 8, 15; above n 161, 6.

[206] An element of stability with respect to territorial control may be required.

[207] Above n 117, 92.

[208] At a basic level this may involve the prevention of crime, the settlement of disputes, and so on. It is reiterated that this obligation only applies to armed groups that have displaced the authority of the state and established control over a territory and population.

[209] Measures required in this regard may include measures to ensure the running of the economy, the collection of taxes to fund public services, and the progressive realisation of the population's economic, social and cultural rights.

[210] Art 54 Fourth Geneva Convention.

[211] *Commentary: IV Geneva Convention Relative to the Protection of Civilian Persons in Time of War* above n 172, 304.

is entitled to require that the local police take part in the maintenance of law and order.[212] Of course, the reality of the situation and the usurpation of the legitimate authority must be acknowledged, and occupation law prohibits any requirement that police officers take part in military operations, or 'participate in measures aimed at opposing legitimate belligerent acts'.[213] An armed group may similarly facilitate the maintenance of public order by allowing local governments to continue operating, thereby avoiding the need to establish a distinct governmental structure.[214] Similarly, an armed group may utilise the existing judicial system, or adopt other pre-existing administration of justice systems, such as customary or religious courts. Of course, the management of existing governmental structures will necessarily impose certain demands on an armed group's capacity, and actual implementation will require negotiation. The territorial state's continuing obligations are recalled, and if an armed group allows the continued operation of state systems, the state will be required, inter alia, to facilitate their continued operation.[215]

It is also possible that an armed group may wish to establish a new system for the administration of justice in areas subject to their control (obligation to provide). In practice, armed groups have adapted their internal court systems, utilised mediation boards for the non-judicial settlement of disputes,[216] or established a system of 'people's courts',[217] and none of these options place significant extra demands on the capacity of an armed group. However, mediation boards cannot be used for criminal cases, and their utility is restricted to relatively low-level instances of dispute resolution, although it is recalled that such disputes may actually form the majority of instances necessitating the attention of an armed group.[218] People's courts may be an alternative option, as they have the potential to keep responsibility for the maintenance of the rule of law within the community, and as such may be independent of the armed group.[219] In India,

212 ibid, 307.

213 ibid, 307.

214 This possibility is also envisaged in the law of belligerent occupation. See above n 117, 58; *The Law of Occupation: Continuity and Change of International Humanitarian Law, and its Interaction with International Human Rights Law* above n 166, 144–45.

215 See above, Ch 7 section I.F.

216 For instance, the LTTE in Sri Lanka and the Mahdi Army in Iraq both established mediation boards or arbitration committees. See 'Thamil Eelam judiciary said a basis for rebuilding northeast' above n 5; 'Iraq's Muqtada Al-Sadr' above n 3, 20.

217 The CPN-M in Nepal and GAM in the Philippines both established people's courts. See 'Courts of Armed Opposition Groups' above n 5, 493; 'Report of the Special Rapporteur on extrajudicial, summary or arbitrary executions, Philip Alston, Mission to Philippines', UN Doc A/HRC/8/3/Add.2, 16 April 2008, para 32.

218 For instance, it is reported that many of the cases heard by the CPN-M and the LTTE related to land, money, or family relationships. See 'Courts of Armed Opposition Groups' above n 5, 493–94.

219 This is not to suggest that all people's courts comply with the requirements of international human rights law.

for example, people's courts are reportedly convened by the Naxalites, but cases are decided by the people.[220] Armed groups may also establish a judicial system similar to that of the state, and the LTTE judicial system is the prime example in this regard. However, the establishment of such a system places significant demands on armed group capacity, and will only be possible for well-established groups.[221] Of course, any administration of justice system adopted by an armed group must comply with the requirements of international human rights law.[222]

(v) Summary

During situations of non-international armed conflict the authority of armed group courts is limited to the prosecution of violations of the law of armed conflict. Outside armed conflict no legal basis for the prosecution of crimes before armed group courts exists. However, this is subject to one significant exception, applicable to situations occurring both during, and outside, situations of armed conflict. In situations where an armed group has totally displaced state authority and exercises stable and exclusive control over a territory and population, the armed group may be granted limited legislative authority, and on this basis may prosecute non-conflict-related crimes. The displacement of state authority results in a legal vacuum necessitating that certain acts of the armed group be regarded as legitimate, inter alia, in the best interests of the population. This application of the implied mandate principle may be regulated by analogy to the law of occupation, which aims to ensure the best interests of the population, while maintaining respect for the displaced sovereign. Limited legislative authority is necessary to give effect to the obligation to protect, which applies when an armed group exerts effective territorial control and requires that armed groups maintain public order and civil life. Legislative authority may be granted to an armed group both during, and outside, situations of non-international armed conflict.

The operation of armed group courts is regulated by the procedural guarantees established under international human rights law and, where applicable, international humanitarian law. If an armed group cannot fulfil these requirements it cannot conduct prosecutions.

[220] See 'Walking with the Comrades' above n 3.

[221] The LTTE themselves noted that: 'In the beginning we were a guerrilla organisation, engaging in hit and run tactics against the Sri Lankan armed forces. We had no stable control over large territories or populations. Therefore we neither had the resources nor the environment to set up and run a proper judicial system. But in 1993, as soon as we were in control of most of the north, our leadership established the Tamil Eelam Judiciary and College of Law.' 'Thamil Eelam judiciary said a basis for rebuilding northeast' above n 5.

[222] See above, Ch 8 section I.A(i).

B. Issues Relating to Detention by Armed Groups

Having examined issues relating to prosecutions undertaken by armed groups, this section addresses the procedural guarantees regulating instances of detention by armed groups, before focusing on issues specific to detention without trial. Other instances of detention—such as pre-trial detention or post-conviction detention—fall within the scope of the above discussion regarding prosecution by armed groups.

(i) Procedural Guarantees Relating to Armed Group Detention

The prohibition of arbitrary detention requires that deprivation of liberty be regulated in accordance with procedures established by law.[223] The principal international human rights law guarantees in this regard are the right to be promptly informed of the basis for detention,[224] and the right to challenge the lawfulness of detention (also known as the right to habeas corpus).[225] These protections are reflected in the law of international armed conflict: Article 75(3) of Additional Protocol I requires that a detainee be informed promptly of the reasons for detention, while Articles 43 and 78 of the fourth Geneva Convention establish a right to appeal the basis of detention. Treaty-based international humanitarian law does not establish explicit procedural guarantees applicable to all instances of non-international armed conflict,[226] although the International Committee of the Red Cross' Customary International Humanitarian Law Study does refer to the procedural guarantees established under international human rights law.[227] Indeed, as procedural guarantees remain applicable during international armed conflict, there does not appear to be any legitimate justification for derogation during non-international armed conflict.[228]

The right to be promptly informed of the reasons for detention is intrinsically linked to the right to challenge the legality of detention.[229] As noted by the Human Rights Committee, 'one of the most important reasons for the requirement of "prompt" information on a criminal charge is to enable

223 International Covenant on Civil and Political Rights, Art 9(1).
224 ibid, Art 9(2).
225 ibid, Art 9(4).
226 This reality underscores the necessity of the co-application of international humanitarian law and international human rights law. See eg Laura M Olson, 'Practical Challenges of Implementing the Complementarity Between International Humanitarian Law and Human Rights Law—Demonstrated by the Procedural Regulation of Internment in Non-International Armed Conflict' (2007–2009) 40 *Case Western Reserve Journal of International Law* 442.
227 Rule 99, above n 17.
228 Jelena Pejic, 'The protective scope of Common Article 3: more than meets the eye' (2011) 93 *International Review of the Red Cross* 212.
229 *Human Rights in Times of Conflict and Terrorism* above n 41, 265.

a detained individual to request a prompt decision on the lawfulness of his or her detention by a competent judicial authority'.[230] As such, international human rights law requires that 'anyone who is arrested shall be informed sufficiently of the reasons for his arrest to enable him to take immediate steps to secure his release if he believes that the reasons given are invalid or unfounded.'[231] Article 9(2) of the International Covenant on Civil and Political Rights establishes that a detainee should be informed of the reasons for detention 'at the time of arrest',[232] while the *Commentary* to Article 6(2)(a) Additional Protocol II states that: 'the accused must be informed as quickly as possible of the offence alleged against him'.[233] The flexibility inherent in an 'as quickly as possible' requirement seems appropriate to the situations discussed herein: it ensures the content of the right to be informed while allowing certain flexibility in response to potentially exceptional circumstances arising in a given situation.[234] Indeed, the European Convention on Human Rights requires that a detainee 'be informed promptly',[235] and not immediately, of the reasons for arrest.[236]

The right to challenge the lawfulness of detention (habeas corpus) has been held to be non-derogable by both the Human Rights Committee and the Inter-American Court of Human Rights.[237] Importantly, international human rights law requires that the detention review process be 'in its effects, real and not merely formal',[238] and as such 'must include the

[230] *Glenford Campbell v Jamaica*, Views, Human Rights Committee, Communication No 248/1987, UN Doc CCPR/C/44/D248/1987, 30 March 1992, para 6.3; *Malofeyeva v Russia* App No 36673/04 (ECtHR, 30 May 2013), para 66. Although these cases relate to criminal charges, the reasoning is regarded as equally applicable vis-à-vis administrative detention.

[231] *Ivonne Ibarburu De Drescher and Adolfo Drescher Caldas v Uruguay*, Views, Human Rights Committee, Communication No 43/1979, UN Doc CCPR/C/19/D/43/1979, 21 July 1983, para 13.2.

[232] Art 5(2) of the European Convention on Human Rights establishes a 'prompt' requirement, while Art 7(4) of the American Convention on Human Rights does not establish an explicit timeframe. It is noted that the term 'arrest', which has a criminal connotation, has been interpreted by the European Court of Human Rights as referring to detention more broadly. See further *Human Rights in Times of Conflict and Terrorism* above n 41, 265.

[233] Above n 23, para 4602. It is noted that this provision refers to criminal charges. However, Art 75(3) of Additional Protocol I, applicable to international armed conflict, requires that '[a]ny person arrested, detained or interned for actions related to the armed conflict shall be informed promptly, in a language he understands, of the reasons why these measures have been taken.' The Human Rights Committee has noted that information for reasons of detention must also be given in the case of internment. See Human Rights Committee, General Comment No 8, 'Article 9', UN Doc HRI/GEN/1/Rev.1, para 4.

[234] This is also consistent with the requirement that a detainee 'be informed promptly' of the reasons for arrest established in Art 5(2) of the European Convention on Human Rights.

[235] Art 5(2) of the European Convention on Human Rights.

[236] *Ladent v Poland* App No 11036/63 (ECtHR, 18 March 2008), para 63. See also, *Malofeyeva v Russia*, above n 230, para 66.

[237] Above n 94, para 16; *Habeas Corpus in Emergency Situations*, Advisory Opinion, Inter-American Court of Human Rights, 30 January 1987, para 40.

[238] *A v Australia*, Views, Human Rights Committee, Communication No 560/1993, UN Doc CCPR/C/59/D/560/1993, 3 April 1997, para 9.5.

possibility of ordering release'.[239] The reviewing authority must comply with the requirements of international human rights law relating to the operation of courts.[240] With respect to the timeframe associated with a review, international human rights law case law generally requires habeas corpus review at the outset of detention.[241] In *Lebedev v Russia*, for example, the European Court of Human Rights held that 'the opportunity for legal review must be provided soon after the person is taken into detention',[242] and delays of six or seven days have been found to be inconsistent with the right to habeas corpus.[243] Exceptional circumstances may justify a delay in bringing a detainee before a judicial authority. For instance, in *Medvedyev and Others v France*, and *Rigopoulos v Spain*, delays of 13 and 16 days respectively were regarded as legitimate owing to the unique circumstances of the case, whereby the accused were detained on the high seas and 'it was impossible to bring the applicant physically before the investigating judge any sooner.'[244] This reasoning seems equally applicable to situations involving detention by armed groups where certain flexibility vis-à-vis the situation at hand may be appropriate.[245] For instance, if a judge is not available in the armed group's immediate area of operations, but the armed group makes positive and immediate efforts to bring the detainee before a judicial authority in another area, this would appear to be reasonable and compatible with the habeas corpus requirement. In this regard it is noted that in *Medvedyev and Others v France* and *Rigopoulos v Spain* the detainees were transported to French territory as soon as possible after arrest, whereupon they were brought before a judge without delay.[246] However, if a judge is not available at all then the armed group cannot satisfy the habeas corpus requirement and must release the detainee.[247] This situation might arise if an armed group does not possess a judge within its membership (including in situations where a judge is in the process of being trained), or if a judge is available in another area but the reality of the conflict indefinitely precludes movement to this area.

[239] ibid, para 9.5. See also, *A and others v United Kingdom* App No 3455/05 (ECtHR, 19 February 2009), para 202.

[240] See above, Ch 8 section I.A(i).

[241] *Human Rights in Times of Conflict and Terrorism* above n 41, 270.

[242] *Lebedev v Russia* App No 4493/04 (ECtHR, 25 October 2007), para 78.

[243] See *De Jong, Baljet and Van den Brink v Netherlands* App Nos 8805/79, 8806/79, 9242/81 (ECtHR, 22 May 1984), para 57; *Torres v Finland*, Views, Human Rights Committee, Communication No 291/1988, UN Doc CCPR/C/38/D/291/1988, 5 April 1990, para 7.2.

[244] *Rigopoulos v Spain*, Admissibility Decision App No 37388/97 (ECtHR, 12 January 1999); *Medvedyev and Others v France* App No 3394/03 (ECtHR, 29 March 2010), paras 127–34.

[245] Certain states have begun to utilise video links so that individuals detained at sea may be brought promptly (if virtually) before a judge.

[246] *Medvedyev and Others v France*, above n 244, paras 131–32.

[247] For further discussion regarding the release of detainees see below Ch 8 section I.B(iv).

(ii) Who can Armed Groups Detain?

The issue of who an armed group can legitimately detain must now be addressed. Of interest herein is non-criminal detention, also referred to as administrative detention, security detention, preventive detention or, in the context of armed conflict, internment.[248] The use of administrative detention/internment is recognised as permissible under international human rights law,[249] and the law of international armed conflict,[250] although its use is tightly regulated and restricted to exceptional circumstances.[251] With respect to non-international armed conflict, Article 5(2) Additional Protocol II regulates the 'internment or detention' of persons without establishing the permissible grounds under which internment may occur.[252] International human rights law restricts the use of administrative detention to 'circumstances where the person concerned constitutes a clear and serious threat to society *which cannot be contained in any other manner*',[253] while similarly the law of international armed conflict permits only the exceptional use of administrative detention,[254] restricted to 'imperative reasons of security'.[255] Importantly, although administrative detention occurs outside normal juridical procedures, it continues to be subject to international regulation.[256] In particular, detention 'must not be arbitrary and must be based on grounds and procedures established by law'.[257] Given the different legal regimes, this section will first look

248 This practice refers to detention outside normal judicial procedures, typically ordered by the executive, whereby the detainee is not subject to criminal charges. See Jelena Pejic, 'Procedural principles and safeguards for internment/administrative detention in armed conflict and other situations of violence' (2005) 87 *International Review of the Red Cross*, and *Human Rights in Times of Conflict and Terrorism* above n 41, 263–64. Issues relating to criminal detention are considered to fall within the scope of the above discussion of armed group prosecution, see above Ch 8 section I.A.

249 *Human Rights in Times of Conflict and Terrorism* above n 41, 263–64. However, administrative detention is not listed as a permissible ground of detention under the European Convention on Human Rights, and is therefore prohibited in the absence of derogation. See Art 5 of the European Convention on Human Rights, and *Al-Jedda* v *the United Kingdom* App No 27021/08 (ECtHR, 7 July 2011), para 100.

250 See Arts 41, 42, 43 and 78 Fourth Geneva Convention.

251 See eg *Daniel David Tibi v Ecuador*, Judgment, Inter-American Court of Human Rights, 7 September 2004, para 106.

252 See further, *Serdar Mohammed v Ministry of Defence*, High Court of Justice, Case No HQ12X03367, 2 May 2014; *Serdar Mohammed & Others v Secretary of State for Defence*, Court of Appeal, Case Nos A2/2014/1862; A2/2014/4084; A2/2014/4086, 30 July 2015.

253 *Davide Alberto Campora Schweizer v Uruguay*, Views, Human Rights Committee, Communication No 66/1980, UN Doc CCPR/C/OP/2, 12 October 1982, para 18.2. Emphasis added.

254 See eg Hans-Peter Gasser, 'Protection of the Civilian Population' in Dieter Fleck (ed), *The Handbook of International Humanitarian Law*, 2nd edn (Oxford, OUP, 2008) 319; *Al-Jedda v the United Kingdom*, above n 249, para 107.

255 Art 78(1) Fourth Geneva Convention. See similarly, Art 42, Fourth Geneva Convention.

256 *Davide Alberto Campora Schweizer v Uruguay*, above n 253, para 18.2.

257 General Comment No 8 above n 233, para 4.

at armed group detention during situations of non-international armed conflict, before turning to situations outside armed conflict.

(a) Situations of Non-International Armed Conflict

In situations of non-international armed conflict, although international humanitarian law regulates internment by armed groups, the permissible grounds for detention are not specified. In order to redress this ambiguity, the International Committee of the Red Cross has referred to the law of international armed conflict and adopted 'imperative reasons of security'[258] as the 'minimum legal standard that should inform internment decisions in all situations of violence, including NIAC [non-international armed conflict]'.[259] This is not to suggest that the international armed conflict rules on detention are, or should be, applicable as a whole to non-international armed conflict.[260] However, the 'imperative reasons of security' standard applies to the internment of civilians in occupied territory, and appears to be an appropriate reference point when considering detention in non-international armed conflict.

The imperative reasons of security standard is itself imprecise,[261] and neither domestic law nor international law currently defines 'imperative reasons of security' with sufficient clarity to enable a determination vis-à-vis the specific conduct necessary to satisfy this requirement.[262] Nonetheless, it is generally accepted that an act of direct participation in hostilities will satisfy the 'imperative reasons of security' requirement.[263] As detention constitutes a means of weakening the opposition forces, there exists a clear military imperative justifying detention of individuals engaged in such activity, and detention on this basis therefore appears consistent with the object and purpose of the law of armed conflict. Reflecting this conclusion the National Democratic Front of the Philippines (NDFP) Policy towards Prisoners of War states that 'for as long as necessary and feasible, we secure [enemy captives] and neutralize their capability of inflicting

[258] This standard is taken from Art 78 Fourth Geneva Convention.

[259] International Committee of the Red Cross, 'Internment in Armed Conflict: Basic Rules and Challenges', Opinion Paper, November 2014, 8. See also, above n 228, 208.

[260] For views in support of the argument that the international armed conflict rules on detention should apply to non-international armed conflict, see Ryan Goodman, 'The Detention of Civilians in Armed Conflict' (2009) 103 *American Journal of International Law* 48; Ryan Goodman, 'Authorization versus Regulation of Detention in Non-International Armed Conflicts' (2015) 91 *International Law Studies* 155–70.

[261] See eg *Commentary: IV Geneva Convention Relative to the Protection of Civilian Persons in Time of War* above n 172, 257.

[262] Above n 228, 209.

[263] *Hassan v United Kingdom* App No 29750/09 (ECtHR, 16 September 2014), *Amicus Curae* brief submitted by Professor Francoise Hampson and Professor Noam Lubell of the Human Rights Centre, University of Essex, para 35; above n 228, 209.

harm to the revolutionary forces and the people'.[264] Indeed, the law of non-international armed conflict accommodates the targeting with lethal force of individuals who directly participate in hostilities.[265] If the death of such individuals is countenanced under the law of armed conflict it seems appropriate that a legal basis for their detention must also exist, given the shared benefits vis-à-vis military advantage and the law's humanitarian imperative which must regard detention as preferable to death.[266]

It may be argued that an armed group's detention powers should extend beyond individuals directly participating in hostilities (ie fighters) to include broader 'security concerns'—such as membership of an opposing party to the armed conflict, or collaboration with the enemy—and it is to be presumed that armed groups themselves desire such authority. Returning to the international armed conflict analogy, the ICRC *Commentary* to Article 42 of the fourth Geneva Convention notes that individuals may potentially be detained if there is 'good reason to think that the person concerned, by his activities, knowledge or qualifications, represents a real threat to its present or future security'.[267]

However, incorporating this broader detention authority into internment is not entirely straightforward, particularly when one considers the issues arising in relation to armed groups.[268] The majority of such groups do not possess sovereign or legislative authority.[269] As such, extending armed groups' detention authority beyond acts of direct participation in hostilities to include broader security concerns raises a number of difficulties, particularly when one considers the lack of certainty associated with the term 'imperative reasons of security': how is this phrase to be determined in the context of non-sovereign non-state armed groups that do not possess any legal authority with respect to the affected population? For instance, how are acts prejudicial to the security of an armed group to be determined? Passing information regarding the armed group to the

[264] Memo of Melito Glor Command on Policy Towards Prisoners of War, 18 June 1988.

[265] Art 13(3), Additional Protocol II. See also, Rule 6, above n 17.

[266] See eg the Martens Clause contained in the preamble to the Hague Regulations. For further discussion, see *Serdar Mohammed v Ministry of Defence*, High Court of Justice, Case No HQ12X03367, 2 May 2014, paras 252–53; Sean Aughey and Aurel Sari, 'Targeting and Detention in Non-International Armed Conflict: *Serdar Mohammed* and the Limits of Human Rights Convergence' (2015) 91 *International Law Studies* 97–108.

[267] *Commentary: IV Geneva Convention Relative to the Protection of Civilian Persons in Time of War* above n 172, 258.

[268] The administrative detention of civilians in international armed conflict is restricted to situations occurring in the territory of the state or to instances of occupation: in such circumstances the detaining authority has an established institutional presence, including legislative authority, and is subject to obligations with respect to the maintenance of public order and civil life; within the state's territory this is an inherent attribute of government. With respect to situations of occupation see Art 43 Hague Regulations.

[269] See further, Ch 8 section I.A(iv).

state could conceivably satisfy this threshold.[270] However, were an armed group to detain on this basis, numerous concerns related to the *nullum crimen sine lege* principle would arise, and there is a clear danger that the 'security' of an armed group could be deliberately misinterpreted in violation of the prohibition on arbitrary detention. In this regard, and recalling the law of armed conflict's basis in military reality,[271] it is perhaps appropriate that an armed group's detention authority be interpreted in a manner that acknowledges the group's lack of sovereignty and lack of legal authority vis-à-vis the civilian population; wholehearted reference to the law of international armed conflict seems inappropriate. Accordingly, an armed group's authority to intern may reasonably include acts of direct participation in hostilities,[272] but would exclude broader conduct related to 'the general war effort' such as political, administrative, or other non-combat activities.[273] However, in situations wherein an armed group possesses legislative authority it may promulgate legislation establishing a basis for administrative detention.[274]

Of course, a grey area between these two forms of conduct will inevitably exist. For example, the production of weapons is not regarded as constituting direct participation in hostilities, 'unless carried out as an integral part of a specific military operation designed to directly cause the required threshold of harm'.[275] In the context of direct participation in hostilities—which legitimises the use of direct lethal force—this is appropriate. However, the situation is more difficult when detention is at issue, and it is submitted that the imperative reasons of security requirement could potentially justify the detention of weapons' manufacturers, if these individuals constituted an imperative threat.[276] So, while a worker in a munitions factory might not satisfy this threshold, an explosives expert with a significant impact on an armed group's military capability might.[277] Significantly, experts are divided 'as to whether the construction of improvised explosive devices (IED) or missiles by non-State actors could in

[270] ie disclosing the identity of group members, the location of arms caches, etc.

[271] See eg Christopher Greenwood, 'Historical Development and Legal Basis' in Dieter Fleck (ed), *The Handbook of International Humanitarian Law*, 2nd edn (Oxford, OUP, 2008) 37.

[272] Acts of direct participation in hostilities include acts targeting protected persons or objects, and are thus not restricted to acts causing military harm. See Nils Melzer, *Interpretive Guidance on the Notion of Direct Participation in Hostilities Under International Humanitarian Law* (Geneva, ICRC, 2009) 49–50.

[273] See further, ibid, 31–36.

[274] See discussion above in Ch 8 section I.A(iv).

[275] Above n 272, 53.

[276] It is emphasised that discussion herein is related to instances of detention, and this argument should not be considered as justification for extending the definition of direct participation in hostilities.

[277] In practical terms it is noted that should an armed group capture this expert they are unlikely to release him or her.

certain circumstances exceed mere capacity-building and, in contrast to industrial weapons production, could become a measure preparatory to concrete military operations'.[278] In the absence of legal clarity regarding whether such acts constitute direct participation in hostilities, detention may arguably be justified. Ultimately, as with instances of detention by state forces, situations such as these must be decided on a case-by-case basis. This proposal seems appropriate given that administrative detention should be regarded as an exceptional measure, 'based on the general principle that personal liberty is the rule'.[279] Interestingly, the NDFP 'Rules in the Investigation and Prosecution of Suspected Enemy Spies' held that 'preventive arrest is prohibited. Arrest based on mere suspicion without firm evidence is prohibited even if the stated aim is to ensure the security of the Party and the revolution'.[280]

Should an individual be detained, international law requires that all instances of detention be subject to review in order to allow the detainee to challenge the lawfulness of detention.[281] Accordingly, a detention review body must be established in order to determine whether an individual has directly participated in hostilities, and thus whether they may be legitimately detained.[282] In situations where an armed group is engaged in an armed conflict with the state, the determination of who is classified as directly participating in hostilities may be made on the basis of the international armed conflict definition of a combatant; adoption of the international armed conflict definition has already been proposed for the purposes of the principle of distinction in non-international armed conflict,[283] and it seems appropriate that the same definition be used to regulate detention. Determining the lawfulness of detention in such situations should be relatively straightforward—members of a state's armed forces typically wear uniforms and carry their arms openly—and may be made on a basis similar to that outlined in Article 4 Third Geneva Convention.[284]

The situation is more complicated when an armed group is engaged in armed conflict with another non-state armed group. Determination of what acts constitute direct participation in hostilities is notoriously

[278] Above n 272, 53, fn 123.

[279] 'Procedural principles and safeguards for internment' above n 248, 380.

[280] NDFP, 'Rules in the Investigation and Prosecution of Suspected Enemy Spies' in NDFP, *Declaration of Undertaking to Apply the Geneva Conventions of 1949 and Protocol I of 1977* (NDFP, Human Rights Monitoring Committee Booklet No 6) 158, quoted in *The Law of Non-International Armed Conflict* above n 27, 303. Sivakumaran notes that 'it is not entirely clear whether the preventive arrest in question relates to the criminal process or to internment.'

[281] See above, Ch 8 section I.B(i).

[282] Marco Sassoli and Laura M Olson, 'The relationship between international humanitarian and human rights law where it matters: admissible killing and internment of fighters in non-international armed conflicts' (2008) 90 *International Review of the Red Cross* 624.

[283] See Rule 4, above n 17. See also, above n 23, para 4462.

[284] Art 4 Third Geneva Convention.

problematic,[285] and the International Committee of the Red Cross' Customary International Humanitarian Law Study notes, for example, that '[a] precise definition of the term "direct participation in hostilities" does not exist'.[286] While a determination may be achievable in certain instances—particularly if direct participation is determined on the basis of a 'continuous combat function'[287] and the group is relatively well organised with a clear allocation of roles[288]—in other cases an accurate determination may be beyond the ability of an armed group. In such situations the presumption of innocence should apply, and the individual cannot be detained. Prima facie, this may appear problematic in terms of practical implementation. However, it is noted that this stipulation is similar to the existing requirement established with respect to the law of targeting which requires that in cases of doubt, individuals must be presumed civilian and protected from direct attack.[289]

The question as to how long an enemy fighter may be detained also arises. In international armed conflict the purpose of detention is 'to exclude enemy soldiers from further military operations',[290] and so prisoners of war may be detained for the duration of the conflict. As military necessity is relevant to the establishment of the grounds for internment in non-international armed conflict, determining the applicable law by reference to international armed conflict may be appropriate. In principle, this would appear to be consistent with the requirements of international human rights law: in *C v Australia* the Human Rights Committee held that 'in order to avoid a characterization of arbitrariness, detention should not continue beyond the period for which the State party can provide appropriate justification'.[291] As the justification for continued detention is military necessity,[292] prolonged detention—potentially until the end

[285] This issue is beyond the scope of this work. See further, above n 272.

[286] Rule 6, above n 17.

[287] Above n 272, 27–33.

[288] ie is divided between an armed wing, a political wing, and so on.

[289] See Rule 6, above n 17.

[290] Horst Fischer, 'Protection of Prisoners of War' in Dieter Fleck (ed), *The Handbook of International Humanitarian Law*, 2nd edn (Oxford, OUP, 2008) 372.

[291] *C v Australia*, Views, Human Rights Committee, Communication No 900/1999, UN Doc CCPR/C/76/D/900/1999, 28 October 2002, para 8.2. This is a consistent feature of the Human Rights Committee's jurisprudence, applicable to all instances of detention, see further *Abassi Madani v Algeria*, Human Rights Committee, Communication No 1172/2003, 21 June 2007, para 8.4.

[292] This issue was addressed in the *Serdar Mohammed* case. The UK High Court concluded that an individual who could be lawfully killed could be detained, but that as soon as an individual is detained authorisation for the use of lethal force is removed and so the authority to detain is negated (paras 252–53). The UK Court of Appeal disagreed with the immediate removal of detention authority, holding that a detained individual 'should generally be regarded as posing an imminent threat, albeit one subject to contingency.' *Serdar Mohammed v Ministry of Defence*, above n 266, paras 252–53; *Serdar Mohammed & Others v Secretary of State for Defence*, Court of Appeal, Case Nos A2/2014/1862; A2/2014/4084; A2/2014/4086, 30 July 2015, para 212.

of the conflict—may be consistent with this provision.[293] It is submitted, however, that such detention must be subject to periodic review. As noted by Pejic, '[o]ne of the most important principles governing internment/administrative detention is that this form of deprivation of liberty must cease as soon as the individual ceases to pose a real threat'.[294] As circumstances change over time,[295] periodic review is required to ensure that the reasons for detention remain valid.[296] In the context of non-international armed conflict, the reasons for detention must be interpreted narrowly, and must take into account both the status of the individual and the prevailing context. Of course, it is possible that periodic review will result in the continued detention of a fighter. In this regard it is noted that a number of non-international armed conflicts have extended over decades,[297] and this reality may raise human rights-related concerns vis-à-vis the prospect of indefinite detention. However, this concern applies equally to prolonged international armed conflicts, and while the law may not be capable of responding to such situations in advance, ad hoc solutions in the form of prisoner swaps or release on compassionate grounds may be appropriate.

(b) Situations Outside Armed Conflict

In general, no legal basis for administrative detention by armed groups exists under either domestic law or international law in situations not constituting armed conflict. However, an exception may exist when an armed group exercises exclusive control over a territory.[298] In principle, if the legislative authority of an armed group is accepted, then there appears to be no reason for precluding the extension of this authority to include administrative detention:[299] international human rights law permits the use of administrative detention for reasons of public security, and in the

[293] More accurately, detention may be justifiable until either the end of the armed conflict, or the end of the detainee's ability to participate in the hostilities. Release of the detainee may therefore be required if they are no longer capable of participating in hostilities, on the basis of injury, for example.

[294] 'Procedural principles and safeguards for internment' above n 248, 382.

[295] Both with respect to the overall situation and the individual concerned.

[296] This is a feature of the law of international armed conflict with respect to civilian internees, and is also required by international human rights law which prohibits arbitrary detention, and therefore requires periodic court control of detention to ensure its continued validity.

[297] For example, the armed conflict between the FARC and Colombia has lasted for over 40 years, while the armed conflict between the LTTE and Sri Lanka lasted for over 20 years.

[298] See related discussion above, in Ch 8 section I.A(iv).

[299] An exception may exist if an armed group exerts controls in the territory of a state party to the European Convention on Human Rights, as administrative detention is not listed as a permissible ground for detention under Art 5 of the European Convention. See *Human Rights in Times of Conflict and Terrorism* above n 41, 95–97, 263.

situations under discussion the armed group is subject to the obligation to protect.[300] Necessarily, however, any instance of administrative detention must be consistent with the stringent requirements of international human rights law.[301] In particular, an armed group must clearly establish the legal basis for administrative detention,[302] and all instances of administrative detention must be consistent with the relevant procedural guarantees, including court review of detention.

(iii) Conditions of Detention

This section will not discuss the requirements relating to conditions of detention in detail.[303] Instead, specific issues will be addressed in order to illustrate the application of a context-dependent approach to international human rights law obligations. Both situations of armed conflict and situations outside armed conflict are addressed.

Article 10 of the International Covenant on Civil and Political Rights requires that all persons deprived of their liberty 'be treated with humanity and with respect for the inherent dignity of the human person'. Although this provision is not listed amongst the non-derogable rights in General Comment 29 the Human Rights Committee stated that it 'expresses a norm of general international law not subject to derogation.'[304] A similar standard is also established under the law of non-international armed conflict: common Article 3 requires that all persons deprived of their liberty 'be treated humanely',[305] and prohibits 'outrages upon personal dignity',[306] while Article 4 Additional Protocol II 'reiterates the essence of common Article 3'.[307] Accordingly, detaining authorities are subject to a positive obligation to ensure that detainees' human rights continue to be respected and protected.[308] In this regard it is noted that the nature of detention places the detaining authority in a position of complete control vis-à-vis a detainee's rights and physical integrity:[309] individuals detained

300 See above, Ch 7 section I.E.

301 See eg General Comment No 8 above n 233, para 4.

302 Art 9(1) International Covenant on Civil and Political Rights; *Amnesty International and Others v Sudan*, African Commission on Human and Peoples' Rights, Communication No 48/90, 50/91, 52/91, 89/93 (1999) para 59.

303 See generally above n 228; 'Procedural principles and safeguards for internment' above n 248; *The Law of Non-International Armed Conflict* above n 27, 292–305.

304 Above n 94, para 13(a).

305 Common Art 3(1).

306 Common Art 3(1)(c).

307 Above n 23, para 4515.

308 Of course, certain restrictions associated with a deprivation of liberty are unavoidable. See eg Human Rights Committee, General Comment No 21, 'Replaces general comment 9 concerning humane treatment of persons deprived of liberty (Art 10)', UN Doc HRI/GEN/1/Rev.1, 10 April 1992, para 3.

309 See for example, *Congo v Ecuador*, Decision, Inter-American Commission on Human Rights, Case 11.427, 13 April 1999, para 83.

by an armed group are subject to the exclusive authority of that group and are, by virtue of their detention, prevented from securing their rights on their own.[310] As such, armed groups are solely responsible for securing the entirety of a detainee's rights, and this obligation applies to all armed groups who detain, irrespective of their capacity level or the level of territorial control exercised. Interestingly, Nkrumah suggests that the humane treatment of prisoners may serve a military purpose beneficial to armed groups:

> If the enemy retains the hope that he can save his life by surrendering, his will to fight will be considerably reduced. On the other hand, if the enemy is unaware of the moderate and humane treatment given by guerrillas to prisoners, he will fight with greater fury, in the belief that there is no escape.[311]

The Human Rights Committee has identified a minimum core of detention-related obligations that 'should always be observed, even if economic or budgetary considerations may make compliance with these obligations difficult'.[312] Given the absolute nature of these minimum requirements, which apply 'regardless of a state party's level of development',[313] it is submitted that they must be regarded as equally applicable to armed groups and must apply regardless of the armed group's level of development.[314] The identified minimum standards include 'minimum floor space and cubic content of air for each prisoner, adequate sanitary facilities, clothing which shall be in no manner degrading or humiliating, provision of a separate bed, and provision of food of nutritional value adequate for health and strength',[315] as well as the 'provision of medical care and treatment for sick prisoners'.[316]

[310] See eg *Juvenile Reeducation Institute v Paraguay*, Judgment, Inter-American Court of Human Rights, 2 September 2004, para 152; *Keenan v United Kingdom*, Judgment, European Court of Human Rights, Application No 27229/95, 3 April 2001, para 91; *Malawi African Association v Mauritania*, Decision, African Commission on Human Rights, Communication No 54/91, 61/91, 98/93, 164/97, 196/97, 210/98, 11 May 2000, para 122.

[311] Kwame Nkrumah, *Handbook of Revolutionary Warfare* (New York, International Publishers, 1969) 113–14. Similarly, Mao stated: 'We further our mission of destroying the enemy by propagandizing his troops, by treating his captured soldiers with consideration, and by caring for those of his wounded who fall into our hands. If we fail in these respects, we strengthen the solidarity of our enemy.' Mao Tes-tung, *On Guerrilla Warfare*, www.marxists.org/reference/archive/mao/works/1937/guerrilla-warfare/ch06.htm.

[312] *Albert Womah Mukong v Cameroon*, Views, Human Rights Committee, Communication No 458/1991, UN Doc CCPR/C/51/D/458/1991, 21 July 1994, para 9.3.

[313] ibid, para 9.3.

[314] See eg General Comment No 21 above n 308, para 4. See also, Art 4(1) Additional Protocol II.

[315] *Albert Womah Mukong v Cameroon*, above n 312, para 9.3. These requirements reflect those of international humanitarian law. See Rule 118, above n 17.

[316] *Rouse v Philippines*, Views, Human Rights Committee, Communication No 1089/2002, UN Doc CCPR/C/84/D/1089/2002, 25 July 2005, para 7.8.

Beyond this minimum standard of treatment,[317] the overall level of treatment required is context-dependent, and must be evaluated in relation to the resources available to the detaining authority.[318] For example, Article 5(2) of Additional Protocol II requires that detaining authorities respect certain provisions 'within the limits of their capabilities',[319] while Article 5(1)(b) requires that: 'the persons referred to in this paragraph shall, *to the same extent as the local civilian population*, be provided with food and drinking water and be afforded safeguards as regards health and hygiene and protection against the rigours of the climate and the dangers of the armed conflict'.[320] Debate exists as to whether the standard of treatment afforded detainees should be equivalent to that of the local population—as explicitly specified in the text of Article 5(1)(b)—or to that of the armed group. While using the local population as a comparator may be warranted on the basis that 'guerrilla fighters may live under harsher conditions'[321] than the local population, in practice it is unlikely that an armed group will treat detainees better than their own members;[322] indeed, to do so may be beyond their ability, based on the presumption that an armed group will provide as beneficial as possible a standard of living for its personnel. Equally, an assumption that the armed group will live under harsher conditions than the civilian population is not always valid; for instance, the civilian population may be mistreated or exploited for the benefit of the armed group.[323]

It would therefore seem sensible that the decisive factors should be whether detainees are treated appropriately on the basis of available resources, and are not deliberately mistreated. As such, it seems appropriate that the guards' standard of living be the comparator.[324] An approach similar to this appears to have been applied by the *Aleksovski* Trial Chamber of the International Criminal Tribunal for the former Yugoslavia. In determining whether guards had mistreated detainees at a detention

[317] In relation to minimum standards the Human Rights Committee references the Standard Minimum Rules for the Treatment of Prisoners, Adopted by the First United Nations Congress on the Prevention of Crime and the Treatment of Offenders, held at Geneva in 1955, and approved by the Economic and Social Council by its resolution 663C(XXIV) of 31 July 1957 and 2076(LXII) of 13 May 1977.

[318] For example, the level of healthcare provided to prisoners will be dependent upon the resources available to the state. A context-dependent approach is also evident in the law of non-international armed conflict. See eg above n 23, para 4580.

[319] Art 5(2) Additional Protocol II.

[320] Art 5(1)(b) Additional Protocol II. Emphasis added.

[321] *The Law of Non-International Armed Conflict* above n 27, 294.

[322] Sivakumaran notes that in practice, armed groups often treat detainees to the same standard as members of the armed group. See ibid, 293–94.

[323] For example, in the Congo, members of the Rally for Congolese Democracy (RCD) are reported as living off the civilian population. See International Crisis Group, 'The Kivus: The Forgotten Crucible of the Congo Conflict' (2003) 11.

[324] See *The Law of Non-International Armed Conflict* above n 27, 293–94.

facility the Court held that although there was a relative lack of food, this was 'the result of shortages caused by the war and affected everyone, detainees and non-detainees alike', and so there was no differentiation between the detainees and the prison staff in this regard.[325] However, this general rule of thumb is subject to an important caveat: the treatment of detainees cannot fall below the minimum required standard. It is foreseeable that an armed group—particularly one engaged in guerrilla activities[326]—may have insufficient access to necessities such as food, water, or shelter, and that their practical situation or lack of external communication capacity, may mean that they cannot facilitate protection of detainees' rights. In such situations armed groups cannot detain and must release any detainees in their custody:[327] the minimum core obligations constitute a mandatory minimum.

In general, satisfaction of the international human rights obligations relating to humane treatment and the conditions of detention should be within the capacity of most armed groups. Regarding humane treatment, the prohibition of torture and cruel, inhuman, or degrading treatment is primarily a negative obligation,[328] and as a matter of internal command and control is capable of being respected by armed groups operating at all capacity levels.[329] Similarly, armed groups at all levels of development should, in principle, have the ability to respect other rights such as the right to food, given that an armed group will have to secure food supplies for their own members.[330] Regarding the infrastructure of detention, while a stationary purpose-built detention facility should be regarded as the preferred option, it is possible that the international human rights law requirements relating to detention may be met vis-à-vis non-permanent, or mobile, detention centres.[331] For example, most detention facilities—including non-purpose-built or mobile detention centres—should have the potential to satisfy requirements relating to floor space, cubic air content,

[325] *Prosecutor v Zlatko Aleksovski*, Judgment, Trial Chamber, International Criminal Tribunal for the former Yugoslavia, Case No IT-95-14/1-T, 25 June 1999, para 173.

[326] In relation to the difficulties associated with such activity, see generally, Ernesto 'Che' Guevara, *Bolivian Diary* (London, Pathfinder Press, 1994).

[327] With respect to releasing detainees, see below, Ch 8 section I.B(iv).

[328] Of course, this obligation does include positive elements, such as training, promulgation of orders, and so on.

[329] Although conditions of detention may amount to cruel, inhuman or degrading treatment.

[330] A similar logic applies with respect to shelter, healthcare, and so on.

[331] During the Algerian civil war, for example, detainees were 'shuttled in small groups from place to place within Algeria' (See *The Law of Non-International Armed Conflict* above n 27, 297), while similarly, individuals detained during the Lebanese civil war were often moved, presumably to avoid detection (see for example, Brian Keenan, *An Evil Cradling* (London, Vintage, 1993)). In Afghanistan general use sites which could be transformed into detention centres—such as mosques, houses, and so on—were utilised (see Qayum Babak, 'Afghanistan: Taliban justice "fairer" than state's', *Institute for War and Peace Reporting* (17 August 2010)).

adequate sanitary facilities, and so on. Of course, minimum conditions will be more difficult to ensure under such circumstances—including when detainees are being moved—but this should not be impossible.[332] However, situations of mobile detention where the detainee is constantly on the move with the armed group are more problematic; for instance, if an individual is detained by a mobile guerrilla group and required to undertake forced marches as the group relocates in response to hostilities, this may implicate the prohibition of cruel, inhuman, or degrading treatment.

Fulfilment of detainees' right to health is slightly more complicated, particularly for groups that do not exercise territorial control. An armed group may satisfy the overall obligation to fulfil by means of the obligation to fulfil (facilitate), fulfil (provide), or a combination thereof.[333] However, unlike the situations referred to previously wherein the obligation to facilitate may be the preferred option for an armed group,[334] in instances of detention, satisfaction of the obligation to provide may in fact be most advantageous. In such situations, directly providing the right to health avoids the need to interact with individuals or entities external to the armed group, a factor which may prove particularly beneficial for mobile armed groups who wish to keep their whereabouts unknown. Direct provision of the right to health during detention is also relatively straightforward from a capacity perspective. In most situations it is provision of the underlying determinants of the right, such as food, water, and shelter that are at issue. These elements correspond both to the minimum standards required during detention, and the level of treatment typically extended to armed group members.[335] In the event of illness or injury, a detainee may be treated in the same manner as a member of the armed group, for example by the armed group's own medic.

At some point, however, resort to the obligation to facilitate may be required. For example, an armed group may run out of medicines and be dependent upon an external organisation for resupply.[336] Similarly, treatment of a detainee may be beyond the capacity of an armed group, and so they may be required to facilitate treatment through an external organisation, inter alia, through cooperation with an organisation such as the International Committee of the Red Cross. In Niger, for example, the

[332] Protection from the elements may be a principal concern. For example, while an armed group and their detainees alike may sleep under a bivouac or in the rough, thereby satisfying the same standard as the armed group comparator, it is uncertain whether this can be considered an adequate form of shelter.

[333] Given the circumstances it is presumed that the obligation to fulfil (promote) is not pressing.

[334] See above, Ch 7 section I.D(i).

[335] See further, above Ch 8 section I.B(iii).

[336] See eg 'Aid for captured Niger soldiers', *BBC News* (London, 27 June 2007).

International Committee of the Red Cross visited detainees held by the MNJ, providing emergency health care and medical aid on a number of occasions.[337] Similarly, during the Cuban Revolution in 1958, Fidel Castro sent a telegram requesting the assistance of the Red Cross:

> After the latest battle in the Sierra Maestra, a great many wounded Batista soldiers remain in our hands. It has always been the rebels' custom to care for enemy soldiers wounded in the fighting in our improvised hospitals, thereby saving the lives of many of them. This time, however, we cannot put our humanitarian principles fully into practice because there are too many casualties. For lack of beds, seriously wounded soldiers are lying on the ground, without even a blanket, and we are unable to provide them with the food which their condition requires. Medicines are in short supply ... We have publicly proposed that a commission of the Cuban Red Cross should come to fetch the wounded and have stated that we are ready to hand them over so that they can receive the treatment needed...[338]

If an armed group cannot ensure a detainee's right to health, whether by means of the obligation to facilitate or the obligation to provide, then they must release the detainee into appropriate medical care: failure to do so may result in a human rights violation.[339] The release of detainees under such circumstances routinely occurs in practice. For instance, in Western Sahara the Polisario Front released two seriously ill Moroccan detainees,[340] while in Sudan the Sudan Liberation Army–Abdelwahid an-Nur faction released a detained Sudanese government official who was ill.[341] In the Philippines it appears to be NDFP policy to release ill detainees if necessary so that they can access treatment.[342] Of course, armed groups exercising

[337] *Annual Report 2007* (Geneva, International Committee of the Red Cross, 2008) 157. See further, 'Detention by armed groups' above n 3, 760.

[338] Telegram from Fidel Castro, Commander-in-Chief of the Rebel Army, 3 July 1958. Quoted in *The Law of Non-International Armed Conflict* above n 27, 275.

[339] See *Hernandez Lima v Guatemala*, Inter-American Commission on Human Rights, Case 11.297, Report No 28/96, 16 October 1996, para 60. See further, Tara J Melish, 'The Inter-American Commission on Human Rights: Defending Social Rights Through Case-Based Petitions' in Malcolm Langford (ed), *Social Rights Jurisprudence: Emerging Trends in International and Comparative Law* (Cambridge, CUP, 2008) 352.

[340] 'Repatriation of two sick Moroccan prisoners', International Committee of the Red Cross, 22 January 2005.

[341] 'Sudan: ICRC visits Sudanese soldiers held by armed opposition group', International Committee of the Red Cross, 27 August 2013. See also, 'Sudan: ICRC facilitates handover of five soldiers in Darfur', International Committee of the Red Cross, 4 December 2013; 'Mali: Four Soldiers evacuated following ICRC visit', International Committee of the Red Cross, 27 March 2008.

[342] '... according to the NDFP, in 2010, four members of the Philippine National Police Special Action Force, who were wounded in an attack by the NPA, were treated as prisoners of war (POWs) and were given first aid by the NPA. In accordance with the NDFP policy on the treatment of POWs, the NPA decided to release them immediately so that they could be brought to the nearest hospitals in Antipolo City'. *The Law of Non-International Armed Conflict* above n 27, 299–300.

territorial control may be able to ensure the continued detention of an ill or injured detainee, if they can be transferred to appropriate treatment outside the detention centre, but within the area controlled by the group.

(iv) The Release of Detainees

If an armed group does not have the capacity to ensure minimum detention standards—including procedural guarantees—then it must release existing detainees and refrain from detaining until it has the ability to ensure that those standards are met. While this may prove problematic from the perspective of the armed group the absolute nature of the requirement must be respected:[343] the law cannot be adapted to the reality of armed groups past its breaking point. It is often assumed that if armed groups cannot detain an individual, then they will resort to summary execution.[344] However, this is not a foregone conclusion, and practice exists demonstrating that armed groups do release captured enemy fighters. For example, Guevara states that '[i]t is a good policy, so long as there are no considerable bases of operations and invulnerable places, to take no prisoners. Survivors ought to be set free.'[345] Equally, the code of the Chin National Front in Burma specifies that:

> As per the nature of [the] revolution that the Chin National Front is waging, prisoners of war should not be detained for [a] long period of time. After interrogating, educating about Democracy and persuading them to support the Chin National movement, the prisoners of war should be immediately released. This should be practiced as the Chin National Front's standard for detaining prisoners of war.[346]

The International Committee of the Red Cross has facilitated the release of detainees held by armed groups on a number of occasions,[347] including in Afghanistan,[348] Mali,[349] the Philippines,[350] Sudan[351] and Colombia.[352]

343 See eg above n 282, 622.

344 See eg above n 87, 371. See also, above n 130.

345 Ernesto 'Che' Guevara, *Guerrilla Warfare* (USA, BN Publishing, 2007) 20.

346 Quoted in *The Law of Non-International Armed Conflict* above n 27, 301.

347 'Sudan: Armed group releases five soldiers', International Committee of the Red Cross, 6 November 2013.

348 'Afghanistan: ICRC facilitates the release of 40 prisoners', International Committee of the Red Cross, 12 February 1999; 'Afghanistan: ICRC facilitates release of twelve South Korean hostages', International Committee of the Red Cross, 29 August 2007.

349 'Mali: three detainees transferred after ICRC visit', International Committee of the Red Cross, 1 March 2012.

350 'Philippines: Two detainees released under ICRC auspices', International Committee of the Red Cross, 19 August 2004.

351 *Annual Report 2010* (Geneva, International Committee of the Red Cross, 2011) 180; 'Sudan: Armed group releases five soldiers', International Committee of the Red Cross, 6 November 2013.

352 *Annual Report 2012* (Geneva, International Committee of the Red Cross, 2013) 372.

Interestingly, a policy of releasing detainees may be adopted by armed groups in order to accrue a military advantage.[353] During the Cuban revolution, for example, a journalist quoted Raoul Castro as making the following speech to detained enemy fighters:

> We hope that you will stay with us and fight against the master who so ill-used you. If you decide to refuse this invitation—and I am not going to repeat it—you will be delivered into the custody of the Cuban Red Cross tomorrow. Once you are under Batista's orders again, we hope that you will not take up arms against us. But, if you do, remember this: We took you this time. We can take you again. And when we do we will not frighten or torture or kill you, no more than we are doing to you at this moment. If you are captured a second time or even a third by us, we will again return you exactly as we are doing now.[354]

If detainees are released it is imperative that measures be taken to ensure their safety. This requirement is explicitly codified in Article 5(4) Additional Protocol II applicable to non-international armed conflict,[355] and must be regarded as equally applicable outside situations of armed conflict: it would clearly be inconsistent with, inter alia, the right to health, if an injured detainee is released without a means of reaching appropriate medical care whether on their own or with accessible assistance, or if a detainee is released in a situation which put them at risk of death or injury from exposure. In certain situations it may be sufficient to release a detainee in the presence of civilians, or in the vicinity of a civilian settlement,[356] while in other situations release through the auspices of an intermediary such as the International Committee of the Red Cross may be required.

C. Summary

In non-international armed conflict international humanitarian law must be regarded as permitting the internment/administrative detention of 'fighters'; ie those individuals who directly participate in hostilities. However, the use of internment is restricted to such persons, and no legal basis exists justifying the extension of internment authority to include acts in support of the general war effort, or non-combat activities. In general, no legal basis for detention by armed groups exists outside armed conflict. However, an exception does exist in situations where an armed group is granted legislative authority.[357] In such circumstances, an

[353] See eg *Handbook of Revolutionary Warfare* above n 311, 113–14.

[354] Above n 87, 371.

[355] See also, above n 23, para 4596.

[356] Provided the detainee is capable of reaching that settlement, and that their presence there will not pose a risk to them (ie if the population of the village is hostile).

[357] See above, Ch 8 section I.A(iv).

armed group may enact detention-related legislation, both in relation to penal prosecutions and, potentially, administrative detention. This authority may apply when a group exercises stable exclusive territorial control, both during and outside non-international armed conflict. All instances of administrative detention are regulated by procedural guarantees, and in particular the right to be informed of the reasons for detention, and the right to challenge the legality of detention.

Both international human rights law and international humanitarian law establish complementary minimum rules for the conditions of detention, based upon the principle that all detainees must be treated humanely. Beyond this minimum standard, the level of treatment is context-dependent. It is proposed that the decisive factors in evaluating this requirement should be whether detainees are treated appropriately on the basis of available resources, and not deliberately mistreated; in this regard it seems appropriate that the guards' standard of living should be the comparator. If an armed group cannot ensure the minimum conditions of detention or satisfy the relevant procedural guarantees, it cannot detain.

II. ARMED GROUPS AND THE RIGHT TO HEALTH

Armed groups often engage in activities that affect individuals' enjoyment of the right to health, either directly or indirectly.[358] For example, an attack launched by an armed group may cause injuries necessitating medical treatment, while more generally, the activities of an armed group may affect access to, or the delivery of, health services for individuals located within their area of operations. For instance, the establishment of a road block by an armed group may prevent individuals accessing health care, either directly or indirectly.[359] As '[h]ealth is a fundamental human right indispensable for the exercise of other human rights',[360] it is imperative that any obligations imposed on armed groups in this regard be determined. Of course, it is also important that any imposed obligations be responsive to the reality of armed groups, and capable of being fulfilled in practice. This section begins by addressing a number of components of the right to health that are potentially relevant to armed groups, namely the concept of progressive realisation, the existence of minimum core obligations, and

[358] It is noted that the full formulation of the right refers to 'the right of everyone to the enjoyment of the highest attainable standard of physical and mental health'. For convenience, this shall be referred to as the 'right to health' herein.

[359] ie the armed group may prevent individuals passing through the roadblock, or the presence of the roadblock may prevent individuals from attempting to access healthcare.

[360] Committee on Economic, Social and Cultural Rights, General Comment 14, 'The right to the highest attainable standard of health (article 12 of the International Covenant on Economic, Social and Cultural Rights)' UN Doc E/C.12/2000/4, 11 August 2000, para 1.

the role of international assistance. The context-dependent application of the right to health is then tested utilising the respect, protect, fulfil framework developed above.[361] The section addresses armed groups both party to a non-international armed conflict, and those armed groups bound by international human rights law obligations outside armed conflict.

A. Armed Groups and the Progressive Realisation of the Right to Health

The full realisation of economic, social and cultural rights is resource-dependent.[362] With respect to fulfilment of the right to health, for instance, significant resources are required, inter alia, to train and employ health care professionals, maintain and operate equipment and machinery, and to provide appropriate education in relation to the main health issues faced by the community. Accordingly, and in light of the significant financial, infrastructural, and human resource constraints faced by states around the world, it is apparent that an immediate unqualified positive obligation to fully realise the right to health would be unrealistic in a number of cases.[363]

Acknowledging this reality, international human rights law establishes an obligation of progressive realisation, which specifies how the full realisation of economic, social and cultural rights can be achieved over time.[364] This is intended to be a flexible device, reflective of and responsive to, the reality of a particular situation,[365] and is determined on a context-dependent basis in light of available resources.[366] Importantly, however, while the progressive realisation clause anticipates that the full realisation of economic, social and cultural rights will occur over a period of time, this cannot be used as an excuse to annul the right. International human rights law requires that immediate and progressive steps utilising all appropriate means be undertaken,[367] and states are subject to a

[361] See above, Ch 7 section I.

[362] Health is a case on point. In 2012, the UK government spent 15.35% of its national budget on healthcare. See Simon Rogers, 'Government spending by department 2011–12: get the data', *The Guardian* (London, 4 December 2012). See further Simon Rogers, 'Healthcare spending around the world, country by country', *The Guardian* (London, 20 June 2012).

[363] See eg *Soobramoney v Minister of Health (Kwazulu-Natal)*, Judgment, Constitutional Court of South Africa, Case CCT 32/97, 27 November 1997, para 28; *Pentiacova and 48 Others v Moldova, Admissibility Decision* App No 14462/03 (ECtHR, 4 January 2005).

[364] Art 2(1) International Covenant on Economic, Social and Cultural Rights.

[365] See eg Committee on Economic, Social and Cultural Rights, General Comment 3, 'The nature of States parties obligations (Art 2 Para 1 of the Covenant)' UN Doc E/1991/23, 14 December 1990, para 9.

[366] See *Minister of Health and others v Treatment Action Campaign and others (No 2)*, Judgment, Constitutional Court of South Africa, Case CCT 8/02, 5 July 2002, para 24.

[367] Asbjorn Eide, 'Adequate Standard of Living' in Daniel Moeckli, Sangeeta Shah and Sandesh Sivakumaran (eds), *International Human Rights Law* (Oxford, OUP, 2010) 253.

clear obligation to take 'deliberate, concrete and targeted'[368] steps in order to 'move as expeditiously and effectively'[369] as possible towards full realisation. For example, to ensure that the progressive realisation clause associated with the right to health is effective in practice, it is required that 'a national public health strategy and plan of action ... addressing the health concerns of the whole population'[370] be adopted and implemented. Thus, in *Paschim banga Khet Samity v State of West Bengal*, the Supreme Court of India held that:

> In the matter of allocation of funds for medical services the said constitutional obligation of the State has to be kept in view. It is necessary that a time bound plan for providing these services should be chalked out keeping in view the recommendations of the Committee [on Economic, Social and Cultural Rights] as well as the requirements for ensuring availability of proper medical services in this regard as indicated by us and steps should be taken to implement the same.[371]

This requirement highlights both the extended time frame associated with progressive realisation, and the fact that (often scarce) resources must be allocated and utilised in the best interests of the affected population. As a result it is submitted that the obligation to progressively realise the right to health should only apply to armed groups with legislative authority; ie armed groups who have displaced the authority of the state, and exercise stable control over a territory and population.[372] Below this point the state will have the principal responsibility to ensure the right to health, while the armed group will not possess legislative authority vis-à-vis the affected population—indicative of a right to act in the populations' best interests—and in practical terms, will generally lack the stability necessary to develop and implement the required plan of action.[373]

For those groups in a position to do so, undertaking tangible measures to progressively realise the right to health—and other rights—may be of military benefit. For instance, Giap notes errors made in the initial stages of the Viet Cong insurgency: 'we mobilized the people for the war without heeding seriously their immediate everyday interests; or we thought of satisfying the immediate interests of the people as a whole, without

[368] General Comment 14 above n 360, para 30.

[369] General Comment 3 above n 365, para 9. See also, *Government of the Republic of South Africa and others v Grootboom and others*, Judgment, Constitutional Court of South Africa, Case CCT 11/00, 4 October 2000, para 46.

[370] General Comment 14 above n 360, para 43(f).

[371] *Paschim banga Khet Samity v State of West Bengal*, Judgment, Case No 169, 6 May 1996, para 16.

[372] See related discussion above, Ch 7 section I.E and Ch 8 section I.A(iv).

[373] This proposal also seems sensible from a practical perspective: it is unlikely that an armed group that does not exercise relatively stable territorial control will prioritise the progressive realisation of the right to health, or other economic, social and cultural rights.

giving due attention to those of the peasants'.[374] From these initial lessons, Giap concluded that the Viet Cong 'had to mobilize the masses for the resistance while trying to satisfy their immediate interest in improving their living conditions'.[375] Similarly, referring to the situation in Somalia, it was reported that: '[f]rom the rebels' point of view, it was in their interest to support assistance for their wounded and displaced populations'.[376] In practice, a number of groups exercising stable territorial control have gradually developed both the services extended to the local population,[377] and their own institutions; prominent examples in this regard include the EPLF in Eritrea,[378] POLISARIO in Western Sahara,[379] FARC in Colombia,[380] the LTTE in Sri Lanka,[381] and Hezbollah in Lebanon.[382]

[374] Vo Nguyen Giap, *The Military Art of People's War: Selected Writings of General Vo Nguyen Giap* (Russell Stetler (ed), New York, Monthly Review Press, 1970) 130.

[375] ibid, 130.

[376] Michael Neuman, 'Somalia: Everything is Open to Negotiation' in Claire Magone, Michael Neuman and Fabrice Weissman (eds), *Humanitarian Negotiations Revealed: The MSF Experience* (London, Hurst & Company, 2011) 84–85.

[377] This is not to imply that these services have been developed in a manner consistent with the requirements of international human rights law, but rather to note that in practice, armed group development of service provision and infrastructure does occur over time.

[378] David Pool, *From Guerrillas to Government: The Eritrean People's Liberation Front* (Athens, Ohio University Press, 2001) 98–104.

[379] 'The Sahrawi have developed a notable administrative structure, which include the election of neighborhood (daria/barrio), camp (wilaya), and national level officials. Schools (K-6) and hospitals are located within each district or camp, with a national level high school, women's school, and hospital.' Michael Bhatia, 'The Western Sahara under Polisario Control' (2001) 28 *Review of African Political Economy* 297.

[380] 'During the 1970s and 1980s, the FARC established its own schools, judicial system, health care, and agrarian economy, and created its own de facto state in remote regions of southern Colombia.' 'Colombia's Civil War: Revolutionary Armed Forces of Colombia (FARC)', *PBS*, www.pbs.org/newshour/bb/latin_america/colombia/players_farc.html.

[381] 'From the 1990s until May 2009, the LTTE controlled large parts of northern and eastern Sri Lanka, the exact contours of which shifted over time as Government forces and the LTTE vied for territorial control. It operated and sought to project itself as a *de facto* State. To this end, the LTTE developed a well-structured international strategy and, in the territory it controlled, established its own police, jails, courts, immigration department, banks and some social services.' Report of the Secretary-General's Panel of Experts on Accountability in Sri Lanka, 31 March 2011, para 33. See also, 'In the beginning we were a guerrilla organisation, engaging in hit and run tactics against the Sri Lankan armed forces. We had no stable control over large territories or populations. Therefore we neither had the resources nor the environment to set up and run a proper judicial system. But in 1993, as soon as we were in control of most of the north, our leadership established the Tamil Eelam Judiciary and College of Law.' 'Thamil Eelam judiciary said a basis for rebuilding northeast' above n 5.

[382] 'Hizbollah over time sought to develop independent sources of funding, which have allowed it to develop an impressive social network for the Shiite community's benefit (including charitable institutions, schools, hospitals and allowances provided to the families of "martyrs").' International Crisis Group, 'Hizbollah and the Lebanese Crisis' (2007) 19–20.

B. The Existence of Minimum Core Obligations

Although the full realisation of economic, social and cultural rights is subject to progressive realisation, elements of these rights must be ensured immediately. In this regard, the Committee on Economic, Social and Cultural Rights has confirmed the existence of 'a minimum core obligation to ensure the satisfaction of, at the very least, minimum essential levels'[383] of each Covenant right.[384] With respect to the right to health, these are considered to include:

- the right of access to health facilities, goods and services on a non-discriminatory basis, especially for vulnerable or marginalized groups;
- access to the minimum essential food which is nutritionally adequate and safe;
- access to basic shelter, housing and sanitation, and an adequate supply of safe and potable water;
- the provision of essential drugs;
- the equitable distribution of all health facilities, goods and services;
- the adoption and implementation of a national public health strategy and plan of action, addressing the health concerns of the whole population;
- reproductive, maternal (pre-natal as well as post-natal) and child health care;
- immunization against the major infectious diseases occurring in the community;
- measures to prevent, treat and control epidemic and endemic diseases;
- education and access to information concerning the main health problems in the community, including methods of preventing and controlling them; and
- appropriate training for health personnel, including education on health and human rights.[385]

Failure to satisfy the minimum core obligation is, prima facie, indicative of a violation of the Covenant,[386] and the General Comment on the right to health states clearly that 'a State party cannot, under any circumstances

[383] General Comment 3 above n 365, para 10.

[384] See also, Committee on Economic, Social and Cultural Rights, 'Substantive issues arising in the implementation of the International Covenant on Economic, Social and Cultural Rights: Poverty and the International Covenant on Economic, Social and Cultural Rights', Statement, UN Doc E/C.12/2001/10, 10 May 2001, para 15.

[385] See General Comment 14 above n 360, paras 43–44. See further, Declaration of Alma-Ata, International Conference on Primary Health Care, Alma-Ata, USSR, 6–12 September 1978, Principle VII(3).

[386] General Comment 3 above n 365, para 10. See also, Maastricht Guidelines on Violations of Economic, Social and Cultural Rights, Maastricht, January 22–26, 1997, para 9.

whatsoever, justify its non-compliance with the core obligations set out in paragraph 43 above, which are non-derogable.'[387] That noted, in exceptional circumstances—due to significant lack of resources for instance—it is possible that minimum core obligations cannot be ensured immediately.[388] However, any exception in this regard is strictly regulated, and in order to attribute failure to satisfy minimum core obligations to a lack of resources, the responsible authority 'must demonstrate that *every effort* has been made *to use all resources that are at its disposition* in an effort to satisfy, as a matter of priority, those minimum obligations.'[389] Applied to armed groups, obligations in relation to the minimum core must be determined in the context of the obligation to fulfil,[390] while the resources at the disposition of an armed group must be regarded as including those of the state, and the international community more generally.[391]

C. The Role of International Assistance

In determining the extent of resources available vis-à-vis the realisation of specific rights the Committee on Economic, Social and Cultural Rights clarified that the phrase 'to the maximum of its available resources' codified in Article 2(1) of the International Covenant on Economic, Social and Cultural Rights 'was intended by the drafters of the Covenant to refer to both the resources existing within a State and those available from the international community through international cooperation and assistance'.[392] International assistance is thus recognised as a legitimate, and at times necessary, means of securing fulfilment of economic, social, and cultural rights.[393] The role of international assistance is particularly pertinent in situations where minimum core obligations are unfulfilled: 'core obligations give rise to national responsibilities for all States and international responsibilities for developed States, as well as others that are "in a position to assist".'[394] The importance of international assistance

[387] General Comment 14 above n 360, para 47.

[388] See eg, *Mazibuko and others v City of Johannesburg and others*, Judgment, Constitutional Court of South Africa, Case CCT 39/09, 8 October 2009, para 56; *Government of the Republic of South Africa and others v Grootboom and others*, above n 369, para 32; *Minister of Health and others v Treatment Action Campaign and others (No 2)*, above n 366, paras 34–39.

[389] General Comment 3 above n 365, para 10. Emphasis added.

[390] See discussion above, Ch 7 section I.D(i).

[391] See discussion above, ch 7 section I.D(i)(c).

[392] General Comment 3 above n 365, para 13. See also, Committee on Economic, Social and Cultural Rights, 'An Evaluation of the Obligation to Take Steps to the "Maximum of Available Resources" Under an Optional Protocol to the Covenant', Statement, UN Doc E/C.12/2007/1, 10 May 2007, para 5.

[393] See eg Marco Odello and Francesco Seatzu, *The UN Committee on Economic, Social and Cultural Rights: The Law, Process and Practice* (Abingdon, Routledge, 2013) 18.

[394] Above n 384, para 16.

is also recognised in the law of non-international armed conflict. Article 18(1) Additional Protocol II states that relief actions shall be undertaken by organisations such as the International Committee of the Red Cross, '[i]f the civilian population is suffering undue hardship owing to a lack of the supplies essential for its survival, such as food stuffs and medical supplies',[395] and this provision is reflected in customary international humanitarian law.[396] Similar to the situation described above regarding the fulfilment of minimum core obligations, relief actions are to be undertaken in armed conflict 'when the responsible authorities can no longer meet the basic necessities of the civilian population whose survival is in jeopardy.'[397]

However, in the specific context of armed group obligations it is submitted that the 'maximum of available resources' must be understood as including not only the resources of the armed group and any available international assistance, but also the resources of the state, recalling that the state is subject to a continuing obligation to ensure human rights protection within its territory.[398] In many situations continuing state services in areas subject to armed group influence or control will be essential to ensuring the right to health. In Sri Lanka, for instance, the state continued to operate health care facilities and other services in LTTE controlled areas.[399] Importantly from a practical perspective, the Sri Lankan government reportedly viewed such service provision as an essential—if tenuous—link to the Tamil population.[400] It is recalled that continued service provision does not necessarily require cooperation between the state and the armed group, and that maintenance of the status quo may be sufficient.[401] That said, in certain situations negotiations between the state and the armed group may be possible; in South Waziristan, for example, the Government of Pakistan reportedly negotiated the running of the area with local Taliban commanders.[402] It is possible that a neutral International Organisation may facilitate negotiations between the state and the armed group.[403]

395 Art 18(1) Additional Protocol II.
396 See Rules 55 and 56, above n 17.
397 Above n 23, para 4878.
398 *Ilascu and Others v Moldova and Russia* App No 48787/99 (ECtHR, 8 July 2004), para 331.
399 Above n 142, 1030.
400 *Rebel Rulers* above n 1, 114.
401 See above, Ch 7 section I.D(i)(a).
402 International Crisis Group, 'Pakistan's Tribal Areas: Appeasing the Militants' (2006) 22. It is unclear whether this arrangement has ceased, and if so, when.
403 For instance, in Senegal, state health teams accompanied by ICRC staff conducted vaccinations in areas subject to armed group control. International Committee of the Red Cross, *Annual Report 2014* (2015) 107.

D. Summary

The nature of economic, social and cultural rights obligations facilitates their application to armed opposition groups by providing an in-built mechanism for acknowledging and responding to differences in resources and capacity levels. While armed groups may not have the capacity or resources to immediately secure the full realisation of the right to health, they are required to ensure the minimum core of the right, and where appropriate can take concrete steps to the maximum of available resources—in a manner similar to states—towards progressive realisation of this right. The specific measures required of armed groups will now be discussed in light of the respect, protect, fulfil framework.

E. The Obligation to Respect the Right to Health

The obligation to respect is a negative obligation, which requires that armed groups refrain from undertaking any act that will negate or undermine the right to health, whether directly or indirectly.[404] As a negative obligation it 'can be fulfilled by an authority simply refraining from action',[405] and fulfilment is therefore primarily dependent upon conduct, and not resources or capacity. As such, the obligation to respect must be regarded as binding upon all armed groups, in all circumstances.[406]

In practical terms the obligation to respect prohibits an armed group from undertaking any action that will interfere with the right to health, such as, for example: an attack on a healthcare facility, intimidation of medical staff to prevent them from working, or disruption of health service provision, for instance, through the cutting of electricity lines or an attack on a medicine supply convoy. By its nature, the prohibition on indirect interference with the right to health is more difficult to discuss at a general level. However, if an armed group establishes a road block at which it taxes the population, it must take appropriate measures to ensure that this does not either act as a disincentive or prevent individuals from travelling in order to access health facilities and services. Broadly speaking, the rules of the law of armed conflict applicable to armed groups in situations of non-international armed conflict reflect the requirements of the obligation to respect.[407] For example, the customary law of armed conflict requires

[404] See General Comment 14 above n 360, para 33.

[405] Tawhida Ahmed and Israel de Jesus Butler, 'The European Union and Human Rights: An International Law Perspective' (2006) 17 *European Journal of International Law* 796.

[406] Presuming of course that the criteria for recognition of the armed group's international legal personality exist. See above, Ch 2 section IV.

[407] However, these obligations are not absolute. For example, while the direct targeting of medical personnel or facilities may be prohibited, proportional damage to such individuals

that medical personnel and medical units be respected and protected,[408] that the wounded and sick be granted access to the required health services,[409] that no medic be punished for performing their duty,[410] and that no attack be directed against hospitals.[411]

F. The Obligation to Fulfil

The right to health subjects armed groups to certain obligations with respect to the population at large; ie those individuals who fall within an armed group's zone of influence, such as individuals living within an armed group's area of operations, or individuals within a territory controlled by an armed group.[412] In such situations, responsibility is divided between the state and the armed group, such that the precise content of the obligation to fulfil is determined on a gradated basis dependent upon the extent of control or influence exercised by an armed group and the corresponding displacement of state authority.[413] Accordingly, when the capacity and influence of an armed group is at its weakest,[414] the state will bear the principal responsibility for ensuring the right to health, and armed group obligations will be limited. However, as the capacity and influence of an armed group develops, and the group displaces the authority of the state to an increasing extent, it will be subject to increased positive obligations, and the balance of responsibility between the state and the armed group will shift accordingly.

As a result of capacity constraints, it is likely that an armed group will attempt to satisfy the overall obligation to fulfil by means of the obligation to facilitate, while ensuring that the corresponding obligation to provide is satisfied by either the state or a third party organisation.[415] In Syria, for example, armed groups have facilitated access for humanitarian agencies providing basic needs such as food, blankets, and medicines.[416] In terms of practical application, an initial manifestation of the obligation to

or institutions as part of a legitimate attack is permitted under the law of armed conflict. The correlation between the obligation to respect and the rules of international humanitarian law is discussed further above, see Ch 7 section I.C.

408 See Rules 25 and 28 respectively, above n 17.

409 ibid, Rule 110.

410 ibid, Rule 26.

411 ibid, Rule 35.

412 The phrase 'zone of influence' is deliberately vague, reflecting the potentially broad effect of an armed group's activities and the absence of a stationary zone of operations.

413 See further, above Ch 7 sections I.D(i) and I.F.

414 During the embryonic stages of an insurgency for example.

415 The provision of third party aid occurs routinely in practice.

416 'Syria: Humanitarian aid, a lifeline for displaced people', International Committee of the Red Cross, 5 April 2013.

facilitate may be the requirement that an armed group inform an external entity—whether the state or an International Organisation—of a health care issue necessitating attention, thereby facilitating protection vis-à-vis the affected individuals' right to health.[417] For example, an armed group may be aware of a remote village suffering from food shortages or a cholera epidemic,[418] and in such a situation the armed group would be required to contact an external entity capable of providing an appropriate response. However, the point at which an armed group becomes bound by this obligation is important: it is not realistic to bind all armed groups as they may not have the necessary links to either the state or an external organisation.[419] However, it seems reasonable that the obligation should apply once an armed group has established contact with the International Committee of the Red Cross or a similar organisation. At this point the armed group will have the necessary link to an external organisation, and from a practical perspective, that organisation will have had the opportunity to inform the group of its obligations under international human rights law.[420]

Necessarily, the extent of an armed group's positive obligations will increase in accordance with the extent of influence it exerts over an area. As such, armed groups may be required to coordinate the provision of health care in their area, in order to ensure that the needs of the population are addressed in a systematic and not ad hoc manner, avoiding duplication in service provision and ensuring equal access to health facilities, goods, and services across the population.[421] This may require that the armed group establish a centralised unit responsible for the welfare of the civilian population,[422] and will also necessitate that safe passage instructions and so on are effectively communicated throughout the armed group.[423] In Syria the Al Nusrah Front established the Sharia Committee of the Eastern Region, responsible for, inter alia, overseeing the delivery of foreign aid,[424] while similarly in Sri Lanka, the LTTE established the Tamil

[417] In Mali, the MNLA informed the ICRC of wounded soldiers' location and condition. International Committee of the Red Cross, *Annual Report 2014* (2015) 171.

[418] Adequate food is an underlying determinant of the right to health.

[419] See above, Ch 7 section II.

[420] See eg International Committee of the Red Cross, *Annual Report 2012* (2013) 267. See further, above ch 7 section II.

[421] See further, Committee on Economic, Social and Cultural Rights, General Comment No 20, 'Non-Discrimination in Economic, Social and Cultural Rights (art 2, para 3)', UN Doc E/C.12/GC/20, 25 May 2009, paras 8(b), 34.

[422] For example, in Sierra Leone, the G5 unit of the RUF 'was responsible for all civilians in rebel territory'. *Prosecutor v Sesay, Kallon and Gbao*, above n 138, para 692. The Islamic State has also established the Islamic Administration of Public Services, responsible for infrastructure and essential services.'The Islamic State' above n 1, 42.

[423] In certain respects this is similar to the obligation of progressive realization. However, at issue is the development of armed groups' capacity and not the development of service provision intended to secure the realisation of individuals' rights.

[424] 'Al Nusrah Front poised to take over last major city on Euphrates River' above n 110.

Eelam Economic Development Organisation which oversaw all development activity, including the delivery of health services.[425] This organisation was superseded by the LTTE's Planning and Development Secretariat (PDS) which was responsible for identifying the needs of the population, and coordinating the work of external organisations:

> [T]he PDS emphasises the fulfilment of basic needs and the need for central planning and coordination. When it comes to the actual delivery of development, however, the LTTE state relies on partnership agreements with international aid agencies and NGOs.[426]

At the most advanced level, an armed group exercising territorial control will be subject to a state-like level of responsibility in relation to fulfilment of the overall right to health. Although this is a potentially resource-heavy obligation—involving progressive realisation—it is possible that it may be satisfied by means of the obligation to facilitate. It is emphasised, however, that it is the overall obligation to fulfil that must be satisfied, and so the context may demand that a balance be struck between the obligation to facilitate and the obligation to provide.[427]

With respect to satisfaction of this obligation in practice, in Sudan the SPLM/A looked to 'international aid organizations to take the lead in the development of a local health system',[428] with the result that towards the latter stages of the conflict 'a three-tiered health system largely funded by foreign aid organizations but amply staffed with SPLM/A personnel was operating in new Sudan.'[429] However, given the potentially detrimental long-term effects vis-à-vis sustainability and the development of local infrastructure—and recalling the need to ensure a region's continuing independent viability[430]—it is perhaps not appropriate for an International Organisation to be called in to establish a parallel public health system.[431] Rather, it seems preferable that, where possible, efforts should be undertaken in order to ensure the continued operation and development of the existing system, and the territorial state's continuing positive obligations may be engaged in this regard. Of course, it may be necessary to supplement existing staff with personnel from an International Organisation, or to utilise externally provided supplies and equipment.[432]

[425] See *Rebel Rulers* above n 1, 110. See also, Iqbal Athas, 'Expanding Tiger civil service', *The Sunday Times* (Colombo, 9 June 2002).

[426] Above n 142, 1033.

[427] See further above, Ch 7 section I.D.

[428] *Rebel Rulers* above n 1, 163.

[429] ibid, 163.

[430] See the discussion relating to interpreting the obligations imposed on an armed group by analogy with the law of belligerent occupation, above Ch 7 section I.D(i)(a).

[431] See eg Caroline Abu-Sada, 'Gaza Strip: A Perilous Transition' in Claire Magone, Michael Neuman and Fabrice Weissman (eds), *Humanitarian Negotiations Revealed: The MSF Experience* (London, Hurst & Co, 2011) 98.

[432] See generally, above Ch 7 section I.D.

While some armed groups may be reluctant to engage with external actors to facilitate health provision, doing so may actually be in an armed group's strategic interest. In Afghanistan the Taliban reportedly saw 'more potential benefits in securing access to medical aid for themselves and their social base than in preventing it',[433] and the provision of medical services was regarded as a means of demonstrating 'able and legitimate government'.[434] Reflecting this focus, when MSF asked the Afghan Taliban for suggestions regarding future projects, a representative responded that '[t]he biggest needs are with civilians, especially maternity care; we can take care of our fighters'.[435] It is recalled that in situations of non-international armed conflict armed groups are subject to an obligation to allow humanitarian access.[436] In practice, armed groups have allowed humanitarian access on numerous occasions, including in Myanmar, Sri Lanka, Sudan, the Philippines, Mozambique, Somalia, Sierra Leone, Yemen, and the former Yugoslavia.[437]

Of course, when the capacity of an armed group is sufficiently developed, it may satisfy its obligations by means of the obligation to provide.[438] In moving towards this point, it is noted that armed group health care provision may be developed gradually. For instance, Guevara described the progressive development of an armed group's provision of healthcare as occurring on the basis of a three-stage process.[439] At the initial 'nomadic' stage, a doctor may travel with a guerrilla group, providing what healthcare is possible under the circumstances. At the next 'semi-nomadic' stage, service provision can be extended to include a mobile or makeshift hospital, facilitating the undertaking of more advanced surgical procedures. At the third stage, a 'true hospital organization is constructed'[440] in areas under the stable control of the armed group.

[433] Xavier Crombe, 'Afghanistan: Regaining Leverage' in Claire Magone, Michael Neuman and Fabrice Weissman (eds), *Humanitarian Negotiations Revealed: The MSF Experience* (London, Hurst & Co, 2011) 57.

[434] ibid, 62.

[435] Quotied in ibid, 62.

[436] See Art 18 Additional Protocol II, Rule 55, above n 17. See further, UN Security Council Resolution 1261, UN Security Council Resolution 1296, and UN Security Council Resolution 1314. See further, above n 129, 87.

[437] See *The Law of Non-International Armed Conflict* above n 27, 333; Marwaan Macan-Marker, 'Kachin refugees in Myanmar get UN relief', *Al Jazeera* (Doha, 19 December 2011); *Rebel Rulers* above n 1, 120.

[438] Examples include the Zapatistas in Mexico, the EPLF in Eritrea, and the FARC in Colombia. See eg: Niels Barmeyer, 'The Guerrilla Movement as Project: An Assessment of Community Involvement in the EZLN' (2003) 30 *Latin American Perspectives*, 135; above n 378, 100; Garry Leech, 'Farc rebel group in peace talks: Is Colombia's 50-year war about to end?', *The Independent* (London, 21 July 2013).

[439] See above n 345, 72–73.

[440] ibid, 72–73.

A similar capacity-dependent approach to the provision of health care is evident in the practice of armed groups. In Iraq, for example, the Mahdi movement provided basic health care in the weeks after the US-led invasion,[441] while in Ethiopia the EPLF established a network of 'barefoot doctors' who traversed EPLF territory.[442] More developed examples include the FARC in Colombia, who have established mobile clinics which provide health care, including dental care and minor surgery, to civilians in rural areas,[443] and Hezbollah in Lebanon who have developed a health care system equivalent to that of the state.[444]

Ultimately, the resources involved suggest that armed groups will most likely endeavour to satisfy the obligation to fulfil through a combination of the obligations to facilitate and provide.[445] For example, while an armed group may operate a network of primary healthcare centres, the state or an International Organisation may operate more advanced hospitals or surgical facilities. This was the situation in Sri Lanka, where the LTTE directly provided primary healthcare to the civilian population, while the government continued to supply the hospitals and pay staff salaries.[446] With respect to the role of third party assistance it is noted that Hezbollah's health system was developed on the basis of extensive financial support from Iran.[447]

The obligation to promote requires that actions be undertaken to 'create, maintain and restore the health of the population.'[448] The Committee on Economic, Social and Cultural Rights stated that such actions include:

> (i) fostering recognition of factors favouring positive health results, e.g. research and provision of information; (ii) ensuring that health services are culturally appropriate and that health care staff are trained to recognize and respond to the

[441] Above n 191, 2. See also, 'Profile: Moqtada Sadr', *BBC News* (London, 19 January 2012).

[442] Above n 378, 100.

[443] 'Colombia rebel army brings healthcare to the jungle', *Al Jazeera English* (Doha, 31 May 2011). It was reported that '[f]or many peasants, the guerrillas are the only ones who have ever helped them.' See 'Farc rebel group in peace talks' above n 438.

[444] 'In fact, the competence and capability of Hezbollah's services have become an embarrassment to the central Lebanese government who cannot provide services throughout the region with the efficiency of Hezbollah.' 'Hezbollah: A State within a State' above n 190, 132. For example, between 1985 and 1987 Hizbollah established two hospitals in Beqaa and Beirut, as well as 17 medical centres, while more recently it was estimated that Hizbollah medical facilities treat over 400,000 patients a year. See Eitan Azani, *Hezbollah: The Story of the Party of God: From Revolution to Institutionalization* (London, Palgrave Macmillan, 2008) 72; 'Hezbollah: A State within a State' above n 190, 132.

[445] It is worth recalling the perceived political benefits associated with direct service provision, as mentioned above, see nn 433–37.

[446] For example, it is reported that the 'LTTE also provides its own services, especially in the form of primary health care and pre-school education, thus creating an element of division of labour between service provisions by the Sri Lankan state and by LTTE state institutions'. Above n 142, 1031.

[447] *Hezbollah: The Story of the Party of God* above n 444, 72.

[448] General Comment 14 above n 360, para 37.

> specific needs of vulnerable or marginalized groups; (iii) ensuring that the State meets its obligations in the dissemination of appropriate information relating to healthy lifestyles and nutrition, harmful traditional practices and the availability of services; (iv) supporting people in making informed choices about their health.[449]

From the above it is apparent that obligations in relation to the obligation to promote are primarily educational in nature, requiring that armed groups raise awareness amongst the population and healthcare workers on issues such as hygiene, nutrition, healthy lifestyles, harmful practices, and so on.[450] With respect to satisfaction of this obligation, it is noted that a large number of armed groups operating across the spectrum of capacity levels engage in propaganda or outreach activities:[451] it is not necessarily the armed group's level of development that is at issue, but rather the availability of reliable health-related information. In this regard International Organisations and non-governmental organisations (NGOs) may play a role thorough the provision of health education training, even if basic. For example, the International Committee of the Red Cross provide training to members of armed groups on issues such as the law of armed conflict and first aid,[452] and a module on health education could feasibly be included in these training sessions. Accordingly, and in a manner similar to the initial application of the obligation to facilitate, the obligation to promote should perhaps become relevant when an armed group engages in outreach activities, and has the ability to disseminate health-related information; for example, after receiving training from an International Organisation, or if they have a doctor amongst their members. Similar to the situation vis-à-vis medical aid,[453] the provision of health-related information may be in the interest of armed groups, forming part of a 'hearts and minds' campaign and demonstrating 'able and legitimate government'.[454]

[449] ibid, para 37.

[450] Based on the list enumerated in: ibid, para 37.

[451] For example, with respect to the Naxalites in India it was reported that 'The movement's ideology is propagated through village meetings, community groups, and theater performances. Indoctrination is done through public meetings, speeches, and in schools.' Human Rights Watch, 'Between Two Sets of Guns: Attacks on Civil Society Activists in India's Maoist Conflict' (2012) 12–13. See further, above n 378, 100; *Hezbollah: The Story of the Party of God* above n 444, 116–17.

[452] See eg 'Building respect for humanitarian action and IHL among "other" weapon bearers', International Committee of the Red Cross, 29 October 2010.

[453] See nn 433–37.

[454] Above n 433, 62. For example, speaking of a desire for information regarding agricultural techniques, a member of the Naxalites in India stated: 'we need urgent help in the agricultural department ... We need people who know about seeds, organic pesticides, permaculture. With a little help we could do a lot.' 'Walking with the Comrades' above n 3.

To summarise, while there is no preference given herein to which authority fulfils the right in question—the important element being individuals' ability to enjoy the right—it is recalled that if an armed group can better ensure the realisation of a right by means of the obligation to provide, or a combination of the obligations to facilitate and provide, then reliance solely on the obligation to facilitate may violate the armed group's obligations under international human rights law. The obligation to facilitate is a means of promoting the realisation of a right, not of abdicating responsibility. Equally, any imposed obligation must be responsive to the context and a clear separation between facilitation and provision may not always be possible: if an armed group has the capacity to treat a seriously ill individual and the movement of that individual is likely to endanger their health, then the armed group will be required to provide treatment rather than transfer the individual to third-party care.[455]

G. The Obligation to Protect

The obligation to protect requires that efforts be undertaken to protect against violations of the right to health by third parties.[456] The Committee on Economic, Social and Cultural Rights notes that this obligation includes, inter alia, an obligation to ensure that privatisation does not negatively affect the availability, accessibility, acceptability and quality of health services; an obligation to ensure that health professionals meet appropriate standards of education, skill and conduct; an obligation to ensure that third parties do not limit individuals' access to health services; and an obligation to ensure that 'harmful social or traditional practices do not interfere with access to pre- and post-natal care and family-planning'.[457] As noted previously, given the requirements related to the rule of law and the maintenance of public order, the application of the obligation to protect to armed groups should be restricted to situations wherein the group exercises exclusive territorial control.[458] In this regard it is noted that violations of the obligation to protect include, the 'failure to regulate the activities of individuals, groups or corporations', 'the failure to protect women against violence or to prosecute perpetrators', and 'the

[455] This requirement is consistent with the Hippocratic oath: 'That I will not withdraw from my patients in their time of need … That above all else I will serve the highest interests of my patients through the practice of my science and my art'.

[456] General Comment 14 above n 360, paras 33, 51. See further, *The Social and Economic Rights Action Center and the Center for Economic and Social Rights v Nigeria*, Decision, African Commission on Human and Peoples' Rights, Communication No 155/96, 13–27 October 2001, para 46.

[457] General Comment 14 above n 360, para 35.

[458] See above, Ch 7 section I.E.

failure to enact or enforce laws to prevent the pollution of water, air and soil by extractive and manufacturing industries.'[459] Further issues arising in relation to this obligation are discussed above in the section addressing armed group prosecution of non-conflict related crimes.[460]

The obligation to protect the right to health places a significant obligation on armed groups, and groups may be unable to satisfy certain elements of this obligation in the absence of external assistance. For example, both a legislative framework and appropriately qualified personnel will be required to regulate the education, skill-level, and conduct of medical professionals, and armed groups may thus be required to enforce existing state laws and to continue to employ state personnel where possible. Similarly, the expertise of external health organisations, such as the World Health Organization, may be required to effectively discourage the continued observance of harmful traditional medical or cultural practices.

H. Summary

The full realisation of the right to health is subject to progressive realisation. This requires, inter alia, the development of a long-term health strategy and plan of action, and the allocation and utilisation of scarce resources in the best interests of the population. As such, it is submitted that the progressive realisation of the right to health should only apply to armed groups with legislative authority; ie armed groups that exercise stable and effective territorial control, whether during or outside non-international armed conflict.

However, elements of the right to health must be immediately ensured by all armed groups, and the Committee on Economic, Social, and Cultural Rights has identified a minimum core of obligations in this regard. Satisfaction of the minimum core obligations form part of an armed group's obligation to fulfil, and may be satisfied by means of the obligation to facilitate, the obligation to provide, or a combination thereof. When fulfilling obligations in relation to the right to health generally, and the minimum core in particular, the resources available to the armed group include the resources of the group itself, the resources available through the international community,[461] and the resources of the territorial state.[462]

459 General Comment 14 above n 360, para 51.

460 See above, Ch 8 section I.A(iv).

461 For instance through organisations such as OCHA, the ICRC, Oxfam, MSF, and so on.

462 It is recalled that the territorial state remains subject to positive international human rights law obligations vis-à-vis the entirety of the national territory.

In relation to armed groups' obligations vis-à-vis the population at large, responsibility for ensuring the right to health is shared between the armed group and the territorial state, with the precise content of each entity's obligation determined on a gradated basis in relation to the extent of control exercised. The obligation to protect can only apply to groups with legislative authority, and it is noted that satisfaction of the obligation to protect the right to health may be dependent upon expertise provided by third party organisations, such as the World Health Organization.[463]

[463] For instance, an armed group may be required to implement legislation regulating pharmaceutical companies, or may be required to monitor the activities of chemists etc.

9

Conclusion

I. SUMMARY OF FINDINGS

NON-STATE ARMED GROUPS exert a significant influence over the lives of countless individuals throughout the world. Although they are often forced to endure unimaginable hardship, life for these individuals does not stop, and they remain entitled to the protection of international human rights law. To date, however, the international legal order has left the activities of non-state armed groups largely unregulated,[1] giving rise to a legal vacuum vis-à-vis the protection of individuals' human rights. This work has attempted to address this imbalance, asking whether recent developments in international law now make it possible for non-state armed groups to be subject to direct international obligations, and in particular, obligations arising under international human rights law. Answering this question was approached in different stages, looking at: the circumstances under which non-state armed groups could be subject to direct international regulation (Part I), whether armed groups could be bound by international human rights law (Part II), and how the attribution of international human rights law obligations would work in practice (Part III).

The possession of international legal personality is an essential component with respect to an entity's direct regulation by international law, and so issues relating to armed groups' acquisition of international legal personality were addressed in Part I. It was established that non-state actors could indeed possess international legal personality, and three criteria necessary to acquire this status were identified: the capacity to possess international rights or obligations, the actual possession of direct international rights or obligations, and independence.

[1] Noting the limited exception of international humanitarian law applicable to armed groups party to a non-international armed conflict. However, as noted in the Introduction, this body of law is primarily concerned with the conduct of hostilities and the treatment of detainees or the sick and wounded; it does not establish rules in relation to the overall protection of the civilian population, such as rules relating to the maintenance of public order and civil life, or the provision of health care or education. See, above Ch 1 section IV.

In order to determine the organisational characteristics required to demonstrate the capacity to possess direct international rights or obligations, the principal entities of concern to the international legal order—states, International Organisations, armed groups, and transnational corporations[2]—were examined. Analysis of the specific characteristics required vis-à-vis each entity's acquisition of legal personality resulted in the conclusion that the capacity criterion is satisfied by the existence of an independent will (also referred to as a *volonté distincte*). Although this requirement will need to be evaluated in a slightly different manner depending upon the entity in question, at its simplest, an independent will is demonstrated by an entity's ability to bind its membership, against their will if necessary. The existence of an independent will is inherent to the organisational structure typically associated with armed groups, and will be satisfied by the existence of a responsible command: ie a central structure capable of imposing internal discipline.

The legal basis underpinning the application of direct international rights or obligations was then examined. Significantly, it was concluded that the *pacta tertiis* principle does not apply to armed groups—inter alia on the basis of their status as non-state subjects of international law—and so armed groups' consent to be bound by international treaty law is not required. The prescriptive jurisdiction theory constitutes the most effective means of applying direct international rights or obligations to non-state armed groups, establishing that states may legislate at the international level with respect to their territory or their nationals. Of course, binding armed groups in this manner first requires the codification and ratification of an international treaty: as it stands, armed groups are only directly addressed by a limited number of international treaties, the application of which is dependent upon an armed group's status as a party to a non-international armed conflict.[3] As such, although this form of application confirms the legal basis for future international treaties relevant to the regulation of armed groups, it is of limited immediate relevance with respect to the overall protection of individuals affected by the activities of armed groups. The customary law and general principles theories are also legally valid means of application. However, they are of restricted utility as they apply only to groups with an already established international legal personality and only involve the application of a subset of

[2] Although not all of these entities are recognised as possessing international legal personality, the potential international legal personality of each has been raised, and it is submitted that they are of relevance herein. It is further noted that transnational corporations are recognised as legal persons under national law, and so specific requirements exist vis-à-vis these entities' acquisition of legal personality.

[3] With the exception of the African Union Convention for the Protection and Assistance of Internally Displaced Persons in Africa (Kampala Convention). The subject-matter of this treaty is restricted.

the potentially applicable international law. Consequently, these forms of application are also of limited relevance vis-à-vis the protection of individuals affected by the activities of armed groups.

The de facto control theory offers a solution in this regard, as it establishes that armed groups may be bound by international law in the absence of direct international treaty regulation. This is significant in that it allows international law to respond effectively to the factual reality of a situation, and ensures that international legal protection is extended to individuals affected by the activities of armed groups. The de facto control theory applies to armed groups that establish an independent existence, as demonstrated by the displacement of state authority. This requirement will be satisfied should an armed group become party to a non-international armed conflict or, outside armed conflict, should an armed group establish control over a territory or population. The displacement of state authority in this regard will be most clearly demonstrated through the exercise of exclusive territorial control. In less certain situations, where control is exercised but is not exclusive, an independent existence may be demonstrated by the commission of internationally prohibited acts coupled with the state's inability to reasonably impose its will; factors relevant in this regard include: whether the acts were committed on a large-scale basis, the temporal frame of the armed group's activity, and the exercise of elements of 'traditional' control over either territory or a population.

Importantly, by making the application of international law dependent upon the displacement of state authority, the de facto control theory treats the non-state armed group in question as a vertical authority. In doing so, the established hierarchy of international legal regulation is maintained. At issue is not an innovative approach to the legal regulation of non-state actors, but rather a modification of the traditional vertical means of application in response to the reality of the situation.

Significantly, the de facto control theory may also be used to determine the extent of the international law applicable both to armed groups with a pre-existing international legal personality,[4] and to armed groups whose international legal personality is established consequent to the de facto control theory itself. The de facto control theory establishes that in addition to being bound by customary international law and any directly applicable international treaty law, armed groups are also bound by the international treaty law specifically applicable to the territory in question, such as localised treaties, and treaties in the field of international environmental law and international human rights law.

Having established that international law may bind non-state armed groups, Part II looked specifically at the application of international

[4] ie armed groups directly bound by international treaty law, such as armed groups party to a non-international armed conflict.

human rights law. It is widely accepted that international human rights law exclusively regulates the relationship between states and individuals subject to their jurisdiction. At the time of drafting, this construction was appropriate: states were the dominant actors of concern on the international plane, and regulating the state-individual relationship constituted the most effective means of protecting human rights. This is no longer true today. While states retain their status as the principal subjects of international law, non-state actors also exert a decisive influence over the lives of countless individuals.

It is therefore appropriate that the application of international human rights law be interpreted in light of the changed international context. This proposition finds support in international case law. In *Reparations* the International Court of Justice held that '[t]hroughout its history, the development of international law has been influenced by the requirements of international life',[5] while in *Legal Consequences for States of the Continued Presence of South Africa in Namibia (South West Africa) Notwithstanding Security Council Resolution 276 (1970)*, the Court applied this evolutionary principle to treaty interpretation: 'an international instrument has to be interpreted and applied within the framework of the entire legal system prevailing at the time of interpretation.'[6] A radical rethink of international human rights law is not proposed. Rather, the application of international human rights law is slightly altered—in response to the existence of a legal vacuum—to bind entities fulfilling the role of a vertical authority. The law is applied in the same vertical manner, overcoming *ratione personae* restrictions.[7] This approach is consistent with both the object and purpose of international human rights law, and the foundation of human rights in human dignity.

In determining the precise scope and content of the international human rights law obligations imposed on armed groups, a context-dependent approach was proposed whereby the precise content of each applicable obligation is determined on the basis of the specific situation at hand, and in particular, the extent of control exercised by an armed group. This approach ensures that international law can respond to all potential situations, and that obligations imposed on armed groups are capable of being fulfilled. In order to regulate the application of obligations in a gradated manner, an adaptation of the respect, protect, fulfil framework is proposed.

[5] *Reparations for injuries suffered in the services of the United Nations*, Advisory Opinion, International Court of Justice, 11 April 1949, 178

[6] *Legal Consequences for States of the Continued Presence of South Africa in Namibia (South West Africa) Notwithstanding Security Council Resolution 276 (1970)*, Advisory Opinion, International Court of Justice, 21 June 1971, para 53.

[7] Where international human rights law treaties refer to the 'State', the application is extended to entities who have displaced the authority of the state.

Accordingly, all armed groups are initially bound by the negative obligation to respect. Dependent upon the circumstances, and as an armed group displaces state authority to an increasing extent, it will become bound by the positive obligation to fulfil (composed of the obligations to facilitate, provide, and promote), while the obligation to protect—which requires legislative authority on the part of the armed group—will only be applied to groups exercising stable and exclusive territorial control. Application of this framework to armed groups centres upon a division of responsibility between the armed group and the state: it is this division of responsibility that ensures the overall protection of human rights.

II. MONITORING MECHANISMS

Of course, if non-state armed groups are to be subject to international human rights law obligations, it is essential that compliance with these obligations be monitored and enforced. It must be emphasised, however, that the absence of an effective enforcement mechanism, or a mechanism capable of authoritatively identifying those armed groups bound by international human rights law, and the scope and content of their obligations, while desirable, is not a prerequisite. Rights and obligations may exist in the absence of effective enforcement. For instance, the enforcement of states' international human rights law obligations is imperfect, and is primarily restricted to those states parties to regional human rights treaties.[8] Similarly, no central authority exists to denote when situations transition to non-international armed conflict, but this does not preclude the application of the law of armed conflict.

Further work in relation to the monitoring and enforcement of armed group obligations is required, but it is noted that a number of possibilities do exist, in particular: judicial regulation before a human rights body, monitoring by the Security Council or a non-governmental organisation, or monitoring by a UN Special Procedure. It is also possible that states may criminalise the commission of certain human rights violations. However, as human rights violations are typically addressed by means of civil and not criminal procedures, this is not discussed further herein.[9]

[8] Of course, the treaty monitoring bodies do monitor states' respect for international human rights law, and issue views on specific cases, but they do not have the authority to issue binding judgments.

[9] It is noted that states do criminalise certain human rights violations, including those committed by members of armed groups, with the criminalisation of the crime against humanity of persecution being a case on point. For instance, Art 7(1)(h) Statute of the International Criminal Court criminalises the crime against humanity of persecution, defined as 'the intentional and severe deprivation of fundamental rights'.

A. Judicial Regulation by a Human Rights Body

Judicial regulation by a human rights body is perhaps the most effective means of ensuring armed group compliance with international law.[10] Possible fora in this regard include the UN Treaty Monitoring Bodies—such as the Human Rights Committee, the Committee on Economic, Social and Cultural Rights, and the Committee on the Rights of the Child—and the regional human rights commissions and courts.[11] Although there are clear benefits to be gained from this approach,[12] one significant difficulty may be identified: these bodies are currently mandated to exclusively address complaints brought against states parties. Accordingly, modification of their mandates to include the regulation of non-state armed groups would be required, for instance through the adoption of an Optional Protocol.[13] However, it is foreseeable that states would object to the regulation of non-state armed groups by human rights bodies, as this may be perceived as placing armed groups on an equal footing with states. For instance, the Inter-American Commission on Human Rights has stated that:

> [I]f the Commission, in violation of its mandate, were to agree to process a denunciation involving some alleged act of terrorism, in so doing it would implicitly place terrorist organizations on an equal footing with government, as the Commission would have to transmit the denunciation to the subversive organization which allegedly is responsible for the act and request that it make such observations as it deems appropriate. Undoubtedly, such organizations would be very pleased to be dealt with as if they were government. But, what government in the hemisphere could tolerate an implicit recognition of quasi-governmental status for an organization of this kind?[14]

[10] In this regard see, OAS General Assembly Resolution 1043 (XX-0/90), 'Consequences of Acts of Violence Perpetrated by Irregular Armed Groups on the Enjoyment of Human Rights', 8 June 1990, wherein the OAS resolved: '[t]o recommend to the Inter-American Commission on Human Rights that in reporting on the status of human rights in the American states, it include reference to the action of irregular armed groups in such states.'

[11] Namely, the European Court of Human Rights, the Inter-American Commission and Court of Human Rights, and the African Commission and Court on Human and Peoples' Rights.

[12] The active regulation of armed group activity would have clear benefits with respect to, inter alia, victims' right to a remedy, ensuring armed group compliance with international human rights law obligations, and developing the law in this area.

[13] It is noted that the possibility exists, with respect to the Inter-American Commission on Human Rights for example, to report on the activities of armed groups. However, this gives rise to the same difficulty vis-à-vis mandate and is not discussed further herein.

[14] Inter-American Commission on Human Rights, 'Report on the Situation of Human Rights in the Republic of Colombia', OEA/Ser.L/V/II.53 doc 22, 30 June 1981, Introduction. For further discussion on this issue see, Inter-American Commission on Human Rights, 'Annual Report of the InterAmerican Commission on Human Rights 1990–1991', OEA/Ser.L/V/II.79 doc 12, 22 February 1991, ch V, Pt 2, 'Groups of armed irregulars and human rights'.

The issue of whether the regulation of armed groups legitimises such groups has been discussed and rejected,[15] and it is further noted that the adoption of an Optional Protocol can only occur consequent to an explicit act of states. Nonetheless, the judicial regulation of armed groups by human rights bodies or courts is not foreseeable in the short-term, inter alia, on the basis of the time required to draft, adopt, and ratify the necessary Optional Protocol.

B. Monitoring by the Security Council

Another possibility is that the Security Council may request that the UN Secretary-General monitor non-state armed groups' compliance with international human rights obligations. Security Council-based monitoring has been successful in relation to the situation of children in armed conflict, and the Security Council has actively—and positively—engaged non-state armed groups in this regard. For example, Security Council Resolution 1261 specified various provisions relating to the protection of children in armed conflict, and requested the Secretary-General to submit a report on the implementation of the Resolution to the Security Council.[16] The Secretary-General's monitoring role was expanded in Security Council Resolution 1379, wherein the Security Council requested that the Secretary-General 'attach to his report a list of parties to armed conflict that recruit or use children in violation of the international obligations applicable to them'.[17] Both state and non-state actors have appeared on this list.[18]

Significantly, in order to be de-listed, states or armed groups are required to prepare action plans 'to halt recruitment and use of children in violation of international obligations applicable to them, in close collaboration with United Nations peacekeeping missions and United Nations country teams, consistent with their respective mandates'.[19] This requires active engagement with armed groups—providing an opportunity to engage armed groups with respect to their international obligations,[20] and to develop strategy to redress any violations—and a number of action plans

[15] See above, Ch 2 section III.A.

[16] UNSC Res 1261 (1999), operative para 20.

[17] UNSC Res 1379 (2001), operative para 16.

[18] Sandesh Sivakumaran, *The Law of Non-International Armed Conflict* (Oxford, OUP, 2012) 534.

[19] UNSC Res 1539 (2004), operative para 5(b).

[20] In this regard it is noted that 'engagement with armed groups on the issue of child soldiers has led to engagement on other humanitarian norms concerning children, as well as on humanitarian norms more broadly.' See Sivakumaran, above n 18, 536.

have been developed to date,[21] consequent to which some armed groups have been de-listed.[22] It thus appears that this process of 'naming and shaming'[23] has achieved some success, particularly in relation to encouraging armed group engagement with international legal obligations. In this regard it is noted that certain armed groups have themselves initiated the de-listing process. In Burma, for instance, the Karen National Progressive Party ('KNPP') issued a statement appealing 'once again to Ban Ki-moon, the Secretary-General of the United Nations, for the name of our armed force, the Karenni Army, to be removed from the list of non-state armed groups utilizing child soldiers.'[24] Importantly, armed group engagement with this process may have a positive impact in relation to other armed groups. For instance, the UN Secretary-General stated that:'[i]t is anticipated that the precedent set by the commitment of the SLA (Minawi) faction in Darfur to an action plan will generate momentum for other armed groups to follow suit.'[25]

It is apparent that Security Council engagement with respect to the monitoring of armed group compliance with international human rights obligations could have significant benefits with respect to the protection of individuals' human rights and armed group compliance with international law. Similarly, albeit at a less high-profile level, non-governmental organisations may engage in such monitoring, and an extension of Geneva Call's mandate in this regard may be desirable.[26] Indeed, it is noted that, in certain circumstances, non-governmental organisations may have greater access than UN representatives precisely because of their lower profile.[27]

[21] According to the website of the Special Representative of the Secretary-General for Children in Armed Conflict, action plans have been signed with 14 armed groups. These groups include: the People's Army for the Restoration of Democracy (APRD) and the Convention of Patriots for Justice and Peace (CPJP) in the Central African Republic; the 'Armed Forces of the New Forces' (Forces Nouvelles/FAFN), the Liberation Front for the Great West ('FLGO'), the Ivorian Liberation Movement for the West of Cote d'Ivoire (MILOCI), the Patriotic Alliance of the Wé People (APWé), and the Patriotic Resistance Union of the Great West (UPRGO) in Cote d'Ivoire; CPN-M in Nepal; MILF in the Philippines; the LTTE in Sri Lanka; and the SPLA, Sudan Liberation Army (SLA) Minnawi, Sudan Liberation Army (SLA) Free Will and Sudan Liberation Army (SLA)/Abu-Gasim in Sudan. See, Office of the Special Representative of the Secretary-General for Children in Armed Conflict 'Action Plans with Armed Forces and Armed Groups', http://childrenandarmedconflict.un.org/our-work/action-plans/.

[22] Those groups de-listed were FAFN, FLGO, MILOCI, APWé, and UPRGO in Cote d'Ivoire. See, 'Annual Report of the Special Representative of the Secretary-General for Children and Armed Conflict, Radhika Coomaraswamy', UN Doc A/HRC/9/3, 27 June 2008, para 16.

[23] See Sivakumaran, above n 18, 533–34.

[24] 'Call for the Karenni Army's name to be removed from the list of non-state armed groups making use of child soldiers in armed conflict', Karenni National Progressive Party, Press Release No 1/08, 12 February 2008. For further examples, See Sivakumaran, above n 18, 536.

[25] 'Report of the Secretary-General on Children and Armed Conflict in the Sudan', UN Doc S/2007/520, 6 September 2007, para 36.

[26] See further, Geneva Call, 'Mission', www.genevacall.org/who-we-are/.

[27] See Sivakumaran, above n 18, 537.

C. Monitoring by a UN Special Procedure

The Special Procedures mechanism established by the Human Rights Council presents another possibility vis-à-vis the monitoring of armed groups' compliance with international human rights law obligations. Special procedures have successfully reported on a wide variety of human rights violations, and have also addressed the activities of non-state armed groups.[28] The creation of a Special Procedure relating to the compliance of non-state armed groups with international human rights law obligations would be a welcome measure, not only as a positive step towards promoting armed group compliance with international law, but also as a means of developing understanding in this area.

III. CONCLUDING COMMENTS

This book has concluded that non-state armed groups may be bound by international law, either by means of international treaty law, or consequent to the de facto control theory—both during and outside non-international armed conflict—when an armed group exists independently of a state. This independence is demonstrated by a state's inability to reasonably impose its will. Importantly, application of the de facto control theory confirms that armed groups are subject to obligations arising under international human rights law. Potential *ratione personae* restrictions are overcome, inter alia, as the application of international law arises consequent to the displacement of state authority, thereby maintaining the traditional vertical means of application.

Application of the de facto control theory allows the international legal order to respond effectively to the influence exerted by non-state armed groups. Subjecting armed groups to direct international legal regulation brings such groups within the international legal sphere, ensuring the effectiveness and relevance of international law. Importantly, application of the de facto control theory also ensures that specific rules regulate the

[28] See, for instance, 'Extrajudicial, summary or arbitrary execution, Report of the Special Rapporteur, Philip Alston, Mission to Sri Lanka (28 November to 6 December 2005)', UN Doc E/CN.4/2006/53/Add.5, 27 March 2006, referring to the LTTE; 'Report of the Special Rapporteur on extrajudicial, summary or arbitrary executions, Ms Asma Jahangir, submitted pursuant to Commission on Human Rights resolution 2000/31, Mission to Nepal', UN Doc E/CN.4/2001/9/Add.2, 9 August 2000, referring to the CPN-M; 'Report of the Independent Expert on the situation of human rights in Somalia, Shamsul Bari', UN Doc A/HRC/24/40, 16 August 2013, referring to Al-Shabaab; 'Follow-up to the report of the Special Rapporteur on extrajudicial, summary or arbitrary executions on his mission to the Central African Republic (31 January to 7 February 2008)', UN Doc A/HRC/14/24/Add.5, 19 May 2010, referring to the Lord's Resistance Army (LRA).

conduct of armed groups, and in particular their interaction with the civilian population, thereby ensuring that individuals' human rights remain subject to international legal protection.

Certain objections from states—arguing that the application of international law to non-state armed groups will serve to legitimise such groups—may be expected. Two factors are relevant in response. First, the application of international law to an armed group does not legitimise the group; rather, it ensures that the activities of the group are subject to direct international regulation, denying the group an unlimited freedom of action vis-à-vis international law. Importantly, the group remains subject to the domestic law of the state, and so the ability of the state to criminalise the activities of the group or its members is unaffected. Second, the application of international law to non-state armed groups during non-international armed conflict is now well accepted, as demonstrated, inter alia, by the universal ratification of the Geneva Conventions of 1949.

At first glance the application of international law on the basis of the de facto control theory may appear novel. However, it has a firm legal basis, drawing upon well-established case law, and furthermore is an appropriate response to the reality of international life. Indeed, states, International Organisations, and other entities currently refer to the human rights obligations of armed groups. For instance, the Security Council has repeatedly called on non-state armed groups to respect international human rights law. This work clarifies the legal basis underpinning this call.

Although this monograph has focused on the international regulation of non-state armed groups, a number of the proposals made herein will apply to any non-state entity that fulfils the identified criteria. As such, the potential international regulation of other non-state actors—and in particular transnational corporations—on the basis of the de facto control theory may be worthy of further investigation.

Further work is also necessary in order to operationalise the proposed legal framework. In particular, research is required in relation to the graded application of international human rights law obligations, in order to establish the boundaries of application (for instance the point at which the obligation to provide becomes applicable) in a manner accessible to armed groups. Clarification in this regard is essential in order to ensure that the law is capable of influencing and informing armed group behaviour. Of course, the most important element in operationalising this proposal is ensuring that armed groups are aware of their obligations. In this regard, the support of states, International Organisations, and national and international non-governmental organisations must be sought. The support of these entities is essential, both with respect to acceptance of the proposal and its dissemination amongst non-state armed groups and other actors.

Bibliography

I. INTERNATIONAL TREATIES AND INSTRUMENTS

African Charter on Human and Peoples' Rights (adopted 27 June 1981, entered into force 21 December 1986) 1520 UNTS 218.

African Union Convention for the Protection and Assistance of Internally Displaced Persons in Africa (Kampala Convention) (adopted 23 October 2009, entered into force 6 December 2012).

American Convention on Human Rights (adopted 21 November 1969, entered into force 18 July 1978) 1144 UNTS 123.

Arab Charter on Human Rights (adopted 22 May 2004, entered into force 15 March 2008).

Charter of the United Nations (adopted 26 June 1945, entered into force 24 October 1945) 1 UNTS XVI.

Consolidated Version of the Treaty on European Union (2010) OJ C83/41.

Constitution of the World Health Organization (22 July 1946, as amended 15 September 2005).

Convention (III) relative to the Treatment of Prisoners of War (adopted 12 August 1949, entered into force 21 October 195) 75 UNTS 135.

Convention (IV) relative to the Protection of Civilian Persons in Time of War (adopted 12 August 1949, entered into force 21 October 1950) 75 UNTS 287.

Convention for the Protection of Cultural Property in the Event of Armed Conflict (adopted 14 May 1954, entered into froce 7 August 1956) 249 UNTS 240.

Convention on the Prevention and Punishment of the Crime of Genocide (adopted 9 December 1948, entered into force 12 January 1951) UN General Assembly Resolution 260 (III) A.

Convention on the Rights of the Child (adopted 20 November 1989, entered into force 2 September 1990) 1577 UNTS 3.

Declaration of Alma-Ata, International Conference on Primary Health Care, Alma-Ata, USSR, 6–12 September 1978.

Draft Articles on State Responsibility for Internationally Wrongful Acts, UNGA Res A/56/49(Vol 1)/Corr 4.

Draft Code of Crimes against the Peace and Security of Mankind (1996).

Draft Code of Offences against the Peace and Security of Mankind (1956).

European Convention for the Protection of Human Rights and Fundamental Freedoms as amended by Protocol No 11 (adopted 4 November 1950, entered into force 3 September 1953) 213 UNTS 221.

Final Act of the Congress of Vienna/General Treaty, 1815.

International Convention for the Protection of All Persons from Enforced Disappearance (adopted 20 December 2006, entered into force 23 December 2010) 2716 UNTS 3.

International Convention on the Suppression and Punishment of the Crime of Apartheid (adopted 30 November 1973, entered into force 18 July 1976) 1015 UNTS 243.

International Covenant on Civil and Political Rights (adopted 16 December 1966, entered into force 23 March 1976) 999 UNTS 171 (ICCPR).

International Covenant on Economic, Social and Cultural Rights (adopted 16 December 1996, entered into force 3 January 1976) 993 UNTS 3 (ICESCR).

Maastricht Guidelines on Violations of Economic, Social and Cultural Rights, Maastricht, 22–26 January 1997.

Montevideo Convention on the Rights and Duties of States (adopted 26 December 1933, entered into force 26 December 1934).

Optional Protocol to the Convention on the Rights of the Child on the involvement of children in armed conflict (adopted 25 May 2000, entered into force 12 February 2002) 2173 UNTS 222.

Permanent Statute of the Free Territory of Trieste, Treaty of Peace with Italy (10 February 1947).

Principles of International law Recognized in the Charter of the Nürnberg Tribunal and in the Judgment of the Tribunal (1950).

Protocol Additional to the Geneva Conventions of 12 August 1949, and relating to the Protection of Victims of Non-International Armed Conflicts (Protocol II), (adopted 8 June 1977, entered into force 7 December 1978) 1125 UNTS 609.

Protocol of the Conference of Paris of 3 November, 1815.

Protocol on Prohibitions or Restrictions on the Use of Mines, Booby-Traps and Other Devices as amended on 3 May 1996 (adopted 3 May 1996, entered into force 3 December 1998) 2048 UNTS 93.

Regulations Respecting the Laws and Customs of War on Land, Annex to 'Convention (IV) respecting the Laws and Customs of War on Land' (adopted 18 October 1907, entered into force 26 January 1910).

Rules of Procedure and Evidence, International Criminal Tribunal for the former Yugoslavia, IT/32/Rev 46, 20 October 2011.

Standard Minimum Rules for the Treatment of Prisoners, Adopted by the First United Nations Congress on the Prevention of Crime and the Treatment of Offenders, held at Geneva in 1955, and approved by the Economic and Social Council by its resolution 663 C (XXIV) of 31 July 1957 and 2076 (LXII) of 13 May 1977.

Statute of the International Court of Justice (adopted 26 June 1945, entered into force 24 October 1945) 1 UNTS XVI.

Statute of the International Criminal Court (adopted 17 July 1998, entered into force 1 July 2002) 2187 UNTS 3.

Statute of the International Criminal Tribunal for the former Yugoslavia, UNSC Res 827 (1993).

Statute of the International Criminal Tribunal for the Prosecution of Persons Responsible for Genocide and Other Serious Violations of International Humanitarian Law Committed in the Territory of Rwanda and Rwandan Citizens Responsible for Genocide and Other Such Violations Committed in the Territory of Neighbouring States, between 1 January 1994 and 31 December 1994, UNSC Res 955 (1994).

Treaty establishing the European Coal and Steel Community (18 April 1951).
Treaty of Peace with Italy (10 February 1947).
Treaty of Versailles (28 June 1919).
UN Basic Principles on the Independence of the Judiciary, adopted by the Seventh United Nations Congress on the Prevention of Crime and the Treatment of Offenders held at Milan from 26 August to 6 September 1985, endorsed by General Assembly resolutions 40/32 of 29 November 1985 and 40/146 of 13 December 1985.
United Nations Convention on the Law of the Sea (adopted 10 December 1982, entered into force 16 November 1994) 1833 UNTS 3.
Universal Declaration of Human Rights (adopted 10 December 1948) UNGA Res 217 A(III).
Vienna Convention on Consular Relations (adopted 24 April 1963, entered into force 19 March 1967) 596 UNTS 261.
Vienna Convention on Succession of States in respect of Treaties (adopted 23 August 1978, entered into force 6 November 1996) 1946 UNTS 3.
Vienna Convention on the Law of Treaties (23 May 1969, entered into force 27 January 1980) 1155 UNTS 331.
Vienna Convention on the Law of Treaties between States and International Organizations or between International Organizations (adopted 21 March 1986, not yet in force) UN Doc A/CONF 129/15.
Vienna Declaration and Programme of Action, adopted by the World Conference on Human Rights, Vienna, 25 June 1993.

II. OTHER INTERNATIONAL AND GOVERNMENTAL DOCUMENTS

'Annual Report of the Special Representative of the Secretary-General for Children and Armed Conflict, Radhika Coomaraswamy', UN Doc A/HRC/9/3, 27 June 2008.
'Committee on the Preamble', Commission on Human Rights, Third Session, UN Doc E/CN4/138, 15 June 1948.
'Draft Code of Crimes against the Peace and Security of Mankind, with commentaries' (1996) *Yearbook of the International Law Commission*, vol II.
'Extrajudicial, summary or arbitrary execution, Report of the Special Rapporteur, Philip Alston, Mission to Sri Lanka (28 November to 6 December 2005)', UN Doc E/CN4/2006/53/Add 5, 27 March 2006.
'Final Record of the Diplomatic Conference of Geneva of 1949', Vol II, Section B.
'First Report of the United Nations Observer Mission in El Salvador', UN Doc A/45/1055, 16 September 1991.
'First Report on responsibility of international organizations by Mr Giorgio Gaja, Special Rapporteur', International Law Commission, UN Doc A/CN4/532, 26 March 2003.
'Follow-up to the report of the Special Rapporteur on extrajudicial, summary or arbitrary executions on his mission to the Central African Republic (31 January to 7 February 2008)', UN Doc A/HRC/14/24/Add 5, 19 May 2010.

'Fourth Report on State Responsibility, by Mr Robert Ago, Special Rapporteur—The internationally wrongful act of the State, source of international responsibility (continued)' (1972) *Yearbook of International Law Commission* Vol II, UN Doc A/CN.4/264.

'Lebanon: Suggested Preamble for the Draft International Declaration on Human Rights', Commission on Human Rights, Third Session, UN Doc E/CN4/132, 14 June 1949.

'Official Records of the Diplomatic Conference on the Reaffirmation and Development of International Humanitarian Law Applicable in Armed Conflicts (Geneva 1974–1977)' Vol XIV.

'Official Records of the Diplomatic Conference on the Reaffirmation and Development of International Humanitarian Law Applicable in Armed Conflicts (Geneva 1974–1977)' Vol VIII.

'Official Records of the Diplomatic Conference on the Reaffirmation and Development of International Humanitarian Law Applicable in Armed Conflicts, Geneva, (1974–1977)', Vol VII.

'Principles of International Law recognized in the Charter of the Nürnberg Tribunal and in the Judgment of the Tribunal, with commentaries' (1950) *Yearbook of the International Law Commission*, Vol II.

'Report of the Credentials Committee', 139th Plenary Meeting, UN Doc A/PV139, 23 September 1948.

'Report of the Independent Expert on the situation of human rights in Somalia, Shamsul Bari', UN Doc A/HRC/24/40, 16 August 2013.

'Report of the independent international commission of inquiry on the Syrian Arab Republic', UN Doc A/HRC/19/69, 22 February 2012.

'Report of the independent international commission of inquiry on the Syrian Arab Republic', UN Doc A/HRC/22/59, 5 February 2013.

'Report of the International Commission of Inquiry on Libya', UN Doc A/HRC/19/68, 8 March 2012.

'Report of the International Commission of Inquiry to investigate all alleged violations of international human rights law in the Libyan Arab Jamahiriya', UN Doc A/HRC/17/44, 1 June 2011.

'Report of the Secretary-General on Children and Armed Conflict in the Sudan', UN Doc S/2007/520, 6 September 2007.

'Report of the Secretary-General on children and armed conflict in Cote d'Ivoire', UN Doc S/2006/835, 25 October 2006.

'Report of the Secretary-General on the protection of civilians in armed conflict', UN Doc S/2009/277, 29 May 2009.

'Report of the Secretary-General's Panel of Experts on Accountability in Sri Lanka', 31 March 2011.

'Report of the Special Rapporteur on extrajudicial, summary or arbitrary executions, Philip Alston: Mission to the Democratic Republic of the Congo', UN Doc A/HRC/14/24/Add 3, 14 June 2010.

'Report of the Special Rapporteur on extrajudicial, summary or arbitrary executions, Philip Alston, Mission to Philippines', UN Doc A/HRC/8/3/Add 2, 16 April 2008.

'Report on the right to adequate food as a human right submitted by Mr Asbjorn Eide, Special Rapporteur', Commission on Human Rights, UN Doc No E/CN.4/Sub 2/1987/23, 7 July 1987.

'Report of the Special Rapporteur on extrajudicial, summary or arbitrary executions, Ms Asma Jahangir, submitted pursuant to Commission on Human Rights resolution 2000/31, Mission to Nepal', UN Doc E/CN4/2001/9/Add 2, 9 August 2000.

'Reports of the International Law Commission on the second part of its seventeenth session and on its eighteenth session', UN Doc A/6309/Rev 1, (1966) *Yearbook of the International Law Commission* Vol II.

'Statement of the Prosecutor of the International Criminal Court, Fatou Bensouda, on opening a new Preliminary Examination in Central African Republic', International Criminal Court, The Office of the Prosecutor (7 February 2014).

'Summary of the Fiftieth Meeting', Commission on Human Rights, Third Session, UN Doc E/CN4/SR50, 4 June 1948.

'Third Report of the United Nations Observer Mission in El Salvador (ONUSAL)', UN Doc A/46/876, 10 February 1992.

'Third Report on the Human Rights Situation in Colombia', Organization of American States, OEA/SerL/V/II102, 26 February 1999.

'Third Report on the Law of Treaties by Mr GG Fitzmaurice, Special Rapporteur' (1958) *Yearbook of the International Law Commission*, Vol II.

'Twenty–fourth report of the Secretary-General on the United Nations Operation in Cote d'Ivoire', UN Doc S/2010/245, 20 May 2010.

African Commission on Human and People's Rights, 'Principles and Guidelines on the Right to a Fair Trial and Legal Assistance in Africa', DOC/OS(XXX)247.

Committee on Economic, Social and Cultural Rights, 'An Evaluation of the Obligation to Take Steps to the "Maximum of Available Resources" Under an Optional Protocol to the Covenant', Statement, UN Doc E/C12/2007/1, 10 May 2007.

Committee on Economic, Social and Cultural Rights, General Comment 14, 'The right to the highest attainable standard of health (Article 12 of the International Covenant on Economic, Social and Cultural Rights)', UN Doc E/C.12/2000/4, 11 August 2000.

Committee on Economic, Social and Cultural Rights, General Comment 13, 'The right to education (Article 13 of the Covenant)', UN Doc E/C12/1999/10, 8 December 1999.

Committee on Economic, Social and Cultural Rights, General Comment 16, 'The equal right of men and women to the enjoyment of all economic, social and cultural rights (art. 3 of the International Covenant on Economic, Social and Cultural Rights)', UN Doc E/C.12/2005/4, 11 August 2005.

Committee on Economic, Social and Cultural Rights, General Comment 18, 'The right to work', UN Doc E/C.12/GC/18, 6 February 2006.

Committee on Economic, Social and Cultural Rights, General Comment 15, 'The right to water (arts. 11 and 12 of the International Covenant on Economic, Social and Cultural Rights)', UN Doc E/C.12/2002/11, 20 January 2003.

Committee on Economic, Social and Cultural Rights, General Comment 12, 'The right to adequate food (art. 11)', UN Doc E/C.12/1999/5, 12 May 1999.

Committee on Economic, Social and Cultural Rights, General Comment 4, 'The right to adequate housing (Art. 11 (1) of the Covenant)', UN Doc E/1991/23, 14 December 1991.

Committee on Economic, Social and Cultural Rights, General Comment 3, 'The nature of States parties obligations (Art. 2. Para. 1. of the Covenant)', UN Doc E/1991/23, 14 December 1990.

Committee on Economic, Social and Cultural Rights, General Comment 20, 'Non–Discrimination in Economic, Social and Cultural Rights (art. 2, para. 3)', UN Doc E/C.12/GC/20, 25 May 2009.

Committee on Economic, Social and Cultural Rights, 'Substantive issues arising in the implementation of the International Covenant on Economic, Social and Cultural Rights: Poverty and the International Covenant on Economic, Social and Cultural Rights', Statement, UN Doc E/C.12/2001/10, 10 May 2001.

'Draft articles on Responsibility of States for Internationally Wrongful Acts, with commentaries' (2001) *Yearbook of the International Law Commission*, Vol II.

Final Record of the Diplomatic Conference of Geneva of 1949, Vol II Section B.

Human Rights Committee, 'Concluding Observations on Lebanon', UN Doc CCPR/C/79/Add 78, 1 April 1997.

Human Rights Committee, General Comment No 13, 'Equality before the courts and tribunals and the right to a fair and public hearing by a competent, independent and impartial tribunal established by law', UN Doc HR1/GEN/1/Rev.1, 13 April 1984.

Human Rights Committee, General Comment No 21, 'Replaces general comment 9 concerning humane treatment of persons deprived of liberty (Art. 10)', UN Doc HRI/GEN/1/Rev 1, 10 April 1992.

Human Rights Committee, General Comment No 25, 'Participation in Public Affairs and the Right to Vote', UN Doc CCPR/C/21/Rev.1/Add.7, 12 July 1996.

Human Rights Committee, General Comment No 26, 'Continuity of obligations', UN Doc CPR/C/21/Rev.1/Add.8/Rev/1, 8 December 1997.

Human Rights Committee, General Comment No 28, 'Equality of rights between men and women (article 3)', UN Doc CCPR/C/21/Rev.1/Add.10, 29 March 2000.

Human Rights Committee, General Comment No 29, 'States of Emergency (Article 4)', UN Doc CCPR/C/21/Rev.1/Add.11, 31 August 2001.

Human Rights Committee, General Comment No 3, 'Article 9 (Liberty and security of person)', UN Doc CCPR/C/GC/35, 16 December 2014.

Human Rights Committee, General Comment No 31, 'The Nature of the General Legal Obligation Imposed on States Parties to the Covenant', UN Doc CCPR/C/21/Rev.1/Add.13, 26 May 2004.

Human Rights Committee, General Comment No 32, 'Article 14: Right to equality before courts and tribunals and to a fair trial', UN Doc CCPR/C/GC/32, 23 August 2007.

Human Rights Committee, General Comment No 8, 'Article 9', UN Doc HRI/GEN/1/Rev.1.

Inter-American Commission on Human Rights, 'Annual Report of the InterAmerican Commission on Human Rights 1990–1991', OEA/Ser.L/V/II.79 doc 12, 22 February 1991.

Inter-American Commission on Human Rights, 'Report on the Situation of Human Rights in the Republic of Colombia', OEA/Ser.L/V/II.53 doc 22, 30 June 1981.

Inter-American Commission on Human Rights, 'Report of the Inter-American Commission on Human Rights on Terrorism and Human Rights (Executive Summary and Recommendations)', OEA/Ser.G CP/CAJP-2126/04, 13 February 2004.

International Committee of the Red Cross, 'Draft Additional Protocols to the Geneva Conventions of August 12, 1949, Commentary' (1973).

International Criminal Court, 'Elements of Crimes' (2011).

International Criminal Court, The Office of the Prosecutor, 'Situation in the Central African Republic II: Article 53(1) Report', 24 September 2014.

International Criminal Court, The Office of the Prosecutor, 'Report on Preliminary Examination Activities' (2012).

International Criminal Court, The Office of the Prosecutor, 'Report on Preliminary Examination Activities' (2013).

International Law Association Committee on the Use of Force, 'Final Report on the Meaning of Armed Conflict in International Law' (2010) The Hague Conference.

International Law Association, 'Committee on Formation of Customary (General) International Law' (2000) London Conference.

International Law Commission, 'Draft Articles on Responsibility of States for Internationally Wrongful Acts, with commentaries' (2001) *Yearbook of the International Commission* Vol II.

International Law Commission, 'Draft Code of Crimes against the Peace and Security of Mankind, with Commentaries' (1996) Yearbook of the International Law Commission, Vol II, Pt Two.

International Law Commission, 'First Report on Responsibility of International Organizations', UN Doc A/Cn.4/532, 26 March 2003.

International Law Institute, 'The Protection of Human Rights and the Principle of Non-Intervention in Internal Affairs of States' (1989) 63 *Institut de Droit International Annuaire*.

OAS General Assembly Resolution 1043 (XX-0/90), 'Consequences of Acts of Violence Perpetrated by Irregular Armed Groups on the Enjoyment of Human Rights', 8 June 1990.

Office of the High Commissioner for Human Rights in Nepal, 'Human rights abuses by the CPN-M: Summary of Concerns' (2006).

Official Records of the Diplomatic Conference on the Reaffirmation and Development of International Humanitarian Law Applicable in Armed Conflicts (Geneva 1974–1977)' Vol VIII.

Proposal submitted by Costa Rica, Hungary and Switzerland on Article 8 para 2(c) of the Rome Statute of the International Criminal Court, Doc No PCNICC/1999/WGEC/DP10.

Report of the Interdepartmental Committee for the Study of Jurisdiction over Federal Areas within the States, Part II: A text of the law of legislative jurisdiction, June 1957, http://constitutionorg/juris/fjur/2fj1–2htm4.

Resolution 10, Final Record of the Diplomatic Conference of Geneva of 1949, Vol I.

Second report of the United Nations Observer Mission in El Salvador', UN Doc A/46/658, S/23222, 15 November 1991.

UK Draft Preamble to the International Declaration of Human Rights, E/CN4/124.

UNGA Res 48/121.

UNGA Res 62/149.

UNGA Res 63/168.
UNGA Res 65/206.
UNGA Res 290 (IV) 'Essentials of Peace', 1 December 1949.
UNGA Res 3452 (XXX), 9 December 1975.
United Nations Assistance Mission in Afghanistan & UN Office of the High Commissioner for Human Rights, *Afghanistan Annual Report 2011: Protection of Civilians in Armed Conflict* (2012).
United Nations Assistance Mission in Afghanistan & UN Office of the High Commissioner for Human Rights, *Afghanistan Annual Report 2014: Protection of Civilians in Armed Conflict* (2015).
United Nations Mission in the Republic of South Sudan (UNMISS), 'Conflict in South Sudan: A Human Rights Report', 8 May 2014.
United Nations Office of the High Commissioner for Human Rights, 'Report of the Mapping Exercise documenting the most serious violations of human rights and international humanitarian law committed within the territory of the Democratic Republic of the Congo between March 1993 and June 2003' (2010).
UNSC Res 418 (1977).
UNSC Res 591 (1986).
UNSC Res 661 (1990).
UNSC Res 1127 (1997).
UNSC Res 1173 (1998).
UNSC Res 1244 (1999).
UNSC Res 1261 (1999).
UNSC Res 1267 (1999).
UNSC Res 1296 (1999).
UNSC Res 1314 (2000).
UNSC Res 1333 (2000).
UNSC Res 1379 (2001).
UNSC Res 1539 (2004).
UNSC Res 1540 (2004).
UNSC Res 1556 (2004).
UNSC Res 1564 (2004).
UNSC Res 1572 (2004).
UNSC Res 1989 (2011).
UNSC Res 2036 (2012).
Zaire, 'Official Records of the Diplomatic Conference on the Reaffirmation and Development of International Humanitarian Law Applicable in Armed Conflicts (Geneva 1974–1977)' Vol VII, CDDH/SR.56, draft art 1.

III. ARMED GROUP DOCUMENTS

'Action Plan between the Moro Islamic Liberation Front (MILF) and the United Nations in the Philippines regarding the Issue of Recruitment and Use of Child Soldiers in the Armed Conflict in Mindanao', 1 August 2009.
'Call for the Karenni Army's name to be removed from the list of non-state armed groups making use of child soldiers in armed conflict', Karenni National Progressive Party, Press Release No 1/08, 12 February 2008.

'Memo of Melito Glor Command on Policy Towards Prisoners of War', 18 June 1988.

'The IRA Court Martial Procedure' in Irish Republican Army, *The Green Book (Book I and II)*.

'SPLM/OLS Agreement on Ground Rules' signed by the head of the UN's Operation Lifeline Sudan southern sector and John Garang, Commander-in-Chief of the Sudan People's Liberation Movement/Army.

National Transitional Council/Free Libyan Army, Frontline Manual (2011).

NDFP, *Declaration of Undertaking to Apply the Geneva Conventions of 1949 and Protocol I of 1977* (NDFP, Human Rights Monitoring Committee Booklet No 6).

IV. BOOKS, ARTICLES AND BLOG POSTS

Abu-Sada, Caroline, 'Gaza Strip: A Perilous Transition' in Magone, Claire, Neuman, Michael and Weissman, Fabrice (eds), *Humanitarian Negotiations Revealed: The MSF Experience* (London, Hurst & Company, 2011).

Ahmed, Tawhida and De Jesus Butler, Israel, 'The European Union and Human Rights: An International Law Perspective' (2006) 17 *European Journal of International Law*.

Akande, Dapo, 'International Organizations' in Evans, Malcolm (ed), *International Law*, 2nd edn (Oxford, OUP, 2006).

Akande, Dapo, 'Classification of Armed Conflicts: Relevant Legal Concepts' in Wilmshurst, Elizabeth (ed), *International Law and the Classification of Conflicts* (Oxford, OUP, 2012).

Alston, Philip and Quinn, Gerard, 'The Nature and Scope of States Parties' Obligations under the International Covenant on Economic, Social and Cultural Rights' (1987) 9 *Human Rights Quarterly*.

Alston, Philip (ed), *Non-State Actors and Human Rights* (Oxford, OUP, 2005).

Alston, Philip, 'The 'Not-a-Cat' Syndrome: Can the International Human Rights Regime Accommodate Non-State Actors?' in Alston, Philip (ed), *Non-State Actors and Human Rights* (Oxford, OUP, 2005).

Amerasinghe, CF, 'International Legal Personality Revisited' (1995) 47 *Austrian Journal of Public and International Law*.

Arai-Takahashi, Yutaka, *The Law of Occupation: Continuity and Change of International Humanitarian Law, and its Interaction with International Human Rights Law* (The Hague, Martinus Nijhoff, 2009).

Arimatsu, Louise, 'The Democratic Republic of the Congo 1993–2010' in Wilmshurst, Elizabeth (ed), *International Law and the Classification of Conflicts* (Oxford, OUP, 2012).

Aufricht, Hans, 'Personality in International Law' (1943) 37 *American Political Science Review*.

Aughey, Sean and Sari, Aurel, 'Targeting and Detention in Non-International Armed Conflict: *Serdar Mohammed* and the Limits of Human Rights Convergence' (2015) 91 *International Law Studies*.

Azani, Eitan, *Hezbollah: The Story of the Party of God: From Revolution to Institutionalization* (London, Palgrave Macmillan, 2008).

Baker, PJ, 'The Doctrine of Legal Equality of States' (1923) 4 *British Yearbook of International Law*.

Bangerter, Olivier, 'Reasons why armed groups choose to respect international humanitarian law or not' (2011) 93 *International Review of the Red Cross* 882.

Bangerter, Olivier, 'Internal Control: Codes of Conduct within Insurgent Armed Groups' (2012) Small Arms Survey Occasional Paper No 31.

Barmeyer, Niels, 'The Guerrilla Movement as Project: An Assessment of Community Involvement in the EZLN' (2003) 30 *Latin American Perspectives*.

Bartels, Rogier, 'Timelines, borderlines and conflicts: The historical evolution of the legal divide between international and non-international armed conflicts' (2009) 91 *International Review of the Red Cross*.

Bassiouni, M Cherif, *Crimes against Humanity in International Criminal Law*, 2nd edn (Alphen aan den Rijn, Kluwer Law International, 1999).

Bassiouni, M Cherif, *Introduction to International Criminal Law*, 2nd edn (The Hague, Martinus Nijhof, 2013).

Bederman, David J, 'The Souls of International Organizations: Legal Personality and the Lighthouse at Cape Spartel' (1995) *Virginia Journal of International Law*.

Bhatia, Michael, 'The Western Sahara under Polisario Control' (2001) 28 *Review of African Political Economy*.

Blin, Arnaud, 'Armed groups and intra-state conflicts: the dawn of a new era?' (2011) 93 *International Review of the Red Cross*.

Bolintineanu, Alexandru, 'Expression of Consent to be Bound by a Treaty in the Light of the 1969 Vienna Convention' (1974) 68 *American Journal of International Law*.

Bond, James E, 'Application of the Law of War to Internal Conflicts' (1973) 3 *Georgia Journal of International and Comparative Law*.

Borchard, Edwin M, 'The Unrecognized Government in American Courts' (1932) 26 *American Journal of International Law*.

Bornkamm, Paul Christoph, *Rwanda's Gacaca Courts: Between Retribution and Reparation* (Oxford, OUP, 2012).

Bossuyt, MJ, *Guide to the "Travaux Preparatoires" of the International Covenant on Civil and Political Rights* (The Hague, Martinus Nijhoff, 1987).

Bradbury, Mark, Leader, Nicholas and Mackintosh, Kate, 'The 'Agreement on Ground Rules' in South Sudan' (2000) Overseas Development Institute, Humanitarian Policy Group Report 4.

Branch, Adam and Mampilly, Zachariah Cherian, 'Winning the war, but losing the peace? The dilemma of SPLM/A civil administration and the tasks ahead' (2005) 43 *Journal of Modern African Studies*.

Briggs, Herbert W, 'De Facto and De Jure Recognition: The Arantzazu Mendi' (1939) 33 *American Journal of International Law*.

Brolman, Catherine, *The Institutional Veil in Public International Law: International Organisations and the Law of Treaties* (Oxford, Hart, 2007).

Brown, Philip, 'The Legal Effects of Recognition' (1950) 44 *American Journal of International Law*.

Brownlie, Ian, *Principles of Public International Law*, 6th edn (Oxford, OUP, 2003).

Brownlie, Ian, *Principles of Public international Law*, 7th edn (Oxford, OUP, 2008).

Casalin, Deborah, 'Taking prisoners: reviewing the international humanitarian law grounds for deprivation of liberty by armed opposition groups' (2011) 93 *International Review of the Red Cross*.

Cassese, Antonio, 'The Status of Rebels under the 1977 Geneva Protocol on Non-International Armed Conflicts' (1981) 2 *The International and Comparative Law Quarterly*.

Cassese, Antonio, *International Law*, 2nd edn (Oxford, OUP, 2005).

Cassese, Antonio, 'The *Nicaragua* and *Tadic* Tests Revisited in Light of the ICJ Judgment on Genocide in Bosnia' (2007) 18 *European Journal of International Law*.

Castel, Jean Gabriel, *International Law: Chiefly as Interpreted and Applied in Canada*, 3rd edn (London, Butterworths, 1976).

Charney, Jonathan I, 'The Persistent Objector Rule and the Development of Customary International Law' (1986) 57 *British Yearbook of International Law*.

Charney, Jonathan I, 'Universal International Law' (1993) 87 *American Journal of International Law*.

Chhikara, Rishi, 'People's Liberation Guerrilla Army of CPI (Maoist)' (2012) Centre for Land Warfare Studies New Delhi, Manekshaw Paper No 35.

Chinkin, Christine, *Third Parties in International Law* (Oxford, Clarendon Press, 1993).

Clapham, Andrew, 'The "Drittwirkung" of the Convention' in Macdonald, R St J, Matscher, F and Petzold, H (eds), *The European System for the Protection of Human Rights* (The Hague, Martinus Nijhoff, 1993).

Clapham, Andrew, 'The Question of Jurisdiction Under International Criminal Law Over Legal Persons: Lessons from the Rome Conference on an International Criminal Court' in Kamminga, Menno T and Zia-Zarifi, Saman (eds), *Liability of Multinational Corporations under International Law* (Alphen aan den Rijn, Kluwer Law International, 2000).

Clapham, Andrew, *Human Rights Obligations of Non-State Actors* (Oxford, OUP, 2006).

Clapham, Andrew, 'Non-State Actors' in Moeckli, David, Shah, Sangeeta and Sivakumaran, Sandesh (eds), *International Human Rights Law* (Oxford, OUP, 2010).

Clapham Andrew, 'Focusing on Armed Non-State Actors' in Andrew Clapham and Paola Gaeta (eds), *The Oxford Handbook of International Law in Armed Conflict* (Oxford, OUP, 2014).

Cochran, Charles, 'De Facto and De Jure Recognition: Is There a Difference?' (1968) 62 *American Journal of International Law*.

Constantineau, Albert, *A Treatise on the De Facto Doctrine* (Rochester NY, The Lawyers Co-operative Publishing Company, 1910).

Corbett, PE, 'The Consent of States and the Sources of the Law of Nations' (1925) 6 *British Yearbook of International Law*.

Craven, Matthew CR, *The International Covenant on Economic, Social, and Cultural Rights: A Perspective on its Development* (Oxford, Clarendon Press, 1995).

Crawford, James, *The Creation of States in International Law*, 2nd edn (Oxford, OUP, 2006).

Crawford, James, *Brownlie's Principles of Public International Law*, 8th edn (Oxford, OUP, 2012).

Crombe, Xavier, 'Afghanistan: Regaining Leverage' in Magone, Claire, Neuman, Michael and Weissman, Fabrice (eds), *Humanitarian Negotiations Revealed: The MSF Experience* (London, Hurst & Company, 2011).

Cullen, Anthony, *The Concept of Non-International Armed Conflict in International Humanitarian Law* (Cambridge, CUP, 2010).

Cullen, Anthony and Wheatley, Steven, 'The Human Rights of Individuals in *De Facto* Regimes under the European Convention on Human Rights' (2013) 13 *Human Rights Law Review*.

D'Aspermont, Jean, 'The multifaceted concept of autonomy of international organizations and international legal discourse' in Collins, Richard and White, Nigel D (eds), *International Organizations and the Idea of Autonomy: Institutional Independence in the International Legal Order* (Abingdon, Routledge, 2011).

De Arechage, Eduardo Jimenez, 'Treaty Stipulations in Favour of Third States' (1956) 50 *American Journal of International Law*.

De Schutter, Olivier, 'The Accountability of Multinationals for Human Rights Violations in European Law' in Alston, Philip (ed), *Non–State Actors and Human Rights* (Oxford, OUP, 2005).

De Schutter, Olivier, *International Human Rights Law: Cases, Materials, Commentary* (Cambridge, CUP, 2010).

Dinstein, Yoram, *The International Law of Belligerent Occupation* (Cambridge, CUP, 2009).

Doswald-Beck, Louise, *Human Rights in Times of Conflict and Terrorism* (Oxford, OUP, 2011).

Draper, GIAD, *The Red Cross Conventions* (London, Stevens & Sons, 1958).

Drzemczewski, Andrew, 'The European Human Rights Convention and Relations between Private Parties' (1979) 26 *Netherlands International Law Review*.

Eide, Asbjorn, 'Adequate Standard of Living' in Moeckli, Daniel, Shah, Sangeeta and Sivakumaran, Sandesh (eds), *International Human Rights Law* (Oxford, OUP, 2010).

Elder, David A, 'The Historical Background of Common Article 3 of the Geneva Conventions of 1949' (1979) 11 *Case Western Reserve Journal of International Law*.

Engstrom, Viljam, 'Powers of organizations and the many faces of autonomy' in Collins, Richard and White, Nigel D (eds), *International Organizations and the Idea of Autonomy: Institutional Independence in the International Legal Order* (Abingdon, Routledge, 2011).

Falk, Richard, 'Janus Tormented: The International Law of Internal War' in Rosenau, James N (ed), *International Aspects of Civil Strife* (Princeton NJ, Princeton University Press, 1964).

Fawcett, ES, 'The Function of Law in International Commodity Agreements' (1970) 44 *British Yearbook of International Law*.

Fierens, Jacques, '*Gacaca* Courts: Between Fantasy and Reality' (2005) 3 *Journal of International Criminal Justice*.

Fischer, Horst, 'Protection of Prisoners of War' in Fleck, Dieter (ed), *The Handbook of International Humanitarian Law*, 2nd edn (Oxford, OUP, 2008).

Forster, Jacques, 'Keynote address by Jacques Forster, Vice-President of the ICRC' (First Meeting of Signatories to Geneva Call's Deed of Commitment, Geneva, October 31–November 1 2004).

Forsythe, David P, 'Legal Management of Internal War: The 1977 Protocol on Non-International Armed Conflicts' (1978) 72 *American Journal of International Law*.

Foxton, David, *Revolutionary Lawyers: Sinn Fein and Crown Courts in Ireland and Britain 1916–1923* (Dublin, Four Courts Press, 2008).

Frowein, Jochen A, 'De Facto Regime' in *Max Planck Encyclopaedia of Public International Law*.

Gaeta, Paola, 'The Dayton Agreements and International Law' (1996) 7 *European Journal of Internaitonal Law*.

Gardbaum, Stephen, 'The "Horizontal Effect" of Constitutional Rights' (2003–2004) 102 *Michigan Law Review*.

Gasser, Hans-Peter, 'Protection of the Civilian Population' in Fleck, Dieter (ed), *The Handbook of International Humanitarian Law*, 2nd edn (Oxford, OUP, 2008).

Giap, Vo Nguyen, *The Military Art of People's War: Selected Writings of General Vo Nguyen Giap* (Russell Stetler ed, New York, Monthly Review Press, 1970).

Goodman, Ryan, 'The Detention of Civilians in Armed Conflict' (2009) 103 *American Journal of International Law*.

Goodman, Ryan, 'Authorization versus Regulation of Detention in Non-International Armed Conflicts' (2015) 91 *International Law Studies*.

Green, Fergus, 'Fragmentation in Two Dimensions: The ICJ's Flawed Approach to Non-State Actors and International Legal Personality' (2008) 9 *Melbourne Journal of International Law*.

Greenwood, Christopher, 'Historical Development and Legal Basis' in Fleck, Dieter (ed), *The Handbook of International Humanitarian Law*, 2nd edn (Oxford, OUP, 2008).

Guevara, Ernesto 'Che', *Bolivian Diary* (London, Pathfinder Press, 1994).

Guevara, Ernesto 'Che', *Guerrilla Warfare* (USA, BN Publishing, 2007).

Guillen, Abraham, *Philosophy of the Urban Guerrilla: The Revolutionary Writings of Abraham Guillen* (Donald C Hodges ed, New York, William Morrow & Company Inc, 1973).

Gutteridge, Joyce AC, 'The Geneva Conventions of 1949' (1949) 26 *British Yearbook of International Law*.

Haines, Steven, 'Northern Ireland' in Wilmshurst, Elizabeth (ed), *International Law and the Classification of Conflicts* (Oxford, OUP, 2012).

Harris, Paul G, 'Common but Differentiated Responsibility: The Kyoto Protocol and United States Policy' (1999) 7 *New York University Environmental Law Journal*.

Hassan v United Kingdom, European Court of Human Rights, Application No 29750/09, '*Amicus Curae* brief submitted by Professor Francoise Hampson and Professor Noam Lubell of the Human Rights Centre, University of Essex'.

Hattenhauer, Christian, 'Danzig, Free City of' in *Max Planck Encyclopaedia of International Law*.

Heller, Kevin Jon, *The Nuremberg Military Trunals and the Origins of International Criminal Law* (Oxford, OUP, 2011).

Henckaerts, Jean-Marie and Doswald-Beck, Louise, *Customary International Humanitarian Law, Vol 1: Rules* (Geneva, International Committee of the Red Cross/CUP, 2005).

Henderson, Christian and Lubell, Noam, 'The Contemporary Legal Nature of UN Security Council Ceasefire Resolutions' (2013) 26 *Leiden Journal of International Law*.

Higgins, Rosalyn, *Problems and Processes: International Law and How We Use It* (Oxford, OUP, 1994).

Jagers, Nicola, *Corporate Human Rights Obligations: in Search of Accountability* (Cambridge, Intersentia, 2002).

Jennings, Robert and Watts, Arthur (eds), *Oppenheim's International Law, vol 1*, 9th edn (Oxford, OUP, 2008).

Jochnick, Chris, 'Confronting the Impunity of Non-State Actors: New Fields for the Promotion of Human Rights' (1999) 21 *Human Rights Quarterly*.

Junod, Sylvie, 'Additional Protocol II: History and Scope' (1984) 33 *American University Law Review*.

Kamminga, Menno T and Zia-Zarifi, Saman, 'Liability of Multinational Corporations under International Law: An Introduction' in Kamminga, Menno T and Zia-Zarifi, Saman (eds), *Liability of Multinational Corporations under International Law* (Alphen aan den Rijn, Kluwer Law International, 2000).

Kay, Bruce H, 'Violent Opportunities: The Rise and Fall of "King Coca" and Shining Path' (1999) 41 *Journal of Interamerican Studies and World Affairs*.

Keenan, Brian, *An Evil Cradling* (London, Vintage, 1993).

Kelsen, Hans, 'Recognition in International Law: Theoretical Observations' (1941) 35 *American Journal of International Law*.

Kelsen, Hans, 'The Principle of Sovereign Equality of States as a Basis for International Organization' (1944) 53 *Yale Law Journal*.

Kelsen, Hans, *Principles of International Law* (New Jersey, Lawbook Exchange 2003).

Kindt, Michael T, 'Hezbollah: A State within a State' in Kindt, Michael T, Post, Jerrold M, and Schneider, Barry R (eds), *The World's Most Threatening Terrorist Networks and Criminal Gangs* (London, Palgrave Macmillan, 2009).

Klabbers, Jan, *The Concept of Treaty in International Law* (Alphen aan den Rijn, Kluwer Law International, 1996).

Klabbers, Jan, *An Intorduction to International Institutional Law* (Cambridge, CUP, 2002).

Klabbers, Jan, 'The Concept of Legal Personality' (2005) 11 *Ius Gentium*.

Klabbers, Jan, '(I Can't Get No) Recognition: Subjects Doctrine and the Emergence of Non-State Actors' in Bianchi, Andrea (ed), *Non-State Actors and International Law* (Farnham, Ashgate, 2009).

Kleffner, JK, 'The applicability of international humanitarian law to organized armed groups' (2011) 93 *International Review of the Red Cross* 882.

Knox, John H, 'Horizontal Human Rights Law' (2008) 102 *American Journal of International Law*.

Koch, Ida Elisabeth, 'Dichotomies, Trichotomies or Waves of Duties?' (2005) 5 *Human Rights Law Review*.

Korowicz, Marek St, 'The Problem of the International Personality of Individuals' (1956) 50 *American Journal of International Law*.

Koutroulis, Vaios, 'The application of international humanitarian law and international human rights law in situations of prolonged occupation: only a matter of time?' (2012) 94 *International Review of the Red Cross*.

Kunz, Josef L, 'The Nature of Customary International Law' (1953) 47 *American Journal of International Law*.

Kuol, Monyluak Alor, 'Administration of Justice in the (SPLA/M) Liberated Areas: Court Cases in War-Torn Southern Sudan' (1997) University of Oxford, Refugee Studies Programme.

La Haye, Eve, *War Crimes in Internal Armed Conflicts* (Cambridge, CUP, 2008).

La Rosa, Anne-Marie and Wuerzner, Carolin, 'Armed groups, sanctions and the implementation of international humanitarian law' (2008) 90 *International Review of the Red Cross.*

Langford, Malcolm, Vandenhole, Wouter, Scheinin, Martin and van Genugten, Willem (eds), *Global Justice, State Duties: The Extraterritorial Scope of Economic, Social and Cultural Rights in International Law* (Cambridge, CUP, 2013).

Lauterpacht Hersch, 'International Law and Human Rights', quoted in Rosalyn Higgins, *Problems and Process: International Law and How We Use It* (Oxford, OUP, 1994).

Lauterpacht, Hersch, 'Recognition of Insurgents as a De Facto Government' (1939) 3 *The Modern Law Review.*

Lauterpacht, Hersch, 'The Subjects of the Law of Nations' (1947) 63 *Law Quarterly Review.*

Lauterpacht, Hersch, 'The Subjects of International Law' in Bianchi, Andrea (ed), *Non-State Actors and International Law* (Farnham, Ashgate, 2009).

Law, Jonathan and Martin, Elizabeth A (eds), *Oxford Dictionary of Law*, 5th edn (Oxford, OUP, 2002).

Lawson, Rick, 'Life after Bankovic: On the Extraterritorial Application of the European Convention on Human Rights' in Coomans, Fons and Kamminga, Menno T (eds), *Extraterritorial Application of Human Rights Treaties* (Cambridge, Intersentia, 2004).

Le Sage, Andre, 'Stateless Justice in Somalia: Formal and Informal Rule of Law Initiatives' (Centre for Humanitarian Dialogue, 2005).

Lewis, Malcolm M, 'The Free City of Danzig' (1924) 5 *British Yearbook of International Law.*

Linderfalk, Ulf, *On The Interpretation of Treaties: The Modern International Law as Expressed in the 1969 Vienna Convention on the Law of Treaties* (The Netherlands, Springer, 2007).

Lootsteen, Yair M, 'The Concept of Belligerency in International Law' (2000) 166 *Military Law Review.*

Lubell, Noam, *Extraterritorial Use of Force Against Non–State Actors* (Oxford, OUP, 2010).

Lubell, Noam, 'Human rights obligations in military occupation' (2012) 94 *International Review of the Red Cross.*

MacGibbon, IC, 'Customary International Law and Acquiescence' (1957) 33 *British Yearbook of International Law.*

Mampilly, Zachariah Cherian, *Rebel Rulers: Insurgent Governance and Civilian Life during War* (Ithaca NY, Cornell University Press, 2011).

Marchegiano, M, 'The Juristic Character of the International Commission of Cape Spartel Lighthouse' (1931) 25 *American Journal of International Law.*

McCarthy, Conor, 'The Paradox of the International Law of Military Occupation: Sovereignty and the Reformation of Iraq' (2005) 10 *Journal of Conflict and Security Law.*

McCorquodale, Robert, 'The Individual and the International Legal System' in Evans, Malcolm (ed), *International Law*, 2nd edn (Oxford, OUP, 2006).
McCoubrey, Hilaire and White, Nigel D, *International Organizations and Civil Wars* (Aldershot, Dartmouth, 1995).
McCrudden, Christopher, 'Human Dignity and Judicial Interpretation of Human Rights' (2008) 19 *European Journal of International Law*.
McDougal, Myres and Reisman, W, 'Rhodesia and the United Nations: The Lawfulness of International Concern' (1968) 62 *American Journal of International Law*.
McNair, Arnold D, 'The Functions and Differing Legal Character of Treaties' (1930) 11 *British Yearbook of International Law*.
McNair, Lord Arnold, *The Law of Treaties* (Oxford, Clarendon Press, 1961).
Megret, Frederic, 'Nature of Obligations' in Moeckli, Daniel, Shah, Sangeeta and Sivakumaran, Sandesh (eds), *International Human Rights Law* (Oxford, OUP, 2010).
Melish, Tara J, 'The Inter-American Commission on Human Rights: Defending Social Rights Through Case-Based Petitions' in Langford, Malcolm (ed), *Social Rights Jurisprudence: Emerging Trends in International and Comparative Law* (Cambridge, CUP, 2008).
Meloni, Chantal, *Command Responsibility in International Criminal Law* (The Hague, TMC Asser Press, 2010).
Melzer, Nils, 'Interpretive Guidance on the Notion of Direct Participation in Hostilities Under International Humanitarian Law' (International Committee of the Red Cross, 2009).
Menon, PK, *The Law of Recognition in International Law* (Lewiston, New York, Edwin Mellen Press, 1994).
Metelits, Claire, 'Reformed Rebels? Democratization, Global Norms, and the Sudan People's Liberation Army' (2004) 51 *Africa Today*.
Milanovic, Marko, *Extraterritorial Application of Human Rights Treaties: Law, Principles, and Policy* (Oxford, OUP, 2011).
Milanovic, Marko, 'Some Thoughts on the Serdar Mohammed Appeals Judgment', *EJIL:Talk!*, 10 August 2015 Available at www.ejiltalk.org/some-thoughts-on-the-serdar-mohammed-appeals-judgment/.
Moir, Lindsay, *The Law of Internal Armed Conflict* (Cambridge, CUP, 2002).
Morrow, Ian FD, 'The International Status of the Free City of Danzig' (1937) 18 *British Yearbook of International Law*.
Muchlinksi, Peter T, *Multinational Enterprises and the Law*, 2nd edn (Oxford, OUP, 2007).
Mugerwa, Nkambo, 'Subjects of International Law' in Sorensen, Max (ed), *Manual of Public International Law* (Basingstoke, Macmillan, 1968).
Muggah, Robert and Jutersonke, Oliver, 'Rethinking Stabilization and Humanitarian Action in "Fragile Cities"' in Perrin, Benjamin (ed), *Modern Warfare: Armed Groups, Private Militaries, Humanitarian Organizations, and the Law* (Vancouver, UBC Press, 2012).
Mullerson, Rein A, 'Human Rights and the Individual as Subject of International Law: A Soviet View' (1990) 1 *European Journal of International Law*.
Murray, Daragh, 'How International Humanitarian Law Treaties Bind Non-State Armed Groups' (2015) 20 *Journal of Conflict and Security Law*.

Neuman, Michael, 'Somalia: Everything is Open to Negotiation' in Magone, Claire, Neuman, Michael and Weissman, Fabrice (eds), *Humanitarian Negotiations Revealed: The MSF Experience* (London, Hurst & Company, 2011).

Nijman, Janne E, 'Non-state actors and the international rule of law: Revisiting the "realist theory" of international legal personality' (2010) Amsterdam Center for International Law Research Paper Series.

Nkrumah, Kwame, *Handbook of Revolutionary Warfare* (New York, International Publishers, 1969).

Nollkaemper, Andre and Jacobs, Dov, 'Shared Responsibility in International Law: A Conceptual Framework' (2013) 34 *Michigan Journal of International Law*.

Nowak, Manfred, *UN Covenant on Civil and Political Rights: CCPR Commentary* (Kehl am rhein, NP Engel, 1993).

Nowak, Manfred, *UN Covenant on Civil and Political Rights: CCPR Commentary*, 2nd edn (Kehl am rhein, NP Engel, 2005).

Nowrot, Karsten, 'Legal Consequences of Globalization: The Status of Non-Governmental Organizations under International Law' (1999) 2 *Indiana Journal of Global Legal Studies*.

O'Connell, DP, *State succession in municipal law and international law* (Cambridge, CUP, 1967).

O'Connell, DP, *International Law* (London, Stevens & Sons, 1970).

Odello, Marco and Seatzu, Francesco, *The UN Committee on Economic, Social and Cultural Rights: The Law, Process and Practice* (Abingdon, Routledge, 2013).

Olson, Laura M, 'Practical Challenges of Implementing the Complementarity Between International Humanitarian Law and Human Rights Law—Demonstrated by the Procedural Regulation of Internment in Non-International Armed Conflict' (2007–2009) 40 *Case Western Reserve Journal of International Law*.

Pejic, Jelena, 'Procedural principles and safeguards for internment/administrative detention in armed conflict and other situations of violence' (2005) 87 *International Review of the Red Cross*.

Pejic, Jelena, 'Status of Armed Conflicts' in Wilmshurst, Elizabeth and Breau, Susan (eds), *Perspectives on the ICRC Study on Customary International Humanitarian Law* (Cambridge, CUP, 2007).

Pejic, Jelena, 'The protective scope of Common Article 3: more than meets the eye' (2011) 93 *International Review of the Red Cross*.

Peterke, Sven, 'Urban Insurgency, "Drug War" and International Humanitarian Law: The Case of Rio de Janeiro' (2010) 1 *International Humanitarian Legal Studies*.

Pictet, Jean S (ed), *Commentary: IV Geneva Convention Relative to the Protection of Civilian Persons in Time of War* (Geneva, International Committee of the Red Cross, 1958).

Pictet, Jean S (ed), *Commentary: III Geneva Convention Relative to the Treatment of Prisoners of War* (Geneva, International Committee of the Red Cross, 1960).

Pool, David, *From Guerrillas to Government: The Eritrean People's Liberation Front* (Athens, Ohio University Press, 2001).

Portmann, Roland, *Legal Personality in International Law* (Cambridge, CUP, 2010).

Rajamani, Lavanya, 'The Principle of Common but Differentiated Responsibility and the Balance of Commitments under the Climate Regime' (2000) 9 *Review of European, Comparative and International Environmental Law*.

Rama-Montaldo, Dr Manuel, 'International Legal Personality and Implied Powers of International Organizations' (1970) 44 *British Yearbook of International Law.*

Ramasastry, Anita, 'Corporate Complicity: From Nuremberg to Rangon, An Examination of Forced Labor Cases and Their Impact on the Liability of Multinational Corporations' (2002) 20 *Berkeley Journal of International Law.*

Reese, Willis LM, 'Legislative Jurisdiction' (1978) 78 *Columbia Law Review.*

Reinisch, August, 'The Changing International Legal Framework for Dealing with Non-State Actors' in Alston, Philip (ed), *Non-State Actors and Human Rights* (Oxford, OUP, 2005).

Riedel, EH, 'Recognition of Bellligerency' in Bernhardt, R (ed), *Encyclopedia of Public International Law, Vol 4* (North-Holland, Elsevier, 2000).

Roberts, Anthea and Sivakumaran, Sandesh, 'Lawmaking by Nonstate Actors: Engaging Armed Groups in the Creation of International Law' (2012) 37 *Yale Journal of International Law.*

Rodley, Nigel S, 'Can Armed Opposition Groups Violate Human Rights?' in Mahoney, Kathleen E and Mahoney, Paul (eds), *Human Rights in the Twenty-first Century: A Global Challenge* (The Hague, Martinus Nijhoff Publishers, 1993).

Rodley, Nigel, 'Non-State Actors and Human Rights' in Sheeran, Scott and Rodley, Sir Nigel, *Routledge Handbook on International Human Rights Law* (Abingdon, Routledge, 2013).

Roxburgh, Ronald, *International Conventions and Third States* (London, Longmans, Green and Co, 1917).

Roxburgh, Ronald (ed), *Oppenheim's International Law*, vol 1, 3rd edn (London, Longmans, 1920).

Roy, Arundhati, *Walking With the Comrades* (London, Penguin Books, 2011).

Rubin, Alfred P, 'The Status of Rebels under the Geneva Conventions of 1949' (1972) 21 *International and Comparative Law Quarterly.*

Salcedo, Juan Antonio Carriollo, 'Reflections on the Existence of a Hierarchy of Norms in International Law' (1997) 8 *European Journal of International Law.*

Sandov, Yves, Swinarski, Christophe and Zimmermann, Brun (eds), *Commentary on the Additional Protocols of 8 June 1977 to the Geneva Conventions of 12 August 1949* (The Hague, Martinus Nijhoff, 1987).

Sands, Philippe and Klein, Pierre, *Bowett's Law of International Institutions*, 6th edn (London, Sweet & Maxwell, 2009).

Santos Jr, Soliman M and Santos, Paz Verdades M, 'Primed and Purposeful: Armed Groups and Human Security Efforts in the Philippines' (Small Arms Survey and South-South Network for Non-State Armed Group Engagement, 2010).

Sassoli, Marco, 'Legislation and Maintenance of Public Order and Civil Life by Occupying Powers' (2005) 16 *European Journal of International Law.*

Sassoli, Marco A and Bouvier, Antoine A, *How Does Law Protect in War? Cases, Documents and Teaching Materials on Contemporary Practice in International Humanitarian Law*, Vol 1, 2nd edn (Geneva, ICRC, 2006).

Sassoli, Marco and Olson, Laura M, 'The relationship between international humanitarian and human rights law where it matters: admissible killing and internment of fighters in non-international armed conflicts' (2008) 90 *International Review of the Red Cross.*

Sassoli, Marco, 'Taking Armed Groups Seriously: Ways to Improve Compliance with International Humanitarian Law' (2010) *International Humanitarian Legal Studies.*

Sassoli, Marco, 'Should the obligations of states and armed groups under international humanitarian law really be equal?' (2011) 882 *International Review of the Red Cross.*

Schermers, Henry G and Blokker, Neils M, *International Institutional Law*, 4th edn (The Hague, Martinus Nijhoff, 2003).

Schoiswohl, Michael, '*De Facto* Regimes and Human Rights Obligations—The Twilight Zone of Public International Law?' (2001) 6 *Austrian Review of International and European Law.*

Schoiswohl, Martin, *Status and (Human Rights) Obligations of Non-Recognized* De Facto *Regimes in International Law: The Case of 'Somaliland'* (The Hague, Martinus Nijhoff, 2004).

Schwenk, Edmund, 'Legislative Power of the Military Occupation Under Article 43, Hague Regulations' (1945) 54 *Yale Law Journal.*

Scobbie, Iain, 'Gaza' in Wilmshurst, Elizabeth (ed), *International Law and the Classification of Conflicts* (Oxford, OUP, 2012).

Sellers, MNS, 'International Legal Personality' (2005) 11 *Ius Gentium.*

Seyersted, Finn, 'Objective International Personality of Intergovernmental Organizations: Do their capacities really depend upon the conventions establishing them?' (1964) 34 *Nordisk Tidsskrift for International Ret.*

Shaw, Malcolm, *International Law*, 5th edn (Cambridge, CUP, 2003).

Shaw, Malcolm, *International Law*, 6th edn (Cambridge, CUP, 2008).

Sivakumaran, Sandesh, 'Binding Armed Opposition Groups' (2006) 55 *International and Comparative Law Quarterly.*

Sivakumaran, Sandesh, 'Courts of Armed Opposition Groups: Fair Trials or Summary Justice' (2009) 7 *Journal of International Criminal Justice.*

Sivakumaran, Sandesh, 'Lessons for the law of armed conflict from commitments of armed groups: identification of legitimate targets and prisoners of war' (2011) 93 *International Review of the Red Cross* 882.

Sivakumaran, Sandesh, *The Law of Non-International Armed Conflict* (Oxford, OUP, 2012).

Somer, Jonathan, 'Jungle justice: passing sentence on the equality of belligerents in non-international armed conflict' (2007) 89 *International Review of the Red Cross.*

Stein, Ted L, 'The Approach of the Different Drummer: The Principle of Persistent Objector in International Law' (1985) 26 *Harvard International Law Journal.*

Stephens, Beth, 'The Amorality of Profit: Transnational Corporations and Human Rights' (2002) 20 *Berkeley Journal of International Law.*

Stokke, Kristian, 'Building the Tamil Eelam State: emerging state institutions and forms of governance in LTTE-controlled areas in Sri Lanka' (2006) 27 *Third World Quarterly.*

Stone, Christopher D, 'Common but Differentiated Responsibilities in International Law' (2004) 98 *American Journal of International Law.*

Szasz, Paul C, 'General Law Making Processes' in Joyner, Christopher C (ed), *The United Nations and International Law* (Cambridge, CUP/ASIL, 1997).

Talbot, LE, *Critical Company Law* (London, Routledge-Cavendish, 2008).

'The Geneva Convention and the Treatment of Prisoners of War in Vietnam' (1966–67) 80 *Harvard Law Review*.

Trechsel, Stefan, 'Why Must Trials Be Fair?' (1997) 31 *Israel Law Review*.

Tse-tung, Mao, *Mao Tse-tung on Guerrilla Warfare* (US Marine Corps, PCN 140 121800 00).

Tuck, David, 'Detention by armed groups: overcoming challenges to humanitarian action' (2011) 93 *International Review of the Red Cross*.

UK Ministry of Defence, *The Manual of the Law of Armed Conflict* (Oxford, OUP, 2004).

Van Wynen Thomas, Ann and Thomas Jr, AJ, 'International Legal Aspects of the Civil War in Spain, 1936–39' in Falk, Richard (ed), *The International Law of Civil War* (Baltimore MD, Johns Hopkins University Press, 1971).

Vandenhole, Wouter and Benedek, Wolfgang, 'Extraterritorial Human Rights Obligations and the North–South Divide' in Langford, Malcolm, Vandenhole, Wouter, Scheinin, Martin and Van Genugten, Willem (eds), *Global Justice, State Duties: The Extraterritorial Scope of Economic, Social and Cultural Rights in International Law* (Cambridge, CUP, 2013).

Villiger, Mark E, *Commentary on the 1969 Vienna Convention on the Law of Treaties* (The Hague, Martinus Nijhoff, 2009).

Vite, Sylvain, 'Typology of armed conflicts in international humanitarian law: legal concepts and actual situations' (2009) 91 *International Review of the Red Cross*.

Walker, Andrew, 'What is Boko Haram?' (2012) United States Institute of Peace, Special Report 308.

Warbrick, Colin, 'States and Recognition in International Law' in Evans, Malcolm (ed), *International Law*, 2nd edn (Oxford, OUP, 2006).

Weill, Sharon, 'The Judicial Arm of the Occupation: The Israeli Military Courts in the Occupied Territories' (2007) 89 *International Review of the Red Cross*.

Weiss, Michael and Hassan Hassan, *ISIS: Inside the Army of Terror* (New York, Regan Arts, 2015).

Wells, Celia and Elias, Juanita, 'Catching the Conscience of the King: Corporate Players on the International Stage' in Alston, Philip (ed), *Non-State Actors and Human Rights* (Oxford, OUP, 2005).

White, Nigel D, 'Layers of autonomy in the UN system' in Collins, Richard and White, Nigel D (eds), *International Organizations and the Idea of Autonomy: Institutional Independence in the International Legal Order* (Abingdon, Routledge, 2011).

Widdows, Kelvin, 'Security Council Resolutions and Non-Members of the United Nations' (1978) 27 *International and Comparative Law Quarterly*.

Wilson, Heather, *International Law and the Use of Force by National Liberation Movements* (Oxford, Clarendon, 1988).

Wilson, Robert R, 'Recognition of Insurgency and Belligerency' (1937) 1 *Proceedings of the American Society of International Law at its Annual Meeting*.

Wolfrum, Rudiger and Philipp, Christiane E, 'The Status of the Taliban: Their Obligations and Rights under International Law' (2002) 6 *Max Planck Yearbook of United Nations Law*.

Yearbook of the International Law Commission, vol II (New York, United Nations, 1966) 219.

Zegveld, Liesbeth, *The Accountability of Armed Opposition Groups in International Law* (Cambridge, CUP, 2002).

V. MISCELLANEOUS, NGO DOCUMENTS, NEWS AND OTHER ORGANISATIONS

'Afghanistan: ICRC facilitates the release of 40 prisoners', International Committee of the Red Cross (12 February 1999).

'Aid for captured Niger soldiers', *BBC News* (London, 27 June 2007).

'Battle for Iraq and Syria in Maps', *BBC News* (London, 10 July 2015).

'Building respect for humanitarian action and IHL among "other" weapon bearers', International Committee of the Red Cross (29 October 2010).

'Central African Republic: A Country in Turmoil', Human Rights Watch (24 March 2014).

'Colombia rebel army brings healthcare to the jungle', *Al Jazeera English* (Doha, 31 May 2011) wwwyoutubecom/watch?v=1hxkoiZVJRQ.

'Colombia rebel army brings healthcare to the jungle', *Al Jazeera English* (Doha, 31 May 2011).

'Colombia's Civil War: Revolutionary Armed Forces of Colombia (FARC)' (*PBS*, May 2002) wwwlb7uscourtsgov/documents/10–37511pdf.

'DR Congo: Situation still very precarious in east of country', International Committee of the Red Cross (21 June 2013).

'FIDH-REDRESS Update on Universal Jurisdiction: Fighting Impunity Worldwide' (Report) (2009).

'IRA kidnappers release industrialist', *BBC News* (London, 7 November 1975).

'Iran's Rohani affirms support for Syria and Hezbollah in "confronting Zionist regime"' *Haaretz* (16 July 2013).

'Mali: Four Soldiers evacuated following ICRC visit', International Committee of the Red Cross (27 March 2008).

'Mali: ICRC visits detainees in the north', International Committee of the Red Cross (31 July 2012).

'Mali: New Abuses by Tuareg Rebels, Soldiers', Human Rights Watch (7 June 2013).

'Mali: three detainees transferred after ICRC visit', International Committee of the Red Cross (1 March 2012).

'"Massive" troop deployment in Nigeria', *Al Jazeera English* (Doha, 16 May 2013).

'Mexican vigilantes drive out religious drug carter from gang-held city', *The Guardian* (London, 9 February 2014).

'More than 191,000 people killed in Syria with "no end in sight"', *UN News Centre* (22 August 2014).

'Nepal: Judged by the people', *The Economist* (5 October 2006).

'Nigeria begins offensive against Islamist sect', *France 24* (Paris, 17 May 2013).

'Nigerian forces target Boko Haram strongholds', *Al Jazeera English* (Doha, 17 May 2013).

'Philippines: Two detainees released under ICRC auspices', International Committee of the Red Cross (19 August 2004).

'Profile: Moqtada Sadr', *BBC News* (London, 19 January 2012).

'Q&A: Mexico's drug-related violence', *BBC News* (London, 25 November 2013).

'Red Command' (*InSight Crime*) wwwinsightcrimeorg/groups-brazil/comando-vermelho.

'Repatriation of two sick Moroccan prisoners', International Committee of the Red Cross (22 January 2005).

'S Leone trio guilty of war crimes', *BBC News* (London, 25 February 2009).
'Struggle for Iraq: In maps', *BBC News* (London, 17 June 2014).
'Sudan: Armed group releases five soldiers', International Committee of the Red Cross (6 November 2013).
'Sudan: ICRC facilitates handover of five soldiers in Darfur', International Committee of the Red Cross (4 December 2013).
'Sudan: ICRC visits Sudanese soldiers held by armed opposition group', International Committee of the Red Cross (27 August 2013).
'Syria Conflict: UK to give extra £5m to opposition groups' *BBC News* (London, 10 August 2012).
'Syria: Civilians in besieged areas in urgent need of relief', International Committee of the Red Cross (24 July 2013).
'Syria: End Opposition Use of Torture, Executions', Human Rights Watch (17 September 2012).
'Syria: Humanitarian aid, a lifeline for displaced people', International Committee of the Red Cross (5 April 2013).
'Thamil Eelam judiciary said a basis for rebuilding northeast', *TamilNet* (30 October 2003).
'The ICRC's mandate and mission', International Committee of the Red Cross (18 October 2010), www.icrc.org/eng/who-we-are/mandate/overview-icrc-mandate-mission.htm.
Abdulla, Namo, 'A Kurdish Village Governed by None', *New York Times* (New York, 24 August 2010).
Adriaan Alsema, 'Profiles: Urabeños' (*Colombia Reports*) http://colombiareports.co/urabenos/.
'Afghanistan: ICRC facilitates release of twelve South Korean hostages', International Committee of the Red Cross (29 August 2007).
Anderson, Jon Lee, 'Gangland: Who controls the streets of Rio de Janeiro', *The New Yorker* (New York, 5 October 2009).
Annual Report 2007 (International Committee of the Red Cross, 2008).
Annual Report 2010 (International Committee of the Red Cross, 2011).
Annual Report 2012 (International Committee of the Red Cross, 2013).
Annual Report 2014 (International Committee of the Red Cross, 2015).
Athas, Iqbal, 'Expanding Tiger civil service', *The Sunday Times* (Colombo, 9 June 2002).
Babak, Qayum, 'Afghanistan: Taliban justice 'fairer' than state's, *Institute for War and Peace Reporting* (17 August 2010).
Barnard, Anne, 'Syrian Rebels Say Saudi Arabia Is Stepping Up Weapons Deliveries' *New York Times* (New York, 12 September 2013).
Barnett, David, 'Jud al Islam claims credit for Sinai suicide car bomb attacks', *The Long War Journal* (12 September 2013).
Barrett, Richard, 'The Islamic State', The Soufan Group, November 2014.
Birke, Sarah, 'How ISIS Rules', NYRblog, *New York Review of Books*, 1 August 2015.
Black, Ian, 'Libyan revolution casualties lower than expected, says new government', *The Guardian* (London, 8 January 2013).
Caris, Charles C and Reynolds, Samuel, 'ISIS Governance in Syria', Middle East Security Report 22, Institute for the Study of War, July 2014.

Chulov, Martin, 'Isis insurgents seize control of Iraqi city of Mosul', *The Guardian* (London, 10 June 2014).
Geneva Call, 'In Their Words: Perspectives of Armed Non-State Actors on the Protection of Children from the Effects of Armed Conflict' (Report) (2010).
Gordon, Michael R, 'US Steps Up Aid to Syrian Opposition, Pledging $60 Million' *New York Times* (New York, 28 February 2013).
Human Rights Watch, '"Being Neutral is Our Biggest Crime": Government, Vigilante, and Naxalite Abuses in India's Chhattisgarh State' (Report) (2008).
Human Rights Watch, 'Afraid and Forgotten: Lawlessness, Rape, and Impunity in Western Cote d'Ivoire' (Report) (2010).
Human Rights Watch, 'All Quiet on the Northern Front?' (Report) (2010).
Human Rights Watch, 'Between Two Sets of Guns: Attacks on Civil Society Activists in India's Maoist Conflict' (Report) (2012).
Human Rights Watch, 'Colombia: Beyond Negotiation International Humanitarian Law and its Application to the Conduct of FARC-EP' (Report) (2001).
Human Rights Watch, 'Indonesia: The War in Aceh' (Report) (2001).
Human Rights Watch, 'No One is Safe: Insurgent Attacks on Civilians in Thailand's Southern Border Provinces' (Report) (2007).
Human Rights Watch, 'Sabotaged Schooling: Naxalite Attacks and Police Occupation of Schools in India's Bihar and Jharkhand States' (Report) (2009).
Human Rights Watch, 'Under Orders: War Crimes in Kosovo' (Report) (2001).
Human Rights Watch, 'War Without Quarter: Colombia and International Humanitarian Law' (Report) (1998).
Human Rights Watch, 'Why They Died: Civilian Casualties in Lebanon during the 2006 War' (Report) (2007).
Human Security Report Project, *Human Security Report 2005: War and Peace in the 21st Century* (Oxford, OUP, 2005).
Human Security Report Project, *Human Security Report 2009/2010: The Causes of Peace and the Shrinking Costs of War* (Oxford, OUP, 2011).
Human Security Report Project, *Human Security Report 2012: Sexual Violence, education, and War: Beyond the Mainstream Narrative* (Vancouver, Human Security Press, 2012).
International Committee of the Red Cross, 'Armed conflicts linked to the disintegration of State structures' (23 January 1998).
International Committee of the Red Cross, 'Internment in Armed Conflict: Basic Rules and Challenges', Opinion Paper, November 2014.
International Committee of the Red Cross, 'Armed Conflicts Linked to the Disintegration of State Structures: Preparatory document drafted by the International Committee of the Red Cross for the first periodical meeting on international humanitarian law' (Geneva, 19–23 January 1998).
International Crisis Group, 'Aceh: Escalating Tension' (Report) (2000).
International Crisis Group, 'Central African Republic: Keeping the Dialogue Alive' (Report) (2010).
International Crisis Group, 'Cote d'Ivoire: "The War Is Not Yet Over"' (Report) (2003).
International Crisis Group, 'Eastern Congo: Why Stabilisation Failed' (Report) (2012).

International Crisis Group, 'Ending Colombia's FARC Conflict: Dealing the Right Card' (Report) (2009).
International Crisis Group, 'Hizbollah and the Lebanese Crisis' (Report) (2007).
International Crisis Group, 'Hizbollah: Rebel Without a Cause?' (Report) (2003).
International Crisis Group, 'Iraq's Civil War, the Sadrists and the Surge' (Report) (2008).
International Crisis Group, 'Iraq's Muqtada Al-Sadr: Spoiler or Stabiliser?' (Report) (2006).
International Crisis Group, 'Iraq's Shiites Under Occupation' (Report) (2003).
International Crisis Group, 'Israel/Hizbollah/Lebanon: Avoiding Renewed Conflict' (Report) (2006).
International Crisis Group, 'Jemaah Islamiyah in South East Asia: Damaged but Still Dangerous' (Report) (2003).
International Crisis Group, 'Lebanon: Hizbollah's Weapons Turn Inward' (Report) (2008).
International Crisis Group, 'Nepal Backgrounder: Ceasefire—Soft Landing or Strategic Pause?' (Report) (2003).
International Crisis Group, 'Pakistan's Tribal Areas: Appeasing the Militants' (Report) (2006).
International Crisis Group, 'Peña Nieto's Challenge: Criminal Cartels and Rule of Law in Mexico' (Report) (2013).
International Crisis Group, 'Rwandan Hutu Rebels in the Congo: a New Approach to Disarmament and Reintegration' (Report) (2003).
International Crisis Group, 'Syria's Kurds: A Struggle Within a Struggle' (Report) (2013).
International Crisis Group, 'The Insurgency in Afghanistan's Heartland' (Report) (2011).
International Crisis Group, 'The Kivus: The Forgotten Crucible of the Congo Conflict' (Report) (2003).
International Crisis Group, 'Turkey: Ending the PKK Insurgency' (Report) (2011).
International Crisis Group, 'Somalia: Al-Shabaab—It Will Be a Long War' (Report) (2014).
International Crisis Group, 'The Huthis: From Saada to Sanaa' (Report) (2014).
International Crisis Group, 'Hizbollah and the Lebanese Crisis' (Report) (2007).
Lederer, Edith M, 'Death Toll in Syria Rises To 100,000 UN Chief Ban Ki-Moon Says', *Associated Press* (25 July 2013).
Leech, Garry, 'Farc rebel group in peace talks: Is Colombia's 50-year war about to end?', *The Independent* (London, 21 July 2013).
Macan-Marker, Marwaan, 'Kachin refugees in Myanmar get UN relief', *Al Jazeera* (Doha, 19 December 2011).
McCarthy, Rory, 'Hamas imposes new Gaza taxes to pay for burgeoning bureaucracy' *The Guardian* (London, 8 April 2010).
McCrummen, Stephanie, 'In Mexico, self defense groups battle a cartel', *The Washington Post* (Washington DC, 10 September 2013).
McDermott, Jeremy, 'Urabeños Flex Their Muscles in North Colombia', *InSight Crime* (9 January 2012).
McGirk, Tim, 'Behind the Taliban's Resurgence in Afghanistan', *TIME* (16 September 2009).

Miroff, Nick and Booth, William, 'Mexico's drug war is at a stalemate as Calderon's presidency ends', *Washington Post* (Washington, 27 November 2012).
Nash, Elizabeth, 'Hostage freed by Eta after 341 days', *The Independent* (London, 15 April 1996).
O'Driscoll, Aylish, ''Urabeños' bring northern Colombia to a halt' (*Colombia Reports*) http://colombiareportsco/urabenos–bring–northern–colombia–to–a–halt–as–police–struggle–to–control–armed–strike/.
Office of the Special Representative of the Secretary-General for Children in Armed Conflict 'Action Plans with Armed Forces and Armed Groups', http://childrenandarmedconflictunorg/our–work/action–plans/.
Pargeter, Alison, 'Islamist Militant Groups in Post-Qadhafi Libya' (*Combating Terrorism Center at West Point*, 20 February 2103) wwwctcusmaedu/posts/islamist–militant–groups–in–post–qadhafi–libya.
Reuter, Christoph, 'The Terror Strategist: Secret Files Reveal the Structure of Islamic State', *Der Spiegel*, 18 Aril 2015.
Roberts, Adam, 'Prolonged Military Occupation: The Israeli-occupied Territories since 1967' (1990) 84 *American Journal of International Law*.
Rogers, Simon, 'Government spending by department 2011–12: get the data', *The Guardian* (London, 4 December 2012).
Rogers, Simon, 'Healthcare spending around the world, country by country', *The Guardian* (London, 20 June 2012).
Roggio, Bill, 'Al Nusrah Front, Ahrar al Sham attack Syrian villages', *The Long War Journal* (17 September 2013).
Roggio, Bill, 'Al Nusrah Front poised to take over last major city on Euphrates River', *The Long War Journal* (13 March 2013).
Ross, Will, 'Nigeria's army gunning for Boko Haram', *BBC News* (London, 7 June 2013).
Roy, Arundhati, 'Walking with the Comrades', *Outlook India* (29 March 2010).
Salman, Rahmeem and Holmes, Oliver, 'Islamic State creates Police Force in Northwest Iraq', *Reuters*, 21 September 2014.
Sengupta, Kim, 'Revealed: What the West has given Syria's rebels' *The Independent* (London, 11 August 2013).
Simpson, John, 'Iraq: Not falling apart Yet', *BBC News* (London, 17 June 2014).
Smith, David, 'WikiLeaks cables: Shell's grip on Nigerian State revealed', *The Guardian* (London, 8 December 2010).
'Sudan: ICRC facilitates handover of five soldiers in Darfur', International Committee of the Red Cross (4 December 2013).
Sundaram, Anjan, 'The Things They Carried: The Congolese Rebel', *Foreign Policy* (4 March 2013).
Taylor, Peter, 'On the trail of al-Shabab's Kenyan recruitment 'pipeline'', *BBC News* (London, 29 September 2013).
Toolis, Kevin, 'Informer: The Life and Death of an IRA Man', *New York Times* (New York, 3 February 1991).
Vulliamy, Ed, 'The Zetas: Gangster Kings of Their Own Brutal Narco-State', *The Guardian* (London, 14 November 2009).
Yadav, Yatish, 'Police vs Maoists: Are Indian Security Forces Strong Against Naxals?', *The New Indian Express*, 25 April 2015.

Index

Abbreviations used in the index
ACom/CtHPR (African Commission and Court on Human and Peoples' Rights)
AP II (Additional Protocol II)
CESCR (Committee on Economic, Social and Cultural Rights)
CRC (Child Rights Committee)
EComHR (European Commission of Human Rights)
ECSC (European Coal and Steel Community)
ECtHR (European Court of Human Rights)
EU (European Union)
GC (Geneva Conventions)
HR (Hague Regulations)
IACom/CtHR (Inter-American Commission and Court on Human Rights)
ICC (International Criminal Court/Statute)
ICCPR (International Covenant on Civil and Political Rights (1966))
ICESCR (International Covenant on Economic, Social and Cultural Rights (1966))
ICRC (International Committee of the Red Cross)
ICTR (International Criminal Tribunal for Rwanda/Statute)
ICTY (International Criminal Tribunal for the former Yugoslavia/Statute)
IIA (International Institute of Agriculture)
IIL (Institute of International Law)
ILC (International Law Commission/ILC Articles and Draft Articles)
Nuremberg Principles (Principles of International Law Recognized in the Charter of the Nüremberg Tribunal and in the Judgment of the Tribunal)
TC (Torture Convention (1984))
TEU (Treaty on the European Union (Consolidated Version) (2010))
UNC (UN Charter)
VCLT (Vienna Convention on the Law of Treaties (1969))
VCLTSIO (Vienna Convention on the Law of Treaties between States and International Organizations (1986))
VCSST (Vienna Convention on Succession of States in respect of Treaties (1978))